CATCHING
LIGHTNING
Without the Bottle

CATCHING LIGHTNING
Without the Bottle

Timothy F. Bouvine

"Tim"

savage
PRESS
A Superior Publishing Company

P.O. Box 115 • Superior, WI 54880
(218) 391-3070 • www.savpress.com

ISBN Number 978-1-937706-12-8

Library of Congress Catalog Card Number: 2014934414

17 16 15 14 9 8 7 6 5 4 3 2 1

Published by:

    Savage Press

    P.O. Box 115

    Superior, WI 54880

Phone: 218-391-3070

E-mail: mail@savpress.com

Web Site: www.savpress.com

Printed in the USA

Dedication

To my son Timothy Jon Bouvine, who inspired me to change my life and pursue a lifelong dream.

To my family and friends who supported, encouraged, and persisted in their desire to see me finish this book, I thank you from the bottom of my heart.

A special thank-you goes out to Casey Tedin Wise for believing in my abilities. Her stellar record of accomplishments and recognition of my writing skills gave me the confidence to complete this writing.

Any lengthy, introverted process like writing a book comes with some price in time, attention, and relationships. I would like to both thank those who stood aside to allow my creative spirit to flourish, and apologize to those who paid the price for my devotion to writing.

—Timothy F. Bouvine

Introduction

Catching lightning in a bottle is a term that has been common in baseball since Leo Durocher coined the phrase in 1941, referring to a difficult feat. The concept broadened through the baseball years to mean a nearly impossible accomplishment. In the context of this book, Blake Benson does indeed capture lightning without the help of a certain kind of bottle. Read on and see what it all means.

1 — Flying High but Living Low

The stifling, steamy air hovered motionless a dozen rows up from the Chicago Cubs' visiting dugout at Atlanta's Turner Field. One could almost feel the slightest breeze coming from the swing and miss of the Cubs batters as the game wore on into the night.

The Atlanta Braves were hosting the Cubs this sultry summer night and the Braves had been in control since the early innings. A four-run deficit in the ninth inning seemed like a sure defeat for the Cubbies. There were no worries over the impending loss, as this year the "North Siders" of Chi town were surprisingly clicking on all cylinders, with a 10-game lead over the rest of the National League Central Division as August opened its doors to major league baseball.

Everything that could go right for their team this season had occurred at a stunning pace. Two separate 10-game winning streaks that featured numerous late-inning rallies had left the team with a "never say die" attitude and a self-confidence that seemed to rattle the opposition that inevitably labeled them as overly cocky.

As the top of the ninth began to unfold, the Cubbies were a bit listless as a road-weary club can be when late summer saps the energy from many players. If the team went down to defeat tonight nobody would be too upset. It was a logical time in the schedule to drift a bit.

The Atlanta closer was lightly tossing the ball in the home team's bullpen with a save situation still a run away, while the normally effective Braves setup man, George Wilson, looked to slam the proverbial door shut and send the Atlanta fans home in a celebratory mood.

Lefty reliever Wilson struck out Chicago pinch-hitter Steve Townsend on three pitches, further damaging the Cubbies' chances, but back-to-back walks had made the crowd a tad squirmy in their seats as the meat of the order came up for Chicago.

A solid line drive up the middle by All-Star first-baseman Tyler Grace brought the Cubs to within three runs and signaled the end for Braves pitcher Wilson. Atlanta closer Jimmy Parsons had plenty of time, not that it was needed to get loose on such a balmy night. The big righty strutted in from the pen with the confidence of a pitcher accustomed to success.

Things also were stirring in the Cubs dugout as some momentum seemed to be building. Potential pinch-hitters began loosening up and sharpening their mental edge as it looked like Chicago manager Buck Mains was examining his lineup card for options while Parsons warmed on the mound.

Chicago Cubs third-string catcher Blake Benson was his usual disinterested self, barely awake in the confines of the Cubs bullpen. Still nursing a hangover from the night before, Benson knew he would likely only be needed to warm up relief pitchers this night. He could do that in his sleep and he was testing that adage in a near literal fashion through the first eight innings.

The 15-year veteran had been an elite performer earlier in his heyday, but he was a "hanger-on" now, uncertain of his future, but unwilling to totally end his career because the money was still so damned good.

The bullpen phone rang and Mains yelled to get Blake into the dugout as he was running out of available pinch-hitters. Benson groggily walked in from the pen to the dugout as Parsons finished up his warm-up tosses.

Cubs clean-up slugger Vince Thomas, batting in his customary four spot, coaxed a 10-pitch walk out of Parsons to load the bases and bring the go-ahead run to the plate in the presence of switch-hitting third baseman Paul Trimble. The veteran Trimble was a solid line-drive hitter with occasional power from the left side even though Turner Field's power alleys were quite deep by present-day ballpark standards.

The potential rally seemed to hit a wall as Trimble flew out meekly to center field, allowing the fourth run of the game to score for the Cubs on a sacrifice fly. Trailing 6-4 and down to their last out, the Cubbies brought long-time fan favorite Sandy Gonzalez to the plate in his normal sixth spot with runners on first and second.

The combatants knew each other well; Parsons had faced Gonzalez countless times and had, in fact, enjoyed a fair amount of success against Sandy. Despite a lifetime .290 batting average, Gonzalez was only hitting .190 against Parsons with very little power production from the slugger that currently sat at 342 home runs in his 16-year career.

Gonzalez worked the count full and as the runners left early with two outs, Sandy fisted a bloop single just over the outstretched glove of the Atlanta second-baseman that was sprinting, his back to the infield, out to right-center field, as he tried unsuccessfully to snare the softly hit, but well-placed ball. Grace came around to score and the Cubs had runners on first and third, but still trailing 6-5, and still down to their final out.

The Cubs had a rookie in the seventh hole, a superb, slick-fielding second-baseman. He wasn't much of a stick at the plate, but the lack of options available to manager Mains dictated that he had no choice but to go with the rookie Luis Santiago, unless Buck felt Blake could come up with a clutch hit.

A few years back it would have been a no-brainer, as the Blake Benson of years gone by was a thunderous bat in the middle of any lineup. Beaten, battered, and bruised, the 35-year-old Benson was a shadow of his former self at the plate, batting a measly .198 with little power left in his one-time lightning-quick batting stroke that used to resonate a recognizable sparkling crack upon contact throughout the ballpark.

Blake could still handle the defensive side of his catcher position and was still superb at handling the frail egos of pitchers, but offensively he was just not quick enough with his bat to succeed against power pitchers like Parsons. Maybe it was a lack of focus or poor conditioning that contributed to Blake's batting demise, but whatever the reason, Benson had slipped to the point of faint recognition to his once All-Star status.

The short-in-stature Santiago stepped in the box and crowded the plate in daring demeanor that challenged the pitcher to come inside. Parsons fell for it and plunked him on the elbow as Santiago twisted his torso enough to protect himself and still leave his arms out over the plate.

The now obviously frustrated Parsons had loaded the bases with the errant pitch and was clearly agitated at Santiago's cleverness. The Cubs had the stellar closer on the ropes and they could feel it as Parsons bounced a split-fingered fastball past the Braves catcher and allowed the tying run to score.

Was there anything that didn't go the Cubs' way this year? The team appeared to be destined for greatness as the baseball gods were uncharacteristically kind to the seemingly perennial snake-bitten Chicago Cubs franchise that had not won a World Series since 1908.

The visitors' dugout was pumped. They wanted to end it here and now and avoid the fatigue of extra-innings as the runners were now on second and third with the eighth-place batter, Tommy Patterson, at the plate. With the pitcher's spot unfortunately coming up next, Braves manager Riley Adams knew the Cubs were pretty much out of pinch-hitting options. Adams wisely forced the Cubs' hand by intentionally walking the bases full again, putting the ball in Chicago's dugout to make the next counter move.

Buck Mains had nowhere else to turn to but Blake and Adams knew it. With the home team enjoying last at-bats, even a tie game would still be in their favor. Parsons should just eat Benson up with overpowering fastballs, but Benson still had an edge hitting over most any available pitcher, albeit probably not by much.

Blake instinctively always looked ahead a couple of batters and he could see this scenario developing before most. Even a tired worn-down Benson still had a sharp baseball mind as he stretched and grabbed a bat in anticipation several batters earlier in hopes of seizing the upcoming moment.

The spotlight was on Blake in this situation whether he wanted it or not. His confidence was sagging low at the plate, but he knew this at-bat would be just as much a mind game as a physical confrontation. This gave him some comfort as he stepped in the box and stared Parsons down as if to say, "I know exactly what you are going to do in this situation and you can't fool me one bit!"

Parsons knew he didn't have to fool Benson. There was no way the has-been could catch up with his fastball anymore. He just shook his head at Blake and then nodded in obvious approval as his catcher gave him the fastball sign. Everyone knew what was coming.

Parsons was his own worst enemy. He forgot he didn't have to reach back for that little extra hump on his heater. He overthrew the first two fastballs and lost control of his pitches as he fell behind in the count two balls and no strikes.

The wily Blake knew he was in the driver's seat as Parsons would have to come right over the plate rather than risk a walk to let in the potential winning run. Blake played with Parsons' mind as he asked for time from the home plate umpire just as the flame-throwing righty was getting set to deliver home with the third pitch.

Blake stepped out of the batter's box, rubbed his three-day unshaven face with his left hand, spat some tobacco juice toward the pitcher's mound and smirked at Parsons, who had a well-deserved reputation as a hot-head that could lose his composure at the drop of a baseball cap. The 6-foot-2 Benson carried a middle-aged paunch around his waist atypical of a major league baseball catcher, but still had the steely eyes of a competitor. As that glare focused on the pitcher, Blake's baseball brain took an educated guess that the closer would come inside with a just above the belt fastball, as many pitchers knew that left-ies like Blake could handle low pitches rather easily, dropping the barrel of the bat as their hands sat right over the inside of the plate. That pitch was easy to turn on no matter what the speed, especially if it came in on the inner half of the plate. Blake's only chance was to pick out a spot beforehand and, if the pitch was thrown in that area, even an over-the-hill 35-year-old could get enough bat speed going to drive the ball somewhere.

Parsons had to come with the cheese and Blake still knew what to do with it, especially if he could sit on that pitch without fear of striking out or falling farther behind in the count. The belt-high fastball arrived gift-wrapped at just the spot Blake was targeting. He ripped a hooking line drive that fell just inside the right-field foul line and rolled all the way into the corner while the bases emptied and put the Cubbies remarkably ahead by three runs. Blake rounded first and somehow managed to build up enough speed to run right out from under his helmet. What hair left on his balding head was flying in the moist Atlanta air as he checked into second base with a double. Blake looked into his dugout as if to say the old man still had it, at least once in a while.

The Braves and their fans were totally deflated at the stunning rally and went down in a whimper in their half of the ninth while the Cubs gleefully celebrated yet another amazing comeback win.

Blake was the unexpected hero of the night as the team continued their celebratory mood in the clubhouse. The post-game spread tasted even better after this hard-fought win.

As the shine of a victory began to wear off, and the adrenaline waned, Blake felt the effects of his hangover, but there was no need to worry now. He knew it would be a party kind of night. The thrill of victory and his starring role made him eager for attention out on the town.

His teammates were his best buddies tonight as the drinks flowed in all the hotspots of downtown Atlanta. Several hours later there wasn't even a sniff of a hangover as Blake knew the best way to get rid of one was to start anew on another.

Somewhere just after midnight Blake hooked up with a group of four women. As the booze and chatter picked up in intensity, he singled out one steaming redhead and began planning his getaway with the next one-night stand of the long road trip away from his wife of 15 years, Kim Benson.

A couple of quick shots of whiskey and he would be set for the night as long as he had the victim of a sexual encounter in sight. He chased down his last shot and entered the near nightly booze blackout stage; his body continued on accustomed to these situations, but his mind was gone for the night. It always came back the next morning, but the gaping holes in recollection were a sick reminder of his powerless alcoholic state.

The night was filled with exhilaration, but in reality it didn't matter as Blake could always find an excuse to drink in excess. Good, bad, or indifferent didn't matter. The results were the same, if not the rationale.

2 — The Airport

Blake hurriedly packed his bags and splashed water on his face. There is no way this is going to turn out well, he thought. Plausible excuses ran through his mind as he scurried unsteadily down the hall to the elevator.

He reeked of whiskey and smoke. His thought process was clouded from lack of sleep and too much booze. All he could think about was getting to the airport before the charter plane took off without him.

I've let the team down again, Blake thought, as feelings of guilt clashed with desperation. We're in the middle of a pennant race and all I care about is getting laid and boozing until the crack of dawn. I am such a worthless piece of shit. I deserve whatever punishment I get this time, he thought, as he hailed a cab.

"Hartsfield Airport" was all Blake could slur and the taxi sped away.

Jesus Christ, he thought. If only I could remember where I left my fucking cell phone last night I could let the team know I'll be there.

Oh shit, he thought as he envisioned the team calling his wife to find out his whereabouts, or, worse yet, Kim calling his unattended cell phone and having a strange woman answer. I'll deal with that later. One lie at a time is all I can handle right now.

"Goddamn, this traffic is fucking ridiculous," Blake blurted out. "Can you turn up the air conditioning? It's so fucking hot and humid in this city."

The cabbie perked up this time as he fumbled for the air conditioner controls and finally turned the knob to full blast. Everyone seemed to like to talk about the weather. It was the perfect small talk.

"Yep, it's good old Hotlanta. Suppose to get some wicked storms today. Front is coming in."

As the cab finally reached the airport, Blake pulled out a 50-dollar bill, handed it to the cabbie, and bolted away as fast as he could.

He knew he would have to get his alibi together and come up with an excuse. He had to try and piece the night together in his mind. Who saw me last night with that redhead? When was the last time somebody saw me? Blackouts, goddamned blackouts! I have no fucking idea, he thought, struggling to deal with the fuzzy details of his binge.

Maybe he could blame it on too many painkillers. He knew that this lie wouldn't account for him not being in his team hotel room, but rather at his one-night stand's pad. It's hopeless, he thought. The truth will have to do. The truth and some serious begging will have to be the game plan once again.

He figured he could get to Sandy. His best friend and teammate could smooth things out with the coaches. He knew he could always count on Sandy.

He had bailed him out so many times without so much as a question. Sandy is it. Blake finally settled on a familiar remedy.

Rushing through the airport, Blake suddenly felt secure in his decision to trust Sandy. It was so reassuring that he decided to get a quick "bump" at the airport bar. It would only take a minute to slam a drink down and settle his nerves. He quickly gulped a double shot of whiskey and briskly walked to the gate where the team would hopefully still be assembling for their trip to St. Louis.

Blake glanced at his watch and figured he had it made. It looked like he had wiggled out of another potential disaster. He knew a fine was coming from his manager, but money really wasn't a big deal to a multi-millionaire.

Everybody laughed off his numerous escapades. Buck would holler like crazy at him and threaten to send him to Des Moines to languish in triple A, but his value to the team as a grizzled veteran was apparent in so many on-the-field ways, if not his off the field antics. He made it through a weekend binge last year in L.A. when Buck was told that Blake had the flu and was resting at the hotel. Two years ago Blake got off with just a fine after a night of carousing in San Francisco caused him to miss the team bus to the airport.

Things were different now, though. His drinking had become steadily worse and everybody knew it. Hangovers were expected in a major league clubhouse and, in fact, were worshipped in warrior type fashion. There was a line not to cross, however, and Blake had ventured across this boundary by sneaking shots of booze in brief getaways to the clubhouse during games and hiding miniatures acquired on numerous airplane trips when he was called down to the bullpen to warm up pitchers. He was reassured by the unlikeliness that a third-string catcher would be needed during game action. He had become so accustomed to his manager's routine that he knew he would play once a week or so when an afternoon game followed a night game. It wouldn't be easy but he could tone down the drinking one night a week.

It was now crunch time for Blake, his confidence growing by the minute as the alcohol gave him some much-needed courage.

He saw Sandy on his cell phone, standing away from the rest of the team with a serious look on his face, outwardly trying to appear unconcerned as his friend was missing, but failing miserably. His teammates knew him too well. Sandy was the type of person who was sincerely a very caring person and all-around good guy, unlike many of his self-centered teammates.

Blake motioned to Sandy to meet him farther down the hallway, away from the rest of the group. A look of relief quickly appeared on Sandy's face, but that look suddenly ran away from his face as an obviously angry Sandy approached him.

"Buddy, you really screwed up this time. Buck is as pissed as I have ever seen him."

Blake's confidence waned as he replied, "Aw come on Sandy, I can weasel my way out of this one too if you'll help me smooth things over with Buck."

"Man, I am done bailing out your sorry ass. Blake, you are not the star you once were. You can't get away with this shit anymore. We're in a pennant race now. This is not the shitty Cubs anymore. There's too much at stake."

"I know Sandy, this is it. I promise to tone it down the rest of the year. You're my best friend and I wouldn't lie to you."

Sandy had heard this "promise" before and knew it did not mean a thing.

Then Sandy boldly proposed a solution.

"Blake, I'll get you out of this mess on one condition."

"Anything," Blake begged.

"You've got to quit drinking cold turkey. Promise me right now that you'll not have one fucking drop of booze the rest of the year. I don't give a shit in the off-season, but this has to stop right now."

"Jesus Christ, Sandy. There's no way I can stomach being on the road without any booze. You hate it too. I'll tone it down, I promise."

"That won't do anymore, Blake. I've had enough. Buck has had enough. The whole gosh-darn team has had enough. There is no negotiating here. You quit right this moment or I'm going to tell Buck that you're out of control and need help. You'll be gone tomorrow and I don't mean to Des Moines. He's this close to releasing you," Sandy seethed at Buck as he moved his thumb and finger oh-so-close together.

Blake had never seen the mild-mannered Sandy this outraged and it made an immediate impression. Blake certainly did not want to go out like this. The embarrassment and humiliation would be unbearable.

"Ok. I know when I've got no choice. You win. No booze for the rest of the season."

Blake's already shaky confidence dissipated from the encounter as the shots of whiskey waned and Sandy could see and feel the pain his long-time best friend Blake was in.

"C'mon buddy. We're in a pennant race and this is our year. Everything is going our way. You're really going to enjoy this. That's my promise! Now let me go over to Buck and mend some fences. You stay out of the way until I get back. We have an hour before we get on the plane. Lucky for you some maintenance issue slowed us up."

Blake leaned against the wall, away from the team's sight. The good news was that he had apparently wiggled out of another jam, but the bad news was he knew he had no more chips to cash in if he got in trouble. Confidence shaken, physically ill from his chosen lifestyle, and faced with the likelihood of a major league career ending, Blake thought this must have been reaching bottom.

Sandy smiled as he approached the crusty manager who wore that never-ending scowl that most managers accumulate over time dealing with irresponsible and immature behaviors intertwined with massive egos in a toxic twist.

"He's here and we've worked things out. Buck, you don't want to know the details. He did the same old thing, but this time I have a stone-cold promise from him that there will be no more shenanigans. He's sworn off the booze for the season."

"Jesus Christ, Sandy. I'd like to believe you, but I can't believe Blake. He has no credibility anymore."

"He knows this time is different, Buck. He knows this is the last straw. I believe him and you need to believe in him too. He is a little shaken right now. His confidence isn't like it used to be during his glory days."

"Glory days? Those days are so far gone I can't even fucking remember them," replied the irritable manager. "Glory days?" Buck couldn't stop shaking his head in disbelief, as he repeatedly mumbled the once apt description of the past Blake Benson.

"Sandy, I have the owner crawling all over my ass on this one. The media is all over the story of Blake's habits and it looks like we don't give a shit about the pennant race. Our general manager is just looking at any old reason to get that stud flamethrower Rodriguez up here and you know it's a luxury that we can't afford, carrying three catchers on the major league roster while our pitchers are battling sore arms. You need to look me straight in the eye and say you believe him this time. I need that from you. Our whole organization respects you, Sandy. I can run with that."

Sandy nodded affirmatively, but Buck did not get to be a major league manager without possessing the ability to read his players. Sandy's body language implied less than a total commitment. He couldn't look him in the eye and quickly scurried away. His endorsement was half-hearted, but Buck figured there was no reason to rock the boat while the team was riding high.

"Sandy, you better keep him in line this time," Buck hollered for all to hear. Buck was less than thrilled, but he had so many issues to deal with that he gladly crossed one off the list for now.

Blake was reassured by Sandy's smooth graceful stride, head held high, with a calm look on his face as he approached. He knew his best friend well enough to know that he was able to smooth things over with Buck. After all, he had seen this play out many times before.

"Thanks Sandy," Blake said to his buddy before Sandy had a chance to speak.

Sandy never said a word as he motioned Buck to join the rest of the team, waiting at the gate for their plane to be ready. The two of them sat just far enough away from the rest of the team that they could speak in private, but close enough to symbolize that they were a unit again.

Blake never used to give a rat's ass what his teammates thought of him personally, but the numerous instances of selfishness and boorish behavior, along with the effects of alcohol on his psyche over the years, made him very sensitive to the seeming disrespect the rest of the team showed him. Blake was a shadow of himself mentally at this point in his career. He knew how the team felt toward him. He could feel it inside, but his paranoia fueled it to excess.

The bitterness inside him was countered by the realization that most of these younger players did not have a clue what it was like to stay in the big leagues for 15 years. They just could not know the physical and mental damage a career does to its athletes. The busted up fingers from years of foul tips, the achy knees from years and years of squatting, the temptations on the road with so much time on their hands and so many willing sexual partners. Not to mention the never-ending marital battles with suspicious wives. Screw them, they just could not know. Blake was at that same point before and his bitterness turned to pity for their lack of understanding.

Blake could feel their steely eyes upon him. The uneasiness ran away from him and passed the baton to sorrow. He knew deep down he deserved all the scorn. His head tilted downward in shame. Boarding the plane could not come soon enough for Blake. The sheltered nature of hiding in obscurity in an airplane certainly would be better than the focus of attention in his present awkward predicament.

The anxiety of the moment was becoming harder for Blake to bear. Still feeling physically ill from his all-nighter and now on top of that, this feeling of anger, sorrow, and shame combined to overwhelm him. Come on, he thought to himself. Let's just get on this plane and without all these eyes on me, I can get to sleep. I can't take much of this anymore.

"Sandy, I'm going to the can for a moment," Blake spoke in obvious discomfort to his friend. "Going to brush my teeth and freshen up a bit. I feel like crap." Blake grabbed his carry-on and headed to the restroom.

Sandy knew his best friend all too well. He loved Blake like a brother, but he also knew that Blake was in a bad place. He had his suspicions on alert constantly regarding Blake and his drinking. Blake had let him down so many times before. Should I trust him this time? He did seem very contrite and sincere, Sandy thought.

Blake took a sharp left turn into the men's room and clumsily scrambled for the spare toothbrush that every drinker seemed to carry with them out of necessity. He looked into the mirror and realized how awful he looked. Time for a change, he thought. After splashing some water on his face and combing whatever hair he had left on his bald-patterned head, he brushed his teeth quickly.

Just as he was getting ready to exit the bathroom and return to his teammates, Blake noticed a few small bottles of liquor in his shaving kit. A boozer knew one could never have too many hiding places. Remembering where you put them was the hard part, but the more spots, the merrier.

For some reason, the spontaneity of the moment caught Blake off guard. Normally he would chug a few down before the plane ride and maybe have one or two drinks on the flight, depending on the time of day. He knew how to play the game to make it look like he was a social drinker, or so he thought. The reality was, his teammates knew he was half-lit much of the time.

The severity of the moment hit Blake hard and he knew he would have to throw these out. It was time for a new beginning. He knew in his heart that this had to stop. However, something else, deep down, intervened and impulse prevailed over reason as it had so many other times.

A couple more shots would not change anything. He could quit when he got to St. Louis. He felt like shit and a couple more bumps would make the flight more comforting. He felt like an anxiety attack was coming upon him knowing that he was still the center of attention in a negative way. What if I freak out on the plane? Blake knew that an athlete could misbehave in almost any manner except for displaying signs of mental illness. Drunk, high, abusive and fighting were tolerated to some extent. Flipping out was not. Being labeled a nutcase was a sure ticket out of the big leagues.

Like any addict, Blake was much more sure of his ability to hide any signs of impairment than reality warranted. These few more shots would only be trouble if caught. Surely, one more deception wouldn't hurt. Nobody would know.

Bathroom stalls were always one of Blake's favorite drinking places. Everybody knew it was rude to invade one's privacy in this somewhat sacred spot. He hurriedly moved into the stall and closed the door. Better get this done quickly, he thought. Three miniature bottles of scotch, brandy, and vodka were opened and swallowed in rapid succession.

Sandy had sat for a few minutes in his uncomfortable airport seat before he realized he knew what he had to do. He just had to find out for sure that his buddy was on the up and up with him.

Feeling both mistrust and apprehension at the same time made Sandy feel very uneasy. He couldn't really trust Blake's word, and yet he innately knew that spying on his best friend was not cool either. As the impeccably dressed, tall and handsome Sandy walked slowly toward the restroom he finally came to grips with the necessary course of action. It was right to find out for sure. His teammates and the organization had a huge stake in this.

The anger slowly built in Sandy's face as he expected the worst. He knew he would have to play detective here because Blake would go to great lengths to hide his alcoholism.

As Sandy entered, he deftly walked on his toes to make a stealth approach. A businessman carrying a briefcase glared at Sandy as he departed the scene. Blake was not in the open area of the restroom. He must be in a stall, he thought. He knew this would not end well. Either Blake would be furious for Sandy spying on him or Sandy would be livid at the betrayal by his best friend and teammate. It was all in this time. He just had to know for sure.

Blake always wore his pricey Nike running shoes because of the soreness in his knees. It would not be a problem identifying which stall he was in. Business or casual attire, Blake stood out with his high tech running shoes. It was a professional necessity.

Sandy knew he had to catch Blake in the act. Blake would quickly hide any devious behavior. He couldn't take a chance of pushing open the door as it might be locked. He had to peer over the top of the stall. It was his only choice.

Bracing for the moment, Sandy identified Blake's footwear and crept slowly toward the stall. Sandy suddenly figured he could tell Blake that he had to hurry because the team was about to board the plane, which would give him some cover for peering into his privacy zone.

Sandy put both hands on the top edge of the stall and pulled himself up to stick his head over the crest as he began to speak.

"Come on Blake, we have to board now," he quietly spoke in a hushed tone, and looked in astonishment as Blake was just finishing his third miniature.

"God damn it Blake, you sonofabitch, I knew I couldn't trust you, but Jesus Christ, only 30 minutes after you just promised me no booze."

Blake knew he was busted. The spontaneity of the moment left him no time to come up with a decent answer. He was speechless as Sandy suddenly belied his calm demeanor with a fit of rage and blasted the door open with a powerful kick. He put both hands on Blake's shoulders and shook him violently.

"This is it, Blake. You're done with the team. There's nothing more you can say. You let the team down, you let your best friend down and Blake, you have to see now that you are letting yourself down too."

Blake still was speechless as the severity of the situation slowly crept in. He had no defense. He was in a state of shock. There were no tears, no pleas, and no anger. Blake just hung his head in shame at his inability to control himself.

Sandy was surprised at Blake's silence. Knowing Blake as well as he did, he figured Blake would pull out the charm one more time to weasel his way out of another mess. The fighting instinct that Blake always possessed was no longer within his spirit. He was broken.

Sandy's rage disappeared just as quickly as it had arisen. He realized that Blake was now a broken man. He hugged Blake and tried to comfort him.

"The organization will take care of you Blake. We'll get you into a rehab place. You'll come out a better man."

"Come on buddy," Sandy spoke in a comforting tone. "It's time to face the music with Buck." He led Blake out of the restroom toward the rest of the team.

The sensitivity of the situation required some privacy. Sandy got Buck's attention and motioned him towards the empty adjacent gate area where the three of them could speak alone.

Buck walked toward the two of them with a quizzical look on his travel-weary face. Buck had assumed this was all taken care of. He had too much to deal with as the sudden realization that more shit was about to hit the fan.

Sandy told Blake to stand a few feet back as he let Buck know the desperate condition that Blake was in.

"I just caught him drinking again in the bathroom. He's out of control Buck, and he realizes it too," Sandy spoke in a quiet tone, anticipating Buck's hot temper would get the best of him.

Buck interrupted Sandy and all hell broke loose. This had been building for a long time and Buck wanted everyone to see and hear his upcoming rant.

A manager is constantly under pressure, even for a first-place team with a healthy lead. The stress of the position usually requires several strategically placed outbursts once or twice a month just to let off steam, but not too often because players will tune you out if it becomes routine. Buck was ready to blow up and this was the perfect opportunity to reclaim authority as Blake's pattern of behavior, followed by token and toothless punishment, made Buck look weak.

"You gotta be fucking kidding me," Buck yelled for all to hear. "Didn't he just promise you he was done with that shit? Is he that fucking dumb that he thought he could get away with it again?" Buck screamed as he pointed at Blake.

"How in the hell can I continue to put up with this bullshit? We've got a pennant race to deal with and I'm constantly babysitting my team. Do we want to win it all or just have a fucking good time? Sandy, you gave me your word this was done," Buck bellowed out as he remembered the half-hearted nod of approval Sandy gave not 30 minutes before.

"I know Skip. Blake has agreed to go into rehab. Let's move past this and get our teammate some help," Sandy's calm demeanor and tone of brotherhood deflected Buck's rage.

"He's done with my team, though. I just can't trust him anymore. There's too much at stake here, Sandy."

Blake stood motionless throughout. He offered no defense for his behavior. He knew there was nothing more to say and he was just worn out, mentally and physically. Blake knew he deserved whatever was coming his way. His body language belied his one-time status as an All Star. There is nothing like the strut of a major league ballplayer when they know all eyes are upon them as they move about in public. Blake now conveyed a homeless person's demeanor rather than that of a star athlete as his shoulders slumped and he continued to look down at the floor.

"Get Marty on the phone and let him handle it," Sandy aggressively spoke, knowing this was a general manager's decision and was hoping Buck could let it go. Marty Anderson was the Chicago Cubs' General Manager who was back in Chicago still trying to make a few more trades to strengthen the club for the stretch run.

"Ok, but get him out of here. He doesn't deserve to be near my club."

"Shouldn't I stay with Blake until Marty arranges for some help for him? I could catch a later flight."

"Fuck him Sandy. He can take care of himself. For Christ sakes he's a grown man," Buck continued without a drop of compassion in his voice.

"Just call Marty right now and make some arrangements for him. Can't you see he needs some help?" Sandy pleaded with the crusty old manager with all of his huge heart.

"Ok. Keep him in sight and I'll make the call," Buck relented.

Sandy could only feel compassion for Blake as he tried to comfort him once again. He put his arm around Blake and guided him to a row of empty black airport chairs.

"Do you want me to call Kim and suggest she meet you when your plane arrives? You might want me to prepare her a bit for what's about to come," Sandy advised Blake as they sat down.

"Thanks buddy. I'd appreciate that. I don't think I can handle her wrath right now. Plus, I lost my phone last night. Just tell her I'm ok and give her the flight information," Blake softly responded.

"Here, you take my phone Blake. Call me on my other phone if you need anything," Sandy whispered to his best friend.

Just then Sandy's phone rang. He recognized the phone number as he was just about to hand it over. It was Marty Anderson.

"Hold on a second buddy. I better take this."

Sandy answered quickly. A player never wanted to keep a general manager's call waiting. They hold a player's future in their hands.

"This is Sandy," the anxious tone in his voice apparent as he opened the conversation. Sandy responded with a succession of affirmative replies.

"Ok, will do, and thank you, Mr. Anderson. Goodbye." The conversation was brief and to the point. The club had arranged for Blake's flight home. He was to be on the 2:30 flight to Chicago. A call would come in a couple of days from a rehab facility. There was a stern message for Blake not to screw this up.

Sandy relayed the message to Blake.

"Just do everything they say and get well. Everything will work out if you just put your life in their hands and do your best. I guess we won't be seeing each other for a while," Sandy said.

Blake rose up to give his friend a hug. "You make sure you keep this team in first place," Blake replied as he tried to keep his emotions intact.

With tears in both of their eyes, the embrace slowly evaporated. They looked at each other one more time and turned away quickly.

Sandy was full of sadness as he rejoined the team. They were boarding the plane now. Goodbyes are always hard, but this one had a different feel to it.

Blake continued to walk until he figured he was a safe distance apart from the team. He slumped down in a chair, put his head in his hands, and cried.

3 — The Devoted Wife

Sandy hesitated as he walked toward the gate to begin the boarding process. He was unsure when would be the right time to call Blake's wife with his other cell phone. This was not going to be an easy phone call. Kim would undoubtedly be upset, but probably not more than already not knowing her husband's whereabouts for almost a day now.

The alcohol problem was a continuous source of friction between Blake and his wife. Kim became aware early on in Blake's baseball career that he recklessly abused alcohol, but felt helpless to stop it. An athlete in his 20s could overcome some of the debilitating effects of overindulgence, but after years of constant abuse, the problems intensified with age.

When Kim met Blake at his first stop in the minor leagues, he was a chiseled athlete with the naive self-confidence of a big league star even though he was just out of high school. As the third pick of the first round of the Major League Draft, it was just a matter of time before he hit the majors. Blake knew the projected timetable. He would breeze through the Rookie League and Class A ball in his first professional season. His second professional season would probably be split between AA and AAA and he correctly figured he would be with the Chicago Cubs at the start of his third season. He had all the confidence in the world in his physical abilities. He just had to learn the intricacies of handling a big-league pitching staff and improving his game-calling skills.

Blake Benson in his mid-30s was a quite different player. He would no longer be looked at as an athlete, but more as a baseball mentor. His physical skills had diminished with injuries, age, and abuse. He was far below his .305 career batting average this season. His power numbers had decreased as well. He averaged 35 home runs and 100 runs batted in during his five-year peak. Later years were statistically less impressive, but were still stellar for a catcher, since the primary talent of a backstop has always been defense first. Offensive production was considered a bonus.

Now he was a part-time, third-string catcher with an aching body and a clouded mind. The desire had waned. Blake often wondered why he still was playing this game. He had more than enough money to last the rest of his life. The travel was exhausting both mentally and physically. Heck, even a pennant race could not get him excited, though he and his team had never won a World Series.

His bloated body was giving him daily signals that his time was running out as a major league player. More importantly, his mental state was in similar decline. He knew that this part of his game was all that he had left. Ironically, he was on a big-league roster solely because he could offer wisdom and experience, but that would only go so far if off-field issues continued. At one point in his big-league career, the superstar was considered a prime candidate for coaching after his playing days were over, but now he could not see that in his future. The game had worn him out.

Kim knew that much of Blake's decline was due to the alcohol abuse. She understood the physical pain a catcher had to endure over the years, but she also figured that a man in his mid-30s should still be in competitive shape if he took care of himself. She harped on Blake to act like a professional athlete and take care of his body, but Blake had the stubbornness of a spoiled superstar who always did what he liked, when he liked. He rationalized that his baseball smarts were really all the team wanted anymore. He saw very little need to push himself physically.

Kim had witnessed firsthand the ravaging effects of alcohol abuse. The wasteful ways of alcohol became embedded in her mind. Her father had been a successful trial lawyer until alcohol began to take away his focus and desire. She also had suffered through her father's diminished mental capacity and loss of confidence. She feared that Blake would continue spiraling down until there was no hope of recovery. Her father had died at the age of 55 from liver disease. He had spent the last couple of years of life in a demented state, with numerous physical and mental ailments. She feared the same would happen to her husband, perhaps at an even earlier age.

Alcohol and road trips were the biggest source of concern and they were indelibly intertwined. Blake had confessed his infidelity numerous times. The loneliness of the road was unbearable for him and the temptations were abundant. Kim was hurt by the infidelity, but tolerated it as long as Blake did not get emotionally attached or financially liable for children. Players' wives had to deal with infidelity on the road. It went along with the territory of fame and fortune.

Kim was always more concerned that Blake's boozing would put him in harm's way. His lack of judgment during his binges could be astounding. Kim did not know all of the dangerous predicaments that Blake had put himself in, but she knew of several because the allegations and rumors had to be addressed by Blake's legal advisers. She was incensed that Blake did not care enough about their marriage to change his reckless ways. Kim was grateful that they did not have any children to be embarrassed by their father's actions, but that was a small consolation.

Sandy finally decided that now was the time to call Kim. He told Buck that the chartered plane would wait a few minutes so he could put this distraction to rest.

"Kim, this is Sandy," he spoke in a deliberately calm tone as he slowly drifted away from the pack of players.

"Sandy, please tell me Blake's okay," she blurted out before he could finish.

"He's safe, but he's going to need some help from all of us." Sandy tried to reassure her of Blake's condition.

"What do you mean, Sandy? Is he with the team right now?"

"No Kim, we had to leave him behind because of his drinking. It's all coming to a head right now. Blake will be in the air shortly to Chicago. Can you pick him up?"

"You know I will. Just so I can knock him upside his head for being so stupid," Kim answered in anger.

Sandy knew he would have to calm her down. He anticipated this reaction, but he also knew this time was different. Blake seemed willing to get help this time.

"Now Kim, Blake's agreed to go into rehab this time. You need to see how down he is. This is the time for compassion. We should find comfort that he's willing to quit, not anger for past deeds," Sandy spoke always as the voice of reason.

"Yes, I know you're right Sandy, but I still feel angry. Why hasn't Blake called me?"

"I offered to call you," Sandy once again covered for Blake. "I gave him my other phone. He'll call you shortly. I just wanted you to know that he's safe and the club is getting help for him. Pick him up at O'Hare and somebody from the organization will call your home in a couple of days with the details on his rehab. I have to run now. Take care of my friend."

"Sandy, you're a true friend. Thank you. I don't know what else to say, but goodbye," said Kim before the call ended.

Kim and Sandy had a very unique relationship. Nearly everyone was attracted to Sandy's calm, laid-back demeanor and classically handsome appearance. Kim and Sandy both knew their proper places in this triumvirate, but their mutual admiration was there for all to see except for one self-absorbed star named Blake Benson.

Blake could see nothing but positives in his longtime friend. Their friendship broke all baseball's customary boundaries. The timeworn adage preached that in baseball "you have many buddies, but no true friends." The business side of baseball was harsh, cruel, and fleeting with one's livelihood depending on outperforming even your closest companions.

Even though she had endlessly prayed for this day, she was not happy at the moment. This was no time to rejoice. There was too much ahead to reconcile. She had stayed with her husband for all these years, convinced of his love for her and hers for him, despite all of the travails her alcoholic husband had put her through. She pulled herself together and got ready for the long trip to the airport. Hopefully, there would be better days ahead now that Blake had been forced to face his demons by his employer.

4 — Day of Reckoning

Blake was so distraught because he was left behind while the team moved on to St. Louis that he headed straight for the airport bar. There was no point in quitting at this moment of self-pity. He knew that he would have to go into rehab, but he felt he might as well enjoy the few drinks he had left in him. There was ample time before he had to be on that plane. A few more belts would knock him out for the plane ride home. It all made perfect sense to his alcohol-soaked body.

He was not looking forward to meeting Kim. Blake did not want to admit that she was right all along nor confront her wrath at his stupidity. He figured enough time had passed for Sandy to call Kim. He was certain of his friend's actions. If he said he was going to do something, Sandy always followed through. In his mind Sandy could do little wrong.

Blake figured now was as good a time as any to call Kim and check on her demeanor. He polished off his drink at the bar and moved to a quiet corner without any audio clues that he was still in a drinking environment. He was an emotional wreck, but he had to get it together for just a few moments.

He punched in his wife's number, seemingly unaware that Kim's contact information was stored in Sandy's electronic address book, and waited for her to answer. He decided to mostly listen at the onset of the call to gauge her displeasure.

"Kim, Blake here, please don't go off on me right now," he pleaded.

"Blake, I'm just glad you're safe. I know most of the details from Sandy."

Anger rose in her voice, but subsided quickly. Now was not the time to display emotion. She knew from Sandy that Blake was in a dangerous state of mind. She worried that Blake could just take off and tie on a real good bender if this wasn't handled right.

"I just don't know what to say, Kim. I have so many different emotions trapped inside of me, but I'm mostly just exhausted," Blake was still trying to "play" his wife. He had become so good at manipulating her throughout the alcoholic process. Despite the toll booze took on Blake, he still knew what buttons to push to defend against her tirades. It was all part of the alcoholic game.

"I just feel nothing at this moment," Blake continued. He knew if she were worried about his mental health, she would back off.

Once again Kim kept calm, fearing the worst. Getting Blake home in one piece was still the biggest concern. She knew what the rehab process was all about from her father's own alcohol experiences. It would not be easy. The medical staff would force Blake to confront many personal issues. That time would come soon enough for Blake.

"I just want you home. Don't worry about anything else right now. I'll pick you up at O'Hare when your plane lands. Is it still scheduled for an on-time arrival?"

Blake had no clue, but answered in the affirmative anyway. He could fix that one later if need be.

"I'll see you when I land," Blake spoke in a matter-of-fact tone. "Goodbye Kim. I'm so sorry," he let out those words and ended the cell phone call at the same moment.

Back to the bar he went and watched as the television showed baseball highlights from the night before. The ESPN commentators were gushing praise on Blake's Chicago Cubs team. All baseball fans knew about the Cubs and their supposed Billy Goat curse. 1945 had been the Cubs last appearance in a World Series. The curse refers to Chicago Billy Goat Tavern owner Billy Sianis and his pet goat that he brought with him to the game. Fans around him objected to the smell of the animal. Subsequently, the goat and his owner were forced to leave. He stated right then that no Cubs team would ever get back to the World Series and supposedly even sent a letter to ownership making that same claim.

The Cubs have had a reputation as loveable losers for quite some time. There have been lean years when they were just awful and there were years where it looked for certain like the team would make it back to the World Series. In 2003 they appeared to be on the verge of a Series appearance before the team faded abruptly against the Florida Marlins. Fans were proclaiming the curse as the prime cause for failure.

This year looked different. The team was 10 games up at the beginning of August. Die-hard Cub fans could remember the collapse of 1969 when the team had a huge nine-game lead over the New York Mets in July but gave it all away. This year's version was not only loaded with talent, but seemingly had the chemistry and desire to win it all.

The team had its share of blowouts as any powerhouse squad should, but there were an inordinate amount of late inning rallies that made this year seem like it must be their season. Everything was going their way. There were the usual aches and pains over a season, but there had been no major injuries. The Cubs' prime rival, the defending World Series champion St. Louis Cardinals, had to endure just the opposite. The Cards had so many early-season injuries that there seemed no way they could compete with the Cubs this year. The Cards always had a solid farm system to keep the team afloat, but unless the Cardinals got healthy soon, they looked like second-best this year.

The Cincinnati Reds were a marginal, middling .500 team. The Milwaukee Brewers were always a couple years away from being a contender and the Pittsburgh Pirates were perennial also-rans. The National League Central Division was there for the taking. Nothing appeared on the radar screen as a threat to derail the Cubs this year.

Of course they would have to beat some quality teams in the playoffs, but the National League seemed down in performance this season. This just had to be their year. Too many events were going their way for coincidence.

Blake sat looking at the screen, drink in hand, and it hit him hard. He had just thrown away his best and probably only chance to play with a World Series team. He could do the math in his head. A 30-day stint at a chemical dependency institution would put him past the September 1st deadline for postseason play. The Cubs organization could not leave open a roster spot for someone with such a risky recovery.

Baseball had been his life. Looking back on it at this sanguine moment, Blake wondered how he ever reached this point. He ordered another drink from the bartender and played sorry for himself for another 15 minutes. Head down, mumbling to himself, and physically ill, Blake looked the part of town drunk, and not big-league majestic idol.

He used to have it all, but now he realized he just forgot how to appreciate all of his gifted life. The years had gradually worn away his love for the game. Blake could only focus on himself and not on the millions of other young men who constantly dreamed of being in his position. He could only look at his knees, his bad shoulder and his hatred of travel. He was stuck in a routine of self-pity. He wanted to get back to the feeling of youth, but he was too depressed with the present. He longed to become reacquainted with the morals that his father taught him such a long time ago.

With both parents dead from a tragic car accident and an only child, Blake had to rely on memories. His parents had been excellent role models and had embedded in his mind the values that Blake knew to be true. He had to get back to that point in his life. He couldn't remember when or where he had started to stray from the straight and narrow. It all just sort of crept in, bit by bit.

Blake blurrily looked at his watch and realized he had better get to the gate where his plane would take him back to Chicago. He had promises to keep. Maybe it will all work out for the best, he thought, as he grabbed his sport coat and slowly made his way to the gate.

There was nothing eventful about Blake's plane ride home. He mumbled a bit about being in economy class, but he understood the circumstances in place. It was not like he was being rewarded. Everything that was coming his way seemed to be punitive. He grudgingly accepted that he deserved what he was getting.

Blake never made eye contact with any other passengers or crew. He was hoping nobody would recognize him and ask for an autograph or a picture. This pain-in-the-butt ritual was just one of many irritations that he longed to get away from. The fascination of fame lasted for only a brief time and was slowly replaced by disgust that grew to unapproachable levels. If anybody noticed him this time, they did not call him out.

His mind and body fell asleep with the comfort of drunkenness, but awoke to the anxiousness of sobriety. Looking at his watch, he assumed they would be landing at Chicago shortly. He felt somewhat comforted by Kim's apparent lack of anger, but was still on guard for a different reception at the airport. He yearned for a long night of sleep in his own bed. Sleep had become Blake's escape from pain and suffering. It was a rare moment to tune out the discomforts of physical pain and mental anguish. At times he would just sleep to avoid confrontation and at other awkward moments he would simply pretend to be asleep.

The flight landed on time and Kim was there waiting for her husband in need. The hug at arrival was terse and awkward, but at least it was a hug. He had feared the worst for half a day now.

Kim knew immediately that Blake was still somewhat under the influence. The scent of alcohol had become a trademark with Blake, much like a brand of cologne with others. His eyes were glazed and reddened by the irritations of alcohol. He certainly did not look like a major league baseball player. His clothes were wrinkled and unkempt. His demeanor was sheepish, not self-confident.

"Blake, let's hurry up and get home. Did you check luggage or is this all you have? You look like shit Blake," Kim said tersely.

"I feel even worse. This has to be about as low as it gets," Blake softly spoke his words in a sorrowful tone. He still had to play the game to keep Kim at bay. It had been so long that he really had no other way to talk to her anymore. Nothing expressed was sincere. It was all manipulative mumbo jumbo.

"Yes, I did check luggage. It shouldn't take long. Let's go to baggage claim and get the hell out of here before somebody recognizes me. Certainly don't want to explain why I'm not in St. Louis with the team," Blake spoke as he rushed to the claim area.

"Just don't make eye contact with anybody, and move along."

"I think I know by now how to play the game," Kim spoke angrily.

"I'm sorry. Please hold my hand Kim?"

"Sure Blake." She knew this was no place for a scene.

The two of them walked hand in hand, but not with the appearance of love one might expect from a married couple. Like much else in their lives right now, this was all about show, and definitely not any tell.

After waiting for a brief but uncomfortable time, the luggage carousel filled with baggage from Atlanta. Blake recognized his instantly and rushed to pick it up instead of waiting for it to come to him.

They began to make their way to an exit when a commotion up ahead caught their attention. People were gathered around an airport television.

"Something big must be happening Blake?" Kim curiously spoke. "Look at all the people staring at the TV screen!"

"Who cares?" was all Blake could reply.

Kim suddenly heard an elderly lady speak in astonishment. "It's the Cubs," the old woman shrieked.

"Did you hear that Blake? The lady said something about the Cubs."

Blake did not respond verbally, but his actions spoke plenty as he rushed towards the throng of people, dropping Kim's hand as soon as he heard mention of the Cubs.

Breaking news flashed from the screen. The broadcaster spoke in her professional tone, but one could see the incredulity all over her face.

"We have this report just in. The charter plane carrying the Chicago Cubs baseball team from Atlanta has reportedly crashed outside the city of St. Louis. There were reports of heavy thunderstorms in the area at the time of the reported crash. Repeating what has just come across our news desk. Wait, we now have confirmation that the charter plane carrying the Chicago Cubs baseball team has gone down. We are receiving reports right now that all on board were killed. Can you confirm that? Yes, we do have confirmation that all on board have perished."

Blake was now close enough to hear the details. Wheeling his luggage along, he stopped to focus on the screen. Hearing the news was all it took for Blake to crumble to his feet. His face ashen, barely conscious, Blake felt about as numb as a person could be and still be alive. Security surrounded the scene and looked after Blake. It took seconds for bystanders to realize that the man being tended to was himself a Chicago Cubs player. Blake Benson was all there was left of this first-place team, even if he was a shadow of his former confident superstar self.

5 — The Mourning

Blake awoke in his own bed the following morning. The aura of comfort, the smell of familiar sheets and the nestled neck formed perfectly by your own pillow were all immediately replaced upon awakening by the pain of loss. The mourning that seemingly takes over every thought in your brain that simply cannot be purged plagued Blake throughout this conscious day.

Kim lovingly brought him some breakfast in bed. She had to force Blake to eat the bacon and eggs along with his standard morning coffee. His body language still spoke of a beaten man. She was grieving as well, but she knew his pain was deeper and required immediate care. She knew most of the players and their wives or girlfriends and of course, Sandy's loss hit her hard as well.

Words were few and far between. What could be said? The shock still had not worn off. It still seemed like the team was just on the road, awaiting return from a long, boring journey that is a 13-game road swing. Hugs triumphed over verbiage this day.

That escape would vanish as outside information couldn't be quarantined with never ending television news. The newspapers were filled with heartbreaking stories from family and fans. The Internet was saturated with the topic and there were the usual conspiracy theories already floating around in cyberspace. The tragedy's sphere of influence was seemingly everywhere in the 24/7 electronically open world.

Blake reasoned he could either deal with his own innermost thoughts in silence or succumb to the media circus. He chose the former. His brain was busy and his heart heavy, but his own feelings seemed to be more manageable than the overdramatic media scrutiny. Grief in the abstract was preferable over visual stimuli that deepened the sorrow.

His only foray into the media world was his opening of the daily paper. Unbeknownst to him, Blake's picture was strewn all over the paper as a bystander captured his reaction to the news at the airport. Cameras were never more accessible now that cell phones with cameras were in the hands of most travelers. It was a very intrusive and emotionally charged picture with Blake vividly displaying mental anguish. This picture would haunt him forever, he thought. It would never be forgotten, but hopefully it could be repressed.

Kim tried to alleviate his pain with gentle expressions that Blake was indeed the fortunate one. What was meant to be comforting turned out instead to be a guilt-ridden reminder that for some unexplained reason, Blake had survived because he possessed character flaws that he was unable or unwilling to control. Nothing made sense in his mind. He was incredibly undisciplined and even immoral at times, but his boorish behavior was somehow rewarded with life, while his dedicated, hard working, extremely professional teammates perished.

Sandy was the one teammate that Blake would miss the most. He wondered how his best friend's family would survive this horrendous ordeal. Blake and Kim had been close to all of the Gonzalez family. Sandy's wife Lisa had befriended Kim from the start of Blake's Cubs career. The Bensons were the beneficiaries of Sandy and Lisa's experience as professional mentors on the lifestyle of a major league ballplayer's family. The Gonzalez children became surrogate kids for the childless Bensons. How awful it must be to lose their father at such an early age; the three children were all 12 or younger. Blake only had to multiply this situation by 35 to realize the scope of this tragedy as most of the players, coaches and media had wives, girlfriends and family who would have to deal with the terrible pain of loss.

At first recollection of the tragedy Blake had forgotten about Mickey Jansen, the head groundskeeper at Wrigley, as it was not part of his normal professional responsibilities to travel with the team. The portly, bald and sometimes crass Mickey had become a favorite of all the players. Jansen was a character out of a bygone era that defined people by their nationalities and saw nothing wrong about using slurs to describe players. It was his way, but he didn't have a bigoted bone in his body. He just had a simpler way of remembering people by their color, nationality, or creed.

Unsuspecting rookies were often goaded by veteran players to go introduce themselves to Mickey. Most players felt it was important to relay concerns about the playing field so it didn't seem too out of the ordinary to the naïve newbies to establish some sort of rapport with the head groundskeeper. They soon became the victim of a huge prank as Mickey would tear them a new asshole and call them any identifiable slur he could amazingly come up with on a moment's notice for having the nerve to "kiss up" to the head groundskeeper that valued himself as more of a part owner of the team than an employee.

Once players got to know Mickey they all loved him. He would do anything for "his" players and had amazing connections around Chicago. The elder statesman could hook you up with anything imaginable in the city of Chicago and he wasn't shy boasting about his power.

Unfortunately, Mickey had been diagnosed with terminal liver cancer and one of his last desires was to mend his troubled relationship with his seldom-seen daughter who lived in Atlanta. Mickey had left Chicago on his own a week earlier to spend some remaining time with his daughter and was returning on the team's charter. The quick and sudden death of Mickey was probably for the better. It was a rare and unique positive sidelight to the tragic passing of so many young men in their prime of life.

The details were just beginning to emerge from the crash although the exact cause would be years away from disclosure, if at all. Amidst the wreckage, the black box was located that would help FAA investigators determine the likely cause. The plane took off from Atlanta in good flying conditions but had run into rough weather as it approached St. Louis in the mid-afternoon heat. Severe thunderstorms cut a broad path through the middle of the country, but it was nothing unlike the many summer flights the team had endured yearly across the country. Some speculated that a lightning strike might have disabled the aircraft or possibly a wind shear as they approached their destination. Nothing was ruled out at this point, but what did it matter anyway? They were all gone and would not be coming back.

The city of Chicago was in deep mourning and disbelief as well. There became an immediate memorial outside of the Cubs' hallowed home, Wrigley Field. Thousands paid visit to the ballpark and flowers mounted at the main entrance. Some fans stayed there all day, tears intermittently streaming down their anguished faces. Jerseys, hats and other memorabilia were mixed in with the flowers to provide a shrine to the fallen team. One little boy, standing in front of the makeshift shrine with his father, left his old baseball glove signed with autographs from his favorite players amidst the flowers. The boy wrote his own message on the glove. "God Bless my Cubs."

The city's leaders, including the mayor, wanted to honor and remember the fallen team, but were unsure how to proceed with dignity and privacy for the families involved. Mayor Thomas Washington met with the Cubs ownership group, and feelers were sent out to some of the senior members of the team's extended family.

There would be a grand memorial at some point, but emotions were too raw at the moment to decide. It was determined that all involved would proceed with caution and with as many people involved as possible to prevent oversights. However, it was apparent that a clear line of authority would have to be established. Everything would funnel through the Cubs ownership. It was their team.

Major League Baseball had the biggest problem: How to honor those lost while at the same time proceeding with the current season with over two months left, including the postseason?

The Commissioner's office had a contingency plan for this type of tragic event. Thankfully, up until now, it had never been put into practice. There would be a one-week moratorium on games to honor those who perished. Logistically, a week's time would be needed to replenish the Chicago Cubs baseball team through an "expansion type draft."

When Major League Baseball had expanded in the past, all other teams were allowed to protect a designated amount of players on their major league roster.

The contingency plan for this tragedy allowed for a similar occurrence. Those that were left unprotected could be picked by the Cubs to form their new roster. A player selected would have 72 hours to report to his new team. It would be a struggle to organize a new squad on short notice, but this was the best alternative to keep the integrity of the season intact and to be as fair as possible to the devastated Cubs team.

Politicians were falling over each other in tribute to the fallen players. The mayor had spoken, but others felt the need to contribute to the public display of affection for the victims. The governor of Illinois, state legislators and members of the U.S. Congress from Illinois were outspoken in their sympathy. The emotionally charged issues of national defense and domestic policy, hotly debated daily, took a backseat to moments of silence and various individual tributes to the memory of the players, their suffering families and all of Chicago. Even the South Siders of the Windy City, forever loyal to their White Sox, were in mourning today for their crosstown rivals.

The president of the United States felt the need to address the nation as he seized upon the moment to bring people together, rather than dividing them with political battles. He deftly recognized baseball as America's summer pastime that binds its citizens in a common bond, each to their favorite team, but collectively in a common pursuit of greatness and loyalty.

"When we grieve together, not as Yankee fans or Dodger fans or Brave fans, but as American fans, the country as a whole rises in spirit to honor our heroes in greater fashion. God bless the families and the victims of this terrible tragedy." The president spoke in glory and attempted to focus on the enormous impact these athletes have on our families and of all the enjoyment baseball brings to the country, past and present.

For one season at the very least, the Chicago Cubs would truly become America's team, even as the attention and focus of a nation was just beginning.

6 — Closure

Blake was still rather in disbelief even after the memorial service, and he felt something was missing as he wandered aimlessly throughout his home. He was unable to concentrate for any length of time and felt compelled to focus in on the abundant awards and trophies that lined his den.

Although most of the recognition was for individual performance, Blake was enough of a professional to understand that his teammates also played an important role in any personal achievements. He had a glazed look in his eyes as he fixed on his National League Rookie of the Year trophy and remembered another young, but more experienced veteran in Sandy showing him the ropes.

Professional baseball at this level was a constant readjustment to scouting reports and other tidbits of information that were passed on in a formal and sometimes informal manner. This characteristic of the game at the highest and most sophisticated ladder of success ensured that there would be plenty of stretches of disappointment. It was so easy to lose confidence as a young player that hadn't gone through the many ups and downs.

Sandy would encourage Blake to study the game and his own self to constantly become aware of subtle changes by opponents. This game was more about learning from failure rather than basking in recollection of personal highpoints.

It was a constant reminder from Sandy that Blake belonged or he wouldn't be here, and that the rookie had more natural ability than 95 percent of the players in this league. All that was missing was the experience and honing of the mental aspects of his game. Sandy reassured Blake that all he had to do was watch and soak it all in and he would flourish.

Blake suddenly snapped out of his trance and came up with an impromptu idea. The immediate plan of action was new, but the thought of visiting the accident site had bounced around his head in a back and forth manner for the past few troubling days.

Without consulting his wife or any Cubs organizational member, he decided to use the many contacts he had acquired from his fame and fortune to arrange a helicopter ride to the crash site just outside of St. Louis.

Blake knew of a pilot that had strong connections to the FAA and he called him to check on his availability and the regulations that protected the sanctity of the scene for investigators. Blake was assured of his access to the site and the helicopter pilot kindly offered Blake anytime availability.

Blake immediately jumped on the offer of assistance and asked if he could go now. Money was never an issue for the wealthy ballplayer and he told the pilot he would just double his normal rate if they could go within the hour.

As if doubling his rate of pay wasn't enough, Blake had become accustomed to others welcoming the opportunity to help a celebrity athlete. He wasn't surprised in the least when others dropped whatever they were doing to accommodate him, and this request was no different as they agreed to meet at the airport in an hour.

Blake hurriedly wrote a note to Kim and snuck out the door before she could figure out what was going on. Blake often responded abruptly and on the spur of the moment, while the analytical Kim surveyed most situations in a more deliberate and rational manner. She would undoubtedly slow Blake down to make certain of the physical and emotional consequences of a rash decision.

Explaining his actions at a later time was something Blake had become expert at in his marriage; although his reasoning was normally dismissed by Kim, it was ultimately accepted if not understood. His wife had come to accept Blake, flaws and all. Some, like the drinking and philandering, were harder to deal with and exacted a deep emotional toll. Blake's instinct to move quickly without much thought was irritating, but not necessarily emotionally damaging to Kim.

Blake arrived at the airport a few hours before dusk to would enable the pilot and Blake to reach their destination in plenty of time before darkness set in.

The two of them met at a predetermined location and Blake immediately thanked the gracious pilot and handed him a wad of hundred-dollar bills.

"If this isn't enough, just let me know," Blake blurted out quickly. He was assured that the stack of hundreds was more than enough to compensate the helicopter pilot for his time and influence on such short notice.

"I remember you helping me out before a couple of times, am I right Paul?"

"Yes Blake, there was that impromptu trip to one of your teammates' celebrity golf tournaments in Ohio, and I think there was one other midnight call that I can't seem to recollect other than the unusual time of night that you got in touch with me," Paul replied a bit sarcastically.

"Yep, I'm a bit of a spur of the moment type of guy, but you obviously know that already."

"Well, you always make it interesting, Blake, and definitely worth my while monetarily."

"Paul, I hope you don't mind if I just sit here and reflect as I try to prepare myself for this upcoming emotional moment? I really don't know what to expect from myself when I get there."

"No problem Blake, I can't even begin to wonder what it must be like for you. We can take all the time you want."

"Thanks Paul, I don't really know what it's like yet either. That's why I've got to go there. You do your thing and I'll just wave at you when I'm ready."

Blake knew they were getting close as he could see the city of St. Louis on the horizon. He steeled up inside and motioned to Paul that he was ready as it would be just a few minutes away now.

There was plenty of open space and a few highways with sparse traffic as they continued closer to the site where the aircraft came down and split apart like a cheap toy airplane from the incredible force of impact.

An eerie sense of how his teammates must have felt as the aircraft went down flashed through his head. Blake had been on so many flights to the Gateway City of St. Louis. They had been bounced around plenty of times with turbulence and approaching storms, so Blake surmised that most of his fellow teammates were likely unaware of the impending doom until the plane spiraled out of control.

Judging by the distance to the airport Blake ventured a silent guess as to the length of rapid descent and was somewhat comforted by the apparent short time it probably took before impact. Most of them probably were awakened by the plunge, but deceased before they had much time to gather their senses.

As Rick picked out a good landing spot, Blake stared in disbelief at the crash site. Not fully knowing what his reaction would be, Blake was cautious and on guard for any outburst of grief. He didn't want to show his emotions in front of Rick, but he fully understood that anything could happen the minute they landed.

The sorrowful Blake glanced over at Rick and asked him to cut the engine with the universal slash sign across the throat. Rick immediately shut down the engine and the blades slowly let go of their deafening sound as a troubling, eerie silence slowly overtook the site.

"Rick, I hope you understand the sensitivity of this moment for me. I just want to walk around in total silence and let whatever feelings come over me dictate my movements. I'll meet you back here when I'm done. I'll be okay. Just let me grieve in private, please."

Rick nodded in agreement without saying a word. It was obvious that Blake was in a great deal of emotional pain at the moment and the pilot knew there was nothing he could say that would help him in the grieving process.

Blake stepped out of the helicopter and made a complete circular turn as if to gather his physical and emotional bearings. The wreckage was nearly gone since the investigators had sorted through whatever was left of the aircraft and moved it to a separate location to try and piece it together. The black box containing all the flight data and communications with air traffic controllers had been located, but it would be months if not years before any conclusive evidence and final determination would be released to the public. It didn't matter to Blake how it happened, but only that it did happen.

There was a crater where the plane impacted and Blake could feel the eeriness of the locale where all of his teammates had perished. It was now a spiritual site that reflected a final ending on Earth for a professional baseball team, a private shrine if you will.

Blake moved about as if looking for some sort of debris that verified all of this in his denial-filled mind. He walked farther away from the impact site and tried to find anything that might have been missed. There was quite a violent storm at the time and Blake figured that winds and the tremendous force on impact could leave debris anywhere within some sort of reason. The investigators were highly professional, but Blake figured there must be something out there that could emotionally cement the finality of it all in his brain.

Off in all directions looking for nothing in particular, but anything of substance, Blake wandered rather aimlessly throughout. There seemed to be an abundance of litter, but most of it was too shredded to make sense of it.

He did find a couple pens with Chicago Cubs emblems on them and surprisingly enough a Major League insignia baseball that somehow was missed. Blake was tempted to pick it up and take it home with him, but it seemed too macabre to collect.

It was all there for him to see, but it was too impersonal to hit home. Off a bit in the distance he was able to spot a shiny reflection that appeared to be partially hidden behind a rock. Blake was drawn to it out of curiosity and in the belief that it may be something of significance.

He picked up his pace and focused in on the glare so as not to lose the sightline. As he approached the bowling ball-sized rock his heart raced a bit in anticipation. Not knowing exactly what he was looking for, but sensing this might be it, Blake picked up his gait to a slight jog.

As he got within a few feet Blake immediately recognized the shining object as a necklace of some sort. He reached down to pick it up and was shocked to see a St. Christopher medal dangling from the necklace. His legs felt wobbly and he suddenly felt nauseated as he knew this medal and to whom it belonged. On the back side of the Roman Catholic medal of St. Christopher was the inscription to his best friend Sandy from his wife and children.

As the patron saint of travelers and to protect against sudden death St. Christopher was popular among Latin American athletes. Apparently the medal had become dislodged from Sandy and wound up too far from the crash site to be detected. Perhaps the rock had just hidden it from view, but whatever the case, the amazing discovery had a chilling effect on Blake as he stared at it in disbelief.

Again, another incredible spiritual moment with his best friend strangely connected to Blake once more. He held the medal close to his chest and knelt down. Blake looked to the heavens and again wondered why. Why had he lived while all his teammates died?

This was the defining moment as Blake let his emotions out and cried incessantly for several minutes. He switched positions and stretched out prone on his back. He stared up to the skies and cried his eyes out until he felt totally empty inside. Finally he picked himself up and walked ever so slowly back to the helicopter pilot who was patiently waiting.

Blake put the medal in his pocket and told the pilot in a soft monotone to take him back to Chicago. He had found closure in the surprising find, and reality set in and set in hard. It was a silent trip home as Blake closed his eyes and never said a word until they parted company.

He thanked the pilot and handed him some more cash out of his pocket without even thinking of the enormous sum he had already compensated Rick for the inconvenience prior. It was over now and Blake could move forward, but still trying to make sense of it all in his head. It was done and it was time to go home to his wife and explain the bizarre circumstances. Emptiness became befuddlement at the whole goddamn crazy circumstance of his survival. The unfittest had survived, proving Charles Darwin wrong in this instance.

7 — Moving On

Putting the memorial service behind them wasn't easy for Blake and Kim. The pain was still too deep, too raw, to move on completely. They did their best to look forward and not in the rearview mirror. Blake's health was just the ticket to shift their focus.

Temporarily lost in the shuffle was his upcoming alcohol rehab stay. Blake didn't want to face up to his problem until it was forced upon him. The tragedy delayed the inevitable, but now was the moment to tackle this debilitating disease head-on. The emotional trauma of the sudden tragedy piled on Blake's troubles and the fear was he might go over the edge unless treatment was done immediately.

Blake had spent countless hours examining his whole life. He couldn't think of anything positive alcohol had done for him despite relishing the high booze provided. Deep down he knew that it was a false high based on deception of his senses. Back and forth, over and over, he examined the how and why of his addiction. He inwardly admitted his alcoholism a long time ago, the kind of secret one keeps to themselves out of pride. The next step would have to be a public admittance of his problem and the scrutiny that would be thrust upon him, unwelcome as it would be.

Cubs General Manager Marty Anderson was too preoccupied with assembling a new team to put Blake's treatment on the front burner. A quick and terse phone call apologizing for the delay in his treatment was all the communication Blake would receive for the moment. Blake certainly understood and regardless, he was in no hurry to be shipped away for a month's stay. Kim however, was adamant that his alcoholism be addressed immediately.

As Kim awoke the morning after the memorial still irritated at Blake for leaving for the crash site unannounced, she bit her tongue and held her criticism when Blake showed her what he had found at the site. The miraculous find sidetracked Kim for a few hours as she and Blake discussed what he had seen and how he felt when he came across the medallion. They both knew it had to be returned to Sandy's family, but for now it was a Benson keepsake. Blake wore the St. Christopher medal even though he scoffed at such foolishness from his non-religious perspective.

Later in the calm of the afternoon, after they had relaxed a bit with some casual reading, Kim approached Blake with that very serious look of a wife who means business.

"Blake, we have to talk," Kim spoke softly, but sternly in the tone no husband wants to hear.

"Kim, I think I know what this is going to be about. Save your breath. The organization has so many pressing issues to deal with right now that I know my situation is far down the list."

"Why do we have to wait for them to act?" Kim simply saw no need for the club to hold their hands in this individual problem.

"I guess we don't," Blake said agreeably. Realizing that he'd just inadvertently set the wheels in motion for immediate treatment, he backtracked subtly.

Blake leaned forward from his favorite living room recliner, slowly stood up and put his battered catcher's hands around Kim's shoulders in a vain attempt to reassure.

"I'm a professional baseball player that wants nothing more than to rejoin his team as soon as I can, but I want the organization to handle this as they see fit. This is as much about them as it is me. I have to be 100 percent compliant. Let's wait for them to make all the moves and then I can just be a good trouper and follow orders completely. It'll just look better to the organization this way."

Kim dislodged Blake's hands from her shoulders in abrupt fashion and spoke in anger.

"No, Blake, this is about you and me. Screw the Cubs. Blake, you know this is pure bullshit, pleasing the Cubs when you know they would cut your ass in a Chicago minute if you were useless to the owners even though you've been incredibly loyal to them. This is about our marriage and our lives. I've stood behind you all the way from the minors to this moment, but this is our problem."

Kim was adamant in her protestation, but only Blake knew at this point in time that he was contemplating beating the booze by himself. His deflections were just a delay tactic, a temporary reprieve before the real war that was coming down the pike would be fought.

Blake took the counteroffensive in an attempt to shift the blame and prey on Kim's normally present guilt. His voice rose in anger this time.

"Remember we're still needed here for others, Kim. Don't be goddamn selfish. Jesus Christ, let's show some compassion for our extended Cub family. We've got a lot of friends here that are grieving terribly."

Blake was always proficient at playing Kim and he was in rare form today at just the right time to stave off the persistence of his wife.

As Kim backed off in retreat, Blake took a moment to reflect once more on his perils. He had inwardly accepted his problem and would soon publicly address the issue with media. He also knew that when he put his mind to something, he rarely ever failed. He was treating this as just another hurdle he had to overcome to sustain his lifelong desire to be a major league baseball player. He rationalized his impending decision by reaffirming to himself that this was something only he could accomplish, nobody else would be there to do it for him. Any well-intentioned treatment programs would still have to be implemented by him and although others could help, it would be up to him to overcome his demons. Only he could rededicate his mind and body to recover what he once had. In the end it was all up to him and him alone.

8 — A Changed Man

The shock of losing all of his teammates had subsided just enough for Blake to reevaluate his life. The immense pain was still present, but somehow through all of the hurt, the guilt and the unexplained insanity of it all, Blake still had the fortitude to look inward.

Blake and Kim were never very religious or spiritual, but for the most part they were, by all accounts, decent loving human beings. A professional athlete has a certain community responsibility and as year-round residents of Chicago, the two were active in fundraising and various charitable organizations.

Blake had accepted his community responsibility, but had not really embraced it. He tolerated the role. He understood it was part of the game that players went along with to interact with adoring fans.

As a naïve, highly touted rookie, Blake had soaked in the admiration, but grew more cynical by the year as fans turned on him as often as the wind changed direction. He had lost sight of the fact that the opposite of love is not hate, but indifference. These fans cared and they expressed their concern passionately, if not always positively.

Blake's epiphany with the fans came about as he became intensely aware of the love the upper Midwest fans had toward the Cubs following the accident. He saw stunned expressionless faces at the memorial. He saw grown men with tears streaming down their faces as their sons looked on in disbelief, never seeing their role models cry before.

If there was a supreme spiritual being overlooking all of civilization, surely he must have been trying to tell one Blake Benson something about his life moving forward. How else could this whole situation make any sense?

Knowing that change must happen is one thing. The mind often tells an alcoholic that he must stop drinking. This time Blake felt a spiritual motivation. He felt reborn, as if the old Blake had died along with the rest of his teammates in that plane crash. He suddenly did not want to be the old Blake. He couldn't even understand how he had become that person.

He now knew he had the motivation to start anew. The problem moving forward was convincing the organization that he did not need an alcohol rehab stay. Blake knew the front office would be calling him soon enough to get him into treatment.

Kim was pressing the matter as well. Blake could feel the walls squeezing in around him. He surmised that he was down to his last day or two before he would be shipped off. Now was the time to be proactive and make his case.

He would have to call Marty Anderson and set up a time to speak with him. Blake had often thought of an angle or manner to manipulate others to fit his agenda. This was going to have to play out differently. He knew he would have to speak from the heart and spill everything out in the open to convince the general manager to let him stay with the team.

Blake always respected Marty even though contract negotiations were always a strain on their relationship. Marty was a no-nonsense guy who seemed a perfect fit for a player personnel man. He never got too close to his players and never became emotionally attached to them.

He evaluated through numbers and had a real talent for recognizing performance trends before anybody else. If he had any emotional weaknesses toward players, it was unknown to anyone. His reputation was solid as a cold hard businessman and he reveled in it.

As if on a whim, but surely with deep predetermined thought, Blake emerged from his bedroom and started the wheels in motion as he hit the Cubs front office on his speed dial. He knew it was time to man up.

Blake knew that he would have to go through Marty's receptionist before he could reach the general manager directly. Cindy Mattson was no slouch either. She seemingly held more clout in the organization than half of the deceased team members ever had. He knew she was aware of his pending rehab stay. Blake correctly figured that the sensitivity of the matter would allow him to get through to Marty.

"Cindy, this is Blake Benson. I know Marty's extremely busy, but this is about my impending alcohol rehab stay. Can I please talk to him right now for just two minutes?"

"Blake, you know the routine. You have to schedule these appointments in advance, even for a phone call," Cindy tersely responded, living up to her reputation as a stickler for details.

"Kim really wants me to get some details right here and now, she's all over me Cindy." Blake was hopeful his wife's name would help matters. "I'm kind of in the crosshairs here Cindy. Please help me just this one time? Please?"

Blake apparently forgot that he had used up several favors in the past from Cindy, but she relented anyway.

"Hold on Blake. I guess I can see your wife's point on this one. I'll transfer you to Marty now."

Blake knew there was no holding back now. It was the bottom of the ninth and his team was trailing by one run. He would have to deliver against the best closer in the business, his own GM Marty Anderson.

"This is Marty Anderson," he spoke gruffly. "I know it's you Blake. What can I do for you? Before you answer I just want to tell you that the organization is very aware of the sensitivity of this matter. We have been in touch with the players' union and are being extremely cautious about any undue speculation from the media. You're very fortunate that Sandy cared enough about you to put you on a separate plane to get immediate help. It's my fault that I haven't followed through quick enough. I apologize for that."

"Marty, I can't begin to tell you how much I've thought about the circumstances leading up to my suspension or whatever we'll be calling it. I know I owe my life to Sandy and I know I screwed up big-time."

"Ok Blake, get to the point of your call," responded the GM, getting back to his official voice after the apology.

"I really need to sit down and talk to you Marty, face to face. I'm really struggling here with the accident. There's plenty of guilt along with trying to figure why I'm alive and the guys aren't."

"I can get you some professional help Blake, but talking to me probably isn't going to do you any good."

"No Marty, this is really a baseball issue first and foremost. You'll understand if we meet. Half an hour is about all it'll take. Fifteen years with the organization should be worth something Marty? Please?"

"Ok Blake, a half hour it is. The emotion of all this has got me a bit off my professional game. Be here tomorrow at nine."

"Thank you Marty, I'll be there first thing in the morning."

Blake spent the entire evening rehearsing his plea to remain with the team and stay sober on his own. He was concerned about appearing too weak but Blake knew he would really have to show some emotion to convince Marty. This time it was sincere. Slowly but surely, Blake had realized the extent of his problem and the new lease on life he had been given by his friend Sandy and by God as well.

Kim immediately noticed how edgy Blake was during the evening. Realizing that Blake often drank to take that edge off, she was concerned about his uncomfortable demeanor.

"Blake, is there something bothering you this evening?"

"Why do you ask Kim?"

"I can't imagine why," Blake continued with obvious sarcasm.

"Well you seem very fidgety this evening and emotionally distant. And it's even more than usual. And don't get smart with me Blake. Man up, this is all your own doing."

"Well, I might as well tell you I have a meeting first thing in the morning with Marty. We're going to discuss my options."

"What options are you talking about Blake? There are no options. You need to get into treatment as soon as possible. You should've been there days ago. I know you Blake Charles Benson and you've been scheming up something."

"Jesus Kim, I told you that the organization has a million things to deal with right now. It's moving along slowly, but we're dealing with it."

"You could've fooled me. It looks like one stall tactic after another. What's your plan Blake? You always have one," Kim spoke with disgust at Blake's past numerous false promises.

"We'll have a concrete plan in place by the end of tomorrow. I promise you that Kim."

"You better Blake. I'm losing patience with you and the Cubs. I'll go around all of you and get you in myself if you don't move quickly."

"I hear you loud and clear honey. I'm ready for resolution too." Blake still somewhat coyly spoke in vague terms and with just enough of an imperceptible smirk gently masking his true face.

Blake was now convinced his wife knew something was up. It all should have been cut and dried by now. He knew one way or another it was going to be a disappointment for one of them. Blake wanted to be a part of this new team right away and Kim wanted Blake to get into treatment. One battle at a time, he thought to himself.

It was not a sound sleeping night for Blake as he continually tossed and turned throughout the night. He must have slept some because he was awoken by a dream he had about his friend Sandy.

Sandy had appeared to Blake in the dream and reassured Blake that this was all part of a plan God had for him. Trust in Him and let the pieces fall where they may. There was absolutely no need to worry. Whatever worked out would be just the way it should have been.

"Trust God my friend, trust God and you will find comfort."

Blake suddenly awoke and lay there in bed trying to make sense of what his subconscious mind had just told him. He was unsure of what it meant. He still did not trust any spiritual message. He looked at the clock beside their bed and realized that he still had several hours to go before he would need to get up. He snuggled up next to his wife and hoped her warm body would give him the reassurance that he needed to fall back asleep.

When he finally awoke at dawn, Blake sprang out of bed and hurried straight to the shower. His anxiety was overwhelming at the moment. He was hopeful that a long, warm shower would allay his uneasiness.

The pulsating warm water was indeed soothing. Blake's anxiety simply wouldn't let him enjoy the moment, however, and he finished up quickly. He was out the door before Kim even realized he was awake.

The morning rush hour traffic was miserable as always in Chicago. Blake's stomach was turning from anticipation of the meeting, and irritation from the slow-moving traffic compounded his anxiety. He simply was worried that his plea would be poorly received by Marty because he would appear too out of control, too sick to be taken seriously.

A drink sure would be good about now to calm the nerves, Blake thought before shaking that troubling and persistent thought out of his head.

After an hour in traffic, Blake pulled in to the Cubs headquarters at Wrigley Field. It was go time and he really felt the adrenaline surge as he entered the building.

Marty deliberately made Blake wait for 15 minutes past their scheduled meeting time of nine o'clock. Always one to be aware of his status, Marty wanted to make sure Blake knew who was boss here. Not all of the intimidation in sports occurs on the playing field.

When Cindy finally told Blake to step into Marty's office, Blake was like a deferential child. He entered timidly as the door was open.

"Good morning Mr. Anderson."

"Hi Blake, how are you today?"

"I'm a bit nervous, kind of like my first spring training."

"Now there's no need for that Blake. We've known each other for a decade or so."

"Marty, I'm not the same person I was 10 days ago. I feel different."

"Well sit down. Can I get you something to drink? I suppose that came out kind of wrong. Would you like coffee?"

"No thanks. I'm good. No need to walk on pins and needles here Marty. We don't need to avoid any alcohol references." Blake cracked a smile to put both of them at ease.

"Ok Blake, let's get to it. When are you going to rehab? I can make a call right now and set it up. It's overdue and I can speak for everyone in the organization here. We all just want you to get healthy and take care of yourself and your family for the long-term."

"Well Marty, about that. This is why I wanted to speak to you personally. Please let me finish before you respond. Ok?"

Blake looked up to see Marty with his hands folded and his head held high with an intimidating scowl predominant on his face. This was Blake's turn at a power play.

"Sure Blake, as long as you stay on the topic of your health." Marty simply wouldn't relinquish any power here.

Marty was still trying to remain in control, but he could see the nervousness in Blake's face. He was curious as to where this was going. Marty fidgeted with his pen and swung back and forth in his swivel chair ever so slowly as he gauged Blake's demeanor.

"I've had a lot of time this past week to reflect and to try and make some sense out of this unbelievable tragedy. I know I've screwed up and I know I've been spiraling out of control for way too long now. I apologize for that."

Blake peered up at Marty to see if he had any visible reaction. He felt awkward at first and remembered that he needed to look Marty straight in the eye.

"I know I can't undo the things I've done, but I can't escape the feeling that I miraculously survived while my teammates didn't, all because I was a drunken fool. There has to be some reason for this turn of events."

Blake again focused on Marty's body language and he could tell Marty was getting anxious. He knew it was time to get to the point.

"Marty, I am 100 percent committed to staying sober. I'm a changed man. I want to be a part of this new team. I want to try and make amends to the organization and to myself. I want to lead this new Cubs team and I can't do that if I go away for rehab. I have never been so sure of anything in my life. I can beat this on my own. I know I can!"

Blake stopped speaking as if to indicate to Marty that it was his turn to reply. Blake had no idea if his plea was falling on deaf ears. Marty stayed true to form and was expressionless throughout.

With great deliberation, Marty slowly stood up out of his chair and looked out the window as if to reflect. He turned around to face Blake and stood over him like a high school principal.

"Blake, all the experts say that you can't do this by yourself. You've acknowledged your problem and that's a good start, but there are usually underlying reasons for all this that you need to work out. I can't go along with this."

"I'm begging you Marty. All that matters is that I stop drinking. All that other stuff is bullshit. Jesus Christ, every little thought or action that we all do is somehow related to our pasts. That is all such bullshit!"

"I am sorry Blake. Maybe you can rejoin the team in 45 days if you do what they say and work on your recovery."

Blake just sat there speechless. He put his head down into his hands and started to cry uncontrollably. Marty walked over to him and put his hands on Blake's shoulders. There was nothing to say. Marty just consoled him with the soft reassurance of a rhythmic pat on his shoulders.

Blake composed himself and felt as if he had taken a couple of mighty swings with his bat, but had come up empty. He would go down swinging if he had to.

He stood up himself and faced Marty directly. With every ounce of emotion he had left in his body, he pleaded one more time.

"Our friend Sandy saved my life with his courage. He went out of his way to make sure I faced up to my problem. I don't know if I would've had the strength to quit drinking had not he and the team died in that plane crash. That event is somehow tied into my recovery. Sandy appeared to me in my dream last night and he told me that it would all work out. That God had a plan for me. This is my plan. I am to lead this team and I can't do it from some stale health clinic, spilling my guts all over the floor to a bunch of strangers."

Whether it was the reference to the beloved Sandy or the outpouring of emotion, Marty appeared to have a different look. He was suddenly sold that Blake could be counted on.

Marty looked straight into Blake's teary eyes and paused while he thought what to say to him next. Marty lifted his right arm and securely placed it on Blake's left shoulder.

The pause gave Blake hope that Marty might be relinquishing. Blake dabbed at his eyes as if to clear them and stared right into Marty's glaze.

"You've got a deal Blake, on one condition. You'll be subject to random testing and there will be zero tolerance from this point on. As Ronald Reagan said, trust but verify."

"Of course Marty, I would expect that," Blake answered quickly to seize the moment.

"Sit down again Blake. I have something to tell you about myself."

Blake felt as if the weight of the world had been lifted off of his shoulders and he plunked down into his chair as if every bone in his body had turned to Jell-O. His relief was quickly replaced by curiosity about what was coming next.

"Blake, I've a pretty good idea of what you're going through. I've been going to Alcoholics Anonymous for 15 years."

"Well, I'll be damned. I never knew that Marty," Blake answered with amazement.

"I'm very well aware it's a personal matter Blake. I also know that there's more than one way to beat this disease," counseled Marty.

"I'm just beginning to understand things about myself as well, Marty. It seems to help just understanding why things are as they are. You know what I mean?"

"You'll have to continue to do some deep soul-searching. It really helps you understand how you got to this point and how you can move forward with clarity. As crazy as it sounds, you have to have a real deep conversation within your own self. At least that's been my experience."

"Thanks Marty. I hope I can continue to rely on your wisdom?"

"Sure Blake. You can't really ever feel like you are doing this alone or it'll eat you up."

Blake paused for a moment and thought of a question for Marty.

"Can I ask you what triggered your willingness to quit?"

"Funny you should ask that, because without my own experience in that regard, I never would have believed you," Marty answered with revelation.

"Well it's like this Blake. Something really drastic has to happen before you want to quit," Marty answered with a strong emphasis on wanting to quit.

"That's what convinced me about your problem. I could sense and feel that desperation in your voice. I knew that the plane accident had triggered emotions in you that you never could have imagined one week ago. Sandy and all of your fallen teammates have given you a new lease on life and a willingness to accept those things that you cannot change. I'm sure you've heard of the serenity prayer?"

"Yes, I have," answered Blake.

"But I still don't know what your trigger was Marty."

"I almost lost my son, Blake. I don't expect you to fully understand this because you're not a father yet. My son was drifting away from me and losing all respect for his father. I simply could not bear to live my life without my son in it. I owe my life to him."

"I'm happy things have apparently worked out for you, Marty."

"Yes they have, Blake, but trust me, there will be difficult moments ahead."

"I'm sure of that Marty, but I now have resolve and determination to stay sober. I never really had that before."

"Blake, I have one question for you now. I've had trouble finding a managerial replacement on such short notice. Now that we are all in so to speak, would you consider being a player-manager for the last two months of the season?"

Blake responded, "I'm flabbergasted. Of course I would be honored to be manager. I come in here desperately trying to remain with the team without going to rehab and now I'm apparently leaving as manager of the Chicago Cubs? Talk about an unlikely ending. This is so great. I won't let you down!"

Marty stood up and shook Blake's hand.

"Well, I would like to have another unlikely ending Blake."

"What's that Marty?"

"How about you bring us a divisional championship?"

"I will do everything in my power."

"Great. Meet me here tomorrow morning at nine and we'll go over some player personnel decisions."

"Sure, and thank you so much for believing in me and giving me this opportunity."

"We're just getting started. There's lots of work ahead of us. Stay sober! Are you sure this isn't too much responsibility for you Blake?"

"Hell no, I need that more than ever now," Blake responded quickly and with authority.

Blake left the office without any immediate recollection of what had just happened. It was like that first trip around the bases after your first major league home run. Reality had not set in yet, but it was sure to follow shortly when he got home.

9 — Putting the Pieces Back Together

Blake sat down next to Marty and thanked him once again for believing in him. Blake was now in full managerial mode. He was happy that his life seemed to have some focus again. Now he would have to help the general manager make some really tough and important decisions for the rest of the season.

Catchers are generally perfect managerial types. They are involved in virtually every decision on the playing field. To maintain a sense of authority, they usually have strong personalities with leadership qualities that are apparent to most everyone on the squad.

Since almost every player comes to bat with the catcher in such close proximity, they tend to be gossip conduits. Blake knew many opposing players personally over all the years behind the plate. He knew personalities, quirks, attitudes and just about every facet of hundreds of players.

Marty was quite aware of this as well. He knew it would be a good idea to pick Blake's brain on potential roster additions from the unprotected list of the rest of the Major League Baseball teams.

"Blake, this is going to be your team so I really want your input here. Of course, the final decision will be mine, but I want you to know that you'll definitely have a say in all personnel matters, for this year at least."

Marty correctly assumed that the more responsibility Blake felt, the more he would be likely to stay on the straight and narrow. It was a delicate balance for sure. Not too much to be overwhelming, but enough to make Blake feel his role was so important that he couldn't let up for one moment in his attempt to stay away from the temptations of booze and partying with the seemingly endless supply of groupies available to professional athletes.

"Well, here's the list. I know you'll be surprised with some of the names available. Some of this is just plain old economics. You let me deal with that. Just give me your best opinion on the current state of mind of these players and where you think they stand at the moment, talent wise."

"Marty, I know more about some of these guys than their wives. Just let me know what you think is important."

Marty interrupted abruptly.

"No Blake, I want you to make decisions on what you deem important to the structure of the team. I don't need to remind you that we still have a big lead and it's possible to put together two months of solid baseball to give our fans a pennant chase run. I know the odds will be severely stacked against us, but we owe it to everyone to do the best we can in honor of our fallen brethren."

"One more thing before I show you this list." Marty took on a serious tone and demeanor as he eyeballed Blake.

"Sure, anything you say Marty," Blake responded in a similar manner.

"Let's keep all this information in house. Understood? It'll be just you and me from here on out."

Blake nodded his head in approval.

"Well, the teams in our division certainly didn't do us any favors, as one would expect. There doesn't appear to be anybody available here that could help us near term. I'm not interested in next year. We need immediate help. Do you agree Blake?"

Blake scanned the list and nothing jumped out at him. He reasoned just as Marty had that teams in their division would be ultra protective.

"Yes, those damn Cardinals would rather sacrifice their season than potentially help us out at all," Blake spoke with obvious irritation in his voice.

Marty slowly rose out of his chair and strolled over to the wall where the team photo of this year's Cubs hung eerily over the deliberations. Someone had surrounded the picture frame with a yellow ribbon in honor. Marty had memorized the list so he just gave Blake some space to look over the names while he stared at the team photo in reverent remembrance while tidying up the ribbon.

"There are some surprises here," Blake's interest rose as he spotted some talented individuals.

Blake's superior baseball intelligence started to kick in as he scoured the list.

"I think it would be best if we took the majority of our pitchers from the American League, if possible," Blake reasoned as he looked up to Marty.

"I was thinking the same thing. The less our division knows about these pitchers the better our chances will be. They'll probably only see these guys twice the rest of the year...not enough time for their hitters to get a good read on their pitches."

"Here's one for sure. I know firsthand about Kyle Jacobson. He was with the team before you became GM Marty. Minnesota obviously isn't going to offer him a contract next year. Crafty lefty that holds runners on well, good team player who will do anything you ask him. He couldn't break a pane of glass with his fastball but he gets guys out. He's 8-5 with an ERA of 3.50."

"Yes, our scouts like him too. Probably could be a number two or three starter in the rotation," Marty offered.

"He's more like a three or four in my opinion," Blake quickly replied without hesitation at Marty's authority.

"Blake, we need to gamble on one guy who could be our number one starter. Obviously no team is going to leave a potential number one starter unprotected unless they're pretty certain he'll never live up to potential or they just made a serious mistake in evaluation. Find me that guy you could work with and possibly catch lightning in a bottle for two months."

"Well, the Yankees left unprotected a guy they drafted in the first round about five years ago who has never lived up to expectations. Rich bastards never have to worry about player development. They just go out and buy the next big-time free agent. Don't need to tell you that Marty. I'm still pissed we got outbid for Bobby McDonald last year," Blake shook his head at Marty, knowing full well the general manager was responsible.

"You mean Randall Hart?"

"Yes, he's a long shot Marty, but he has skills that have never been refined."

"He's a big, tall righty who hits 95-96 on the gun with his four-seam, but sloppy slider around 85 that could be tightened up some. Mix in a changeup and he could be special. Of course control has been an issue."

"Marty, rumor has it that he's a head case too. At least that is what I hear from their catcher Magnuson when he talks about some of his challenging pupils. Keith doesn't have much patience with prospects," Blake said with a chuckle, knowing all too well how difficult some young pitchers can be.

"I think he's worth a shot Marty."

"Now I want you to look at the back end of our bullpen Blake. Pick a couple of guys you think just might be good enough to close out some tough games. Let's see if we can find one lefty and one righty for setup and closer roles. Doesn't matter which order."

"Baltimore left unprotected a decent setup man. Lefty Guillen has a weight problem, but he has the stuff to get those big outs. Again, control seems to be an issue. I guess that's the main reason a lot of these guys aren't protected. I'll have my hands full, but again we're only looking at a two- month window. Just have to get in a short groove and ride with it."

"I guess I should have asked you this earlier. Are you ok with Mark Douglas as our pitching coach? I'm thinking of bringing him up from Des Moines to steady our number one pitching prospect in triple A. I know you're familiar with Woody Williams from spring training. The kid looks to be the real deal and Douglas really has the kid's ear. I think it would be a good fit."

"That works out just fine. Mark's a good guy and has patience. Williams is ready, Marty."

"Ok. It's closer time. I don't have to tell you how important that role is. Find me a guy that's not afraid to pitch with the game on the line Blake."

"I bet you'll be surprised at my next thought. The Mariners didn't protect Bowman. I know he's always been used in the middle innings. He's a sidearm slinger who doesn't throw hard and has been typecast as a one-inning middle-of-the-game guy. Sandy talked about him from his minor league days. He always said the guy was a fearless competitor as a closer in the International

League, but MLB teams just couldn't project him as a closer because he could barely break 85 on the gun. The guy is just tough to square the ball on."

"I'll have to trust you on that one Blake. That one just seems to be a reach. We'll see. Now just circle about a dozen more possibilities with an accompanying note about each pitcher. We plan on carrying 11 pitchers on the staff until September call-ups. I'll check back with you later and follow up on some of these names. In the meantime I have an organization-wide conference call to discuss our prospects in the minors. Go get some lunch and meet me back here at three and we'll go over positional players."

"Yes, I've a lot to contemplate here with this list. I'll look it over long and hard. See you back here at three."

Blake figured he would just grab some fast food and return to the team's facilities to finish his lunch. He still could not handle being seen in public after the tragic accident.

Rumors were already circulating about the real reason Blake was not with the team when the plane went down. The Cub organization released a statement declaring Blake had to leave the club in Atlanta to take care of a "personal family matter."

Blake knew the truth would have to come out soon but he was grateful that the team was covering for him. Blake had always enjoyed a strong relationship with the media in town and they likewise kept it secret for now, at least officially. They knew about it, but it was "off record" for now to many local scribes.

The quick trip to the fast food joint and back alleviated another problem. Sitting down at a nice restaurant carried with it a certain temptation that Blake thought prudent to avoid. He seldom ate out without an alcoholic beverage or two. He suddenly realized that his patterns of behavior would have to change, at least in the short term.

Blake studied the unprotected player list like an eager college student. He found a nice quiet corner at the team's headquarters. He sprawled out on the soft sofa and nibbled at his mediocre burger and fries.

The solitude of the moment allowed Blake to return to reality. The rush of excitement that ran through his body as he was discussing potential roster moves was replaced by a realization that this was a near impossible task. Even a 10-game lead could not be protected by a plethora of castoffs. He briefly and fleetingly thought perhaps it would be best to disassociate from this assuredly colossal failure.

On the other hand he was desperately seeking redemption, both personally and with the organization. He would be portrayed as a gutless coward by the media if he abandoned his past and future teammates. Knowing he had to take a stand focused Blake again on the task at hand.

There was some offensive talent on this list. Sure, nearly all of them were past their prime and have been worn down by the on and off the field antics of major league baseball. Being in a pennant race with a 10-game head start on the field surely would interest some capable veterans.

As Blake studied the list he came across a 10-year veteran who had languished with a deplorable Kansas City Royals club. Slick fielding shortstop Luis Rivera came up through the minors with the Royals organization and immediately was an All-Star. He had put up great offensive numbers to go along with his fielding prowess early in his big-league career. He averaged 20 homeruns and 90 RBI to go along with his near .300 career batting average through the first half of the decade. He signed a $60 million six-year contract and apparently lost all of his competitive desire. He was set financially and the team was consistently glued to the basement of the American League Central Division. Blake thought this could be the perfect situation for him to regain his drive.

Another name just irritated the hell out of Blake because of their past history. John Bartlett was a real pain in the ass to Blake and to the Cubs as a whole. He built up his reputation as a catcher with the rival Cardinals club, but was traded two years ago to the New York Mets. Like many Midwesterners, Bartlett just could not handle New York and apparently his wife couldn't either, as she left him right around the period he was traded to the Mets.

Blake and the team had battled with Bartlett throughout the past decade. He plowed Blake over at the plate in 2006 in a brutal collision that landed both of them on the disabled list. Blake remembered at least a half dozen times where Bartlett initiated a bench-clearing brawl between the two rivals. He had a sharp tongue and a nasty demeanor, but he was as competitive as hell, Blake thought to himself. Maybe the change of scenery would suit him well. Every good club needs a player like Bartlett who is hated as a rival, but admired as a teammate. Blake reasoned he could put up with Bartlett for two months anyway. He knew "The Rat," as Bartlett was nicknamed by opposing teams, could handle the pitching staff as well as Blake himself.

Blake glanced at the Chicago Cub decor clock on the wall and realized it was time to meet with Marty again. He was surprised decisions had transpired as well as they had so far. Blake knew there would be conflict. Knowing that he owed so much to Marty, he reasoned that he would defer to the general manager's knowledge. He wasn't exactly dealing from a position of strength in this scenario.

Marty clearly had other matters on his mind when Blake reappeared at the GM's office. Nobody with half a brain would want his job in this situation, thought Blake. The tragic accident had ripple effects throughout the organization. Player personnel decisions in the minors were rushed to the forefront as the big league club would dip into their farm system for a few players for these last two months, and replacements throughout the system had to be organized.

"Marty, I'm guessing we'll want to focus on National League position players for just the same reason we focused on American League pitchers. For the most part, familiarity with the arms in this league will be a big factor."

"Great minds think alike Blake, my thoughts exactly."

"Before I forget, here are the rest of the pitchers' names that I circled. Fire away at me with your thoughts Marty."

"No, we'll finalize the pitchers later. I'm really curious about your opinion on some of these positional players."

"You and I might either get a chuckle out of my first thought or we might start planning to hurt the sonofabitch for all the shit he's put us through."

"I know where you are going Marty. Glad you are taking the rational approach here and not letting emotions get the best of you. Bartlett has to be taken by us. His attitude has kind of gone to hell with his personal life, but he would take a great load off of your shoulders Blake, both physically and mentally. His leadership skills would allow you to manage from a safe distance both emotionally and without being a constant presence in the locker room."

"Marty, I might cold-cock him on arrival just because I'd like to even things up, but then he'll be one of us."

"I gotta be there for that one. If I was 20 years younger I'd take a shot at him too," Marty retorted.

"I know we agreed to focus on National League players, but the Royals have a talented shortstop available who just might regain some focus over here for a couple of months. If we're trying to win the lottery here, he probably would be our likeliest ticket. Rivera would strengthen us up the middle and would be a good mentor to Arroyo if you call him up from Iowa."

"I like it so far. I suppose we should find some speed for centerfield and then we'll have our middle set. We can work outward from there." Marty was testing Blake a bit as well. These were the easiest decisions as these names stood out.

"Wilson can flat-out outrun the baseball. I hear the Dodgers aren't happy with his offensive production. Jesus, if we could just get him to hit the ball on the ground more often, he could approach .280 with 70 stolen bases over a full season. Are his wheels ok Marty?"

"Our most recent scouting reports show him nursing a calf muscle problem. We'll get an update and select him if his health isn't an issue."

"I'd like at least two potential bombers anyway. Power hitters are notoriously streaky, but a hot streak for a few weeks could make all the difference in the world. I suppose the opposite is true as well, but we're rolling the dice here, right Marty?"

"The weather will still be hot here at Wrigley for at least four weeks so everybody will be a potential slugger if the winds keep blowing out as they have this summer. If we're lucky enough to get into the final series with a chance or God blesses us with a playoff series, we sure could use some quick strike options. Don't see much power out there though, Blake."

"Well you and I have been critical of the Marlins' coaching staff and their offensive philosophy. They take guys with potential power up from their system and turn them into opposite field slap hitters. That never made much sense to me."

Marty quickly concurred. "Those darn morons ruin more minor league talent than anyone around. I think I know where you're headed with this Blake. Are you sure you aren't after my job? That's some excellent analysis Skipper!"

"That first baseman Arnold is a physical specimen. We've got a chance to get some real power production out of him. He has hands of stone unfortunately, but we could get by with a sub-par fielding first baseman.

"Another guy who's weak defensively, but could deposit a few balls on Waveland Avenue, is that Marlins' left fielder Rodriguez. Real streaky, but the hot streaks he gets on are Sports Center material. He can really get on a roll, but when he's not, he's a complete rally-killer. We have a lot of power arms in our division and he crushes the heat. These two could be our four- and five-hole boppers if we do our work with them. I suppose you're bringing up Hutchinson from Des Moines to be my hitting coach, huh Marty?" Blake got a little off track as he began to think about his staff.

"Actually I'm more inclined to bring up Hank Hanson from double A. I really like his approach to hitting and he seems to connect more with his players from a personal standpoint. Hutch's a great guy, but he seems disinterested this season. I think it'll be his last with the organization."

"I like Hutch too Marty, but he's past his prime as they say, with his teaching skills. Sandy had heard good things about Hanson from some of his Latin buddies that worked with Hank in the minors."

"Well Blake, we've got a good start here and we don't want to overdo it here. We still have one more day to evaluate. Again, give me a list with a small surplus and let me pick the rest. I'll go over it with you before any decisions are made. I want you to write a few notes about each player, even the ones you don't want. When you're done with that, just write four words at the top of the page that you'll want to define your club. I'll take it from there."

"Blake believes in you," the excited manager blurted out suddenly, then just as quickly apologized for such quick thoughtlessness and lack of professionalism.

"I'm sure I'll come up with a more profound baseball-type description tomorrow," Blake said with the sincerity that fit in line with Marty's request.

"Don't apologize Blake," said Marty. "I like it, Blake's Believers sounds pretty good to me."

"That sounds good to me Marty. Say, how long before I can assemble the guys and get started on some workouts? I'm curious as to a couple of things though. As a player-manager, what kind of workload split do you think will work best? Also, what date does everybody have to report by?"

"I'm glad you asked the question about your role. I think it'll work best if you continue the role of the back-up catcher that fills in once or twice a week. You'll have your hands full managing a group of relative strangers. Just get to know them a little more in depth and leave the everyday catching to your buddy Bartlett. I'm just kidding Blake, about that last remark."

"It makes perfect sense Marty. I'm not exactly tearing the cover off the ball anymore the past few seasons. Now what about the other questions boss?"

"The Commissioner's Office and the Players' Union have agreed on 72 hours from selection. You should have everybody in place by Tuesday of next week. Unfortunately, we have to open up our home stand the next day. It's far from ideal, but the league has to get the ball rolling again to make up ground and keep the World Series from approaching Thanksgiving. My God, I long for the old days of a mid-October finish to the whole season. The money in the game is killing us all."

"It should work ok. Baseball is baseball. Most of these guys could do their jobs in their sleep and sometimes it looks as if they are," Blake smiled as he finished his words. This was the first time a smile had been born again on his face since the accident. Marty noticed it as well and smiled back.

"Blake, this is going to be good for all of us. Let's get this started, but never forget where we came from. God bless our fallen team in heaven."

10 — Doing it His Way

The euphoria of returning to baseball so soon was quickly replaced by the somber task of revealing to Kim that he was not going to rehab. He knew she would be furious, in part because his word meant very little to her.

Blake knew this time was different. He had convinced Marty that he was going to stay sober. It turned out he had more in common with Marty than he ever knew. Kim had been on the other side of the problem, both with her father and with Blake. She would certainly look at resolution differently than two old boozers, and guys to boot.

Blake was actually disappointed that traffic was non-existent in the middle of the day. For once, he would have preferred a slow ride home. He pulled his black Mercedes into the driveway and contemplated conversation with Kim. Her rich red Cadillac Escalade was still in the garage. He thought the present was the best time to explain that he was going to do this his way now that he had received approval from the Cubs management, and while he was in a good mood from his meeting with Marty.

With a bounce in his step and a gleam in his eyes, Blake confidently opened the front door and immediately hollered out to Kim. Upon hearing no response, Blake walked hurriedly upstairs to the bedroom looking for his wife. He peered into the room and noticed her packing a travel bag for him.

"Are you trying to get rid of me?"

"I just thought I'd get a head start on some personal items for you. Did you work out the details with the front office? I've got about two weeks of clothing and essentials for you."

"Sit down Kim. We've reached an agreement, but I don't think it'll be one you'll like."

Blake tried very diligently to maintain a sense of calmness. He guided her with his hands towards the bed and gently caressed her exposed slender arms with both hands.

"I'm confused Blake. What could be an issue? It's cut and dried. The only variable is where and when?"

"Kim, I know we're in this together and I know you've stuck with me through some very awful times. I always appreciate your loyalty."

"Blake, what is it? Just get to the point. I can tell something is amiss. Just spit it out. No trying to sugarcoat this, please?"

"I'm 100 percent committed to staying sober like I never have before. The shock of living while everybody else died has put a huge new dynamic in all of this. By all accounts, I should be dead right now. You don't think that has a huge impact on how I view my life, our lives?"

"I'm satisfied you want to stay sober this time. I also know there are huge obstacles still in your path. There are factors that you don't even know about yet that the doctors will bring out of you in treatment," Kim said.

"Well, about that. Kim, I might as well just tell you. I'm not going into treatment and I have Marty Anderson's approval. Turns out that Marty has been going to AA for years and nobody knew about it to my knowledge. He believes in me and I hope you will too."

"Why do you always think decisions are made by you? Don't I have a say in this? What about MY approval?"

Kim was furious as she sprang off the bed and threw Blake's unclosed luggage across the room in disgust. She spun around to face Blake and her reddened face stood out like a ripened tomato in a snow bank. Her eyes flashed with anger.

"I've had it Blake. It's always about you and never about us. Well, this decision is mine alone. I'm leaving you!"

"The club has named me player-manager, Kim. Could there be a better tribute? Please don't leave. I'll need all of your support to stay sober. I'll do anything short of leaving the team to go into rehab. Tell me what else I can do? What else we can do?"

The news about managing struck Kim hard. She always worried what Blake would do when his playing days were over.

"Marty made you the manager? You really think you'll be up to that Blake? With everything else you'll be dealing with? Why would you want to pile on more responsibility in this personal crisis?"

"C'mon Kim, you know me. I actually work better with challenge. I think that's been part of my problem. I've been drifting aimlessly with little responsibility on this team. I knew I could catch one day a week practically in my sleep. There was nothing to inspire me. Even a pennant race wasn't doing it because I was playing such a bit part."

Kim's emotions slowly calmed down. She sat back down on the bed and contemplated her threat to leave.

"Do you really want my advice Blake? Isn't your mind already made up?"

"Only on doing it my way and not going into a rehab facility. Only on forever wanting to stay married to you. We can work on other matters together."

The words of devotion melted Kim's heart and dissipated her anger. She reached out to Blake and held him ever so tight. She still had that stern look in her eyes as she asked Blake a compromising question.

"Blake, will you go to AA meetings? If we need spiritual advice, will you come with me to talk to a priest?"

"For you I will, honey. For you I will."

Blake felt a huge load released from his mind. Maybe Sandy was right when he said in the dream that everything would work out just fine.

As he walked hand-in-hand with Kim out of the clothes-strewn bedroom with the issue apparently resolved, Blake suddenly realized that most of the external elements had been put to rest. Now it would be time to focus on baseball. As much as Blake hated dealing with emotional issues, on the flip side, he relished everything about baseball at this moment in his life.

Just over a week ago Blake despised the professional baseball lifestyle. Now he could see just how blessed he had been all these years. The tragic accident and the renewed vision of life had transformed him. He knew there were many challenges ahead, but now he was back in his element. It was going to be about baseball from here on in and that is where Blake felt most at ease.

"I can't wait to get to the ballpark tomorrow Kim," Blake gushed as he eagerly anticipated the dawn of a new day, both literally and figuratively.

His eagerness caused him to overlook the obvious obstacles to his sobriety that lay ahead. For now those challenges were miles away in thought and in practice.

Those demons would patiently wait their turn. For now the demons were content on lurking in the shadows. The timing of temptations would be their key to tripping the recovering addict up. It would come all in the demons' due time as they had been down this road before with Blake and others.

11 — Back in the Comfort Zone

To the average baseball spectator the dugout of a ballpark looks like a plain wooden bench protected from the natural elements and fans, friend and foe alike. However, to the players it is more like a strategic lookout and a social medium.

Players bond in the dugout, passing time as the game of baseball moves along at its own pace, dictated by the preferences of batter and pitcher. Some study the players, the pitcher in particular, like hawks, waiting for a moment of weakness to seize upon their prey. Just a barely perceptible movement of the glove hand or a position of the throwing elbow can tip off a batter to what pitch will be coming next.

Other players relax by mentally straying away from the game as the conversation flows from baseball to finance, sex, other sports, or any other distracting topic, while at the same time appearing to be involved in the game at hand.

Some veteran players who have seen or been a part of thousands of games can do both as their highly trained professional eyes can follow the action intensely while conversing on many a topic. Grizzled old vets are as comfortable in this setting as a ballplayer can be. This is their home, their sanctuary and their workplace. It's a ballplayer's comfort zone.

Blake leaned back against the dugout wall and took in all the sights and sounds as his team worked out for the first time. His players had come from all over, but the standard baseball regimen applied.

Pitchers run and shag fly balls from batting practice. They stretch their highly valuable pitching arms out with lengthy, but controlled throws.

Hitters take turns stepping into the batting cage to crisply take their swings at moderately paced batting-practice tosses from middle-aged coaches.

Infielders get their work in between all of the activity as they get accustomed to all the nuances of the playing field.

Players have been through this routine so often that they sometimes appear to be robotic. The atmosphere of batting practice is often very loose as music soothes in the background and players smile and joke around while they hone their skills.

It isn't like football when set plays have to be coordinated. The players perform as individuals, but in a team concept. Each player is individually responsible for fine-tuning his baseball skills. If an individual performs well, the team normally prospers accordingly.

As a player-manager, Blake had to do a little of both. For now he was content to visualize the talents of his team as they worked out. He had scheduled a team meeting after the workout to try and form some cohesiveness as a group.

Blake never liked managers that were aloof. He was going to be involved in everything. As a player-manager, he would make sure that all his players knew they were in this together, but they would be treated individually like adults. Blake was looking forward to meeting each one of his players in a private setting. He wanted players to feel welcome in his office because he knew that he could only get to know these ballplayers if they relaxed and let their personalities out into the open. These individual meetings would come before the first game tomorrow night.

It was impossible to be fully prepared after one workout, but this was the best the league could do given the circumstances and the timetable.

Blake knew he would have his hands full right away. He was certain that most of the new players would be upset at being left unprotected by their past teams. That would be a slap in the face to their pride. He was also fairly certain that very few players like to be uprooted with less than two months left in the regular season with a makeshift team that was very likely only a temporary baseball job. Blake himself figured only a handful of them would be back the following season.

At least the several players who were Cub farmhands including premier pitching prospect Williams would be ecstatic about their promotion to the big league club. These players had this goal in mind for years. The new players had a couple of days to bask in it all even if they had to hide their emotions in order to show respect for the deceased and their families.

As Blake stepped out of the dugout he could see that there was talent on the playing field. It definitely wouldn't hurt that the club had a 10-game cushion in early August, but Blake knew that could dissipate in a couple of weeks. Baseball history was full of late season collapses. The sport is conducive to streaks, both good and bad. Losses can pile up in a hurry as a slump can suddenly become contagious throughout the lineup. Such is the hazard of playing day after day, with few breaks in the schedule.

Catchers seem to have an eye for pitching talent. Most importantly, catchers tend to know what makes different pitchers click. Veteran backstops have seen it all. They have dealt with the flaky pitcher, the know-it-all pitcher, the timid and the brash, and they react accordingly. Blake was fortunate, based on his lengthy career, that he knew how to mold a pitching staff on the fly. He knew that effectively handling a pitching staff, and the bullpen in particular, goes a long way in defining a manager's success or failure.

Blake switched roles and stepped into the batting cage to take his hacks. He bantered back and forth with his third base coach who was struggling to groove his batting practice pitches.

"Bobby, can you please throw one right down the middle? I have to make a good impression on these guys."

"It's too late for that Coach. These guys already know what a horse's ass you are Blake."

"I am a new man, Bobby. I am a new man. Now flip me a cookie."

Blake drove the next toss deep into the left field seats, well beyond the 10-foot-high ivy-cloaked outfield wall. He strutted out of the cage and yelled again as loud as he could.

"Blake Benson is back. Blake the rake is here to stay! Baseball's going to be fun again!"

Raking is a term that describes nothing but line drives and Blake was reveling in his impressive hitting display.

The workout finished in the sweltering late afternoon sun and Blake instructed his team to meet in the clubhouse in 15 minutes. It was time to judge the tone and temperament of his team.

12 — Ready to Lead

The whole team was gathered in the clubhouse. It was an eerie setting as the names of the deceased Cubs were still posted at each station. It was an obvious oversight, but the urgency of assembling a new team so quickly exceeded all other factors.

The new faces of the franchise were subdued. Players were somewhat familiar with each other, but the protocol for such a strange turn of events was decidedly unclear. It was definitely time for their new leader to set some standards of conduct for this delicate situation. The clubhouse setting where 25 former and now deceased Cubs used to gather a mere two weeks ago had a church-like feel to it as the new group assembled.

Blake sat in his office, contemplating what to say and how to say it. He leaned back in his chair and reflected on his former teammates, digging inward for inspiration.

He knew baseball was business-first for many players. Many, if not all, of the players assembled would have little connection to those lost. It just did not seem appropriate to Blake that he should not refer to his fallen comrades, but it couldn't be the main focus of his presentation either.

It came to Blake that he should rely on his late best friend Sandy one more time. Everybody knew about Sandy, either from a personal encounter or from numerous media accounts of his stellar reputation. Blake knew he had to form a link from past to present somehow. It was unavoidable, but he had to make sure his new team had its own identity apart from the fallen Cubs.

Blake felt he should save that for last. He thought the practical things should come first in case the scene became emotional. He knew these guys must have a bunch of unanswered questions regarding simple everyday matters like the locker oversight. Nobody even knew where to put his professional gear.

He knew it was time to perform his first managerial function. It was team meeting time.

Blake opened the door to his new office and walked confidently to meet his new team. He wanted to present himself as an authoritative figure, but remain one of the guys. There's a reason player-managers have been few and far between. It's difficult to combine two very different roles. The distinction becomes less and less clear, and confusion mounts when players blur the separate tasks of player at one point and manager at another.

"Welcome to Chicago men. First, I'd to apologize for not having your lockers ready yet. I hope you can appreciate the difficulties at hand here in this very unique situation. Just grab the one closest to you and we'll work out the details as we go."

Blake was interested to see any type of reaction or resistance from the players. He could sense from a few grimaces that there would be some griping. Players are a pampered bunch. Their status requires little decision-making of their own. Menial tasks are delegated to others.

"It's obvious that we're all in a difficult situation here. It's bullshit to expect us to be ready to play a game tomorrow. We're going to have to figure this out on the run and in a hurry. Mistakes will be made so bear with us."

Team meetings are a necessary evil. Often they occur when a squad is struggling. As a last resort, expressing emotions sometimes brings a group together. This was uniquely different though. There was no blueprint for this scenario. Frustrations had not built to the boiling point yet. Most of the newly formed team was still bewildered by it all. Silence prevailed throughout the beginning of Blake's speech. All were hesitant and unsure.

"The good news is that we have a 10-game lead right now. Another bit of news that should make you happy is that the Commissioner's Office just informed me that you all will be eligible to claim the full playoff share if we hold on and win our division. Boys, that would be $65,000 in your pocket in case you aren't aware of the latest playoff share."

For the first time a collective audible cheer filled the room. Whoops of approval filled the air. There is nothing like money to bring people together in spirit.

"The bad news is that this will be a very difficult task. You guys all know how fast a 10-game lead can disappear. We have no time to figure out our pitching staff and with the postponements due to the plane crash, we'll have to make up a whole shitload of games that'll surely create havoc for our arms. All I ask is that we all do our best and remember that we're representing our major league brethren here that died doing what we all do every day. It easily could have been any one of you on that plane as well."

Blake immediately noticed the glances of several of his players. They obviously were aware of his good fortune of not being on board. He figured some had heard through the grapevine that he had been sent home on a different plane because of his lurid behavior. That seemed to be Blake's cue to tackle the issue head-on. It was time to let his players feel what he had been feeling this past week. Hopefully it would have a positive impact on them.

"I should've been on that plane too. I didn't have a good reason not to be on that trip. I'd been in a very bad place mentally for quite some time. That morning, one player and close friend had the courage, and the concern, to try and save a buddy from slowly killing himself with alcohol. That one player and friend was Sandy Gonzalez. Most of you know what a great player and a great man he is."

Blake caught himself using Sandy in the present tone and his emotions started to get the best of him. He lowered his head so the players wouldn't see him cry, but it didn't matter as his voice cracked with emotion for all to see and hear.

"A great man he was," Blake sadly corrected.

Blake paused to compose himself. It was a very awkward moment for the players assembled. The silence seemed to echo loud and clear, as crying clearly made all men uncomfortable.

"Sandy made sure that I got the help that was needed to stop me from drinking. It was his insistence that I had to stop then and there that made me miss that plane. What he couldn't have known at that time was that this quirk of fate would indeed give me the courage to quit. Losing all of my former teammates and my best friend Sandy has given me a new lease on life. It's made me appreciate what a great gift we all have. It's a gift to be able to play major league baseball and we should never forget that. We need to take care of our bodies so we can enjoy this gift as long as we can."

If there was any doubt before, it was clear now that Blake had the close attention of everybody in the room. Blake had inadvertently shifted the focus from himself and his former teammates to each and every one of the players in the clubhouse. It was brilliantly delivered, if not planned.

"We'll have a very unique opportunity to be part of baseball history here. The attention that we'll all be receiving from the national media means that each and every one of you will have a glorious opportunity to shine professionally. Let's make the best of it, men. We could be in for the time of our lives. Whatever the case, it won't be boring. None of us will be playing out the string in September. I for one just hate that last month with a passion if there's little to play for."

There were nods of approval as many of the veteran players felt the same way about September.

"Tomorrow night it all begins. I'll be meeting with each of you in my office before the game tomorrow. Everyone must be here on time. We've had too much time off as it is. The whole team needs to be in the clubhouse by 2 p.m. sharp."

With that announcement, Blake turned around and headed for his office. He shut the door behind him, slumped down in his swivel chair, swung around away from view and wondered to himself how he came across to his team. He was emotionally spent. It was time to go home to his wife and hopefully spend a nice, quiet evening at home.

13 — Game On

It felt like Opening Day all over again as Blake pulled into Wrigley Field for their first game after the accident. He knew it would be a media circus and planned his stealth entry into the ballpark before his arrival.

There were media trucks everywhere. Not just the usual ESPN for a sporting event, but CNN, Fox, and other major networks. This was definitely a national event. Rumblings of a presidential visit had been circulating for a day or two. Judging by the security around Wrigley, it seemed more fact than rumor.

Blake knew the media hounds would be circling the wagons looking for answers regarding his somewhat mysterious absence from the team flight that crashed. His agent advised him to come clean as soon as possible or there would be unending speculation and gossip.

Blake decided to schedule a press conference tomorrow before the second game of their rescheduled series with the St. Louis Cardinals. There would be enough to deal with tonight. For everyone's sanity, the Cubs just had to get through that first game back before moving on to their manager's personal issues.

Blake felt anxious, but he recognized that feeling as a star athlete. This was usually a good sign for him. He had spent far too long the past few years as a relaxed third-string catcher that understood his role as a spare part. He welcomed the fear of failure that had shadowed him all those years when he was expected to carry the team with his performance. It drove him then and it felt like it was doing the same now.

His next major managerial move would be the upcoming individual meetings with his players. Blake was looking forward to these sessions. He needed to feel their level of enthusiasm for this awkwardly bizarre scenario. Surely, the players would be looking at Blake for some guidance as well.

A well-managed baseball team usually has clearly defined roles for its players. This allows each player to first of all accept his role, and then to prepare physically and mentally for his situation as it develops during a game. Blake knew his players would want to know where they fit in on this newly assembled squad.

Blake knew this could not happen in this brief time period. He would just reassure his players that their performance in this narrow window of opportunity would define their roles. Hopefully, this would motivate 25 players to take each game appearance very seriously. The two-month dash for the division title should be more than enough to keep his players hungry.

As Blake sat in his office he recognized the symbolism of his individual meetings. His first face-to-face sit down would have to be with his one-time rival, catcher John Bartlett. The former Cardinals and Mets backstop had so many run-ins with Chicago teams of the past that Blake conceded he regrettably knew him all too well.

This would be different though. They were now on the same team and although Blake would have clear authority over Bartlett, he knew that the veteran catcher would be invaluable to his pitching staff as most of the pitchers were from the junior circuit, the American League. It was time to clear the air and become allies, not enemies.

Blake picked up his cell phone and let his coaches know he was ready to visit with Bartlett. An avid boxing fan, Blake transferred a pair of boxing gloves from his player's locker to his new manager's office. He liked to pound the punching bag every once in a while and he felt it was good for hand-eye coordination, vital for a catcher. Blake smiled as he put the gloves on and waited for his one-time nemesis. It seemed like a good icebreaking tool.

The tall, muscular Bartlett, his face weathered like an old baseball glove, entered the room with a hesitant look on his face. The apprehension was easily felt from both participants, but immediately disappeared with the boxing glove ploy. Bartlett smiled as he took one look at his manager, donning his boxing gloves and took a defensive pose.

"Bartlett, I've been waiting for years to take a shot at you," Blake's smile deflected the tone of his voice.

"I kind of figured you might Skipper. That's why I walked in so hesitantly," John laughed as he sized up the situation. "I almost paid a teammate to walk in unannounced to set him up for any booby trap, but the word was already out about our loving relationship," Bartlett smirked as usual in reply.

Blake tossed his gloves aside and shook the hand of his new teammate.

"Glad to be on the same side for once. You sure are a pain in the ass to compete against."

"Likewise, I'm sure," Bartlett retorted in his usual antagonistic, perpetually smirking manner.

"Sit down John. It's time to mend some fences and move on. I need your invaluable experience here."

Bartlett looked puzzled as he leaned backward in his chair. He never lacked confidence and his demeanor always seemed to reek of casual indifference. Blake knew firsthand that this wasn't his on-the-field attitude by any stretch of the imagination.

"Skip, you have all the experience in the world and then some as a catcher. Why do you need me?"

"I have a difficult role here John, as player-manager. I have a feeling it's going to be mostly as manager from here on out. You have more left in the tank than I do and the bulk of my time and attention will be focused on keeping this unit satisfied and together for two months."

"I suppose, but you know the hitters in this league as well or better than I do," Bartlett responded in a tone that suggested he didn't really mean it.

"Well, I'm afraid I've been negligent regarding the baseball knowledge as a third-string, part-time catcher with a serious drinking problem. I just haven't paid attention to advance scouting reports like I used to."

Bartlett nodded his head as he finally grasped the situation, understanding the mental and physical pain the long-time catcher had endured.

"I hear you Skip. The road has been tough on me too. I guess we both can lean on each other for advice. I don't think we'll butt heads."

"No, I'm going to defer to you regarding the pitching staff and the calling of games. It's what you've always done best, besides getting under people's skin," Blake laughed.

"Thank you for the compliments on both ends," John never could reply without some type of edge in his voice.

"I also want you to be a sort-of assistant coach with us John. I need you to be my eyes and ears for the morale of our team. You come to me with anything that might be boiling under the surface, okay?"

"Sure and thank you for the honor," Bartlett replied with sincerity in his voice for once.

"I'm going to start Jacobson tonight. Are you familiar with him at all?"

"Not much except for his reputation as a crafty lefty with experience."

"You got it John. That's why I'm going with him tonight. There's a whole lot of attention on us, for now anyway."

"Should be a piece of cake, right Skip? I know these Cardinals like the back of my hand."

"I figured as much. You're still feuding with them."

"I can't stand their front office people, but I respect Coach Leighton. I'm still mad as hell at him for trading me, but I respect the man. I'd like nothing better than to whip their ass down the stretch and prove to them that they screwed up in letting me go. I hated New York too as you probably know."

"John, just make sure you stop in here after every game. I want you to be very involved in this. You meet with our pitching coach Mark Douglas and start working on a rotation and some sort of bullpen setup for now. I need to meet with 24 more guys. I really am glad to have you on the roster."

"I'll get on that right away, Coach."

Bartlett left the office displaying the same sour demeanor he wore entering. Blake surprisingly felt very comfortable with his new number-one catcher and virtual assistant. He felt he should meet with Luis Rivera next as he would be the leader of the infield at shortstop. He was another veteran that could be a conduit to another very important faction, the Latin American players.

Latin American players were often misunderstood. They had been stereo-typed as emotional and moody players as a whole, but Blake always felt as if there were just cultural differences that had to be constantly addressed. He knew Rivera could help address the situation on a daily basis and keep everyone on the same page. As he called Rivera in, Blake was hopeful that his second meeting would go as well as the first.

"Luis, come on in and sit down. What's it been, like five years since we met at the All-Star Game?"

"That sounds about right. What should I call you now that you are my manager?"

"Call me Coach, Skipper, Skip, Blake, anything but Mr. Benson."

"Okay, but it sure seems weird."

"Luis, this whole thing's weird, but we've got no other choice. The show must go on, as they say."

"Coach, how can I help you? I'll do anything you want."

"How about banging out a couple of dingers tonight and making all the plays at short?"

"Does that mean I'm starting at shortstop?"

"Of course it does, Rivera. Don't tell me you've lost your confidence. You've always been one of the best hitting shortstops in the game."

"Thanks, but I haven't been tearing the cover off the ball for a few years now."

"Well it's a new beginning for all of us Luis, myself included. Ten days ago I hit bottom. I didn't give a shit about baseball or anything other than boozing. I feel that's all behind me now."

"Just what do you expect from me, Coach?"

"Just play ball like I know you can. Don't focus on numbers. Enjoy this pennant race. There's going to be a huge spotlight on us, Luis. If you shine for these two months, I'm sure your career will take off again. The good news is you're out of Kansas City. It's difficult to motivate yourself to play every day when the organization can't get their head out of their ass. You and I both have a new lease on life."

Luis smiled and appeared to appreciate the pep talk. He now stood up confidently and shook Blake's hand.

"You give a good pep talk Coach! I feel appreciated and it feels like something special could happen if we stay together."

"There's just one more thing, Luis. I would really appreciate it if you take a leadership role with your fellow Latin players. I don't pretend to know or understand what they're feeling and how it differs from me. Will you keep a close eye on the situation and help me understand what they're experiencing?"

"Of course I will Skipper. A lot of my brothers take failure differently. You surely know this game is all about handling failure in a positive way. I'll keep you informed."

"My office is always open for you Luis. Starting tonight, just try to enjoy the spotlight that you've been deprived of all those years in KC."

Luis left Blake's office feeling very much appreciated once more. He felt better about being in Chicago. Blake was right. It felt good to be out of Kansas City and in the limelight.

Blake methodically went through each individual meeting explaining to his players there simply was no blueprint for this scenario. He urged patience to every one of them and encouraged all to come and see him personally if there was any problem.

The pitchers were all polite and proper as they cooperated with the formality of the meeting. However, they understood that their pitching coach would be their main conduit. Pitchers can be a strange group, definitely a huge part of a team's success, but separate in outlook and regimen from everyday players. If the pitching coach had their back, then all was well in their world. The manager was simply the decision-maker that put them in the game or removed them for another.

Blake assembled his coaches and went over the lineup card for the first game back. He asked pitching coach Douglas how he thought the bullpen should be managed for this first game. It was agreed upon Jacobson would likely go no more than five innings and it would be prudent to get as many pitchers involved as possible for this first game, as they all needed some game action to get back in their groove.

"Let's just see how each player handles the limelight tonight and go from there," Blake said. "We'll meet after the game and discuss different options. We've all been in this game long enough to know that it's dangerous to base opinions on short-term performance. I just don't know what other option we have with the limited time frame we're handicapped with."

The assistant coaches all nodded their approval and were as hesitant as Blake regarding the upcoming process of evaluating.

"Well, the game should be the easy part guys. Let's get back to our livelihood and our playground."

Blake took a moment to reflect on the absurdity of it all as he sat in his manager's chair staring at the lineup card in disbelief. It was actually all about to happen.

"Well it's only one game, isn't that what they say fellas?" Blake smiled as he let silence take over the room

Baseball doesn't lie to you over 162 games. Perhaps it does over 10 or 20 games or even 30 or 40, but not 162. Blake took just a bit of comfort in the fact that the Cubs only had 53 games left.

"Let's take the field and see what the hell we got ourselves into. It should be a circus out there tonight, but we have to remember the seriousness of the situation. My old teammates will be honored tonight and the least we can do is respect the moment."

The nervousness was entrenched in Blake's stomach. He hadn't felt like this for a long time. As he made his way down to the playing field, he wondered how many games this feeling would last. The whole scene would be surreal at Wrigley tonight. It was going to be a memorable moment in baseball lore.

14 — Reality Bites

A person that didn't know the circumstances surrounding this game would have thought it was a World Series event. The atmosphere belied a regular season game. While there were network trucks, cameras, and media everywhere, and the fans filled the ballpark much earlier than normal, the mood was reverent and respectful, not joyous in anticipation of a home team triumph.

Blake received a huge ovation when he stepped out onto the playing field, but most of the others were strangers to the fans. They had Cubs uniforms on, but they were outsiders still. Fans usually welcomed a player or two obtained in a trade, but this was exponentially different. Twenty-four new players filled the roster, with Blake being the lone familiar face.

Surviving family members were honored before the game and Sandy's widow threw the honorary first pitch. The president was in attendance as suspected, but he maintained a low profile as the game approached. He had a press conference downtown in the afternoon, but wanted to try and keep the focus on the players, both old and new. He met with surviving family members in private as well in an attempt to console.

However, there was a dilemma brewing that had to be addressed. The fallen team members had already been memorialized. A respectful tone was expected for the first game back, but it was also a signal that it was time to move on. The fallen heroes would not be forgotten, but the reality of the situation started to set in. These were the new Cubs and it was time to look forward without dwelling on the past. This was how Major League Baseball was going to continue on.

The mood became a bit more celebratory as game time approached. Chants of "Let's go Cubs" began to circulate in unison. It was a beautiful warm and rather humid night with just a whisper of wind as the home team took the field.

The four game series with the Cardinals began with the Cubs holding a 10-game lead over their rivals. Blake was hoping for a split of the series as the Cards had to catch them. Salvaging a split would signal to the Cardinals that this Cubs team was not going to be a pushover.

Jacobson set the Cards down in order in the top of the first. Every player in the Chicago dugout seemed much more comfortable now that they were back to playing ball. The game was second nature to them. The crazy off-the-field issues were the difficult part for ballplayers.

Blake nestled in his corner of the dugout and kept a reserved demeanor for the beginning of the game. He just wanted everyone to settle down and relax a bit after the emotional pregame activities. Displaying a sense of calmness came easy to Blake. He was aware that he would have to light a fire under his team every now and then, but that was somewhere down the road.

The Cardinals had their ace pitcher Salvador Torres on the mound as the league-mandated mourning period suspended the playing schedule five days. The delay allowed all of major league baseball to realign their pitching staffs for the final two months.

Torres threw heat with precision. A mid-90 miles per hour fastball that came somewhat from the side put the fear of God in right-handed batters as the Cards' right-handed flamethrower loved to pitch inside to intimidate the opponent. Blake figured his only hope tonight was for the warm southerly winds of Wrigley to blow out to center field, as the stud pitcher seemed to either strike batters out or allow fly balls. Mother Nature looked to be cooperating on a hot humid night that enabled baseballs to soar majestically in these weather conditions.

Desmond Wilson, the speedy outfielder selected from the Dodgers, gave the crowd a thrill in the bottom of the first as he took a hanging slider from Torres and lofted a fly ball that somehow carried over the right field wall. The pesky switch-hitting outfielder was constantly being instructed to hit the ball on the ground to take advantage of his speed, but nobody was going to complain on this night as his home run gave the Cubs a 1-0 lead. Nobody realized at the time that it would be the only run the home team would produce this night at homer-friendly Wrigley.

Torres found his groove about the third inning and he mowed down the Cubs with his assortment of off-speed pitches to go along with his heat. There's not a more helpless feeling in the baseball world than facing an All-Star pitcher on top of his game.

Jacobson kept his team in the game for five innings, departing for a pinch-hitter with a 3-1 deficit, but the Cubs bullpen fell apart in the latter innings and St. Louis romped 8-1.

Blake had little managing to show off in this disappointing loss. The one-sided contest did provide one opportunity. He was able to substitute freely and get almost everybody involved and back in the flow of live game action.

The Chicago fans were as silent as the Cubs' bats. The respectful cheers slowly faded away as the game got out of hand. It was a lengthy contest as the substitutions slowed the game to a crawl at times. By the eighth inning, Wrigley was less than half-full. If any fan had dreams of a comeback they were either intoxicated with too much ballpark beer or painfully ignorant of the Cardinals star's pitching prowess.

The difficulty of the task at hand had been unmercifully unleashed with the reality of a completed game. The Cubs looked every bit the part of an expansion team, which in effect they were, and certainly not like a first-place team with a sizeable lead in August.

Blake tried to reassure the team after the game that it was only one of many, but the mood in the clubhouse reflected another story. An expansion-type team had no business competing for first place in August. There was simply not enough talent and an absence of cohesiveness on such a makeshift squad.

Blake retreated to the confines of his office and tried in vain to stay positive. Baseball was full of ups and downs, but he could see the handwriting on the wall.

He had always lived by the motto that a player should not take his game home with him. He showered and headed for the comfortable confines of his house, determined not to let Kim know his innermost doubts.

15 — Opening Up

Kim was at the door waiting to give Blake a hug as he arrived home. She long ago decided it was best not to attend the games at Wrigley. There were the usual obnoxious fan comments that got under her skin and she didn't want baseball to define her life.

She had her own friends and interests outside of baseball. It was foregone that she would always be known as major league baseball star Blake Benson's wife. At one point in her life that was quite a thrill, but she had grown as a person and wanted her own identity.

There was no need for a second income and definitely no desire for a full-time commitment that a career would entail. Kim decided that involvement in charitable activities would be the outlet to channel her own ambitions. Her social legacy would be recognized as a selfless, productive member of the overall Chicago area community.

Kim was much more sociable than Blake and she took advantage of his celebrity status to gain her entry into philanthropy circles, but she definitely desired to help others in a positive well-meaning way. She would always be there for Blake in a supportive role. She knew all too well about the many ups and downs of a baseball player. Many a big-league player would give credit to his wife for contributing significantly to his much-needed strong mental attitude.

Kim knew that the game didn't go well and Blake would need some reassurance. He had a tendency to sulk, and alcohol was always Blake's preferred remedy of choice to wash away the pain. He would certainly need a different outlet from now on.

Blake opened the front door and was pleasantly surprised to see Kim greeting him. His pleasantness suddenly shifted to suspicion as soon as he entered. He thought Kim was keeping a close eye on him, afraid he might be tempted to drink tonight. Blake knew he better get used to the suspicion. He had a well-deserved track record. Three strongly mixed brandy Cokes used to be his nightly post-game tonic.

"Hi honey, I suppose you saw the score?" Blake's voice was timid and a bit discouraged.

They met in a lengthy embrace followed by an affirmative nod from Kim.

"Yes I did. Are you going to be okay?

"Do you mean am I going to drink tonight? I can see the way you're looking at me."

Kim suspected Blake would be tense and short with her so she didn't bite at his antagonistic response even though she greatly desired to snap back in her own terse manner. She still carried voluminous scars from Blake's drinking and the philandering behavior that often takes over an addicted person.

"I just knew you'd be down tonight, that's all," Kim replied dishonestly. She was concerned that Blake would be tempted, as any wife would be.

"It wasn't the score that bothered me as much as the lack of connection between players. Everyone's a stranger to each other and so unattached. It's just weird. It felt like nobody cared about the honor of replacing my former teammates."

"Blake, you know that you've told me so many times not to base anything on one week, much less one game. You know it's going to take time. These are uncharted waters. Take your coat off and I'll give you a neck massage. That usually relaxes you."

"Thanks Kim. I guess I'll need some other relaxation mode now that I'm sober. You think your hands can survive a nightly massage?"

Blake finally hinted at a slight smile as he sat down in the elegant and spacious living room of their majestic home, complete with state of the art electronic gadgets but still extremely well proportioned and tasteful, thanks to Kim's astute home decorating eye.

"I know I can't bring the games home with me honey. I've got other things on my mind besides. I have a press conference tomorrow. It's time to come clean on my alcohol problem."

"I agree Blake. You don't have to spill your guts. People will be respectful of your medical privacy. Just disclose that you've been dealing with this problem and that's why you weren't on the plane that went down."

"That will probably just lead to more questions. I've got to tell the whole story and get this behind all of us. I'll tell the media that my alcohol problem finally reached a boiling point on the last road trip and the club was concerned enough about me to send me home to tackle the issue."

"Okay, draw the line there and ask them to respect your privacy as you deal with it. Hopefully, their detective noses won't be stimulated by the unanswered treatment option, but we both know that's not likely to happen."

"Thanks Kim, I appreciate your input. If they press any further I'll tell them off the record and hope that they appreciate the sensitivity of the subject. I think I have enough good standing with all of them to come to some type of an agreement. They don't want to be isolated professionally as well. The media understands the rules of the game."

"That reminds me. You said AA meetings were an option. When are you going to start? It would be nice to go with you, but I'm fairly certain that's against protocol. To be honest with you Blake, I'm worried about your upcoming road trip. The road has always been one of your biggest demons."

"I'll check with Marty to see about attending a meeting before we hit the road. I've heard they're open to anyone so I could find meetings to go to when

I'm traveling. Yes, those motel rooms are like prison cells. You just feel like you want to escape and do anything other than sitting in there staring at the ceiling, but realizing that the minute you step out of the room the temptations become even more potent."

"How about that neck massage you offered? Kim, can we not talk about anything deep for a few hours?"

It turned out to be a rather restful night. Blake tried not to think about baseball, but of course that was futile. At least he got a good night's sleep as he prepared for round two of managing.

This was going to be another taxing day. Blake felt anxious, but he was hopeful that his disclosure at the press conference would lessen the mental load he had been carrying around for over a week. Slowly but surely, Blake had felt more at ease with himself and his problems. He didn't feel the need to totally hide himself from others, either physically or mentally, but he wasn't quite ready for total transparency of his feelings even though he possessed a bit more self-respect in his clean and sober state.

Blake could sense that he was returning to his roots in a number of different ways. His outlook was more positive. He just felt better physically and emotionally. It was difficult to put a finger on it, but he felt that he was returning to the person he used to be before the harshness of baseball life had turned him into a bitter man. He knew that the average man on the street couldn't relate to the troubles of a star athlete. Making millions playing a kid's game seemed, on the surface, a dream job, but Blake knew any position that leaves others clamoring for your place on the pedestal put enormous pressure on oneself to perform as well. Unfortunately for Blake, relieving that pressure through alcohol had changed him in so many ways that it was difficult for others to remember the Blake Benson they once knew, much less himself.

Blake left for work the following morning confident that his disclosure would dampen speculation. He knew there was plenty to worry about regarding his team. Anything tacked on to the squad's emotional state would take some additional toll.

He had contemplated consulting his personal attorney before he waded into the media pool, but he just couldn't see any need for it. His agent was content with the developing situation. He still felt confident his baseball lifelong relationship with Chicago would make this something of a formality.

Maybe it was still the shock of all that had happened lately, but Blake had clearly misjudged the scope of attention on the developing story. Perhaps it was more than myth that the month of August was always considered the "scandal month" when news networks would focus incessantly on one event and milk it to death.

Blake was surprised to see the large contingent assembled for his press conference, but he still had not grasped the national attention that was coming his way like a runaway train.

The Cubs' own Sherry Williams, in charge of such publicity manners, opened up the press conference by confirming the standard rules of procedure. Blake would read a statement and then take a few questions before he had to get ready for tonight's game.

He sat amidst the glare of numerous cameras and read from his prepared statement. The constant clicking of camera shutters sounded like an orchestra as Blake continued on with his neatly arranged words.

"Thank you all for coming today. I felt it was important for my club and for my overall health to announce the reason why I was not with the team when the accident occurred. For the last several years my behavior was negatively affected by a problem that was spiraling out of control. My teammates had been covering for me for some time as I neglected my professional duties. Alcohol had always been a part of my life, but it had completely taken over my daily activities by the time the team left Atlanta. My teammates and the coaching staff had seen enough of my irresponsible behavior and had sent me back home to Chicago the morning of their accident to deal with my alcohol problem. I will forever be grateful that they took this overdue action that saved my life that day and preserved my life for the future. I feel an extreme sense of responsibility to remain alcohol-free and lead my new Chicago Cubs team for the rest of this season. I hope you will respect my privacy as I deal with my personal health problems in the manner that my family and the organization have settled on. Thank you. I will now take your questions."

Blake pointed to a very recognizable face from Sports Illustrated and gave him the floor.

"Rick Reynolds from Sports Illustrated. Blake did you ever play baseball under the influence?"

"Rick, well, you know I haven't played much the last couple of years," Blake tried to deflect the question with a poor attempt at humor. He was definitely caught off guard by the question.

"Well, I suppose there was still alcohol in my blood, but I don't feel I was ever intoxicated and incapable of performing."

Reynolds interjected again and tried to pin Blake down on the question.

"Did you ever take a drink in the bullpen or clubhouse while the game was going on?"

Blake was suddenly grasping the severity of the questions. All he could think about in the back of his mind was a possible suspension. He had overcome too much already to be knocked down by the Commissioner's office.

"I don't think it's necessary to go over all of my indiscretions here Rick. It would take us up to game time if I attempted to recall all of my misdeeds. The important thing is that I've acknowledged I have a problem and am dealing with on a daily basis as I continue my recovery."

Blake began to squirm in his chair and hesitantly pointed in the direction of Tim Conroy of ESPN. His nervousness and agitation were now clearly out for all of the suspicious media members to see and feel.

"Tim Conroy, ESPN here. Blake did you make any promises to your former manager before the team left for St. Louis? If so, have you lived up to those promises?

Blake became even more visibly agitated as he began to answer the question. He was now convinced that somebody had leaked the alcohol rehabilitation plan. He suddenly realized how naïve he had been.

"Well I'm not going to reveal the contents of a private conversation, but I can tell you that I am now, and will continue to live up to commitments that were made to my former team and my new team."

Fifteen years in the big leagues dealing with media types of all kinds had clearly taught Blake how to handle questions on his feet. He was not entirely accurate, but he did not lie either.

Blake regained some composure with that cagey answer and sat up straight in his chair. No more mister nice guy. His antennae was up and he could play the media game with the best of them.

He had always felt more comfortable with the local media so he looked for his old pal George Blanchard of the Chicago Tribune. He could see the pudgy old scribe sitting comfortably in the front row, apparently disinterested in it all. Blake felt the urge to prod his old buddy chewing on the butt end of a cheap cigar.

"Now come on Georgie. Don't tell me you don't have any questions for your friend of 15 years?" He pointed Blanchard out and begged for a question.

Attorneys are taught early in their legal career to never ask for a question that you don't know what the answer will be. Stupidly, Blake had fallen into a similar trap that he set for himself.

"Sure Blake, I have a question. We all know how close you were with your old teammate Sandy. Would Sandy approve of your plan of action regarding your treatment and recovery?"

The roller-coaster ride with Blake's demeanor continued as he fought back tears at this unexpected question. After a momentary pause and a wipe of his eyes Blake stood up and answered abruptly.

"That was uncalled for. That's it fellas. It's time for our game."

Sherry Williams quickly interjected; ready to defend Blake when needed and obviously well prepared in the expected duties of her position as director of media relations.

"Mr. Benson has professional duties to attend to. I'm sure you all understand. He'll be available after the game. Thank you ladies and gentlemen."

Blake hurriedly scampered out to the playing field, aware that this press conference had not gone well at all. The pressures were beginning to mount in his head as he realized that not only would he have to deal with managing and playing, he would have to deal with those nosy bastards of the media. Not to mention the most important issue, the ever-present temptation to resort to artificial means to deal with stress.

The vise was already beginning to tighten on Blake and it was only game two. His hands were shaking as he started to hit some grounders to his infielders in preparation for the game.

Slowly, but surely the years of preparing for game action had taken over his muscle memory and his mind. The ballgame itself was quite the tonic for complete distraction.

16 — Freefalling

Game two against the Cardinals went very much like the series opener. The Cubs' Randall Hart, previously of the Yankees, gave the fans plenty of evidence regarding his draft availability. Hart had no command of his pitches and the Cardinals were just waiting him out as he compiled six walks in three innings. He had his usual strikeout an inning with his high heat, but walks, wild pitches and an occasional base hit were enough to knock him out in the fourth inning trailing 6-1.

The bullpen kept the final score within reason, but it was difficult to tell if they pitched well or if the Cardinals felt like they didn't need to score any more. The Cubs' bats were impotent too as the final score of 8-2 didn't actually reflect the one-sidedness of the game. Mop-up duty is always difficult to assess because of the lack of urgency by the opposing team to score in a non-competitive contest.

The atmosphere in the ballpark and dugout was tepid at best. There was so little to cheer about that the fans were more interested in the trite fan participation of the wave and punching beach balls around the stands than anything happening on the field.

Blake felt helpless in the dugout, but he knew he had to be careful not to show it. He tried to stay upbeat and encouraging. He couldn't shake the helpless feeling so he decided to put himself in the game and give Bartlett a break behind the plate.

The final three innings went much faster with Blake catching. He flew out to medium left in his only at-bat, feeling good that he was able to make contact after not playing for so long. Rust is always the baseball player's worst enemy.

The 10-game lead was now down to eight with a doubleheader scheduled tomorrow. It was bad enough to assemble a pitching staff this late in the season without having to deal with two games in a day. There just seemed to be more trouble adding up down the road. The hope now was to just salvage one game of the four-game series and keep some breathing distance between his team and the Cards.

At least the post-game press conference went smoothly. The national media had left town and it was mostly a local press crowd after the night game. It was more a pity party than a professional press conference. The local scribes didn't even press the issues from earlier in the day.

Blake threw out the usual cliché answers, but the veteran reporters could already see and feel the despair in his voice. If ballplayers could perform on the field in near robotic fashion, bored in seemingly endless repetition, reporters could match them in professional custom with their standard questions.

The results didn't get any better after the doubleheader the following day.

The Cardinals swept the double-dip and the series to move within six games of the lead. It already had the feel of a funeral procession, and the team was lifeless and despondent once more.

This would be Blake's first real test as a manager and as a recovering alcoholic. The mood of the clubhouse was testy and the beer was flowing pretty freely after three days of futility.

Comments started to surface that reflected the players' true feelings about being forced to play for Chicago this late in the season. The respectful tone that prevailed in the opening days was replaced by surliness and defeatism. There was a sense of victimization as the new Cub players felt abused by the haphazard process and by Major League Baseball.

Blake could have really used a beer or two or 12 after the long afternoon in the hot sun. His past reaction to an event like this four-game swoon was to drown his sorrows in alcohol and lighten everybody up with distractions away from the game. He would have to look for a new outlet now. That beer sounded so good from the clubhouse all the drive home. The incessant urge to drink overburdened his mind.

Just as he was about to pull into his driveway Blake's cell phone rang and he was surprised to hear the voice of the legendary manager of the Cardinals, Don Leighton, call out his name.

"Blake, this is Don Leighton of the Cardinals. I bet you're surprised to get a call from your division rival," the St. Louis manager said in his slow-paced Southern drawl.

"Not after today coach. We've been pretty generous to you guys."

"Blake, I just wanted to express my admiration for the sacrifice you're making for the Cubs and to encourage you to keep your head up. It's a difficult job you have ahead of you. All of Major League Baseball owes you a debt of gratitude for keeping the credibility of the baseball season intact through this troubling time for you and the Chicago community."

"That's very classy of you Don, and I wouldn't expect anything different from you given your longstanding commitment to the game. Now I just hope we can give your club a battle the rest of the way."

"Just keep your team together and constantly remind them what they are sacrificing for the game of baseball and your former teammates. You have my deepest sympathies for your loss. Take care of your health, Blake, and we'll see you down the road."

Blake ended the call with a sincere thank-you and entered his house with a better taste in his mouth than any beer could have given him. That phone call came at just the right time to remind Blake that any respect attained from such a legendary man as Leighton made sobriety worthwhile.

17 — Sandy on the Brain

Blake was tussling with several emotions as he entered the house. The phone call was rewarding emotionally, but Blake did not want to be seen as some type of victim. His brain told him to stay away from alcohol, but his heart ached for the soothing feeling booze gave him. Kim was there to offer moral support. She could not let Blake become despondent over the deepening situation, fearing he would turn to booze one more time to ease the pain.

Blake was still struggling with the question posed to him yesterday at the press conference. He had always wanted to please Sandy. He projected an image that every athlete strove for. His laid-back demeanor, friendliness to all teammates, and hard-working professionalism made Sandy the ideal professional athlete. While others, including Blake himself, were fooling around with strange women on the road, Sandy was devoted as ever to his marriage. He simply seemed immune from temptation.

Kim could feel Blake's discomfort as he sank into his favorite reclining sofa.

"Why are you so distracted Blake? You seem a million miles away."

"Well, it's that stupid intrusive question that was asked yesterday. I can't seem to get it out of my mind."

"You mean the one you didn't answer?"

"Yes, it really hit home. It's got me questioning whether Sandy would approve of my approach to sobriety, as you asked."

"Jesus Christ Blake, you didn't seem to care that much what I thought. Why do you care so much about Sandy's opinion? The man is dead. You'll never know that answer. Just deal with it."

"You're right Kim. Still, I wonder if he'd approve."

Kim was downright angry now. She threw the kitchen towel that was draped around her waist toward Blake and spoke in that high-pitched tone that always accompanied her anger.

"Why do you think that man was a saint? If you had spent half the time trying to please your wife as you did Sandy, maybe we would have a better marriage. He was like a god to you guys. The man had his demons too. He just hid them better than the rest of you playboys."

Blake was too focused on his inner thoughts to question Kim's implied meaning.

Truth is Kim admired Sandy as much as anybody. In fact, she admired him too much, but she still was jealous of the time and attention Blake showered him with. That sort of reverence was supposed to be directed toward her. The relationship puzzled both Blake and Kim. Blake just knew he loved the man, but he often wondered why he was so infatuated with him. Kim was just jealous at apparent misdirected love.

"I know you're right honey, but I can't seem to shake it. The man simply was my hero and mentor. With all my flaws so out in the open for all to see, I just respected Sandy's well-deserved reputation and professional standing in the community."

The rest of the evening was quiet and uneventful. Blake took up reading in his den and unsuccessfully tried to suppress the still-unanswered question in his head.

Kim kept a watchful eye on Blake. She still did not totally trust his commitment to sobriety. She believed his words, but she knew deep down there were a hundred more questions buried in Blake's soul that he had yet to uncover, let alone answer.

The morning brought another of those mysterious questions to light. Blake had noticed that every dream he had experienced lately had him in an intoxicated state.

It was deeply troubling and confusing to him. Last night's dream had him hiding his drinking from Sandy. The two of them were having dinner on the road at a posh restaurant. In the dream Blake was sure that Sandy didn't know he was drinking when they were out. Blake had always seemed to be hiding his drinking in these dreams, but Blake himself knew he wasn't sober. The confusion had reached a point where Blake had a semi-conscious feeling that would cause him to be unsure himself if he was sober as he awakened from sleep.

He had not shared this with Kim yet as he feared she would misinterpret these dreams as a warning that he was close to drinking again. Blake couldn't be so sure himself. He didn't know the answer, but he was going to find out.

The next day, as Blake drove to Wrigley to begin their last leg of the home stand, a three-game series with the last place Los Angeles Dodgers, he was feeling even more overwhelmed. On top of a four-game skid that saw their lead shrink to six games in just three days and a lifeless squad that still didn't know their teammates' first names, he now was having to deal with his subconscious thoughts as he plowed straight ahead through another day at the office.

Hopefully a last place team that had been out of the race for months now would be an easier match-up for the Cubbies. The Dodgers had recently jettisoned their big name players in a trade with the New York Yankees and were going with young prospects themselves. Blake was confident things could not get much worse.

18 — Sparks Fly

The start of the series with the Dodgers had an all too familiar tone. Until the squad received some decent starting pitching, it was next to impossible to exhibit some excitement in the dugout and on the field. Los Angeles jumped out to a 6-0 lead after three innings and the downbeat mood just couldn't dissipate from the confines of the Chicago dugout.

Once again Blake had no choice but to preach patience. This approach was getting stale and Blake could sense it himself. The sense of despair was already entrenched with this team after only four games. He needed to light a fire under his team soon, but he did not know how what his next step should be. Blake was desperately looking for some inspiration as he glanced around the ballpark.

Baseball has its slump busting customs. Wild nights out on the town could release some of the built-up tension, but this was more common on the road. There was the overused team meeting approach that usually turned into a bitching session. The manager could go berserk on the field and get tossed out of the game on purpose to fire up a team in the doldrums, or destroy the post-game meal spread to get his message across. Blake had seen more than his share of these scenarios and realized that they failed more often than not. At best a tantrum would be only a temporary fix, but any improvement would be welcome at the moment, regardless of its duration.

As Blake sat in the dugout pondering what he could do to light a fire, he looked over at his new teammate and old nemesis John Bartlett when it suddenly hit him. Nothing could bring a team together like a bench-clearing brawl and nobody was better at instigating a fight than the Rat, Bartlett. The inspiration was right beside him all the time, but it wasn't until Blake heard Bartlett heckling the Dodger pitcher before it finally hit him right between the eyes.

The tricky part was manipulating events to make it appear as if any fight was spontaneous and not pre-planned. If the fight appeared staged the spread of emotions wouldn't ignite throughout the rest of the team.

Blake figured this game was another lost cause and a quick glance at the scoreboard showed that the second-place Cardinals were rolling again today. The lead would be down to five games before the end of the day. He felt the sense of urgency. Another week of these results and it would likely be all over.

Blake sat on the bench, chewed his bubble gum faster in distress, his blood pressure rising by the minute as Dodger line drives laced the playing field. The Dodgers were making this look way too easy. His fatigued pitcher committed the cardinal sin of looking in the dugout, practically begging to be taken out.

Blake was steaming now. This pitcher just got himself a ticket to Des Moines, but Blake was going to make him stay in there and eat up some innings to protect the rest of the pitching staff. He sent his pitching coach Mark Douglas to the mound to relay the message.

The beating continued as the Dodgers built a 10-0 lead. After the inning mercifully ended, Blake motioned for his catcher to meet him up the runway to the clubhouse.

Blake looked at Bartlett sheepishly and smiled. He threw his wad of gum on the floor and revealed his plan.

"Bartlett, I can't tell you how many times I wanted to knock you out because of some of your bullshit antics out there on the field. You've started more fights than Don King. I've no idea how often you started a fight on purpose, but I would be willing to bet it was more than once."

"Skip, I think I know where you're going with this. Just leave it all to me. You're looking at the master."

"I've got just one more thing Bartlett. Don't make it so obvious that the guys smell a rat."

"Was that supposed to be a joke with my notorious nickname that I'm quite proud of, actually?"

"I wish I was that clever. Now go out there next inning and start scheming."

Bartlett had a long list of options to choose from. He even kept a little book with some of the details from his best plots, like an artist treasures their best work.

He knew that his pitcher was toast and was probably destined for a one-way ticket out of town after tonight. With that in mind he walked out to the mound to start the next inning and started up a conversation with the soon-to-be-demoted pitcher.

"Can you believe Benson has you still out here? That sonofabitch has no more business managing than my crabby-ass mother-in-law. He's just being a huge prick right now and wants to use you to set some kind of example. That's bush league bullshit."

Bartlett rubbed his sleeve across his sweaty brow, peering just slightly at the guinea pig pitcher for any suspecting reaction, and continued on.

"Now I don't want you to get hurt out here now. Just follow my lead and I'll get you off this mound in a few batters."

Bartlett walked back to the batters' box realizing that he had just set the stage for another chapter in his book. He had several options to choose from depending on what would happen next.

Noting that the meat of the order was due up this inning for the Dodgers, his priority was grooving a fastball for the power-hitting LA catcher Domingo Martinez. Bartlett couldn't stand the prima donna stud catcher and the feisty Chicago backstop had no problem working up hatred for Martinez, who stood at 6 foot 4 and 225 pounds with a muscular build that was only matched by his enormous ego. The former number one pick overall was special and the kid knew it.

The first batter popped up. Bartlett had called for five straight fastballs. The perplexed pitcher called him out to the mound after shaking off the catcher several times.

Bartlett walked briskly to the mound in a huff, ripped off his cage mask in obvious anger as his raging eyes looked square into the young pitcher's gaze.

"I told you to trust me on this. I've only been in this league 15 fucking long seasons kid. I know all the tricks. Just follow me."

Martinez strutted up to the plate as only he could. Bartlett mumbled in anger to Martinez about his pitcher.

"The kid's so fucked up. Benson wants him to work on his fastball and all he wants to do is toss up breaking balls."

Bartlett crouched down and the kid shook him off again.

"This kid just doesn't get it Martinez."

Then Bartlett hollered out to the kid.

"God damn it, do you want to rot out there kid? I'll kick your fucking ass right here, right now."

Three fastballs came right down the pike with Martinez fouling off the last one after taking the first two in disbelief of Bartlett. There was no pressure in a 10-0 rout so Martinez dialed in on another expected fastball and crushed it well over 400 feet on to Waveland Avenue.

Bartlett knew Martinez' slow home run trot irritated the hell out of the opposing teams so he just patiently waited for Martinez to circle the bases. When he finally touched home plate, Bartlett let him have it real good.

"Hey asshole, are you showing up my team? You're a goddamn punk Martinez!"

"Be quiet old man, before I hurt you." Martinez smugly turned away from Bartlett.

The Rat was glad Martinez took the bait, but he had to show anger, not appreciation. He picked up Martinez' bat and flung it toward him, striking the arrogant superstar in the back.

"You're lucky I didn't shove that bat up your ass, you classless wetback."

That was the racist trigger to a bench-clearing brawl. Martinez turned and raced toward the Cubs' catcher, bat in hand. Bartlett never hesitated, plowing straight ahead. He had learned long ago that it was better to be the aggressor in these battles. Wearing catchers' gear and a mask didn't hurt his cause either.

Martinez swung the bat at Bartlett and the wily old vet threw caution to the wind, planting himself right on the chest of the slugger. He speared the youngster with his mask and wrapped his arms right around Martinez' torso effectively tying up the Dodger player and neutralizing the swinging weapon.

Blake was anticipating the confrontation from the top step of the dugout. As soon as he saw the two of them steaming toward each other, he sprung out onto the field to protect his catcher. The dugouts emptied in full fury as both teams raced to the tussle. The bullpens usually arrive late to any brawl, but they didn't want to miss out either. No player ever wants to be seen as a coward. Bruises from a brawl are seen as a badge of courage.

Martinez' strength began to take over as he flipped Bartlett over and began to pummel him with rapid-fire punches. Bartlett lay defenseless just outside the visitors' on-deck circle with his hands over his head as the rest of the players scrambled to intervene.

Baseball fights typically consist of wrestling moves. The players need to protect their hands, arms and shoulders to preserve their careers. Winners would be losers if their hands were broken from a devastating punch. So as the two teams square off, generally nobody intervenes unless a mismatch develops. Normally, the combatants are cordoned off as cooler heads attempt to prevail. Sudden rage outranks logic for a brief time before players realize they're gambling with their livelihood.

This time Blake felt obligated to protect the instigator acting at his behest. He also disliked Martinez as much as Bartlett did. So without hesitation, Blake plowed over Martinez to get him off of his catcher.

Suddenly the unwritten baseball rule of protecting the tools of your trade went out the window as players from both teams piled on and did their best to protect their teammates who were all coming to the rescue.

The Wrigley Field faithful were clearly enjoying the sudden passion that was emerging. The score was embarrassing, but the fighting spirit that had been lacking so far aroused the fans. The standing ovation that followed the fight resonated with the Chicago players. They finally acted as a unit and the raucous crowd appreciated it.

As order prevailed and the umpires regained control, one by one the Cubbies walked up to their starting catcher Bartlett. Some patted him on the shoulder, some on the rump and a couple of others even helped him take off his catching gear. He was tossed from the game by the umps along with Martinez, but he was instantly anointed team leader by his aggressive action.

Blake gained instant cred as well, coming to Bartlett's defense. Being a player-manager certainly helped in this instance. Blake still had some physical presence as a current player. He was glad to help out, especially since his covert actions had started the fracas. Managers seldom get involved, but a player-manager had to make a decision about what role to play in this circumstance.

True to his word, Bartlett got the kid pitcher out of the game. The lengthy delay meant that a new pitcher would be needed, as custom dictated that it was not healthy to reheat a pitcher after such a long break from activity.

The naïve pitcher never knew what role he played in the uprising, but it didn't matter since he was dispatched to the minors, likely never to be heard from again at the major league level.

The game ended quietly with the Cubs on the losing end again, but this time the mood in the clubhouse was different. The back and forth banter that defines a major league clubhouse had emerged from the rubble of another one-sided defeat that defied the custom that a losing clubhouse should remain subdued.

The "Rat" had added another chapter to his book. Blake sure felt a lot better about this episode with Bartlett on his side for once. Maybe they had turned the page from a tragic novel to an uplifting drama.

19 — Coming Together

Blake wore his stern game face as he entered the clubhouse after another lopsided loss, but he quickly turned all smiles as he entered his private manager's office. He looked in his full-length mirror across from his cluttered desk and smirked in delight. The plan had worked like a charm, but he knew events like this were only temporary. The foundation had been laid for team unity, but there was more work ahead. All the fights in the world could not make up for continuing losses. They had to start winning and competing.

Blake opened his office door and searched for Bartlett.

"Bartlett, get your ass in my office. I'll meet you there in a minute."

"Sure thing Skipper. Do I need to bring a bat for self-defense?"

"By the look of things out there on the field, you don't really need any weapons," the manager said in praise of the catcher's scrappy fighting ability. "I just want to hear your side of the story in case I get a call from the Commissioner's Office."

When Blake returned to his office, he found Bartlett firmly planted in the manager's chair that was clearly more comfortable than the other seats in the office. He could plainly see that Bartlett was milking his performance to the hilt.

"Ok, Bartlett, let's get back to normal here. Get your ass out of my chair," ordered Blake as he shut the door behind him.

"Come on Blake, my plan worked to perfection other than me taking a pounding from Martinez. I deserve a medal of honor or something. I'm just trying to enjoy the moment before the pain settles in."

"You're right and believe me, I'm thankful for your dastardly deeds today. If you do nothing else the rest of the way, you'll have earned your paycheck for the rest of the season. But you know it's just like everything else in this game of baseball. It's only one of 162 games and we have to turn the page and build on what was accomplished today."

Bartlett shrugged his shoulders in agreement. "Damn baseball. You just can't enjoy the moment for more than a few minutes. Well at least I can chronicle it in my instigator book. Damn thing should be worth a fortune someday."

"I don't want to question your methods, but why did you have to call him a wetback? You did call him that didn't you? The Commissioner's Office is really sensitive to that shit. If word gets out to the media, there could be some pressure on you."

"Of course I called him that. I was trying to start a fight. You have to know what will set somebody off. Martinez struts around like he's some god. I'm sure he's been embarrassed all his life about his poor upbringing and now he wants to shove it in everybody's face. I probably could have a rewarding career as a psychologist after baseball," the pugnacious catcher said with a smile.

"Okay, but we have to get a plan of action here if shit comes our way. I can expect some kind of communication from New York on this," said Blake.

"You worry way too much Blake. The prick Martinez called me a fucking queer a while back and said that's why my wife left me. I don't think New York will want to touch that subject with a 10-foot pole either."

"Did he really say that to you Bartlett?"

"It doesn't matter Skipper. That's my story and I'm sticking to it. This instigator and fighting shit isn't all about fisticuffs. You have to play the bullshit games too."

"Ok, I'll relay that message if I have to. Now let's get on to the bigger issue. How do we build on this temporary feeling of togetherness?"

"Listen to those guys out there," Bartlett said in reference to the buzz and chatter coming from the clubhouse.

"They're probably telling each other how they kicked someone's ass out on the field or that they had some poor guy shaking in his spikes in fear of him. I'm sure there will be a week's worth of exaggerated claims of bravado."

"Well those guys out there respect you even more now, Bartlett. You're their leader on the field. Milk it for all it's worth to bring these guys together. Use this to bring out all of their personalities. The more they get to know each other and their quirks, the closer they'll be. There really isn't enough time left in the season for people to tire of each other unless, of course, we continue to lose."

"Don't worry about it Blake. I'll definitely have some fun with it. This'll be the easy part. Winning games is another story."

"You rest on your laurels for a couple of days and I'll catch the next few games. It looks like you might have a couple of bruises to deal with. Get into the trainer's room and get everything checked out. It's sure great having you on my side. You're not a rat, you're a teddy bear, a Cubbie."

"Thanks Blake. That definitely is a first. I've never been called a teddy bear before and thanks for the couple of days off. These old bones don't feel so hot right now."

"Now get out of here and make sure the team knows I have your back too. Tell them I just wanted to get all the facts straight in case the Commissioner calls."

20 — Clubhouse Banter

Blake arrived at Wrigley even earlier than usual before the middle game of the series against the Dodgers. The anticipation of entering a game with even a slight advantage gave a little more spring in Blake's step this day.

The Cubs were turning over the five-man pitching rotation today and starting what might conceivably be their number one pitcher. Conversely, the Dodgers had a minor league call-up pitching for them as a last minute replacement for one of their starting pitchers that went on the disabled list with a bum elbow. Today's game just had a better feel to it for Blake.

For the first time since he became manager Blake was not the first one to arrive at the ballpark. He interpreted that as a good sign. As he sat in his office with the door open he began to hear laughter and good-natured ribbing between players. This is what he was accustomed to in a major league clubhouse. The somber and timid mood that prevailed before was awkward and unusual.

Blake was prepared to catch today, but it still came as a surprise to hear that Bartlett and Martinez had both been suspended so soon after the brawl. They each received three-game suspensions. Bartlett could appeal, but since he was going to take the next few days off anyway, he decided to accept the suspension immediately. At least the tawdry details of the skirmish had not made the sports pages. This club certainly didn't need any more distractions.

Bartlett wasn't surprised at his quick suspension. His reputation had been tarnished some time ago. He took his share of verbal abuse from the other players while receiving his treatment from the club's top trainer for bruises from the fight. In fact, he relished the attention he always received from his shady tactics. He soaked in all of the abuse with a smile, occasionally throwing out some barbs of his own, while the trainer worked on his aching body.

Outfielder Bryce Burroughs was brought over from San Diego in the special dispersal draft. He was a player with marginal major league skills, but his forte as a versatile ballplayer made him more valuable than his body of work suggested. He also was notorious as a clubhouse prankster and team clown but had been noticeably silent as a Chicago Cub. The events of the previous day seemed to unshackle his vibrant personality. Burroughs walked over to Bartlett, sat down next to him and let loose with a synopsis of the tussle yesterday laced with sarcasm.

"Eighty-year-old John Bartlett of the Chicago Cubs went toe to toe with 24-year-old Domingo Martinez in a surprising close sparring match yesterday at Wrigley Field. The cagey veteran catcher, already suffering from the effects of dementia, threw caution to the wind and potential quality of life of his few remaining years to preserve the honor and integrity of his teammates by throwing an ethnic slur against the young stud catcher of the Dodgers. He further enhanced his sterling reputation by spearing the muscular foe with his catcher's mask before the two could square off. Bartlett reportedly told his teammates that being brought up in the medieval ages trained him to defend the honor of his comrades by whatever force is necessary. Unfortunately, the elder statesman is confined to a wheelchair today, courtesy of the fists of Mr. Martinez."

"Very good Burroughs, I've been wondering when your comedic skills were going to come out. You're supposed to keep us loose. They certainly didn't bring you here for your baseball ability."

"That hurts old man. Did the club bring you here to teach the youngsters how to slur the opposition?"

"Of course they did," replied Bartlett. "It's about all I've left at this point in my career."

Miguel Guillen lay 10 feet from Bartlett, plopped out on another trainer's table, silent as always while he received treatment on his aching left shoulder. The overweight lefty reliever looked anything but a professional athlete as his huge girth spread out on the table. It caught everyone off guard when Guillen joined in the banter. He had been quiet, but that was about to change dramatically.

"I would've protected you Bartlett if I could've gotten there faster. Even though you slurred my country, you're my teammate and my compadre."

"Thanks lefty, I don't think I could ever count on your fat ass to get there in time, but thanks anyway. It's good to know what you're thinking every once in a while Guillen. Don't wait for the next fight to speak up, compadre."

"I would Bartlett, but I feel you do enough talking. I like to listen to you. It teaches me what not to say," Guillen said with a wry smile.

The rest of the guys in the clubhouse erupted in laughter. The spunky character Guillen just spoke what the others had been thinking for some time now.

Bartlett laughed right along with the guys.

"I guess we got ourselves a comedy team now. Guillen can play the straight man and Burroughs can deliver. They're regular Abbott and Costello. Or maybe it should be the other way around. Guillen certainly looks more like Costello."

Just then Blake interrupted to congratulate the team on remembering what a clubhouse is supposed to look and feel like.

"Now let's go out there today and resemble a major league team. It's time to go out there on the field and just let everything fly like you guys have been doing all of your professional life. No thinking allowed. Just react and have some fun."

21 — Footloose and Fancy Free

The relaxed atmosphere was just what the doctor ordered as the Cubs played their first complete game in all facets, a 4-2 win over the Dodgers. The team played baseball just like each one of them had done thousands of times before with no emphasis on their unique status, and no expectations.

Kyle Jacobson threw seven solid innings, mixing up his pitches well and living every bit up to reputation as a very crafty lefty. Blake truly enjoyed catching Jacobson as his pinpoint control made it easy on Blake's old knees. It was pitch and catch with a purpose.

Miguel Guillen came in to pitch a 1-2-3 eighth and T.J. Bowman protected his first save opportunity with a stellar ninth, striking out the first two batters he faced and inducing a feeble grounder to end the game. The crowd roared in approval as the team basked in sun-soaked Wrigley Field and in its first win as the "new" Cubbies.

Desmond Wilson got a chance to show off his speed for the first time when he torpedoed a triple down the right field line. There was just a slight bobble by the Dodger outfielder as he corralled the ball in the corner. Wilson reacted instantly to the bobble and dove head first into third just in time to beat the tag. The center fielder then scored the first run of the game on a sacrifice fly by Reggie Rodriguez.

First baseman Jim Arnold led off the fourth inning with a screaming line drive that hooked around the left field foul pole for a home run. The third base umpire ran straight down the left field line and appeared to have a good look at the flight of the baseball as he signaled home run. Dodger manager Frank Cisco ran out to the field protesting the call so Blake followed suit to make sure Cisco wasn't the only one to have the umpires' ears. A quick video review confirmed the call and the home team seemed to be in control for once. The game of baseball takes on a different feel when played with the lead.

Small ball proved to be the difference as the Cubs plated two runs in the sixth inning after the pitcher Jacobson advanced both runners with a perfect sacrifice bunt. P.J. Wilson failed to bring the runners home as he struck out chasing a low and away slider, but second sacker Pedro Arroyo picked up his teammate with a two-run single over the outstretched arms of the LA shortstop and into left-centerfield that provided the Cubs with the winning margin.

Blake struggled at the plate, but he contributed with his defense and pitch calling. There were hundreds of decisions to make as a catcher in pitch selection and location. His smaller-in-number managerial decisions all came through for him on this occasion. It was a splendid day all around.

The post-game atmosphere was loose as well. Victory has a way of taking your mind off the negative thoughts. The manager was answering questions to the media about the game, but the players were immersed in anything but baseball as the topics ranged from beautiful scantily dressed women in the stands to monetary investments by the millionaire players. Ironically, success on the field often comes about by shifting the focus to anything but baseball. The players were now in full reactive mode and their skills were flourishing by keeping their brains empty. Such is baseball life after a good day. The problem lies in the length of the season and the certainty that there will always be a multitude of not-so-good days. Tomorrow always comes and presents another day of opportunity and challenges. The Cubs would have to repeat this performance tomorrow or the negative thoughts would creep back in.

The trick for players is to enjoy the moment and try not to look ahead. The professional knows and understands the highs and lows that will inevitably challenge each and every one of them throughout the season. Having the experience and confidence that one can withstand the pressures is all one needs.

The act of winning feels liberating as it clears the mind and lessens the tension ever so slowly like a balloon with a small leak. A long winning streak eventually takes all the air out and produces a very loose team that usually creates good results if the talent is there as well.

Conversely, each loss fills a bit more air pressure into the balloon and tightens the whole team atmosphere. If a squad stretches a half dozen or more losses in a row, the tensions accumulate, pressuring the nearly full balloon to capacity. If the balloon pops all hell breaks loose with players, coaches, ownership and the media at each other's throats.

Blake was praying for another pressure-leaking performance tomorrow as the Cubs tried to win back-to-back contests for the first time, and defeat the Dodgers to claim the rubber game of the three-game series.

22 — Road Trip Angst

Despite the inaugural managerial win, the press conference was fairly mundane for Blake as he launched into full cliché mode. Inside he was beaming, but the duty of feeding the press the stale, overused quotes took the fun out of the victory for a short while. He knew he had to downplay this victory. There would simply be too many games left to feel outwardly giddy about this particular result, as rewarding as it was for Blake personally.

The drive home provided time for Blake's usual post-game reflections. He had been trained long ago as a professional baseball player to let go of the day's game as soon as possible. Good or bad, the season was too long to dwell on what had been. The focus had to stay on the immediate future and that was tomorrow's game and the upcoming road trip. The team would be flying out right after the game for their first long road trip and its perils, temptations, and travails.

It had all been fairly easy up until now for Blake to stay sober. The comforts of home and the company of Kim took the edge off the anxiety that had often led to the self-medicating use of alcohol. Both Kim and Blake were acutely aware of the upcoming trip, but had avoided any mention of it even though the anticipation and anxiety hung in the air like a bad smell.

Kim had previously offered to accompany the team on the road, but Blake knew that would send the wrong signal to the rest of the Cubs. Anonymity was the timeworn code of the road, and the wife of the manager would be seen as a spy on ballplayers' post-game activities.

Blake knew the topic would undoubtedly come up during the evening at home so he decided to initiate the conversation shortly after arriving.

Kim congratulated him on his first win as a manager with a lengthy embrace. She followed that with a sultry kiss that emboldened Blake to initiate the topic that was like the big elephant in the room, which had been figuratively stepped around for quite some time.

"Man, did I need that honey! That kiss and that first win. We both know there are many challenges ahead, but I guess the first big test will be this upcoming road trip. It won't be a piece of cake, but I can handle it now that I have this responsibility. Failure isn't an option, Kim."

Blake looked Kim straight in the eye and tried to reassure her that it would be okay, but she remained hesitant. She knew this time was different, but she had been down this troublesome path before with unkept promises.

She wanted to believe in her husband, but she felt he was going about his recovery in ignorance about the disease of alcoholism. Denial of all the numerous factors that attracted Blake to booze only temporarily diverted the opportunistic demons that would have to be content to wait for their moment of opportunity to trip Blake up.

Kim wrapped her arms around Blake's neck, returned the look straight into his eyes and tried to assess the real confidence Blake possessed, not just empty words.

"I know the road has always been a troublesome part of your professional baseball career Blake. Have you ever really examined closely why you feel so uncomfortable on the road?"

"Not really," answered Blake in a matter-of-fact fashion.

"This is why I feel so worried about your recovery. You haven't gone to any meetings yet and looked inward to find some answers for your past behaviors."

"I guess that'll take some time to figure out honey, right now I just want to concentrate on baseball and rely on willpower to avoid the booze. There'll be plenty of time for that in the winter."

"You sound just like my dad, Blake. This disease isn't simply a case of willpower. You just don't get it! That's why I'm worried," Kim wanted to scream but tempered outright anger and frustration in her voice with her guarded, but obviously irritated, response.

"Kim, I'll call you at the first sign of any craving. Your voice will be enough to get my head straightened out."

"Alcohol hasn't always been your only temptation on the road, Blake. I seriously doubt you will be thinking of me when you get the sexual urge. Your guilt will take over and you will avoid me like always."

"Kim, the booze led me down the wrong path that way too. It's like the chicken and egg thing. The booze always came first and then the other shit followed because I knew I fucked up."

"Blake, that's exactly what I mean when I said you have so many things to figure out inwardly before you can tackle this completely."

She turned away from him and flung Blake's light summer Cubs jacket in disgust, throwing it to get her point across as the coat landed softly on the living room sofa.

"Well, it's not going to get solved tonight babe so why don't we just have a quiet evening together while we can?"

"Fine," Kim responded tersely, but without any hint of anger in her tone of voice. She knew when she had been beat.

She had seen this side of Blake way too often before. It was pointless to argue with such a stubborn man.

The evening that followed their intense discussion was quiet indeed, but the house was dripping with tension that made the quiet unsettling, not soothing. The couple was miles apart in thought, but keenly aware of each other's dissatisfaction with the evening's proceedings. Blake wanted Kim to trust him, but Kim knew trust wouldn't be enough to keep her husband on the straight and narrow.

After a few hours of reading and a nightcap of ESPN Sports Center, Blake strolled to the bedroom alone as Kim spent most of the night on her laptop, surfing the Internet in an electronic escape from reality.

Blake lay in bed unable to sleep with thoughts and fears scurrying through his head. He knew inside that Kim was right about everything. She almost always was. He knew that his stubborn insistence on staying sober would be his only hope in the short term. Resolve, plus his loyalty to past teammates and long-time close friend Sandy, were his short-term ticket to sobriety. He tried to convince himself that he could handle whatever came his way, but that little inward voice inside still gave Blake trepidation in an underlying, but ever-present mode.

Blake had to get his thoughts toward baseball as he lay there writhing in emotional pain. Tomorrow, the Cubs would have to garner some momentum before hitting the road. Another victory would win the series and mark the beginning of an upward trend. We have to win tomorrow. We just have to. Baseball again had soothed his pain. Blake was soon asleep.

23 — Down But Not Out

It was the type of August day that makes fans long for the cool fall breeze of Lake Michigan. Hot and steamy Wrigley Field was sure to live up to its reputation as a hitter's park in the summer months with a strong, thick southerly blast of hot air blowing out to the fences this getaway day for the Cubbies.

Wrigley Field has dimensions that are slightly more favorable to power hitters than pitchers, with distances of 355 feet down the left field line and 353 feet to the right field foul pole and the power alleys only 368 feet in both directions. The center field distance tops out at 400 feet.

However, it is the wind direction that classifies the park on any particular day. Winds off Lake Michigan that prevail in the spring and fall turn Wrigley into a pitcher's park as the wind blows in toward home plate. Conversely, when the summer months bring a strong southerly flow, the ballpark turns into a hitter's paradise as fly balls easily sail out of the park.

This oppressive summer day was sure to bring its share of home runs to Wrigleyville. The best strategy for this day would be to play error-free baseball with few walks allowed. Balls were sure to fly out of the park. The best a manager could hope for would be solo homers allowed to limit the pain and damage.

Blake had seen countless summer games in these conditions at Wrigley. It was imperative to keep his team from becoming overconfident with a lead or too despondent over a large deficit. These almost always turned out to be among the strangest games of the year.

Today's starting pitcher Randall Hart struggled in his Cubs debut. His overpowering velocity could be beneficial in these conditions, but his wildness and penchant for allowing fly balls could be disastrous as well. Blake would have to watch him closely in the heat and humidity for any signs of tiring, if he indeed made it far enough into the game to tire. This had all the makings of a bizarre game.

Sure enough, the contest started out like the slugfest that any longtime Wrigley fan had grown accustomed to over the course of many summers. The Dodgers plated four runs in the first on only two hits. A leadoff walk, followed by an infield single, set the stage for the Los Angeles power hitters. Hart came back to strike out the next two batters before an error by Cubs shortstop Rivera allowed a third runner on base and extended the inning. On a normal day the routine fly that Dodgers left fielder Trevor Hulsing sent to center field would have ended the inning with Hart and the Cubs unscathed. Today, it turned into a grand slam and the Cubs came to bat in the bottom of the first already trailing by four.

Through the first four innings the Cubs managed only two solo home runs, one by Blake and the other by first baseman Jim Arnold. The Dodgers had long since knocked Hart out of the game as his penchant for allowing fly balls doomed his cause on this day. Four home runs allowed by Hart had powered the Dodgers to a 10-2 lead midway through the game.

Blake had tried his best to keep the team inspired despite the big lead. Nobody appeared to give up as the lore of Wrigley Field on a day when the wind was blowing out was also well documented by years of big comebacks.

"Do you guys see how the ball's flying out of here today? My grandma could go deep today. We've got a big inning or two in us today, I'm sure of it. I've got a plan for the rest of the game, guys. It's a bit out of the ordinary, but what the hell. It kinda describes our year anyway."

Blake motioned to pitching coach Mark Douglas to meet him in the runway just out of the dugout.

"Now don't go thinking I'm crazy Mark, but how many innings you think Bowman can give us today? I know he's our closer, but today's conditions are made for his sinker. We'll worry about tomorrow later. I really want this game for some momentum for our trip."

"Well, he had an easy inning yesterday. Doubt if he's gone more than two for some time. If it goes well and these guys are swinging for the fences early in the count like they probably will, I think he could go three or maybe four."

"Well get his ass on the phone and tell him to get up and loosen that arm, but tell him to take it easy in the pen. It shouldn't take more than a handful of tosses to get loose today. Let him know he's in for the duration today or as long as he can go. And make goddamn sure he knows that it'll be all sinkers today. He can come get me behind home plate if he objects. I don't even want strikeouts today, just quick groundouts."

The Cubs went out quietly in the bottom of the fifth and Bowman entered the game in the top half of the sixth. Blake strolled to the mound to make sure his instructions would be followed. He took his mask off as sweat was still dripping from his brow after his at-bat from moments ago and covered his mouth up with his glove as he muttered to Bowman.

"Look at me for Christ sakes T.J. I'm too fucking old to be squatting down behind home plate for very long in this heat and I'm sure the rest of the guys would like it too if you'd just get them off the field in a hurry. These Dodger guys just want to jack balls out of the park today. Just give 'em sinkers all day and we'll see what they do with it. We're going all sinkers now, got it?"

Bowman never did talk much and he quickly nodded in agreement with his skipper and stood on the rubber just waiting for old man Blake to get in the crouch position.

The plan worked to perfection as the LA batters swung early and often. Eight pitches later, the Cubs were back in the dugout as Bowman induced three ground ball outs.

Now it was up to the offense to get rolling. The Dodger starting pitcher was beginning to labor in the heat and his pitches lacked the zip from earlier innings. Most experienced major league players could intuitively sense the diminished capacity of their vulnerable prey.

Two singles and a walk later, the Cubs were in business with the scent of momentum on their side as the pitcher seemed to be on the ropes. The eighth place batter, Luis Rivera, was up, with the pitcher's spot in the on-deck circle. Blake really didn't want to be forced to pinch hit for Bowman so he was thrilled to see the bases loaded. Without an open base and with an eight-run lead the Dodgers went right after the light-hitting Cubs shortstop Rivera.

The Cubs dugout came to life as Rivera deposited a hanging slider into the bleachers directly down the left field line for a grand slam. The eight-run deficit was cut in half in just a moment's notice and the team could sense they were on the verge of something big.

A new LA pitcher was summoned from the bullpen and with some damage already done this inning, Blake was able to let Bowman hit for himself and leave him in the game. The relief hurler put out the fire in the bottom of the sixth. But it felt like a new game now as the Cubs took the field in the seventh.

The Dodger batters still hadn't figured out Blake's game plan and were flailing away at Bowman's sinker. They went out in order again, this time on six pitches, as the shortstop Rivera flawlessly handled three grounders.

The crowd was starting to get into the action after the seventh inning stretch and an always- uplifting rendition of "Take me out to the ballgame."

Blake gave the fans a thrill with a two-run homer that was just over the glove of the leaping left fielder and into the basket area that signified a home run. He pumped his fists in exhilaration as he rounded the bases and he answered the curtain call from the adoring crowd. The deficit was now a mere two runs on this day in the windy city of Chicago. The excitement was building, but the Cubs could do no more damage that inning.

It took only two innings for the Dodger bench to figure out the strategy. The LA hitters were much more patient in the eighth and ninth innings and a weary Bowman struggled his way to the finish, allowing one run in the ninth to leave the deficit at three for the bottom of the ninth as the Cubs left two runners stranded in their half of the eighth.

The Cubs knew they would have to rally against the Dodger closer who was no slouch. Six-foot 5, 270-pound Ryan Thurston took the mound with the confidence of a successful closer. His fastball reached into the upper 90s, but control could be an issue for him at times.

He blew away the Cubs leadoff batter Wilson on three straight heaters. The atmosphere in the dugout switched from boisterous to quiet as Wilson struck out. The mood heightened a bit as second baseman Arroyo walked, giving the crowd and the team just a bit of hope.

The next batter struck out on a wicked split-fingered fastball, but fortunately Arroyo had reached second on catcher's indifference one pitch earlier, allowing the Cubs batter to reach first as the strikeout pitch went through the catcher's legs and all the way to the backstop. With runners on first and third and one out, the Cubbies left fielder Rodriguez lined the ball off the shortstop's out-stretched glove into center field for an RBI single that cut the deficit to two.

The crowd went ballistic as the home team looked like it might snatch victory from the jaws of defeat. The tying runners were on base and the winning run was coming to the plate with a definite home run threat in Jim Arnold. The fans and the Cub bench had a feeling it was going to be all or nothing with Arnie. He always swung hard just in case he hit it, but he struck out more than anyone on the team.

"Arnie! Arnie!" The crowd chanted as the right-handed slugger came to the plate.

There was no secret to this match-up. It would be velocity against power. Arnold swung mightily and missed on the first pitch, as he couldn't catch up to Thurston's high heat. He dug right back in and looked to connect this time with the upper 90s heater that the Dodgers closer was firing up to the plate. The result was the same on the second pitch and it looked like poor Arnie was over-matched in this situation.

The crowd was still hoping for the best as big Jim fouled the next pitch off straight back, a sure sign that Arnold was beginning to time the fastball.

Thurston took a deep breath on the mound and wiped the brow with his road gray Dodger jersey sleeve as if to gather just a bit more power to muscle one by Arnold. Thurston then began to think just a bit too much as he stared in for the catcher's sign. Figuring that Arnold would have to continue to cheat a bit on his swing to catch up to the high heat, Thurston convinced himself that a slider was in order. He shook off the catcher's sign for a fastball and let go with a 90-mile-per-hour slider that hung just a bit over the plate.

Arnold was indeed fooled by the pitch but there was just enough weight back in his hands that he got the ball airborne to straightaway left field. On a day like today, that was all he needed as the ball carried in the gale winds and into the bleachers for a walk-off three run homer and a dramatic comeback Cubs win.

Blake and the rest of the team sprang up from the dugout and sprinted to home plate in the jubilation of a come-from-behind victory. They mobbed big

Arnie as he touched home plate and continued to jump alongside him as he slowly made his way toward the dugout.

Blake was screaming at the top of his lungs even though it was debatable if his teammates could hear him.

"That's what I'm talking about! Never say die in this park fellas. We can't quit, We WON'T QUIT! You gotta believe. You gotta believe."

It was the perfect ending to the home stand and the crowd loved it. Nobody wanted to leave Wrigley. This moment was too special. The fans continued to chant for the Cubs to make a curtain call. The team was more than happy to oblige as they all came out to a rousing standing ovation that lasted over five minutes before the crowd slowly began to file out of the ballpark.

The clubhouse was hopping with music and beer for the victorious team as the players answered the media questions with a bit more emphasis on this jubilant occasion.

Blake finished his post-game press conference still on a high from the comeback win when rather suddenly his demeanor went from pure satisfaction to angst. The big rally reminded him that on past occasions like this he would get totally drunk in celebration.

He saw the players enjoying their beer and Blake just wanted that feeling of jubilation to continue as it had done in the past with a night of all-out drinking. It was the best way possible to start out a road trip in the past. A night of partying on the plane trip that would immediately follow, plus a few hours out on whatever town they were flying to, would be an uplifting morale booster until the stark reality of a hangover would set in like an unwanted visitor that wouldn't leave.

Blake fondly reminisced on past adventures until he realized that he had to block this out of his mind. This path was extremely dangerous. It was more than dangerous. It was lethal, as Blake's history could attest.

While his teammates partied all night long on the thrills of victory, Blake shut himself off from the rest of the squad. It was not an easy night for Blake as he put his headphones on and listened to soothing music for the duration of the flight to New York, where the Cubs would begin a three-game series with the Mets.

He scurried off to the team hotel as quickly as he could upon arrival and asked his coaches to organize everything on this night. They could sense something was bothering Blake, but didn't feel comfortable asking him what was wrong. They just agreed in unison to take over for Blake.

The demons had waited their turn and were primed to pounce on their weakened prey.

Major league players are accustomed to their accommodations on the road and rarely need any guidance. It didn't seem like any big deal to the rest of the team as the coaches led their way to the team hotel. They still were too busy enjoying their night with the help of alcohol to be bothered with any managerial mini-crisis.

Blake immediately settled in his room and called Kim to help him refocus on what was really important and to take his mind off the impulse to drink. The struggle was beginning to rear its ugly head already on the road.

24 — Looking Inward

The night from hell finally ended for Blake. Kim's voice had settled him down some, but the itch to drink was with him throughout the night as he tossed and turned in his hotel room bed.

Blake was puzzled by his reaction to the game as he tried to make sense of the past 24 hours. He wondered if the upcoming road trip had made him so unsettled, or perhaps it was the game. Maybe it was the separation from Kim?

He had always possessed a curiosity about the human mind. Blake knew that baseball was such a mental game. As typical with any competitive athlete, he was always looking for an edge on the competition. This would be different though, as he looked at himself critically. It was one thing to delve into the abstract and something entirely different to peel away the layers of denial that distract from honesty.

He had a few hours in the morning to refocus his mental state before the rest of the team would be checking him out as well. A long, warm shower seemed to refresh his head as well as his body. Blake decided he would spend some time each morning analyzing his feelings and thought process from the day before. He knew he had to get a handle on himself if he ever was going to stay sober for any length of time.

He walked over to the window and stared out over the New York City landscape. The picturesque view quieted his mind. The restlessness, the anxiety, and the confusion slowly slipped away from his busy brain as he began the process of self-examination.

The dramatic victory had given Blake a sense of self-satisfaction. His baseball instincts were indeed spot on. He had always felt strongly that he understood the game as well as anybody, if not better. Was he really that self-confident deep down? Why did he feel such euphoria at the result?

Maybe it was the daring, unconventional approach to the situation that gave him such a sense of satisfaction? Did he have to stick out his neck like that just to prove a point to himself and to others?

Did that sense of justification make him so ecstatic that he wanted to drink to enhance that feeling or was it his innermost demons questioning his abilities? Blake had heard the term self-sabotage before. Perhaps this was his psyche tempting him to prove that he was no good and undeserving of any accomplishment?

Blake had always felt there was some cycle to his behaviors. This pattern of predictability must show something. For now it was just important to accept this responsibility of self-awareness. It felt good to bare his soul. This will become a daily ritual. It feels cleansing, he thought.

Just then his cell phone alerted him of a call. It was pitching coach Mark Douglas checking on Blake. He hesitated to answer at first, but he knew no response would set off some red flags.

"Hey Mark, what's up?"

"Blake, I was just checking to see if you saw the Chicago papers today? You're a hero this morning. You might as well enjoy it while you can. I thought we could meet over breakfast to talk about our pitching staff. That daring move you pulled off yesterday has us scrambling a bit to piece together our bullpen."

"What the hell was I thinking, Dougie? It must have been the heat. Please remind me to keep my ass planted on the bench next time it gets so damn hot! Sorry to put you in a bind with your guys. Heard any guys bitching about it? You pitchers are always so gosh darn self-centered," Blake spoke with a laugh.

"Guys are just worried about their livelihood. They don't want to jeopardize their arms with two months of chaos. You know how it is Blake. Pitchers always think managers know nothing about what they're going through."

"Well that's why I've got you, Mark. You have to convince them that there's a method to my madness."

"Pray tell Blake, just what might that be?"

"Give me 30 minutes Dougie, and I'll come up with something," Blake said again with a bellowed laugh. "I'll meet you down at the motel restaurant in half an hour and we'll figure out something."

Blake often flew by the seat of his pants before thinking it through, but this was different and he knew it. Every decision he made from here on out affected the whole organization. The higher ups would surely let him know if he was screwing up, but Blake could be a stubborn cuss too. He was well aware that power struggles would come into play at some point and he would have to deal with it. For now, he had enough on his plate as he dressed and entered the elevator to take him to breakfast.

Blake shot Mark a text from his cell and waited for him just outside the entrance to the restaurant. Blake always tried to look busy in public as he fumbled with his phone. He learned a long time ago not to make eye contact with other guests. It was a sure way of inviting fans to approach him. He felt that these moments were his down time and that there was plenty of time at the ballpark for him to please the public.

Mark smiled as he approached Blake. The pitching coach was the one doing the evaluation this morning as Mark sized up Blake's demeanor to see how he was carrying himself. From outward appearances it all looked normal as they waited to be seated.

"It's just a bit different from Des Moines, huh Mark? The Big Apple still blows me away. The prices in this city are sinful."

"You must have forgotten that I used to play in this hellhole of a city, Blake. I was with the Yankees in 1980, all of 25 days in this not-so-friendly city."

"Sorry, how could I forget your cup of coffee in the Bigs?" Blake responded with a wry smile.

"Well the way I look at it, there are thousands of guys who would die for 25 days in the majors, Blake."

"Well-played my friend. There was a time when all I could do was dream about stepping onto a major league field. How soon we forget how fortunate we are."

The two requested an out-of-the-way table and their wish was granted. The perks of status as a major leaguer never ceased to amaze Blake. He could count on the fingers of one hand the number of times his wishes were not accommodated when he was out in the public arena.

As Blake perused the menu he deemed it necessary to explain himself right away to Mark for his behavior last night.

"Thanks for covering for me last night. I have to thank the rest of the coaches this morning too. Something just hit me after the thrill of victory wore off. Alcohol related as you might guess."

"Blake, you didn't give in to the temptation did you?"

"No Mark, I didn't, but it sure was tough not to. It just hit me like it never has before. All three weeks of sobriety," Blake said with a self-depreciating smirk. "Let's talk baseball Mark. That always gets my mind off the inner struggles."

"Whatever you say Blake, it's cool by me. Don't ever hesitate to call me or knock on my door if you want to talk. I had an uncle who passed away from the poison so I know a little bit of the continuous struggle."

"Thanks Mark. I may take you up on that sometime. Now let's deal with our staff and the screwball who messed up your bullpen a bit yesterday."

"Bowman is out for at least three days I suppose. Do you have any ideas on a replacement?"

"Well just shoot me if I make no sense at all from here on out. You can put me out of my misery," Blake shot back as he smiled to make sure Mark knew he was joking.

"Guillen could close in a pinch I suppose, but I wouldn't want to rely on him every night. Do you think he could handle it here in the big lights of New York City as a temporary fix, Blake?"

"He's no spring chicken so he better be able to handle it for one or two nights, but yeah I wouldn't want to rely on him too often in that role. The Mets always have a ton of lefty sticks in their lineup."

"So Skip, we go with him until T.J. rests up?

"I suppose," Blake replied tentatively. There was an awkward pause in the conversation before Blake threw out a barnstorming idea.

"I like this kid Bowman. People I respect said he could do the job even though many so-called experts didn't think so. How about moving him into the rotation?"

"You mean starting rotation Blake? I'm not sure he's ever assumed that role before. I suppose he does have enough pitches to make it through the lineup several times. Yes, I think he could give us six good innings every time out based on what I've seen so far."

"Who would he replace if you had your way Mark?"

"Hart, I guess. He just doesn't seem to get the art of pitching despite his power arm."

"Does Hart think too much in your opinion? I have my own thoughts based on catching him and thinking about his mound presence."

"Yes, I think he loses focus and his thoughts wander. That seems to mess up his mechanics. He can't repeat his delivery with all of his pitches."

"Then let's try and make him a closer. No thinking. Just have him throw power fastballs for one inning. Can you get him to repeat his delivery if he stays with the same pitch 95 percent of the time?"

"There's only one way to find out. I'll give it my best shot. Do we have the option of experimentation with the Cards breathing down our necks and getting closer by the day?"

"Probably not, but I'm going to take a ton of chances down the stretch. I don't care if Marty gets pissed or if the media hangs me out to dry. This is a one-shot deal here Mark. I ain't gonna manage after this year."

"Let's set it up then Blake. Pressure isn't really on us. Who could expect us to win with the talent we have here anyway? Even with our 10-game head start, we're still huge underdogs."

"Yeah what the hell does anybody else know? I'm going to talk to the rest of the coaches this morning and set the tone. We're throwing away the staid and overused baseball book and going all out with every crazy option we can think of. Screw the book!"

"Just remember these players have longer term interests, Blake. We owe it to them to keep them healthy and in charge of their careers."

"That's a point well taken. Let me know if I take this gambling approach too far. I've been known to lose focus myself on the overall picture. I guess we all are self-centered at times, not just pitchers."

"It's the nature of the beast Blake. This business is survival of the fittest."

"Well then, let's enjoy our overpriced breakfast and take on a new approach at the park today. We're going all in my friend. We are going all in!"

25 — You Gotta Believe!

Blake was set to unveil his new and unconventional approach to his teammates in the clubhouse after batting practice. He knew there would be skeptics, but deep down, Blake was beginning to see and believe in divine providence for all of the unbelievable events that led up to this moment.

The manager was a long-time baseball fan who appreciated the history of the game. He could think of no better place to unveil his innovative game plan than the home of the New York Mets.

It was in 1969 that the "Miracle Mets" accomplished what was believed to be impossible. That franchise suffered miserably throughout the '60s, mired in last place and engulfed in futility. In their first seven seasons as a franchise, the Mets finished no higher than ninth place in a 10-team league.

The 1969 Mets somehow managed to win the World Series, ironically overcoming a nine-and-a-half-game deficit in mid-August against the Cubbies in what has been declared the biggest choke job in Chicago sports history.

The Mets began to use the slogan "You Gotta Believe" in 1973 as that team rallied from seven games behind in September to reach the World Series before eventually losing to the Oakland Athletics four games to three in the best-of-seven format.

While this Chicago Cubs team was six games up in first place with August half over, it was a foregone conclusion that this makeshift squad with leftover talent would wilt in September and succumb to the vastly superior Cardinals team.

Blake was intent on installing a similar mentality to his team. He wanted to get his players to believe as well. The smaller the sample size, the more likely very unpredictable events could happen in baseball. Only the best prevail individually and as a team in a 162-game schedule, but 35 or 40 games could produce just about any result.

The mood was upbeat in the visitors' clubhouse as the team now looked forward to games rather than dreading them. Batting practice was full of laughter and taunts as the players flexed their muscles with prodigious blasts into the bleachers. The sweltering heat that plagued Chicago had drifted on to the East Coast just in time to follow the Cubs around on their road trip.

Blake was running around on the outfield grass talking to various cliques that tended to form as batting practice progressed.

Pitchers shagged fly balls as a group, outfielders gravitated to their own and infielders just stayed out of harm's way as they kept one eye on missiles launched from the batting cage.

Blake approached each grouping the same way. With a smile on his face and a confident but not cocky stroll, the manager wanted to intrigue his players as he declared to each huddled group that he wanted to explain a new approach in the clubhouse after BP.

With everyone accounted for and off the playing field, Blake stood high atop a wooden bench and removed his baseball cap. The sweat was still dripping down his face from batting practice. As he wiped his face with a towel, he began with a familiar phrase.

"Guys, we've all heard more than we'll ever want to about the baseball book. You know the one that says we can't steal if we're up by six late in the game, that piece of crap paper that says we have to play for a tie at home, but a win on the road. Or the unwritten rule to never intentionally put the winning run on base late in the game. I could go on and on. You've heard 'em all I bet. Well, beginning tonight we're going to start writing our own book of baseball for the Chicago Cubs and rule number one is that there are no rules. So therefore, any rule after that just doesn't exist. If there are any other questions, just revert back to rule number one."

Blake got down from his perch above the huddled mass of players. He moved around the room in an attempt to connect with them all.

"We're going to have some fun with it fellas. This isn't a joke however. Winning is still our ultimate objective, even more so with this new style. We could follow the baseball book and still die a slow death or maybe, just maybe, throw out that damn book and hang on to our lead. Counting tonight we have 36 games left. You veteran players know anything can happen over such a short period. I want us to make a statement to anyone watching that nothing is out of bounds for this team and all our opponents can kiss our ass if they don't like it. Let's face facts here. The position baseball put us in sucks. I can't sugarcoat it anymore. We're renegades from here on out and we're going to give 'em hell. I'm not talking dirty here, just an approach that frees us from the usual time-worn boundaries. It's my hope that we can come together as a team in a short period of time and accomplish something that no other group has ever done in the history of baseball. Get out your erasers guys, a new book is coming. Better yet, just throw that damn book in the garbage and pretend it never existed."

Third base coach Lenny Paxton interrupted at this point, asking Blake if he could address the group. Blake acquiesced gracefully, but perplexed a bit at his coach's intent.

"Now I know what you guys are thinking," blurted out Paxton. He stood up high for everyone to see as he set them all straight on the new approach.

"This doesn't mean you guys can steal when you want, or swing away when you feel like it. Everything still will go through the coaches first. It just means that we, as a team, will look at all of the unwritten rules that we've suffered through as players over all the years and see if they really make sense. We welcome any and all suggestions or thoughts."

Lenny stepped down and motioned to Blake to continue on with his speech to the group.

"We can have some fun with it guys," Blake smiled as he kept the players interest. "Now look at the old rat bastard Bartlett over there. You think he might have some opinions about this? He's forgotten more about baseball than most of you'll ever know."

"Thanks coach, I think," replied Bartlett wryly. "Yes, come to think of it, I've got a shitload of grievances against that fucking book. Where do I begin? It never seems better than a 50-50 proposition anyway. The damn weathermen can do that and they're horseshit at their job."

Blake approached Bartlett and gingerly put his right hand on his catcher's still injured shoulder and stopped him before he got going in a diatribe.

"Well, for today we'll just table the thoughts. This'll be great fodder for trips. We can all question the so-called great baseball minds over the years and their apparent reluctance to go against the norm. But if something comes to your mind during the next couple of days, just bring it on!"

Blake pulled his lineup card out of his back pocket and held it up for all to see.

"This is my first move. I'm going to go with an unconventional batting order. Starting tonight, I'm putting my three hottest hitters at the top of the order without any concern for speed or bat control or any other factor that usually comes into play when making out an order. And my pitcher will hit eighth at times. That should put at least four good threats in a row up to the plate after the first go-through of the lineup. How many times have you seen where a club was just dying to get their number three or four hitters up to the plate just one more time late in the game, only to just come up short by a batter or two? I'm hoping that at least once or maybe twice down the stretch this will pay off by getting our best sticks up to the plate one more time in a crucial situation."

"I love it," screamed Bartlett as he stood up for emphasis. The old and bruised catcher turned to Blake and walked right up to him and playfully punched him in the stomach. Blake flinched when the old vet Bartlett cocked his arm, perhaps out of habit dealing with the Rat in the past, or just never sure what the crazy catcher would do next.

"I now renounce every bad thing I said about you before we became teammates Skipper. Believe me there was a whole chapter devoted to you in my own book."

"We'll have to compare notes then, Bartlett. I had a contract written up in my locker that offered a reward to anybody that took you out of the game when we were enemies. I'll have to show it to you sometime. My price tag will show you how badly I wanted you busted up."

The laughter was bouncing off the walls of the room as the rest of the team clearly enjoyed the back and forth banter.

"Ok, let's settle down here," Blake struggled to regain control of the room. "There'll be more to come. Let's go out tonight and keep the fire burning."

The evening game moved along briskly in the New York heat. Neither team was able to generate much of an offense as the pitchers stayed in control. There seemed to be little sense of urgency to compete as the game rolled along tied at zero. Games often had a flow like this until someone broke loose out in front.

Blake was dragging as he caught his third game in a row. This would be his last start as a player for a while since Bartlett's suspension would end tonight. He had a pretty good feel for this game behind the plate. That was the advantage of being a player-coach. He could physically see the stuff that his starting pitcher possessed tonight. The futility of himself and his teammates against the New York pitcher gave him the sense that this would be a low-run, tightly played game.

The Mets took a 1-0 lead in the sixth inning with back-to-back two-out doubles, but Blake wasn't too disappointed. The New Yorkers had an awful bullpen, which would now be exposed as the Mets pinch-hit for their pitcher in their half of the sixth.

The Cubbies had the top of the order coming up in the top of the seventh and they immediately rallied with consecutive singles to lead off the inning.

The Mets were expecting a bunt as normally light-hitting second-sacker Petey Arroyo came up batting third in Blake's unconventional order. Petey had been swinging a hot bat for the last week, but was an unlikely three-hole hitter nonetheless.

The gambling manager knew Arroyo would hit the ball on the ground somewhere even though the pitcher was likely to throw a high fastball making it difficult to bunt. Petey had a slashing swing that kept his hands above the ball and Blake liked his chances with New York fielders running all over the infield expecting a bunt.

Blake flashed the hit-and-run sign to third-base coach Paxton who relayed the sign to Petey. The runners on first and second stared at Paxton to also pick up the sign. Blake knew it had to work on this play, as the Cubs would only enjoy the element of surprise on the first pitch.

The runners broke with the pitch and the high fastball was slashed past the startled first baseman who was charging on the play expecting a bunt. The right-handed Arroyo did just what Blake expected, as his inside-out swing favored a ball hit to the vacant right side of the infield. One run scored and the Cubs had runners on first and third after the play.

The successful execution of the daring hit-and-run play energized the Cubs as they tacked on two more runs to take a 3-1 lead into the bottom half of the seventh.

As the Mets fans sang "Take me out to the ballgame," Blake warmed up a new pitcher for his team. Woody Williams had cruised through most of his six innings, but the Cubs manager proactively replaced Woody with Miguel Guillen. Blake knew the bottom half of an inning, after the visiting team scored several runs to take the lead, often inspired the home team to immediately rally. It was a good time to shut the door with a different style of pitcher.

The big lefty Guillen promptly shut down the Mets, as his command was impeccable tonight. The fastball had life and the curveball was biting as he set them down in order.

Blake felt good as his proactive move panned out perfectly. He thought of leaving Guillen in for the eighth, but he had been hoping for this type of performance out of him for some time and wanted Guillen to gain confidence from this outing. Blake didn't trust Guillen to repeat this half-inning performance. It was a mistake he would soon regret.

After the Cubbies stranded a couple of runners in a scoreless eighth, the Mets came to bat looking to overtake a team they felt they would handle easily. If they didn't know it at first, the New Yorkers definitely knew now that this Cubs team had some fight to it.

Ryan Washington took over for Guillen and promptly walked the first batter. The bullpen was in a state of flux because Bowman was switching to a starting pitcher, while the new closer Hart would not be ready to assume his role for a couple of days after throwing four innings yesterday in a starting spot.

Blake knew he was in a bit of a bind and was already second-guessing his decision to take out Guillen as he walked to the mound to calm down Washington. The talk did little to remedy the situation as he walked the bases loaded.

The next visit was far from encouraging. Blake was pissed at the young reliever's unwillingness to challenge hitters with his stuff. He huffed his way to the mound, angrily pulled off his mask and chewed the timid pitcher out right in front of all to see. Blake wanted the youngster to get pissed off and showing him up publicly was usually a managerial no-no, but Blake didn't care.

Washington steamed up in a hurry. Whatever venom Blake spit out, it sure lit a fire under the normally somewhat timid reliever. His demeanor changed drastically as the reliever threw nothing but straight smoke past the next two batters, striking each of them out swinging on four pitches.

Two-time batting champ David Russell came to the plate for New York chomping at the bit. This was the type of situation he thrived in and he calmly delivered a bases-clearing double down the left-field line. The go-ahead run just slid in before Blake applied the tag as the runners got a good two-out jump right off the bat.

Washington steamed his way through the following batter with another punch-out. He angrily walked toward the dugout and threw his glove against the back of the dugout wall before exiting up the runway to the clubhouse.

Blake was still steaming as well and he didn't care for his pitcher appearing to show him up by storming his way up to the clubhouse.

Bartlett was taking this all in stride as he appreciated outbursts of anger. He walked up to Blake and asked him what he had said to Washington.

"Jesus Blake, you really set him off. What did you say?"

"I called him a goddamned pussy that didn't belong in the big leagues."

"Well, I guess he pitches better pissed off. He threw much better after you chewed him a new one."

"I'm ticked that we're behind, but at least he seemed to get the fucking message. Russell is just a beast in those situations. I can't fault him for that at-bat. Just the others."

"I'll go talk to him, Blake, and set him straight on the bush league antics, but make sure he knows that you were just trying to get the best out of him. Guess what? It worked."

"Thanks, I screwed up too, taking out Guillen. I've got more important things to worry about now. We've got to come back."

Blake took a look at his lineup card to see who was available to pinch hit, as the pitcher was due up this inning. He sheepishly noticed that the top of the order might be coming up again. His vision for the new formula was about to get tested.

Blake led off the inning. He was running on fumes by now, but he was very motivated and still full of piss and vinegar from his meeting with Washington.

The Mets closer, Hamilton, came in to try and shut the door. He was a typical hard throwing closer with a split-finger fastball as his out pitch. It came in knee high looking like the heat, but the bottom would fall out of it. With his 93-mile-an-hour heater, the batter had to trigger his swing a bit early and the splitter induced quite a few embarrassing swings as it tumbled into the dirt, nowhere near the strike zone.

His problem this season was that he could not get ahead of batters with his fastball. The command just wasn't there so hitters were not as susceptible to the splitter if they were ahead in the count. His ERA stood above four runs a game, so there was hope for a much-needed comeback.

Blake knew his job was to just get on base and he was hoping Hamilton would have control issues this night as well. It was time to take a few pitches to see what Hamilton had.

His approach worked like a charm as Hamilton walked him on five pitches. Blake knew a pinch runner was in order for him, but once again the team was short-handed, this time because Bartlett was still suspended.

The boo-birds were out in full force in New York as Hamilton had blown a number of saves already this season. The fans here could be especially brutal and Blake could feel the tension all over Hamilton's face as he cautiously moved off first with his one-way lead.

The shortstop Rivera stepped up and took the opposite hitting approach. He sensed Hamilton would groove a fastball to get ahead after struggling with the first batter. He guessed correctly and lined a single up the middle to put runners on first and second with no outs.

Unfortunately, the pitcher was due up and Washington was still in the clubhouse. He never figured he would be back in the game. Blake was handcuffed by the lack of available pitchers in the bullpen and although he needed runs here, the pitcher could also be called on to bunt.

Blake asked for time from the second base umpire and slowly walked toward the first base coach to stall for a minute or two while the club scrambled to get Washington back onto the field.

Washington hurriedly grabbed his helmet after receiving notice that he better get down to the dugout this instant if he wanted to remain in the big leagues.

Fortunately, Washington was an ex-shortstop who could handle the bat some. He laid down a perfect sacrifice bunt to put the tying and go-ahead runs in scoring position.

The number nine batter was intentionally walked to load the bases and set up the double play as unlikely lead-off hitter Jim Arnold came to bat. The hefty first baseman was in a hitting groove, but he looked out of place at the top of the batting order. Baseball tradition made it difficult envisioning a power hitter as a lead-off man.

This would be Blake's first and biggest test of his new strategy. His hottest hitter was at the plate in a crucial, late-inning situation. If Blake went by the baseball book, the power-hitting, slow-footed Arnold would have been batting in the middle of the lineup.

Blake stood on third base shouting encouragement to the big but strikeout-prone slugger. Arnold had come through in a similar situation just a few days ago. Hopefully, he would have that confident short stroke needed against Hamilton.

Hamilton threw pretty hard, but it was his splitter that made him a solid major league closer. That pitch is difficult to block for the catcher with the tying run on third base and the bases loaded, Arnold felt Hamilton would come in with a fastball on the first pitch to get ahead in the count.

Jim had set in his mind that if a first pitch fastball came in anywhere near the upper half of the strike zone, he would attack.

The pitch sailed out of Hamilton's hand with what looked like a fastball spin on the sphere as it approached home plate. The thigh-high pitch centered the plate and Arnold drilled a two-base gapper into left center field that cleared the bases and unleashed a chorus of boos from the disgruntled Mets fans. New Yorkers were never shy about shouting obscenities in a public setting, as they chased Hamilton from the mound spewing venom.

Henry Rodriguez greeted the new thrower with a single that plated Arnold and gave the Cubs a 7-4 lead as Blake's way continued to shine. Rodriguez certainly wasn't your typical number two hitter either.

The mood in the stands was surly as the Mets tried to rally in the ninth, but Washington kept his foul demeanor and attacked the strike zone. Just for good measure, Blake walked out to the mound and cussed out his pitcher again.

Blake turned away from Washington and walked back to the batter's box with a smile on his face, but he was determined to keep his delight away from his pitcher's view as he squatted down awaiting the first pitch of the inning.

The fans and the Mets felt like a beaten team as they went down meekly. Blake always felt that it was difficult for a team to win the same game twice. The Mets thought they had the game in hand, but the blown save dealt a severe mental blow, as always.

Customized handshakes and head slaps were in abundance as the Cubs celebrated their hard-earned victory over the Mets.

More importantly, a new tone was set and for at least one night, Blake had believers as the players began to think that they had not such an ordinary man for a manager. Maybe this man had stumbled across a new way of thinking that could shake up the baseball world.

You gotta believe.

26 — Rewriting the Book of Baseball

Blake arrived at the Mets' ballpark early and in a carefree mood for the evening game. The anxiety that had overcome him yesterday was long since an afterthought. The focus was on keeping the momentum going and keeping the team loose.

The urge to drink could come over him at any moment, but fortunately his cravings didn't persist for too long, maybe an hour or two, before distractions seemed to get his mind off of temptation. All appeared fine, especially when he was back in the saddle at a ballpark.

The Cardinals were six games behind in the standings after they also took two of three games in their latest series against the Milwaukee Brewers at Busch stadium in St. Louis. There would be the curiosity to scoreboard watch to see how other teams are doing from here on out, but Blake worried that could be detrimental. He knew it was always best to stay concerned about your own efforts until at least mid-September when hardly anybody could resist checking out the competition.

If the Cardinals were winning that particular day, the Cub players could feel extra pressure to keep pace, and if the Cards were losing, Blake's team could let up. He was determined to not let either scenario play out. Baseball was extremely mentally challenging by itself without the added influence of worrying about other teams. The time for scoreboard watching comes in middle-to-late September, not in August; though it's almost universally discouraged, but seldom practiced.

The visiting manager's office door was closed and occupied by Blake's full coaching staff. The coaches stared at each other as they waited for Blake to speak. It seemed odd to have a meeting after the team appeared to be turning the corner. These types of strategy sessions seemed to arise during losing streaks.

Blake broke the ice as he reclined in his office chair.

"Gentlemen, I want your honest opinion here. I want each of you to write down a realistic percentage chance we have of winning this division. No bullshit here. I want pure honesty. Each of you'll get a separate piece of paper and there's no need to write your name on it. Won't matter one iota what percentage you give as long as you're honest."

Blake handed out separate sheets to all seven coaches and waited for them to write and drop in his baseball cap. One by one the coaches folded up their sheets and dropped them in.

"I know you guys are wondering what the hell I'm doing here. You'll understand in a few minutes."

Blake had a playful smirk on his face as he studied the responses in his chair and held his thoughts to himself as he looked over them briefly.

"Well the consensus here seems to be about a 25 percent chance. I suppose that's about right from my perspective. The high was 50 and the low was 10 so we have a real optimist in the bunch. Nobody said zero so I guess nobody's too pessimistic. I probably should let the 50 percent coach take over my job," Blake said with a wry smile.

The manager stood up and circled the room before explaining his rationale for the survey.

"We have to take some pretty big gambles over the next six weeks. I suppose we could do everything by the book as we've all probably done 95 percent of the time in our baseball lives, but that would just be a slow death in my opinion. The Cardinals' talent and our lack of it would probably overtake us by mid-September. We've got to surprise the hell out of some advance scouts and keep opposing coaches guessing. Hell, we even have to keep all of us coaches guessing. Nothing is out the window here. There'll be no such thing as a stupid play and no mistakes by the book. We're throwing that sonofabitch out."

Blake got overly excited and yelled out in emphasis.

"We're going to Vegas baby and we're coming back broke or on top of the baseball world. We've all seen some crazy things in baseball. What have we got to lose? This franchise is due for some good fortune. C'mon, over a hundred years of baseball futility and now a freaking plane goes down and wipes out the whole team except for a stumblebum drunk who didn't deserve to live. Maybe there's a message in all this craziness somewhere?"

His coaches initially seemed a bit taken aback by his out of character, bubbly enthusiasm. The normal laid-back Blake Benson was off in the distance somewhere, momentarily displaced by a ranting and raving idealist.

Third base coach Lenny Paxton interrupted the monologue and wholeheartedly agreed with his Skipper.

"I've been so sick of that baseball book for half of my professional life. It always seemed just like a cover your ass playbook and I don't like it. Take a stand with your own conviction and instinct and live with the result. I'm totally with you, Blake. This could be the only advantage we have over anybody. Let's free ourselves from this bondage and keep everybody guessing. It's better to be lucky than good, right?"

"Glad you feel that way Lenny. Any other opinions from you guys besides it's time to get the straitjacket out for your manager?"

"You know I'm on board Blake," replied pitching coach Mark Douglas, hinting at their previous meeting.

All seven coaches nodded their heads in approval without saying anything.

It was clear that there still was some convincing to do with the remaining skeptics, but they knew who was boss.

Blake reassured them that they could throw out anything they wanted. It would all be up for consideration, but the manager emphasized that it would all go through him first.

Blake was on a roll and he kept on going.

"We're not stopping here either. We're going to get the players involved in this too. Everybody will have a say-so. Good ideas can come from anywhere. Shit, I'll even listen to the broadcast booth and the know-it-all sportswriters. The more the merrier."

Blake stopped at this point as he could see his enthusiasm was wearing a bit thin on his coaches. The proof would be in the pudding as they say. Putting your professional life in the hands of the baseball gods required a great leap of faith. Blake was now a believer in some spiritual force. The huge task ahead was convincing the others. Belief could be a powerful force, but it required some tangible proof first. The non-believers would have to see results.

Tonight's game would be the beginning.

27 — The Media Catches On

It was pure coincidence that Blake unveiled his new strategy in New York. Yet another seemingly benign event like a regular season baseball game suddenly took on mythical proportions as the media began to sense the team was riding a wave of destiny.

New York City is the media capital of the world. The city is like none other in terms of attention and scrutiny. Legends have been made in New York and heroes have become villains.

There seemingly was no in-between in New York. Opinions were expressed openly and decisively. One was a hero or a bum. The media fueled this dichotomy. It was a timeworn method of gaining public attention. Of course negativity sells too, but feel-good stories seem to reach a wider audience.

Blake's Chicago Cubs had more than their share of human interest on their side with the plane crash and improvisational reformation of the team in mid-season. Now it became apparent to the media powers that something different was developing here.

Of course winning three in a row helped, especially with two drama-filled comebacks in the last inning. Now there were signs that this renegade manager was going to try and shake up the baseball world with instinctual decisions rather than following the norm.

Blake tried to keep his change of strategy out of public view, but the New York media would have none of it. The strangeness of the batting order raised more than a few eyebrows. There were no amateurs here in the Big Apple as the best of the best reside in New York and could instinctively smell a big story.

Blake kept his thoughts to himself, but a few of his players let it be known that this was just the beginning of some unconventional moves devised by their leader. He knew that this would all come out eventually, but he mistakenly forgot to tell his players to keep the news in-house.

Every managerial decision was now under intense scrutiny. Blake had the New York media questioning his every move after the second game of the series produced more unconventional maneuvers.

The Cubs were desperately hanging on to a 4-3 lead in the bottom of the ninth as the second game of the series neared its end. Blake's team had played small ball to perfection as they jumped out to a 4-0 lead after four innings.

The power hitters Arnold and Rodriguez stunned the Mets on successful bunts and came around to score on a pair of groundouts after a successful sacrifice bunt had moved them up. The speedy Wilson stole second and third after a leadoff walk in the third and came home on a sac fly to make it 3-0. Luis Rivera delivered a run-scoring single on a rare two-out hit-and-run with Petey

Arroyo scampering all the way from first on a ball that flared down the left field line.

Blake laughed all the way up the runway after Rivera's hit. He felt like a hot blackjack player in Vegas going against the odds, still coming through with winning plays.

"Might as well run with it while we're hot," Blake shouted for all to hear after the hit-and-run play. Teams almost always attempt this play with one or no outs in an inning to get a potential run to third base. Blake looked at it as an opportunity to get a run home on a single with two outs and the speedy Arroyo on first.

The Chicago starting pitcher Terry Riley had begun to wilt in the still oppressive heat wave that enveloped the East Coast. Their lead had dwindled to a scant one run. After six innings the manager brought in Guillen again, confident in his ability to shut down the Mets' abundant left-handed swingers.

Blake instructed Bartlett, who was back from suspension, to demand from his pitcher that he throw strikes and to live with the consequences, good or bad.

Guillen looked sharp in his first two innings of relief. The left-hander eyed Blake as he walked to the dugout after the bottom of the eighth, sidestepping the chalk line as many superstitious players do. Guillen rarely pitched more than one inning in this specialized era of baseball. Two was stretching it, especially after his one-inning stint last night.

"Gimme one more inning big guy and I'll give you the next two nights off," Blake pleaded with his hefty lefty. "I'll even buy you a couple a beers tonight if you hold 'em for one more. You're sharper than nails right now and I want to run with ya for one more."

Blake remembered last night and his hesitation to take Guillen out after he dominated in his one inning. Blake had seen too many managers push their luck by continually bringing in fresh arms every inning regardless of how the previous pitcher threw. If one of his pitchers looked to be in a groove, he wanted to run with it.

Still holding a precarious one run lead in the bottom of the ninth, Guillen took the mound to hold off a Mets rally.

The first two batters flied out harmlessly, but Blake knew that the last out was always the hardest to get. Rather than relax it was imperative to bear down even more intensely as one base runner could totally flip the mood on the bench.

Sure enough, as if on cue, the next batter split the outfielders and pulled into second base with a double. Trouble strolled up to the plate in the presence of David Russell, who hurt the Cubbies the night before in a late game situation.

Blake asked for time from the home plate umpire and slowly walked to the mound to talk to Guillen and Bartlett.

"We're gonna put the winning run on base here guys. It's just another example of the bullshit book. They've got nobody left on the bench to hit for the next guy, and you own lefties Guillen. Trembley couldn't hit your curve if his life depended on it. Don't be afraid to throw it again and again to him. You've got to get Trembley though. After him it's a different story. Throw the breaking ball for strikes and let's go buy your beer, big boy!"

Bartlett stuck out his right arm to signal the intentional pass and repeated the effort four times as the lefty threw batting practice tosses to the catcher safely outside of the left handed batter's box. The partisan crowd booed, the sportswriters questioned, and the radio and television announcers all commented on the "forbidden" strategy of putting the winning run on base in the bottom of the ninth.

Guillen walked behind the pitcher's mound to regain focus. He took a deep breath and then stood on the rubber, glancing in for the sign he already knew was coming.

Bartlett flashed a number of signs decoying the tying runner that was on second base for fear that the runner could tip off the batter to the next pitch coming.

The big lefty snapped off a curve as the manager demanded, and Mets lefty swinger Paul Trembley took for a called first strike. It was not a surprise that Guillen started him off with a breaking ball and the lanky pull-hitter knew that wasn't his pitch to hit.

The scenario repeated itself to perfection as the hefty lefty clipped the low and outside corner with a perfect bender that Bartlett framed nicely for the home plate umpire.

Ahead in the count, it was not unusual for a pitcher to show the hitter a fastball that was well out of the strike zone to set him up for the next pitch. It was all part of the cat and mouse game that detailed virtually every at bat. The tension of the moment heightened the game within the game as Bartlett surprisingly asked for time from the home plate umpire and walked out to his pitcher very slowly, as if to give Trembley more time to think about it. Bartlett knew all about this guy and his tendency to outthink himself.

Bartlett simply wanted to tell his pitcher that no matter what the signs were, he should throw a curve. The wily veteran catcher was determined not to flash the same set of signs for three pitches in a row, as a preventive measure against sign stealing.

Bartlett shifted inside to suggest a high and tight fastball that Trembley figured would set him up for a breaking ball outside on the next pitch.

Guillen's pitch came in high and tight to the inside like a fastball would suggest. As the batter was beginning his stride into the pitch, the ball broke sharply down and across, freezing the batter. The natural tendency was to flinch for just a millisecond as the fear of the baseball takes over the electrical circuits in the brain, preventing any reactive measures.

The umpire bellowed out a called strike three as Trembley dropped his bat in frustration at taking three strikes without even attempting a swing. The victorious Cubs emptied their dugout in jubilation and began the winner's procession of high-fives and unique handshakes while the New York crowd belted out a thunderous collective boo toward their floundering losing home team.

Blake had defied the odds one more time, increasing his managerial credibility almost daily now.

The postgame press conference was now almost entirely focused on Blake's brazen decision-making. He was becoming the story within the story and he didn't mind one bit. Blake was quick to laud his players first, but he knew that one of the manager's most important roles entailed taking the pressure off his players. The scrutiny on him left ballplayers to do what they do best, just play ball.

Blake's cell phone rang and he immediately recognized the ring tone of his wife Kim. His conference was over and he was in his office basking in the delight of a victory as he answered.

"Hey, honey. Did you see the game? It sure was a nail-biter."

"Of course I did Blake. Why do you have to put yourself on the line like that all the time? The announcers were questioning your sanity all the way through that last at-bat."

"Just as long as they don't give an answer," Blake laughed as he delivered the punch line.

"Kim, I just call 'em as I see 'em and so far, so good. I know it won't work all the time, but for now it sure feels great to make the right move."

"Don't get too caught up in yourself Blake. I'm just following your baseball advice to not take the wins too highly and the losses too low. Those mood swings have always been a thorn in your side."

"Thanks Kim, I can always count on you to bring a man down to size right quick," Blake answered with sarcastic praise. "I know you're right, though. I'll call you when we get back to the hotel. I have to follow through on a promise to Guillen."

"Ok Blake, just don't forget that promise you made to yourself." She reminded Blake of his sobriety pledge.

"You got it honey. You keep me focused please. I have a feeling this media thing is about to get out of hand a bit. Feeling this good has led to trouble before. I've got to stay down to earth and humble. Call ya in a bit."

Blake got ready to head back to the hotel when Bartlett sent him a text message to meet him and his newfound Mexican hero Guillen at a club to satisfy the young man's desire to let loose tonight.

Blake shot back a text requesting the hotel bar instead. Being seen at a club in New York would entirely change the focus of his team. He knew he could have none of that.

What he didn't know was that the hotel bar would bring other distractions as well for the man of the hour in New York City.

28 — The Spotlight of the Big Apple Works Both Ways

Blake arrived at the hotel bar in an excitable celebratory mood. Guillen and a few other pitchers had already started their post-game drinking, but were reminded quite quickly by pitching Coach Mark Douglas that an afternoon game awaited them in just over 14 hours.

"Not for me coach. Skip gave me the next few days off. Plus, he's going to buy the beer. It doesn't get any better than that."

"You still got curfew young man and some running to do tomorrow. I don't want to be running by your side with a bucket, catching your puke."

"Relax Coach Dougie. I'll be professional. I'll throw up in the clubhouse," Guillen joked.

Blake arrived at their table with spring in his step and a big smile on his face. He circled the table and slapped hands with his teammates.

"What a night fellas. That kind of game toughens us all up. I know we have to forget about it in a few hours, but for now it sure feels good. Just one game though. Shoot, let's just enjoy the moment."

"Blake, Fat Man over there has been salivating at the mouth waiting for you to buy him his reward booty. Look what you started, Blake, everybody is going to want free booze as a prize. Pretty soon we'll have a bunch of alcoholics on our team," Bartlett once again spoke without thinking about Blake's condition.

Blake beat Bartlett to the punch as he recognized the Rat's rarely embarrassed face.

"Relax Bartlett, I know firsthand it takes years and years of winning and losing to become a drunk. We only have less than two months left," retorted Blake.

"Not if we keep winning all the way to the Series," Guillen jumped in with his giddy and far-fetched reply.

"How many of those have you had already, big boy? We're getting a little ahead of ourselves now. I'm not saying we can't do it, but I wouldn't want to bet my mortgage on that. Back to Earth guys, who wants a drink? I'm buying and I suppose I'll have to get an extra one or two for tonight's hero," Blake reached in his back left pocket to grab some cash.

"It'll be an early night for me again, boys. I'll hang with you for a bit, but I gotta get out of here. I feel real good and I got that feeling that I want to feel even better, if you know what I mean. Man, this atmosphere gets me jacked up. Look at the women in here tonight. You guys better be careful. That goes for you too Guillen. If you miss curfew those beers I'm buying will be coming right back my way plus five bills."

Blake was walking that fine line again between manager and teammate. He knew the boys liked to have fun and blow off some steam, but he had to distance himself from the guys too. There would be many important decisions to make in the next month and he had to stay somewhat detached and capable of denting some egos if he had to.

The waitress came and took their order. Blake recognized her from previous trips. The tall blonde looked even finer this time. His senses were all in high gear tonight as he dropped two crisp hundred dollar bills on her tray, gave her a smile and a wink, motioning to her to keep the change, eyeballing her throughout her enticing stroll back to the bar.

The players all took note of Blake's flirtatious demeanor. It wasn't difficult to digest that the manager was testing all temptations tonight, albeit holding them at a safe distance for the time being.

Mark Douglas reminded Blake of his scheduled appearance on NBC's Today Show early tomorrow morning. The pitching coach felt the tempting vibes emanating from Blake's eyes and was becoming concerned.

"Skipper it's time for you and I to head up to our rooms and let these young studs loose. The night belongs to them. Tomorrow belongs to us."

"I suppose you're right Dougie boy. I'm batting a thousand today. No sense ruining my perfect night. We'll see you guys bright and early at the ballpark."

Before the manager could get too far away, Guillen stood up and offered a toast to Blake.

"To the best manager in baseball," shouted the exuberant lefty.

The group gladly chimed in and clanked their glasses in approval before swallowing long and hard.

Feeling high from the beer and his performance, Guillen begged Blake for one more beer.

"Now I get you big lug. The bullshit toast was a ploy for one more freebie. Sure I'll get you another one just so I can add to your misery tomorrow."

Blake looked around for his eye candy. The waitress was nowhere to be found so Blake walked up to the bar and ordered Guillen his favorite brew.

Nothing appeared unusual as he picked up the bottle of beer. Blake was accustomed to the bright staring of adoring fans. It was second nature to him by now. He knew eyes were always upon him. Tonight was no different.

He squeezed his way back to the table and handed over the beer to his new pitching hero.

"Pitch like that all the time and I'll supply you with beer until you lose that great physique of yours, young man," Blake said, sarcastically referring to the lefty's recurring weight issue.

Blake and his pitching coach stepped out together and hopped in an elevator to their rooms. It was fairly late, but Blake knew he should call and say good-night to Kim. Her voice had a way of easing him into sleep.

The adrenaline of the evening was beginning to settle down. Blake suddenly realized how exhausted he really was. He clumsily fiddled for his room key amongst a wad of cash in his pocket. As he finally entered the room, Blake immediately plopped on his bed as he called Kim to wish her a goodnight.

"Hello Mrs. Benson. I just got back to the room. Do I ever feel tired now. How are you? I hope I didn't wake you."

"Blake, I was just laying here in bed waiting for your call. I've been watching ESPN and seeing all the publicity you and your team are getting now. I love it, but it makes me kind of nervous too. Are you okay with it?"

"Well it's great for the guys. It's a big self-confidence booster as long as it doesn't go to their heads. For me it's old hat in a lot of ways, but new in responsibility with the whole team and all."

"I just worry about all the extra pressure Blake. You sure you're ok with it?"

"Well so far, so good my dear. Did I tell you I'm going on the Today Show in the morning?"

Blake was always proficient at changing the subject on a dime. Truth be told, he wasn't sure he could hold up, but he couldn't let on to his wife. It mattered not, as Kim recognized his old diversionary tactic.

"No you didn't Blake. That shows that you guys are becoming more of a human-interest story and not just a sports headline. Jesus, I hope you brought some decent clothes, Blake. It's national TV and all."

Blake laughed at the sudden concern.

"I guess it's okay to you if I look like shit on ESPN, but not the Today Show!"

"Well, yes honey, there's a different standard there. Is it taken care of?"

"I got the concierge at the hotel to set me up earlier today. It's all good. The NBC limo will pick me up early tomorrow morning and drive me to Rockefeller Center. I'm trying to just enjoy the attention and to realize it's good for the boys. I guess the organization must like the positive attention as well. I hope we can keep it up."

"I know you have been on some Chicago media outlets outside of a baseball perspective, but this must be a first. At least as far as I can remember, it is. Do you know the approach NBC is taking with the questions?"

Kim was once again showing her unyielding concern for Blake. Despite his oft-described grizzled veteran status, Blake could be woefully naïve at times outside of his baseball perspective.

"What could they possibly ask besides baseball stuff and maybe my drinking? It's all old news now. I can handle it. The tough part is over. Everybody knows my condition by now."

"Okay Blake, but just don't be surprised by any new angle the questions might take you. Those national media types have an agenda or they wouldn't have asked you on their show. Be ready to open a vein or two. That's all I am saying."

"It's a piece of cake, my dear. Now it's time to go to bed. Love you and look for me in the morning on the show."

"Goodnight Blake. I love you too. We'll see you on the show in the morning."

Blake settled in bed and took a minute to reflect on the wild events of the day. It really couldn't have gone any better, but he knew that tougher times were ahead. They happened to be on the right end of baseball good fortune that he had seen hundreds, if not thousands of times before. It just felt different because he was the man in charge this time. Be prepared for the worst and hope for the best. It's always been the best slogan for an athlete. It was nothing different than he had experienced so often.

He continued his nightly ritual of stacking all the available pillows on the left side of his body and leaning emphatically in that direction to keep pressure off his throwing arm. A catcher could never be too careful with his throwing arm, even an old beat up part-time player-manager.

Blake started to doze off knowing that his experience was comforting him as he turned over on his non-throwing side, as usual, to fall asleep. It would be just another day in the life of a professional baseball player tomorrow. Just one more day, it was nothing to worry about.

Blake nestled in his bed and wondered where this journey would take him next. He didn't have to wait long before he would abruptly find out.

29 — The Media Strikes Back

Blake stirred to the repeated beeping sound of his hotel room radio alarm clock. Four hours sleep was just barely enough as he rolled out of bed.

Baseball was all he could think about this morning. Going for the sweep of the Mets this afternoon before heading on to Pittsburgh to take on the Pirates in a three-game series was next up on the baseball agenda. Coming back to play the following day's game so soon after their dramatic win could go both ways. Blake was confident that the momentum would carry over and propel the team, but he worried about the focus of his players after a celebratory victory. Letting go of games was always one of the toughest aspects of professional baseball, whether good memories or bad.

At this early moment of a new morning, Blake wished he had declined the interview at NBC's Rockefeller Plaza. His ego liked the national attention, but all he wanted to think about right now was baseball and the pennant race. The recent play of his team inspired Blake to no end to think of ways to continue their recent swing toward success.

After showering and dressing quickly, Blake was ready to be picked up by his limo. He called down to the front desk to alert the hotel staff. The concerned voice on the other end of his line quickly interrupted.

"I hate to be the one to bring this to your attention, Mr. Benson. Have you seen the morning edition of the Post?"

"No, I haven't," replied Blake quizzically. "Why would you ask that?"

"There's a picture of you holding a bottle of beer on the front page."

"What the hell? Why would that be on the front page? I don't get it."

The now increasingly nervous voice at the other end tried to explain to Blake.

"The title says, is this man a fraud? It refers to something about your drinking alcohol after pledging not to."

"Jesus Christ, this makes no sense whatsoever. I'll be right down to take a look at it."

Blake rushed to the elevator and anxiously awaited its arrival. He was in a state of disbelief as the elevator finally reached his floor. None of this made any sense as his elevator descended rapidly.

'Let me take a look at that please," Blake tried to be polite as he struggled to make sense of it all.

The newspaper implied Blake was back to drinking and had the picture to prove it. Blake immediately recognized the beer as the brand that Guillen drank.

"I was just buying my winning pitcher from last night's game a beer. They can't be serious with this? Those fucking camera phones are ridiculous. I bet this came from somebody's smart phone. I never saw anybody from the press around."

"Mr. Benson, your limo is here," the concierge said.

"Okay, tell them I'll be out in a minute. I've got to do some serious quick thinking here."

Blake knew the picture was legit. He couldn't claim that he was a victim of a false photo. To top it off he had to go on national television shortly. He sat down in the lobby and tried to remain calm. He realized he needed to call the general manager right away and explain the situation. Then he would call his agent to see how he should play this. It would certainly come up in the interview. No laws were broken so he didn't see a need for a lawyer. He suddenly knew that he would have to call Kim right away too, but first he had to defend himself to the Cubs general manager. He was flustered, but his thinking remained sound as he stood and walked out of the hotel.

Blake immediately asked the driver to close the soundproof glass door. He had Marty's number on speed dial and quickly placed his call. It was very early back in Chicago, but this was an emergency.

"Hello, is that you Blake? Why in God's name are you calling at this hour? Please don't let me down here. You're not in trouble are you?

"Sir, I didn't let you down, but we've got a situation here. I'm not drinking again Marty. I promise you, I'm not drinking again."

"Okay, I believe you. Now tell me what it's all about," replied the still groggy voice of the general manager.

"There's a picture of me with a bottle of beer in my hand on the front page of the New York Post. I was just buying one for Guillen. I promise. They're making it look like I'm lying about my sobriety. And I've got to go on the Today Show in less than an hour. Jesus, Marty, what do I do?"

"First of all you have to remain calm and poised. Get a grip on it Blake. If you're innocent, you've got nothing to be worried about from the organization. We'll stand behind you as long as you tell the truth."

"Okay. You're right. I've done nothing wrong and I have to show everybody that I'm not a liar. I'm not playing games here. I'll just look confident knowing that I've nothing to hide. Thanks Sandy. I'm sorry to cut you off here, but I've got to make two more quick calls. You were the first."

"Okay Blake, stay calm. You're doing a great job and I'm proud of you."

Blake said goodbye and called Kim. She was very upset, but she believed Blake this time. She knew he was going out for a bit with his team. Kim was the media savvy person in the family. She told Blake to call his agent, Charley Feldman. He would know better than anybody else how to handle it. In today's media age, most top pro athletes had a public relations entity to handle such situations. Blake called Charley's cell phone. Even at this odd hour, within seconds his agent had returned Blake's troubled call and laid out a plan.

As Blake neared the TV studio, he gathered himself together mentally. He had responded quickly and efficiently and alerted all the right people. His confidence was restored and he felt reassured that he could answer all upcoming questions in a professional and convincing manner.

He had been awake for less than two hours and he felt as if he'd gone through a whole day already. Blake did some primping on his appearance as he waited for the limo to arrive at his destination.

It didn't take long for Blake to notice the media gathered outside of Rockefeller Plaza. He knew he was on the hot seat here, but while he was frayed on the edges 45 minutes earlier, he now was sure he could handle the heat.

He was peppered with questions immediately upon arrival as cameras invaded his personal space. He stood proud and calmly declared his innocence. He instructed them to be patient and watch the show. His explanatory answer would stop all of this silly speculation.

Blake's groove was back on as the makeup crew worked on his appearance while he waited for his interview to begin. Sure, there would be some who wouldn't believe him, but the people that mattered were in his corner. It's no different than being a visiting player at the home team's ballpark. They hate you for being the opposition. It's not personal and those that won't believe him were saying more about themselves than him.

Blake looked confident and dapper as he was called to the studio. The concierge had set him up well. There was no better place for buying new clothes than New York. It was go-time and Blake was well prepared.

The stunningly beautiful Today host, Kathy Cronin, welcomed Blake to the show and prepared him for the upcoming segment. They would get the photo out of the way first and then move on to the resurgence of the team following the horrific plane crash.

Blake smiled and nodded in agreement. There was a tinge of nervousness in his demeanor as he was a bit out of his element, but he tried to reassure himself that it was the same as Sports Center, only a different focus.

"Welcome back to the Today Show. Our next guest is Blake Benson. You may know him as the only surviving member of baseball's Chicago Cubs. The rest of his teammates were tragically killed in a plane crash that Blake narrowly avoided. Blake is currently the player-manager of the newly revamped team that is hoping to hold off their rivals in the National League Central Division to advance into the playoffs. Blake is here to discuss his team and the remarkable personal adventure that this accident has forced him to deal with."

"Good Morning Kathy," Blake politely interjected to greet his host.

"Good Morning Blake. It's nice of to join us on your busy road trip to New York."

"My pleasure," he smoothly responded.

"Now Blake, you've dealt with some personal demons in the aftermath of the accident that killed all of your teammates and coaches, along with members of the traveling media, I might add. Why don't you explain to our audience?"

"Well Kathy, I missed the fatal plane flight to St. Louis from Atlanta because I'd finally hit bottom in my excessive drinking. The team had basically suspended me and sent me home on a different flight to deal with my problem or I was done with the organization. I'd screwed up big-time and I was in a bad place."

"It was a terrible ordeal for you Blake, and the whole city of Chicago, all of major league baseball in fact. However, something good has come out of it, right? Why don't you explain to our audience?"

"Kathy, I was forced to deal with my drinking problem. I'm not entirely convinced I would've gone sober without the life-changing realization that losing all of my teammates brought. I'm not a terribly spiritual person, but I had to believe that I survived for a reason. I believe that reason was for me to right some very serious wrongs that I'd committed over my drinking years. Thanks to the Chicago Cubs organization, they allowed me to rejoin the team as a player-manager as long as I stay sober."

"I'm glad you mentioned that Blake, because today's edition of the New York Post has a photo with you holding a bottle of beer last night. They've implied that you're a fraud. Have you started drinking again?"

"No. No. No," Blake replied emphatically. "I understand newspapers are in the business of making money. A photo on the front page like that would sell some papers. Let me explain."

"Please do," Kathy interjected.

"Some of you out there may not follow baseball too closely, but we had a very exciting win against the Mets last night. Our winning pitcher deserved a lot of credit for an outstanding performance. I offered to buy him some beer as a token of my appreciation for his superb effort. I'm sure the media will be checking out my story, so I know the audience will hear the truth. I was just buying a beer for last night's hero, Miguel Guillen, and apparently somebody with a smart phone caught it as I was carrying it back to our table. I was actually just leaving since my pitching coach reminded me I had to get up so early for this appearance. How do you guys do it Kathy? It's unnatural to get up this early," Blake responded with a charming smile. He was in control.

"So you vehemently deny that you were drinking last night?'

"Kathy, that's right. I can't say I haven't been tempted to drink again, but so far so good. I'm going to stay sober and I'm going to do my very best to uphold the tradition and the dignity of the Cubs and Major League Baseball to finish out this troubling season. Who knows, we may surprise a few people."

"Yes, let's transition to your team's surprising and daring play of late."

"Gladly," replied Blake.

The two of them laid out the framework for the team's inspired play of late and they continued to talk baseball for the remainder of the segment. Blake was clearly proud of his boys. Talking baseball was enjoyable again after the troublesome personal matter was brushed aside with Blake's professional response.

Kathy thanked Blake again for the appearance and the red light of the cameras dropped off indicating that they were off the air. The two of them exchanged small talk with Blake fondly recalling Kathy's days as a sports reporter years ago in Cincinnati. The conversation continued for a moment as the host had to be back on air in a matter of minutes, but she wanted to tell Blake something.

"Blake, I just wanted to applaud your efforts here. I've dealt with my own substance abuse problems and I know what you're going through. I just have a word of advice, though. You probably need to stay out of places that can get you in trouble, even if they are entirely innocent. You know what it's like being a public figure. I've heard the media has been following you around since you arrived in town looking for some dirt. Be careful."

"Thanks Kathy," Blake replied with a stunned look.

He naively assumed that nobody would want to give him trouble as he dealt with his personal issues. After all these years in the limelight Blake still didn't get it. Some people just want to tear you down, to belittle your efforts in order to feel better about themselves. He was beginning to understand that he needed to re-examine many of his habits to see how they might reflect poorly on his new role as manager of the Chicago Cubs and as a person in recovery.

Blake left in his limo feeling like a huge load had been lifted off his shoulders. He relaxed for a few moments, stared out the window and admired the hectic pace of a bustling New York City. It reminded him that there were so many people that busted their butt everyday to better themselves and their families. He reflected in amazement at how professional athletes like him get so caught up in their own world without appreciation for the hundreds of thousands of people that deal with real-life issues daily. His career was fantasy-like. Sure there were pressures, but he was truly living the dream as a major league baseball player.

Blake's focus turned to the upcoming game this afternoon as the limo driver fought the traffic on the return to the team hotel. He needed to get back to his element and daily routine. This extra crap was not for him. It was time to think baseball and nothing else.

30 — The Worm Turns Quickly

Blake arrived at the ballpark later than usual as a result of the media appearance. He immediately didn't like what he saw from his players. It wasn't unusual to sense a lack of enthusiasm for an afternoon game following a night game, but the mood was incredibly subdued.

Blake gathered his coaches together to let them know he wasn't happy about the apparent lack of leadership shown by Blake's staff in his absence. The coaches defended themselves by claiming a valid lack of hierarchy established by the manager.

Blake could see their point, but he wanted someone, anyone, to take the initiative and let the chips fall where they may. It simply was an area that hadn't been thought through so Blake addressed the situation by naming third base coach Lenny Paxton as next in line in his stead.

The players were certainly aware of Blake's problems this morning, but didn't seem very concerned. They knew the true circumstances behind the photo and understood well the sometime unscrupulous methods of the media. His team spewed most of their venom at the vultures of the press.

Many of his players had simply partied too much the night before. Establishing camaraderie was one thing, but excessiveness was entirely something else. Blake understood their exuberance. He felt it too last night, but how could he put a limit on this in the future?

The game was a complete downer as the team fell flat on its face in a 5-0 defeat. The Cubs could only garner four measly singles. The lack of runners made it virtually impossible for Blake to jump-start his team with aggressive tactics. There was little enthusiasm, no mental toughness and very little positive in the loss. Blake had seen this before on road trips so he decided to downplay the obvious lack of spirit in the effort. The ups and downs of baseball demanded a level head.

"Two out of three on the road isn't bad, guys. Winning the series is our number one immediate objective on each trip so we can't dwell on today's game. I just want to say one thing so we can improve ourselves in the future. We have to maintain our focus each and every day from here on out. I let this team get a little out of hand last night. It's my fault and it won't happen again. Let's get on that plane to Pittsburgh and start another winning streak."

Blake's address to the team following the disappointing outcome seemed to go over well. The players generally didn't care for that rah-rah stuff and appreciated that Blake didn't overreact in a fit of anger. The team was well aware they had let themselves down. Lesson learned and stored in its collective memory bank.

The mood picked up as the team boarded the plane. The lingering effects from too much partying the night before dwindled to next to nothing as the Cubs looked ahead to the next series.

The Pirates were very middling as usual this year. It seemed like they were always reshuffling in a youth movement and pointing toward the future. They were always tough at home, at least against Chicago. This Cubs team certainly couldn't be looked at as a favorite against any foe, something Blake was always quick to point out lest his team get complacent.

As Blake looked at the standings after today's game, he could still see his squad on top of the Cardinals by five and a half games, depending on the Cards game tonight. More importantly, on a personal level, the media frenzy of New York was in the rearview mirror. His photo was apparently a one-day 24-hour news cycle event, a very troubling one indeed for Blake, but soon to be yesterday's news.

Summer was indeed beginning to wind down. You could feel it in the air as the team took the field the following night in Pittsburgh. The stifling heat had vanished and the nights were becoming visibly longer as August moved on.

It was Blake's first inkling of summer's impending departure. The good news was that he was in a pennant race. He had too often been on teams that were just going through the motions by the time September rolled around.

The troubling news was that despite this team being less than three weeks old, these players had been playing this season for six months now and were starting to show some wear and tear. The dog days of August lingered on in summer's last gasp, before the change of seasons.

Blake was up for this game tonight. He didn't want to start going in the opposite direction again. He could feel his team was geared as well. Plus, he was turning over the starting rotation again. His number one starter Jacobson would be toeing the rubber in the Steel City.

Blake was sitting this one out, but he was in the game mentally from the get-go, looking for a spark to set the trend for the series. Perhaps he was over-anxious or the baseball gods were turning against him, but his managerial decisions were all wrong this night.

He tried to get things going with a hit-and-run play with one out and a runner on first. However, Rodriguez' one-hop smash headed up the normally vacant middle of the infield, suddenly becoming an easy double play for the Pirates second baseman. The fielder was already moving toward second to cover the bag when the Cubs runner left first base early. A sure base-hit up the middle, unluckily for the Cubbies, suddenly became a rally killing double play. All the Pittsburgh middle infielder had to do was field the smash, step on nearby second, and fling the ball to the first baseman to retire Rodriguez and end the inning.

A surprise bunt attempt by the power hitter Arnold with a runner on first turned into a double play as well, as his drag bunt was popped up and turned into an easy twin killing, ending a possible fourth inning threat.

Jacobson pitched well and was holding his own, down 2-1 in the seventh inning, when he ran into a spate of trouble. Two singles and a walk loaded the bases. As the bullpen warmed up, Blake decided to stay with Jacobson after a trip to the mound. If Guillen was available he might have gone to him in this situation, but he stuck with Jacobson one batter too long.

Pittsburgh's power hitting left fielder Rudy Torres deposited a hanging slider into the bleachers at PNC Park, thrilling the small crowd in attendance. The grand slam sealed the victory for the Pirates and sent the Cubs into a two-game losing streak.

The offense was stagnant again as the club was suddenly devoid of any power, mustering up seven singles in this 6-2 loss. Blake tried to remain calm, but his worry was starting to show. The Cardinals had won two in a row, trimming the Cubs' lead to four games. With the Redbirds breathing down their necks, the team could tighten up again or just plain accept their obviously overwhelming talent disadvantage.

Back at the team hotel after the game, Blake lay in bed trying to think of something that might turn the tide again in his favor. He tossed and turned without any remedies coming to mind. Even his nightly hotel ritual with the strategic placing of the pillows took on a separate life of their own in scattered disarray.

Professional baseball is all about routine. That sometimes leads to complacency, as an athlete can begin to accept poor results if they are repeated enough. The trick, according to an experienced veteran like Blake, was to keep the mind fresh and the body would follow in a positive direction.

After Blake had realized his alcohol problem, he began to read profusely on bad habits and how they form. It took a mere three weeks to develop a habit and possibly settle into a routine, good or bad.

Blake always respected the traditions of the game to a point, but as a catcher, he was determined to look for the little things that can make a difference in output. He thought that some players got into a rut this way and needed a change to refocus their mental state.

He certainly didn't like the way the team was swinging the bats right now. Too many guys seemed to go up to the plate hacking away without some kind of game plan. It was like batting practice with every guy up there swinging away mindlessly at the pitches thrown to them.

Blake knew pitchers and catchers tended to recognize patterns quicker than others. He sensed that pitchers were purposely throwing first pitch breaking balls and other pitches just outside the strike zone. The Cubs were swinging undisciplined at first pitches way too often.

Blake made his decision shortly thereafter. There would be no batting practice the rest of the series. It was mostly symbolic, but he wanted to get them out of their bad habit of swinging at every pitch without any purpose. Players could do whatever they felt like doing before the game, but they had to do it together. It wasn't rocket science, but it was different. He didn't care if some would belittle the effort as pure superstition; he wasn't going to repeat the same crap over and over again and expect different results.

After his customary goodnight call to Kim, he shut out the lights and hoped that his players could start hitting the ball again. The pitchers had held up their end of the bargain this trip. It was time to shake things up a bit.

31 — The Best Laid Plans
Somehow Go Wrong

Baseball streaks have a mind of their own. Logic, strategy, and calculations simply are a waste of time. Blake Benson knew this to be true as a player, but he was now learning it as a manager as well. That lesson would come shortly, but for now the newest quick fix was about to be implemented.

Blake was going to give the guys a history lesson on one Dick Allen. He was quite the loose cannon to be sure, but he had the guts to question one of major league baseball's timeworn traditions of batting practice.

Allen played in the 1960s and '70s at a time when society in general and players in particular began questioning authority on a regular basis. His views were tolerated mostly because of his enormous talent, but he met resistance as well. One of his quirks was the avoidance of batting practice. He thought it was a waste of time and surely ineffective in preparation for games because of the huge difference in pitching speed in batting practice compared to live action. Allen was known to show up on the field less than half an hour before the game would start, declaring he was ready to go at that late moment.

The man was a complete stud as a baseball player, even if a troublemaker in the eyes of some. He got away with it because he could. Perhaps the man was ahead of his time.

For the most part, the cancellation of batting practice for the next two games was viewed as a welcome change. There would always be some that felt that they needed these swings to stay sharp, but this certainly wasn't unheard of. Rain and travel delays had cancelled batting practice before, but that was out of necessity, not design.

A few of the players had heard of Allen's enormous talent and more had heard of his troublemaker image. Some were even sympathetic to his cause. In late August, on a long road trip plagued with fatigue partially as a result of steamy weather, the idea carried even more weight. The only question was how to fill up the time.

Blake stood before them and asked for ideas. "Well, now that we've got that out of the way, we need to find something we can do together for an hour or two. Do any of you geniuses have suggestions?"

Big Jim Arnold stiffly lifted out of his chair in the visitor's clubhouse room in the Steel City of Pittsburgh and clumsily spit out a unique possibility. The 6-foot 5-inch, 250-pound Arnold, with a full red beard, stood out like baseball's version of Paul Bunyan. The Wisconsin native liked to spend time on the road in various bowling alleys across the country.

"How 'bout we all go bowling? I know the owner of that bowling alley just up the freeway from here. A quick call and I'm sure he can set us up. We could be there in 30 minutes and still be back in plenty of time for the game. It sure takes my mind off of baseball for awhile."

Blake couldn't stop laughing at the suggestion.

"Arnie, are you kidding me? We've got guys in here who have no idea what you're talking about. Just because you were raised in Wisconsin where bowling alleys outnumber churches doesn't cut it in this clubhouse. They ain't from Wisconsin, big boy. Inner-city folk and Hispanics don't bowl much, in case you haven't noticed."

Miguel Guillen shouted out at the top of his beefy lungs at Blake's stereotypical response.

"Coach, I like to bowl. I might be the only Mexican that does, but I know I can bowl good enough to whup your behind coach!"

Laughter erupted with that retort and continued on for nearly a half a minute as the cackles ebbed and flowed until Blake interrupted.

"Okay Senor Guillen. You've got your wish and judging by the hoots and hollers going on around here, the rest of you like the idea too. What the hell, let's go bowling!"

Arnold made the call to his bowling buddy and the team headed off to the local Pittsburgh lanes. Cabs were plentiful at the ballpark. It sure must have been a strange sight to see 25 ballplayers hop into several cabs just hours before the opening pitch was to be thrown.

The spur-of-the-moment decision brightened the mood of the team beyond Blake's wildest dream. The team was like a bunch of high-school students skipping school as they stumbled their way around the unfamiliar alleys of a bowling hall.

The team was back in plenty of time for the game. The short trip had a lasting impact. Further bonding was formed by their collective misdeed and, if nothing else, broke up the monotonous routine.

The clubhouse was locked to create an illusion of privacy. Blake had instructed security to keep the doors shut. For all any outsider knew the team could have been enduring one of those old-fashioned team meetings that the media liked to report. Fans just ate up that team-meeting angle. Whenever the players wanted to distract the reporters from what was really going on, they would just secretly let out that a team meeting was in order. The press would run around trying to decipher the subject of the meeting like Kremlin spies. It was a great distracting tactic.

As the players were finally getting ready to take the field, Blake held them up for one last word of advice.

"Guys, I'm not sure if you figured out what my real purpose was in breaking our routine. Besides giving you a little mental and physical break, I wanted to get rid of that swing at every pitch mentality we get in batting practice. We've got to be more patient at the plate, work the count in our favor, and get a pitch that we like instead of swinging at the pitcher's pitch. If we do that, we should hit with some more power and knock in some runs for a change."

"You're a sneaky sonofabitch Skipper," replied Bartlett. "I wish I would've thought of that. It makes sense to me." Bartlett nodded as he spoke.

"Shit, you're not the kind of endorsement that carries a lot of weight, but I guess I'll take it Bartlett," said Blake. "Let's have a game plan at the plate tonight. You've all seen this starting pitcher before and we've got scouting reports up the wazoo on him, so it shouldn't be a puzzle to anybody. Don't fish at his borderline pitches unless you have to."

The unusual pregame routine worked to perfection as the Cubs plated five runs in the first inning, highlighted by a bases-clearing double by Bartlett.

However, a streak has a mind of its own and the Pirates kept clawing away at the deficit until they took the lead 8-7 in the bottom of the sixth. The home team had the baseball gods on their side. Softly struck, but well-placed hits, always just out of reach of Chicago fielders, piled up in succession. There was nothing Blake could do about the loss but shake his head as the Pittsburgh bullpen closed out the win.

It stood to figure in baseball streakology that one area would be fixed only to see another problem pop up that wasn't expected. The Cubs pitching didn't hold up, bad luck and all.

Fortunately, the Cardinals also lost. The lead was still at four, but it was precarious. At least it felt that way to Blake as he swiveled around in the visitor's manager chair, contemplating the third and final game of the series tomorrow night. He turned his focus to Mark Douglas, his pitching coach, and spoke.

"I've got my boy Bowman going tomorrow. It should be good if we swing the bats like we did tonight. I feel good about this one. We certainly need it before our squad heads to Milwaukee. Then it almost will feel like home since we get a ton of fans at Miller Park."

The night passed uneventfully for a welcome change. The team had gone through worse on that first home stand and responded quite well before hitting this little slide. There was no panic and little anxiety as the team seemed to enjoy the respite from New York and all of its distractions.

Blake kept his word about skipping batting practice again the following day, but he kept the squad at their place of work this time. He was beginning to regret their little venture to the bowling alley. Every quirk is fine and dandy when you are winning. Losing always puts a different spin on departure from the norm.

A confident Cubs team took the field the following night only to see their swagger wane as they played their worst game of the season in a 7-3 loss. Bowman pitched well as a starter, but the defense was atrocious. The tone was set in the first inning as two errors by the shortstop Rivera led to three unearned runs. The club fell apart defensively with five errors and several fundamentally incorrect plays.

Blake was livid after the game. The team had never seen him this upset, but the manager knew this type of performance was unacceptable and had to be addressed immediately. He gathered the team together in the visitor's clubhouse and let his team have it. His face reddened with each passing profanity. "God damn it guys, we simply cannot have any more days like this one. We don't have enough talent to overcome these mistakes. Fuck, nobody does, not even the fucking New York Yankees." He reached for his baseball cap and flung it against the wall. Then he took the gum out of his mouth and threw the wad as far as he could in emphasis.

"This shitty play is just a lack of concentration. It has nothing to do with your abilities and everything to do with thinking about anything but the game. Shit, we only have to concentrate three hours a fucking day. It's just three fucking hours. We're not brain surgeons here. We can't have this anymore. We won't or changes will have to be made."

Blake stormed to his office and slammed the door in disgust. This time it was no act; he was generally pissed off at the whole team today.

After a 15-minute cool-down period, third base coach Paxson knocked on Blake's door. He entered the room even though there was no reply. He could still see the disgust on Blake's face as he sat down.

"Tough one today, huh Skipper?" Paxson said.

"Yep, even though we've struggled before, I never saw this carelessness until today. I was just thinking we're starting to turn the corner here and then this happens. It makes me sick. Are we just kidding ourselves here? These guys aren't professional enough or talented enough to win. Shit, that's why we got 'em in the first place. Nobody else wanted 'em."

"I suppose you're right, Blake," replied Paxson.

After a momentary pause the third base coach spoke up again, this time with more emphasis.

"But you saw something in them that made you think they could be better than they've been. Your years of experience and shrewd eye for talent saw something that hadn't been developed yet, for whatever reason. I think you can get it out of them. Won't be easy and might take some patience, but you can get it out of them if you coach them right. You have that ability Blake."

"Thanks Lenny. You're right and I needed that wake-up call. It's my responsibility to bring out their talents and professionalism. I asked for this chance knowing full well the challenges it presented."

Blake stood up and glanced out at the team as they were preparing for their flight to Milwaukee.

"I suppose I better get ready myself. We've got a plane to catch. Oh that's right, they wait for us in the big leagues 'cause we're so fucking special," Blake blurted out sarcastically.

At least now the manager was smiling.

"Lenny, I really thought we were gonna win today. I guess that's why it hurts so much. Goddamn baseball. You think you've got one thing figured out and another thing pops up to bite you in the ass. These streaks kill me. Fifteen years in baseball and they still make no fucking sense to me. I never saw this defensive lapse coming. It wasn't even on my radar. Guess I better look out for whatever shortcoming might pop up tomorrow. Did you see any signs of this play coming Lenny?"

"No Blake, I never sniffed a scent of it. Just one game my friend. Remember it's just one."

Blake picked up a piece of paper and rolled it into a ball. He tossed it into the garbage can beside his desk and spoke with conviction. "I just threw it away. That game is gone. Maybe I should've flushed it down the shitter? Might be more appropriate," Blake broke out in laughter this time.

"Okay Lenny, speaking of the shitter, let's move on to Milwaukee. Just kidding, I love the place."

Blake knew his third base coach was from Milwaukee. The good-hearted kidding was a welcome sign to Paxson. Blake was back from the dark side and more like his old self.

"Na coach, you got it right the first time, but this trip it's going to be special. We're gonna turn it around once again. I can feel it. Let's get outta here. Pittsburgh blows, at least this stop anyways."

32 — Sleepless in Suds City

Road trips have a tendency to slide into despair as the wear and tear of travel takes its toll on players and coaches alike. Tempers get short, fatigue builds as routines get altered and performance often suffers. This trip was no different.

Blake was hopeful that the proximity of Milwaukee to Chicago would ease the burden of travel as they touched down at Mitchell Airport. The team appeared, on the surface anyway, to be in fairly good spirits as they bused to the hotel.

The lead over the Cardinals was dwindling with each Chicago loss, daily it seemed, but the Cubs were still in first as August wound down. The calendar would soon switch over to the last full month of the season. September signaled the stretch run and the cementing of rosters for the postseason. Any player acquired after the last day of August would not be eligible come playoffs.

The proximity to the deadline made communications between Blake and Marty Anderson almost a daily occurrence. The minute the plane touched down, Blake's cell phone alerted him to a new voice message from the general manager. It certainly didn't feel out of the ordinary to hear from Marty. Blake held off calling back as was his custom. Talking personnel was awkward at best, particularly if the team was in his presence. Blake preferred the solitude of his hotel room for these types of calls.

Blake was surprised to hear some anger in Marty's voice as he finally returned the call from the comfort and privacy of his room.

"Blake, it's about time you got back to me. This time of year it's crucial to be in touch constantly. Do you understand that?"

"Sure Marty, I just thought I could be more open if I waited until I got to my room," Blake couldn't even finish before Marty interjected again.

"You let me handle that Blake. I can speak in code as well as the rest of 'em. I'm sure you can too, if needed."

"Jesus Marty and I thought I was having a bad day. It's kind of late. Maybe we should talk in the morning when we both are refreshed. This ain't starting off too well."

"I wish we had that luxury, but the clock is already ticking on my end. I put Rivera on waivers to see who might be interested in him and the Yankees claimed him. Now, you know I can pull him back, but our scouts have been following their organization for some time and they like a few prospects in their system that might be available and can help us in the future. You know everyone's been pushed ahead quicker than expected, or warranted too, for that matter."

"Shit Marty, are you asking my permission to trade him or just giving me a heads-up?"

"Well Blake, it might appear as if we're giving up. Do you think we'd be signaling that or will your teammates think that, in your opinion?"

"First of all Marty, I haven't been that impressed with Rivera's attitude since he's been here, but we've got nothing to replace him with. There'd be a huge hole in our infield."

"I think we can squeeze two prospects from the Yanks, one that we could move to another team in the off-season to get us a quality replacement right now."

"Really Marty, and who would that be?"

"We've got a claim on Sanchez from the Padres. He's a free agent at the end of the season and they're out of it so they want to move him now."

"Shit, that's a no-brainer from my end. That kid is a stud. He's motivated too by contract issues. Why wouldn't we take a career .300 hitter with great range at shortstop? He'd definitely be an upgrade."

"Keep it quiet Blake. We've got to make this deal first with New York to get the player the Padres want."

"Why wouldn't New York just deal with San Diego directly for Sanchez? Everyone knows he's better than Rivera at this stage of their careers."

"Blake, it's all tied in to the waiver process. He'd just be blocked by another team. The damn Yankees will just throw all their money to get him down the road, but nobody's going to help those bastards out now."

"Sounds great Marty, I'm sorry if I came across kind of pissy a few minutes ago. I'm tired and we're not doing too well at the moment."

"That's okay Blake, just stay in touch. Answer your goddamn cell phone! And I've got just one more thing Blake, before I let you get off the phone. No more last minute trips to the goddamn bowling alley. I heard about it. I've got my connections too. We've got too many people watching us now to screw this thing up with bullshit bush league pranks."

"Just trying to keep my team loose Marty. It won't happen again. I'm truly sorry about that one, but I did have very good intentions."

"We all do Blake, but let's stay professional here. We don't want to become a joke, especially now that the national media is focusing on us."

"Gotcha sir, I guess it's time to call it a day. We'll get back on track tomorrow."

"'Night Blake, I'll keep you informed on this waiver deal."

Blake ended the night with an unlikely prayer. He had never been particularly faithful to God or whatever supreme power might be responsible for this crazy world, but he simply felt he couldn't do this alone. The prayers were coming more frequently as the struggles increased. He was feeling the pressure and the scrutiny of this whole nightmare as he pulled the bed covers over his tired body.

He stared at the ceiling of his hotel room. That silent voice deep inside of him was re-emerging once more. The self-doubt and anxiety seemed to move the ceiling lower and lower until it felt like it was right on top of him, suffocating any positive feelings that were left inside.

He was trapped in his own self-doubt with nowhere to go at this time of the night to relieve the anxiety. The sudden fear of a panic attack began to race through his brain, followed by the instinctive desire to resort to alcohol to remedy the situation as he had done countless times before.

Blake knew he had to call his wife right now to get centered once again. Fortunately, Kim answered and talked him through the anxiety. She was his natural stress reliever and full-time remedy that never wavered from her supporting role.

All those years of boozing and fooling around on the road had clouded his moral judgment. As his body jerked to indicate sleep was near, Blake could only think of how foolish he had been finding false comfort and temporary relief through his sinful ways. He somehow forgot that the love of his life could provide real and long-lasting comfort if only he had opened up to her in times of need.

33 — Suds City Swoon

The dawn signals a fresh start for a new day and a hopeful end to past miseries. Baseball, more than any other sport, typifies this opportunistic outlook, as 162 games allow ample opportunity for redemption.

The standings reflect the whole season, marking progress or a lack of it, but the unknown future almost always gives an athlete or a fan hope that better performances lie ahead. The long drawn out campaign was holding fewer and fewer games as the season reached its final stages, but there were still enough contests left to overcome any dry spells.

With the Cubs' lead down to a mere three games over the Cardinals, Blake's team was feeling the pressure along with weariness as they prepared for the last leg of the nine-game road trip. Three games at Miller Park in Milwaukee would bring a welcome end to the current sojourn.

The good news for this series rested with the legions of Cubs fans that spill over from Chicago to make the atmosphere in this ballpark unlike most others, as the split of fans from the two teams usually sifts out at about 50-50.

The close proximity to Chicago also brought players' wives and girlfriends, a welcome sight to road-weary players and coaches. Kim usually drove up with several other wives, but there hadn't been enough time with this new collection of players to really form any bonds. She decided to fly in just to see for herself how Blake was handling the pressures of the road.

The fans from Chicago enthusiastically welcomed the visiting club as they took the field for the opening game of the series. It was a rainy day in Milwaukee, but the retractable stadium roof at Miller Park saved the evening. The enclosed space made for a boisterous atmosphere as the noise reverberated throughout the ballpark.

Blake's boys came out storming in the first inning, putting up a five spot in the top half and thrilling the many Cub fans in attendance, but the joy was short-lived as the Brewers came back with five runs of their own in their half of the inning.

These games in Milwaukee always seemed to feature a seesaw effort as if both teams responded to their equal fans in attendance. Chants of "Let's go Cubs" would be immediately responded with "Here we go Brewers, here we go." It was always the boisterous Chicago fans that initiated the chants, but the hardy Milwaukee fans would never let the Chicagoans take over their field without a fight.

Back and forth the two teams went, along with their respective fans, before Milwaukee took over down the stretch as the bullpen battle went to the Brew Crew. The final score of 12-10 put stress on each team's bullpen, but more importantly to the Cubs, the loss, coupled with a Cardinals win, brought the lead down to a paltry two full games.

Blake was in a surprisingly good mood after the game, in anticipation of the expected move shortly to acquire Sanchez. He spoke to the team in a positive and encouraging tone before one of the Brewers' clubhouse guys walked in and broke some news to the team.

Holding a fresh new Sports Illustrated, the old clubhouse hand threw his magazine on a bench and told the team to look at the cover.

The portly, balding 60-something man named "Pops" told his clubhouse visitors that he knew why their team was in a funk.

"Look, you guys made the SI cover with your New York showing last week. That'll show you guys to make a splash in the big city. Now you've put the biggest sports hex on your team that there is. It even tops your Billy goat jinx."

Blake rushed over to view the magazine cover and broke out in uncomfortable laughter.

"Looky here, the headline says it all," Blake spoke with a sarcastic tone and threw the magazine down in disgust as the laughter ran away to be replaced by irritation.

"Benson resurrects Cubs with daring play" was the headline.

"Why do they have to focus on me? And to use that resurrected wording. That's downright disrespectful to my former teammates. And now we can't win a game!"

Blake was always surprisingly uncomfortable as the center of attention. The stereotype of an inflated ego that was normally attached to superstars in any sport certainly didn't apply to him. He was flattered as a young prospect, but that quickly faded as increased publicity was accompanied by increased scrutiny. Inside Blake always knew that he had enormous personal flaws that were better off hidden.

The clubhouse attendant, seemingly unaware of his irrelevance, interjected regardless. "But it's not your fault, Mr. Benson. That SI curse has taken down many a team and individual. You should take it out on them."

"Pops, maybe you got something there. At the very least it might focus the guys and get everybody on the same page. It would take the spotlight off me too. God damn it it's their fault."

Blake figured they might as well have some fun with it. He would do just about anything to avoid a doomed and dejected clubhouse.

"Where the hell is Guillen? Somebody go get that hex expert. He always has some answer for superstition and curses. It never fucking made any sense, but he's got strong opinions. Guillen will know what to do. He's probably enjoying the postgame spread with a couple of beers. Bring him to me, but let him finish his meal and a few beers first. Guy's gotta get his groove on first before he can think straight."

Within a half hour Guillen reemerged in the clubhouse with a towel still wrapped around his increasingly thick torso. He liked to shower and then eat his spread naked. Nobody ever had the nerve to ask him why. The screwball lefty wiped his hands on the towel that now looked more like a bib than anything else.

"You called for me Skipper? For what do I enjoy this pleasure? I heard something about needing my cultural expertise on a pressing matter. Somebody throw me another brew please. I need to get in the right frame of mind to educate you simpletons."

"Guillen, you're always spouting off about ways to get rid of bad spirits and such. How about hexes? We've got ourselves a huge problem here. Take a look at the Sports Illustrated cover over there," Blake motioned with his hand to the magazine lying on a bench nearby.

"Oh, that's a bad hombre. That SI jinx is some nasty shit. Sure explains a lot of what's been going around the last few days though. Now I know why that Brewers sonofabitch took me over the fence today. I could feel the bad vibes in my pitching hand as soon as I let go of that changeup. Spirits must've lifted that pitch thigh-high. It was supposed to be below the knees. Looked perfect too when it left my hand, but the gods raised it up some. Those bastards must be Cardinal fans!"

"That's in the past. We've got to get rid of this thing quickly, before the Cardinals catch us. I came to you first, but if it's too big for you Guillen, I can find someone else," Blake playfully nodded to his chunky lefty reliever.

"Skipper, do you want the best or just the rest man? You go elsewhere and you go right down the tubes. Or should I say we? Let me go sit on my throne while I come up with something. Gimme that piece-of-shit magazine. I need something to read while I do my business. Maybe there's something in there about me?"

"You better hurry up amigo or I go to my Dominican guys. We can't wait all day," Blake said, clearly enjoying the playfulness of the moment, while still allowing him to believe, ever so slightly, that there could indeed be a cure to be found in Guillen's repertoire of cultural remedies.

Guillen reappeared soon after with a mixture of good and bad news. Holding his cell phone in his hand, he told Blake the bad news first.

"I'm really only an expert in the spirits. My jinx expertise is not so good. I can't lie to you and the team Blake. I'm like 0 for 10 in my jinx removal tries. They weren't even close. No can do."

"Jesus Christ Guillen, you had to go to the can just to tell us that?"

"No Skip, I just wanted to see if SI had anything nice to say about me."

The room was roaring with laughter, but Guillen cut it short with his reply.

"I've got good news too. My cousin down in Mexico is a curse expert. That's his career, man. He's good at it too. The sucker makes more dinero than me. I'll call him right now."

"You do that Miguel. We'll just sit here and wait for your cousin to save the season for us."

Guillen sat down and began his conversation with his cousin Enrique. After minutes of chatter, the portly left-hander put his hands over the phone and gave Blake the news.

"He's got a cure, but says it will cost 1,000 U.S dollars."

"Give me that goddamn phone."

Blake grabbed the phone from an unwilling Guillen and began to holler at the pitcher's cousin.

"Listen you slimy bastard, you've got a chance to help a major league team. Money should be the last thing on your greedy mind."

Blake's face turned even redder as he listened to the cousin's reply and then apologized sincerely to the man. Blake handed the phone over to Guillen and put both of his hands around his pitcher's neck.

Guillen just smiled back at Blake and said in jest, "You wouldn't hurt your star pitcher now would you?"

"He said he offered to do it for free as a courtesy to his cousin. You were setting us up for a lousy grand?"

"Hell yes," replied Guillen. "I would've tried for more, but I didn't think you'd go any higher Skipper. I was just playing with you guys. Bartlett's the one that gave me the idea. That guy sure knows how to get under people's skin."

"I never would've believed you until you threw out Bartlett's name. Now I do. So, what's the cuz gonna do about it?"

"Again it's good and bad Blakester. Turns out you can't do anything about a curse on Tuesday, bad karma or something. It's Tuesday now. We're after midnight. He promises to release the curse first thing Wednesday. He's got all the ingredients down there, but he just needs to track down an issue of SI first."

"I suppose we can hold out for one more day. Maybe we can get a rainout or something for tomorrow night's game."

Guillen was clearly enjoying the attention as he belted out another line in Blake's direction. "My cousin don't do no rain dances man. He can only handle one cure at a time Skipper."

Blake turned the mood in a serious direction as he put an end to all the goofiness. "We still have hope on our side. Let's not forget that. Things can change on a dime. It's time to put fun and games aside. We'll be okay. Just believe guys, just believe."

Blake was referring to the expected acquisition of Sanchez, but he couldn't let on. It was no sure thing either, but he knew Marty was an excellent dealmaker.

"We'll see you all tomorrow. Get a good night's rest fellas. This road trip is taking its toll on all of us. Visit with the wives and girlfriends that came up from Chicago."

Unfortunately, the following night's game was more of the same. The team played a good, solid game before bowing 4-3 to the Brewers. The contest ended on a sour note as the soon-to-be-traded Rivera lined out with the bases loaded to end the game.

Rivera threw his helmet in anger toward the dugout. It glanced off the feisty Bartlett who threw it right back at him and the two had to be separated.

Player emotions were raw, as one would expect after a tough loss and a fight involving teammates. It was eerily quiet and subdued, bordering on defeatist, as the media was let in.

Rivera was motioned to Blake's office where the manager gave him the news that he had been traded to the Yankees. Blake assured him that the trade had nothing to do with his fracas with Bartlett. He informed Rivera that the trade had been in the works for 48 hours.

Within moments of Rivera's departure, the team and the media were informed that the talented Sanchez would be coming over from San Diego. The news could not have come at a better time for the morale of the squad.

The pain of continued losing dissipated some as the news spread. The Cardinals lost as well, so the lead still stood at two games heading into the series finale.

The long road trip would soon be coming to an end. At least the team was assured of remaining in first place when they arrived back in Chicago, as the two-game lead could only be dwindled in half at the worst.

And it was almost Wednesday. The curse could end anytime soon, according to Guillen's cousin. At this point, it was about the best news the team could come up with, silly superstition or not.

34 — Getaway Day Gone Wild

Nearly everyone on the team was in high spirits before the Wednesday afternoon game at Miller Park in Milwaukee because today was getaway day signaling the return home to Chicago. All were looking forward to the friendly confines of Wrigley Field as soon as the matinee contest concluded.

Blake felt confident as well as relieved to be heading home. He had survived his first road trip as a player-manager without resorting to drink or infidelity. He struggled a couple of times, but his sobriety prevailed and his duties as manager seemed to go off without a hitch. Blake was never too worried about the on-the-field managerial task. He had supreme confidence in his baseball instincts and knowledge. It was the intangibles and the off-the-field surroundings that would test his weaknesses. He knew there was plenty more to come in that department, unfortunately.

A loose but somewhat shaken squad took the field that afternoon. There was nothing like getaway day to brighten team spirits. Many players simply are happy to get away from each other for at least several hours each day as personalities grind back and forth looking for an outlet. Losing often certainly does not help civility on any squad.

The sense of things will get better when we get home' temporarily alleviated the built-up tension of continued failure. Homemade food, good rest, and all the other amenities of home could do wonders for a struggling player and team. The professional baseball player generally believed in the tonic of home.

Blake was playful as his teammates prepped for the game. It was an obvious attempt to brighten the team's mood. He clowned around about the expected removal of the Sports Illustrated cover jinx that was promised by Guillen's cousin for today.

Blake hollered for all to hear at Guillen as the slow-moving Miguel lumbered onto the field. The pudgy lefty didn't care too much for an afternoon tilt after a night game. An overabundance of food and cheer usually made for a grumpy Guillen until the contest approached his normal expected entrance in the later innings.

"Guillen, you better have gotten this jinx thing straightened out with your cousin or your fat ass is going to be running nonstop for the next week. You'll look like a Mexican supermodel by the time I let up if you don't remove this fucking jinx," Blake playfully hollered at the miserable looking Guillen.

"Relax coach, it's a done deal. There's no way we can lose today, according to Enrique. He said he wouldn't be surprised if we didn't run off 10 wins in a row. The dude said it was his best work ever. Now let me go lay down somewhere until my Mexican power arm is needed."

"Sure thing Guillen, get your rest and don't fall asleep on your fucking pitching arm like you did last week, you crazy bastard. These umpires are catching on to my delaying tactics and if you're not in the shitter you're asleep somewhere. Try to stay just a bit enthused. Is that too fucking much to ask?"

Blake was just clowning around with Miguel as he knew the kid would pitch until his arm fell off for his Skipper. Characters like Guillen are what make the game fun for all and keep the atmosphere playful and loose.

"You can count on me Skip. Just move around as slow as me and I'll have plenty of time to get this Olympic body ready. You just need to slow down and enjoy the moment Skipper. Got it?"

"Yeah I got it right here big guy," Blake gestured toward his groin and slowly walked away.

The newly acquired Rickey Sanchez would not arrive in time to play today, but would be ready to go when the team opened a 10-game home stand on Thursday. There would be very few off days from here on out because of the logjam of games that had to be made up after the weeklong moratorium following the tragedy.

Most of the team appeared to be enthused about the Sanchez addition and were relatively surprised at the aggressiveness of GM Marty Anderson as he seemed to be going all out to scrape out at least a Division title for the Cubbies. Any worries about appearing to give up with the trade announcement were immediately replaced with the news of the highly regarded Sanchez.

A bright sunny day soaked the playing surface and the stands at Miller Park as the Cubs tried to end the team's losing skid and stay at least two games ahead of the second-place Cardinals.

A high priest would have been a believer in Enrique's powers if he watched Wednesday's game. Everything the Cubs touched turned to gold as the team collected a season-high 20 hits in the 15-3 never-in-doubt victory. Bloopers, liners, and big flies, it didn't matter; everything found a hole in the Brewers defense.

Guillen woke up in the fifth inning and saw his squad comfortably ahead 10-1. He stood up and went through the sign of the cross motion, mumbled something about his whacked out cousin, and went back to sleep. He would crow about it on the short trip home, but for now his body still needed some recovering.

Every time it had looked like the team was ready to fall apart the squad would somehow respond in a positive way. Whether it was the baseball gods, Enrique or just the luck of the game, the team was resilient. There was some character building in his team and Blake found plenty of reason to smile as he neared his residence. He certainly knew there still was a long ways to go.

The home stand would be another crucial step, as the New York Mets, the Pittsburgh Pirates and the Milwaukee Brewers would invade Wrigley Field in the next 10 days. These were the same squads the Cubbies faced on their road trip and Blake knew that his team had a bit of an edge the first time around due to unfamiliarity. There would be no such luck for these return engagements. The adjustments would start to come fast and furious as tendencies and strategies became apparent to advance scouts.

Blake knew he had to stay one step ahead of those guys all the way. It would be time to sit down and anticipate the counterattacks that he knew were coming, but for now he just wanted to unwind behind closed doors with Kim and enjoy the solitude and comforts of home.

35 — Looking Back but Moving Forward

A road-weary Blake walked though his front door desiring peace and quiet and nothing else. However, his anxious wife wanted to rehash the troubling experiences for her husband in another attempt to force Blake to accept the futility of defeating this illness on his own.

After several long embraces that were desperately needed by both parties, Blake left his luggage at the door and settled into his favorite reclining sofa as Kim handed him a bottle of water. He was interested in solitude and internal reflection, but Kim would have none of that.

After several minutes of small talk and neighborhood gossip, Kim slowly moved toward her husband and balanced her athletic, shapely body on the edge of the sofa. She clasped both of Blake's hands and her voice took on a more serious tone as she proceeded to gauge her spouse's demeanor to figure out if she should delve a bit further into his current mental state.

Kim cautiously moved ahead testing the waters with a relatively innocent question even though Blake's eyes were shut in an emotional distress signal.

"Do you feel much differently coming home from this road trip than the others now that you have more responsibility Blake? Or do you feel better without the physical destruction of alcohol? I'm just kind of curious."

Blake sat motionless in silence before he blurted out in anger, "Kim, I'm in no mood to be psychoanalyzed. I do feel better physically, but I'm also much more emotionally drained. Can we just leave it at that until morning? Everything doesn't have to be done this instant within your irrational sense of urgency. For God sakes, I'm not going to leap off a cliff tonight! I'm okay, just tired that's all."

"You're right Blake there's no immediate need, but we will discuss this. You simply can't put this off or repress your feelings. It'll eat you up if you don't acknowledge your emotions. The first thing after breakfast in the morning we have to look at some things. And don't you sneak off to the ballpark before we get a chance to talk about this," Kim sternly warned her husband.

"Tomorrow Kim, we'll do this tomorrow. I don't want to, but I'll open up a vein in the morning. How 'bout you just put on some classical music for me? For some crazy reason your obsession with that music has rubbed off on me and it sort of clears my mind."

"I'd love to lose myself in some music right about now too. You just sit there and relax and I'll put away your luggage and fix you something to eat. I think I can come up with just the right music for you, honey. My obsession, as you call it, actually gives me the knowledge to apply the right sound to calm your nerves."

Kim politely subdued her inquisitiveness for Blake's need to come down from the road. For the rest of the evening she did nothing but acquiesce to her husband's wishes. Her time would come in the morning. She was edgy, as any kind of delay to her concerns struck a compulsive nerve in her brain, but after all these married years she knew her husband well enough to ascertain when to fold her cards for another day.

The following morning brought out a fresher and less irritable Blake, but Kim stayed disciplined and true to form, reminding her soul mate that they should meet out by their swimming pool after he finished his breakfast, prepared elegantly by Kim as always.

Like a schoolboy sent to the principal Blake reluctantly wandered outside to meet Kim lounging by the pool and reading the morning paper as the sun played peek-a-boo with the clouds on a crisper morning than a mere two weeks ago.

"Did you enjoy your breakfast honey? I made your favorite, as I'm sure you noticed."

"Of course I did Kim. You always start me off with my favorite breakfast the first morning home, but yes, I loved it and appreciate your thoughtfulness."

Blake enjoyed French toast and bacon with one fried egg and, like his other sports superstitions, he never felt just right until he had his favorite breakfast meal cooked the same way every time. Any alterations were frowned upon and could even set Blake off if he was on a hot streak. Kim wasn't the only one in the Benson household that could be obsessive at times.

"You're welcome. Now please sit down here for a few minutes and I'll let you get to the park. No talking baseball now, please. You need to pretend that you have no other responsibilities than recovering from your alcoholism. It's that important to you and to us."

"You think I don't know that Kim? It's constantly on my mind. Hell, even when I sleep I have dreams about me drinking. I can't get away from it."

"That's exactly why I think you need to go to some AA meetings as you promised. Until you get some things figured out you will struggle. It doesn't mean you can't stay sober your way, but unease about your thoughts and feelings will affect you in other detrimental ways too."

"Okay, perhaps you're right. I'll check into it with Marty. He knows where and when these meetings take place. I really need to get to Wrigley now. We've got another big game today."

"Yes Blake, they're all big games," Kim answered with dripping sarcasm. "Before you go, why do you think the road bothers your psyche so much?"

"I've got to go Kim. Maybe it's just the loneliness or maybe it's my anxiety. Fuck I don't know, but I just feel out of sorts and the only way I've ever known how to get back to some kind of normalcy was to hit the booze. It took away the edginess that was driving me crazy. Now I've really got to go."

Kim stood up and reassured her husband that it was good to express these inner revelations.

"You just need to figure yourself out and I think you'll be comforted by understanding all of your previous harmful and destructive reactions," Kim professed, then waved her husband off as if to signal him that it was fine for him to leave now.

Blake kissed her goodbye in an impersonal habit-like way and hurriedly turned to scamper away from his irritating husbandly duty.

"Blake, now don't you forget to find out where and when the next AA meeting will be. You know I'll ask you the minute you step in the door tonight."

Blake raised his right hand in acknowledgement as he traipsed farther away in both physically and emotionally manner from the troublesome topic.

Kim was encouraged that Blake didn't totally dismiss her insistence on opening up to her and, hopefully, eventually to others. Cautiously optimistic, she walked back into their home in a good frame of mind.

Little did she know that Blake would talk himself out of the commitment while he sped towards Wrigley Field anxious to clutter his mind with numerous baseball decisions. Blake was very thankful for distractions on a day like today, when placating his wife took precedence over his preferred method of self-treatment.

He was troubled by the overhanging dilemma of being true to himself at the expense of his marriage. Kim was probably right in the abstract, but Blake knew himself better than anyone on this planet. It would be his way and the results would speak for themselves. Stay sober and prove he was right or slip up and acknowledge the errors of his ways. In the end, it was all up to him.

36 — Home Sweet Home is not a Cure-all

It is extremely difficult to stay in the present and not look ahead in the game of major league baseball. Home stands and road trips were natural delineating points and the temptation is always there to project how each one will play out.

Despite years of realization that prognosticating seldom works, there is something in the makeup of humans, and athletes in particular, that innately searches for likely results in the near future. Blake often succumbed to this even though he scoffed at "schedule analysis" in the abstract, convinced of its futility, but in practice he couldn't resist.

With a slim two-game lead over the Cardinals as August was nearing its close, Blake liked his team's chances to stay at or near the lead for the next 10 games as Wrigley Field would be the host. The teams invading the north side of Chicago were not exactly the cream of the crop, but then again, neither was this makeshift Cubs team, a factor that an inexperienced manager like Blake seemed to overlook as he was surmising the situation while driving to the ballpark.

Skipper Blake Benson was anticipating a loose and relaxed Chicago Cubs team to show up for the inaugural series of the 10-game, 11-day home stand against the New York Mets. He fully expected his squad to be rejuvenated by the comforts of home, but once again Blake seemed to forget that this newly assembled team didn't have any roots planted in the Windy City as of yet. For the rest of the year this ball club would be vagabonds living out de facto road trips for the last two months of the schedule.

The manager was surprised to see a tired and somewhat dejected group of guys assembled before the opening game against the Mets. The day started out with plenty of sunshine, but by the scheduled afternoon game time of twenty minutes after one o'clock, the skies turned dull gray and sprinkled intermittent drizzle. Perhaps it was the weather or the culmination of travel that often seemed to hit the day after arrival home, but nonetheless it was a lifeless bunch at the start of the contest.

There had been a fair amount of joking about the exorcism of the SI curse and Guillen's cousin Enrique who was the team hero at the moment, but it certainly lacked the vigor of the previous day. The team was flat and Blake could feel the lack of enthusiasm as his team fell behind early 3-0.

Fortunately for the home team the umpiring crew contained an arrogant prick that was the scourge of almost every major league player. The source of aggravation was the long-standing smug demeanor of crew chief Lance Rockford who was behind the plate in this contest pissing every player off once again. His inconsistent strike zone frustrated players, as did his apparent lack of professionalism as he domineered over any and all players with his pompous behavior.

There was the usual bitching about the balls and strikes and, as always, the response from Rockford proclaimed this was "my strike zone and it's up to you peons to figure it out, not me.' His reputation as a complete pain in the ass was well-deserved, but he was fair and treated all players the same. The major leaguers just figured he was a frustrated jock that never could measure up athletically and took it out on those that did achieve greatness by advancing to the highest level of professional baseball.

The man seemed to relish conflict and went out of his way to confront anybody that questioned his competence or absolute power. Rabid fans were not even exempt from his wrath, as he was known to try and intimidate ballpark security to eject rowdies from the stands.

Throw in a humid late summer day with frustrations building and it was the perfect recipe for dynamite, as Rockford called John Bartlett out on a check swing without even asking for help from the first base ump on a borderline call.

Bartlett, with his surly reputation as an instigator and possessing a sarcastic wit that belonged on a comedy stage more than a baseball diamond, reacted as one would expect and immediately swore at the home umpire with a swipe that questioned the arbitrator's manhood.

Rat Bartlett dropped his bat in mock display at the ump's feet and muttered a few choice words at the trigger-happy Rockford.

"Lancey boy, even you with a miniature dick shouldn't be so insecure and power hungry to not even ask for help on that call," Bartlett whispered in his ear as he walked behind the home plate umpire on his way to the dugout.

The smart-ass catcher expected an angry reply and he got an earful himself as Rockford pulled off his mask and charged at Bartlett, who was still moving away with his back to the pissed-off ump.

"Turn around you gutless bastard, Bartlett. I'm the only prick in charge here. You're a bigger sonofabitch than me, but I'm the only one that can toss your slimy ass out of here. You're gone," shouted Rockford as he emphatically threw his right arm toward the official scorer's box, indicating that he'd tossed the starting catcher from the contest.

Bartlett knew it was coming, but he still wanted to get his money's worth out of this one. He abruptly turned around and smirked at Rockford, tossed the chew from his mouth in the same motion that the power-hungry ump had moments before displayed. The chaw landed in the box seats, but the fans didn't seem to mind the crude act as their anger was focused at Rockford.

Bartlett got nose to nose with the umpire and spit was flying between the two as they went back and forth with their insults.

Blake tried to intercept before Rockford tossed him, as all good managers attempt to do in their duty to protect their players from disqualification and likely eventual league disciplinary action. However, the main combatants were too ticked off and had way too much prior history to intervene in time.

Blake tried to separate his catcher from Rockford to spare him from further punishment. Bartlett was always under a microscope from the league office, plus he wasn't too far removed from his earlier suspension for his confrontation with Martinez and the Dodgers.

An angry Blake threw Bartlett aside and got tangled in Rockford's face immediately in an attempt to change the ump's focus toward him. Blake had no problem getting worked up over an umpire that was all too familiar to him, having that spent plenty of time catching in close proximity to the cantankerous Rockford behind home plate.

Blake was rationally aware of the situation because he himself was Bartlett's replacement and the last available regular catcher on the squad. Blake knew the dangers of only carrying two catchers on the active roster, but preferred the flexibility of an extra arm in the bullpen for a pitching-limited team.

However, the snarly Rockford got the best of Blake too, with his own personal attack toward the Cubs player-manager that was highly unprofessional, but par for the course for a power hungry and tenured umpire safely protected from corrective actions by his union.

"I liked you better when you were a drunk has-been, Benson, than a sober never-will-be major league manager past this fucked up season. You should've been on that plane, you sorry-ass loser," barked out an angry Rockford with his umpire's mask strategically placed on his head to avoid detection from lip-readers.

A furious Bartlett heard that below-the-belt reply and got in Rockford's face before Blake and the rest of his coaches could restrain the already-ejected Bartlett.

Blake responded in kind to Rockford and dropped in a few choice words that invariably drew an almost automatic ejection, but there was no way Blake was going to let that classless retort go unpunished.

As events calmed down between the home plate umpire and Blake, the atmosphere suddenly perked up in the dugout as Bartlett made sure the rest of his teammates knew what the universally disliked Rockford had said about their manager.

The Cubs rallied around their ejected manager and played inspired baseball the rest of the way, overcoming the 3-0 deficit and ultimately prevailing 8-5. With the switch of an umpire's hand gesture the team had awoken from its slumber and suddenly played like a pennant contender even though they were hampered by the play of emergency catcher Jim Arnold, a capable first sacker, but a lousy last-ditch replacement behind the plate. The Cubs were fortunate that their New York opponent did not have much team speed to exploit the situation. Acting manager Lenny Paxton wisely went with left-handers out of the bullpen for most of the remaining game to keep base runners honest.

The clubhouse was once again filled with good-natured ribbing after the game, as only a win can overlook shoddy managerial decisions. It was no fault of Arnold that he was put in this untenable situation. The blame was Blake's for getting tossed and for carrying only two catchers. It's a gamble to only have one extra catcher on a roster, especially in the National League where pinch-hitting decisions and in-game maneuvers are widely practiced.

All was forgotten as the inspiring come-from-behind win overshadowed everything else. Arnold would take the blunt of teasing for his adventurous play behind the plate, but a win is the ultimate tonic. Mistakes made during the game are forgotten like one of Blake's alcoholic blackouts of the past, as long as the good guys come out ahead in the final score.

The good feeling persisted throughout the four-game series with the Mets and the club was having a great time holding on to their slim lead over St. Louis. Miguel Guillen was peacocking each day claiming credit for the release of the curse and subsequent winning streak that reached four games before the series finale Sunday afternoon. However, at this point Blake once again saw the team's fortunes change on a dime with a deflating blown save by closer Randall Hart.

Hart had been perfect in save opportunities since his role had been switched to the bullpen from the starting rotation. He appeared to be enjoying his one-inning-at-a-time workload that enabled him to throw all-out for a short time and not have to worry about stamina.

Just as the Cubs were about to sweep their first series since their makeshift inception, the team sunk back into old ways with the emotionally damaging loss as Hart blew a 4-2 ninth inning lead. Hart's sudden loss of control saw him walk the bases loaded with nobody out before allowing a bases-clearing two-bagger that propelled the Mets to a 5-4 win.

The home team still had a two-game margin over the Cards, but the distance suddenly felt precarious; late-inning blown leads often lead to a quick loss of overall team confidence. Blake allowed himself a rare show of clubhouse dejection as he hung his head in silent disbelief before realizing his role was to keep the squad upbeat despite baseball's notorious turns of emotion.

"Okay guys, that was a tough one, but we all know these things happen throughout the course of the season. Let's turn the page and start a new chapter tomorrow when the Phillies come to town. I'm guessing Guillen's cousin must have gone on vacation because something weird just happened out there on the field," Blake lamely attempted to joke away the pain.

"Don't worry Blakester, I'll reach him after my postgame spread erases my anger and frustration. Couple of beers and this one will be a distant memory," retorted Miguel, even though his voice lacked its usual spunk.

Blake suddenly realized that he couldn't erase his pain in the old medicinal manner and slammed his office door in disgust, surprising all occupants of the Cubs clubhouse. The area had been awash in cheer a mere four hours ago, but was now more like a morgue as the team collectively mourned what could have been.

The Cubs general manager must have sensed the distress signal emanating from Blake's office. Marty Anderson called down to see how his manager was coping. Marty just had a feel that it wasn't going well for Blake at the moment and sought to reassure him with a brief chat.

Blake picked up the phone with hesitation as he struggled to regain control of his emotions. He was well aware that the call was from his boss as the caller ID signaled the GM's office.

"Hello Marty, this one was a tough pill to swallow. I hope you understand my pissy mood. Why do the losses hurt so much more than the thrill of victory provides?"

"Blake, that's a time-worn question that has eaten away at many a coach. You just gotta let it go. Isolated incidents we can handle. Just do your best to limit the damage," Marty spoke with grandfatherly comfort to his manager.

"I know Marty, but it's how I handle it that's my concern at the moment. Say, let me ask you a question? When's that next AA meeting? I'm not comfortable with how I feel at the moment."

"Do I need to be concerned Blake? Are you okay? I can cover for you for a few days if you need."

"Don't worry about me Marty."

Marty interjected immediately, "It's my job to worry about you Blake."

"I'm just having one of those moments Marty. I'm sure you can relate."

"Gotcha, let's get you in to one of my AA meetings tonight. I guarantee it'll help with the uncertainty that comes with dealing with it in near isolation. Stay right where you are. Just shower and get dressed and I'll be down there in an hour. Call your wife and let her know. We'll get you home by 10 so you might as well grab a bit of the postgame meal to tide yourself over."

Blake thanked his boss for the concern and gave his approval as he mulled over the upcoming meeting in his brain. Doing something felt better than doing nothing at all. The immediacy of the unsettling moment had passed, but knowing that there was more where that came from signaled to Blake that he had done the right thing.

It was time to see what this approach was all about and whether it was really for him or not.

37 — Mood Swing Methodology

Blake explained to Kim over the phone that he was having a difficult time today. He confided to his wife he would like some help in dealing with the expected, but often untimely setbacks that the game of baseball delivers in cruel fashion.

"I was feeling high as a kite Kim, everything was falling into place, and then in one inning I fell into an unexpected and unexplainable hole that I previously would soothe with booze, but I knew I couldn't do that now and it somehow made me even more distraught."

"Blake, look at this as a good thing, a learning experience. I've said to you many times that you couldn't fully recover until you understood the keys to your drinking. Now how are you going to seek out help?"

"Marty called down to my office right after the bitter ending of the game. It was if he expected my reaction almost before I did. The eeriness of the moment somehow affected me in a deep manner."

"He caught you off guard, Blake, and you just let your true feelings flow before your mind normally shut down those emotions. I've seen it before in my family."

"Could be," Blake retorted, as he stubbornly still resisted any outside observations.

His male pride was still too strong to admit that others might have a better understanding than him. It was his way of remaining in control of his life at a time when others were seemingly making inroads.

First it was Marty and now it was Kim that better understood what was happening to him and even before Blake could barely make sense of it. His brain was still in an alcoholic state of mind even though he had been sober for nearly three weeks now.

"Whatever the case, I'm going with Marty to an AA meeting tonight if nothing else than to satisfy my curiosity," Blake stubbornly held on to his pride with the qualified reply.

"I'm very relieved to hear that Blake. Just go with an open mind and for God sakes don't hold your emotions inside. You'll never figure it out until you explore the disease and share with others in the same boat. You'll feel cleansed when you let it out, Blake."

"Marty's going to be here any second now so I have to go," Blake replied tersely and untruthfully. "I should be home a bit after 10. See you then."

Blake was back at it again, cutting off his emotions just when it appeared he was losing control, and unwilling to let Kim have the upper hand in her understanding of what he closely guarded as his thoughts.

He leaned back in his office chair and began to self-examine for a few moments until Marty came down to the clubhouse. Blake was craving the mind-numbing effect of alcohol at a time when he knew more than ever that he had to stay in charge. It wasn't just him anymore. He could let himself down as he had in the past without too much worry, but now he was responsible for the whole Chicago Cubs organization and, ultimately, the legacy of his fallen teammates.

The overwhelming sense of responsibility stiffened his spine and he rose out of the chair with newfound determination. For a moment, Blake tossed about in his head the thought of canceling his commitment to partake in an AA meeting, but realized that would probably set off more alarms to Marty than Blake deemed desirable.

Marty knocked on Blake's door and the manager quickly responded.

"Okay Marty, let's get this show on the road before I change my mind. Let's try to not look too serious as we make our way to the elevator."

Marty was struck by the urgency in Blake's demeanor. He thought it would be prudent to discuss in private the expected protocol at an AA meeting. He followed Blake to the elevator while deftly motioning with his right hand to the meandering eyes of the remaining team members that were taking their time in leaving the premises.

As they entered the vacant elevator, Marty pulled Blake aside with a calming tug at his sport coat.

"Just chill out a bit and relax Blake. We aren't going to a prison. This is all very informal and 100 percent nonjudgmental. You think these people haven't seen or experienced it all? They're just trying to make sense of the whole process of sobriety themselves. It's a learning experience for everyone involved and you can count on their support just like your teammates. Just like Sandy."

Once again, that word did it all. The mere mention of Sandy's name seemed to solidify Blake's resolve.

"Yes, I guess you're right Marty. How can I expect to gain anything out of this if I put up such a resistant wall? Let's see what this is all about. What can I expect when I get there?"

"Now I know it will feel that all eyes are upon you because you're new and you're famous, but these folks really don't give a shit. Everybody's equal in their eyes. We share an overwhelming common bond."

"I'd like to slowly work my way into the conversations. I hope I can watch and soak it in for a bit? I'll pick the time to open up, ok Marty?"

"Don't worry about a thing Blake. Nobody is pressuring anyone in here. Give me a moment to explain your presence and just stick by me. I'll take care of everything. You just speak when you want or not at all. If you need me to interject on your behalf just tap me on the shoulder."

The two of them pulled up in a taxi. Marty didn't want any showboating here and felt an ostentatious vehicle would just send the wrong message. It wasn't like they were hiding their presence, but rather downplaying their material worth at a place where it was very important to emphasize their shared affliction rather than differences.

Blake walked alongside Marty until the two of them approached the rather mundane building that hosted the sharing of such important pent-up emotions. It seemed like a major league all-star team playing on the sandlot, but he surmised that like baseball, the game itself or in this analogy, the game of life overshadowed any brick and mortar.

The super confident Blake of the baseball diamond retracted like a shrunken turtle as the manager slowly began to walk in the shadow of his boss the nearer the two got to the meeting room in the basement of an old Catholic church nestled in the North Side neighborhood of Chicago.

Marty waved at a few of his recovery colleagues as he entered the dimly lit room, but ushered Blake to the seating area before speaking in private with two tall, gruff-looking graying men that Blake guessed were somehow in charge of the upcoming proceedings.

After a brief chat with the leader of the session, Marty reunited with Blake and updated him with news that offered some much needed comfort.

"Well, they say you're welcome here any time and they could care less what you do for a living, Blake. To them you're just a drunk trying to beat something that has battered them all. I told ya they couldn't care less. They've got bigger issues to face themselves."

"I've never felt better being labeled as an alcoholic, rather than a star. There's something liberating about being nothing special. Marty, thanks again for everything and I mean everything!"

"Just sit back and relax, Blake and take it all in for a bit. You're in for quite a show of emotions, struggles, and persistent demons that plague everybody in this room at times. Listening is good and I mean really listening to their issues. I should say our issues. You will learn quite a bit if you really pay attention."

As the room filled with people of all sizes, shapes, and ages, Blake suddenly began to realize the scope of the disease of alcoholism. He didn't feel so special right about now, but rather humbled at the state of his life at this particular moment. He was beginning to let go of the shame, confusion, ignorance and ever-present doubt that he carried around with him all the time. There suddenly was not any doubt that he was an alcoholic too, not anymore.

Marty and Blake sat quietly, listening intently the whole time. Two hours passed with numerous topics and emotions shared by all in some form or fashion. For Marty and Blake it was just about listening, observing and feeling the deep emotional struggles presented during the two-hour meeting.

Blake left the session a different man than the one who entered just a couple of hours earlier. The struggles hit home and hit hard. He was not alone, nor was he some kind of deep mystery. He was just like millions of other alcoholics living day-by-day in this country and abroad. Many others just like him shared his thoughts and his doubts.

Mood swings, drinking dreams, doubts and fears. You name it, they had it too. A sense of calm permeated his psyche after he left the building. Blake was not sure he would be back there, but he knew for damn sure that this night was a step in the right direction as he stepped into the waiting taxicab with Marty for the ride back to Cubs headquarters. The stillness of the dark, moonlit night offered an appropriate setting for reflection as Blake gazed out the rear side window, silent the whole trip back, but without the edginess that clung to him before the meeting like a pesky fly follows a warm human body.

Blake was in such a calm state when they arrived at the parking lot outside Cubs headquarters that he had to think for a moment why he felt the need to go to an AA meeting several hours prior. He thanked Marty and professed progress this evening.

Now it was time to return home and fill in the details for his wife. Normally that would annoy him, but tonight he looked forward to it. Blake actually could verbally express his feelings better now that he had heard what others were feeling as well.

This should go well, he thought as he sped around the corner and skillfully maneuvered his sporty car up the driveway and into their spacious garage.

38 — Satisfaction not Guaranteed

Kim was somewhere between awake and deep sleep on her favorite reclining sofa with the latest Cosmopolitan magazine gently nestled against her chest. Unbeknownst to Kim, Blake whooshed through the foyer of their home without fear of awakening his wife.

Normally Blake would enter quiet as a mouse longing for a quick and quiet respite absent of meaningful conversation, but this time he wanted to be heard as a soothing sense of pride filled his inner self.

Despite apprehension about his first Alcoholics Anonymous meeting, Blake overcame his angst and felt strong, momentarily throwing aside his self-perceived lack of success in dealing with his disease. He was anxiously looking forward to sharing his experience with Kim rather than his normal withdrawn self.

Perhaps it was simply an urge to show Kim that he could deal directly with his plight rather than a true desire to connect with his wife, but nonetheless it was an emotionally open Blake that sought out the nearly dozing Kim.

Blake's eyes searched out Kim although she barely made out his presence in her foggy near sleep. It was totally out of character, but he initiated the conversation, oblivious to the non-attentive condition of his wife. His tone of voice was noticeably upbeat as he addressed Kim as though he was talking to himself out loud.

"Well Kim, I did it. Never thought I'd follow through on it, but I actually enjoyed my AA meeting tonight. I'll admit I was nervous and apprehensive, but I felt the need to hear others talk about their struggles."

Kim slowly regained her clarity of thought from the dimness of quasi-sleep and asked her husband to say again what he had just uttered for confirmation.

"What, you can't believe what you just heard or are you just waking up?" Blake was momentarily irritated at the initial resistance.

"Both, I thought I heard you say that it was an enjoyable meeting, but that totally caught me off guard," replied Kim as she slowly lifted out of her recliner to welcome her husband home with a somewhat tepid hug.

After a quick embrace, Blake gently maneuvered his wife ever so slightly away from him and spoke while looking directly into her eyes.

"I feel much better just hearing others experiencing the same emotions, the same questions and continued doubts. I didn't say a word all night. I just listened and absorbed it all in."

Kim abruptly interjected and separated from Blake with agitation in clear display.

"Why didn't you participate? Just listening won't allow you to complete your recovery. It requires total capitulation and submission to your disease. That doesn't mean only listening. Don't you get it Blake?"

"Why are you bursting my bubble? God damn it, I finally feel good about letting my pride go a bit and you fucking put down my approach as usual. Jesus Christ Kim, give me a fucking break. Do you always have to push me further and faster than I'm willing to go?"

An obviously irate Blake spun around his head in disgust and threw the car keys that he was still gripping in his right hand violently across the room.

Kim quickly realized she had struck the wrong tone in reply, but her indignation at Blake's reluctance to take her counsel one more time continued to raise her ire as she spouted back.

"Damn it Blake, it doesn't always have to be your fucking idea. Others, especially me, can see things that you won't or can't face."

Blake spun around and faced Kim directly from a safe distance and struck an over-played nerve from Kim's past.

"This isn't about you, it's about me! It's my booze problem, my lack of interest in my profession and my daily struggles. You always look at issues from your perspective and yours just isn't mine. You can't bully me into submission. My timing is my choice. My methods are my choice. Just fucking let me do it my way, right or wrong. I know me better than you know me. Always have and always will Kim."

Blake's wife knew all too well her husband's discontent with his perception that she too often tried to control his emotions and subsequent decisions, but she couldn't resist her own chafing retort.

"Blake, your denial of the reality of your emotions and behaviors just leaves you incapable of self-reflection. Your stubbornness always gets the best of you and wins that internal tug of war. It won't work that way Blake, it won't work."

She stomped all the way upstairs and stepped more forcefully on ascent, each and every step of the elegantly spiraled staircase until she reached the top, and shouted down to Blake.

"Sleep on the couch or in one of your glory rooms," Kim sarcastically screamed. There were numerous shrines that ostentatiously displayed her husband's numerous personal accomplishments over the years, mostly from seasons long since passed by before his playing career careened off track.

As Kim disappeared from sight, but not yet quite out of sound, Blake opened the refrigerator in a failed attempt to change his mental focus. He was piping hot and visibly agitated as he ripped open the refrigerator door with excessive and unnecessary force.

There was tonight's dinner in clear display, a still slightly warm grilled rib eye steak, his favorite cut, neatly snuggled in Saran wrap There was an abundance of exquisite foods staring at a somewhat disinterested Blake who could only focus on the bottles of beer that lined the back of the refrigerator.

His first impulse was to grab one of those cold bottles and chug it down in a dual delight of thirst quench and stubborn defiance. He further dared disaster by tightly gripping his favorite brand before he realized the error of his ways and slid the beer back out of sight.

Still shaking from the argument and the closeness of succumbing to the sudden flight to drink, Blake unsteadily found his way to a nearby kitchen chair. His head sunk into his chest as he replayed the previous five minutes, searching for clarity of remembrance rather than his impulsive reactions to distress and discomfort.

Blake slowly regained his composure and normally calm demeanor. Clarity made a return trip to his brain as he traveled to reflection from impulse.

Kim had always pushed him to higher levels. Blake understood that her personality traits were indeed good for him in balanced fashion. She put issues to the forefront where Blake continually nudged them to the back burner in an inconspicuous manner for another day's denial, where hopefully the troublesome issue would be replaced by yet another and soon forgotten.

He begrudgingly admitted to himself that his wife was right in that internal voice that shields all others from acknowledgement out of stubborn pride. Blake still wished that Kim would have simply given him credit for a step in the right direction while Kim's impatience demanded an immediate response that entailed a total commitment.

Blake eventually returned to the refrigerator and grabbed a bite to eat. His steak, now cold, was still delicious washed down with a Coke as he ignored his wife's demand and joined Kim in their spacious king-sized bed. She was physically and mentally distant in the vastness of the bed as he turned his back to his wife and fell asleep, but not before transferring his thoughts to the upcoming home series against the Philadelphia Phillies.

At least Blake would be back in his realm at Wrigley. He took some solace in that thought as he slowly drifted into deep sleep on an unexpectedly tumultuous night.

39 — Laughter is the Best Medicine

Blake's drive into Wrigley and the start of the upcoming series with the Philadelphia Phillies occupied the manager's thoughts as he tried to put aside his personal issues while weaving through slower traffic on the Kennedy Expressway.

The freeway was an excellent venue for introspection as driving with traffic congestion had become second nature to many Chicago residents. Blake's thoughts ebbed and flowed with the stop-and-go congestion, but never strayed too far from his home life, even as he contemplated his managerial strategy for the next few games.

He finally accepted that his wife was right in substance, if not in style. Tact was never Kim's strong suit and in retrospect it was not surprising that she objected so quickly without considering his own trait of cautious step-by-step involvement.

Blake also had his tendency to do just enough to ward off criticism while Kim tended to rapidly apply an all-out method attacked "yesterday."

As he pulled into his reserved parking space at the ballpark, Blake internally reaffirmed his desire to put his team first and block out his personal issues.

Even with the devastating series finale loss, his squad was more than holding its own in the standings maintaining a slim two-game lead over the Cardinals who were following the same winning pace as the Cubbies the past week.

External attention was creeping their way again, as how could anyone root against this makeshift team except for die-hard fans of the St. Louis Cardinals? They were media darlings whether they liked it or not. Some players enjoyed it and some did not, but they all had to deal with it now and likely in the near future as well, unless the bottom fell out of their postseason chances.

As if one Sports Illustrated cover feature wasn't enough, there were rumors floating around amongst media types that the national publication would be in town again this week. Another possibility mingling about was a reality-type show on ESPN or another national cable outlet.

Blake didn't mind the national attention for his boys and likewise, for his fallen former teammates, but he would put his foot down on a reality show. There was enough gimmickry and circus-type attention with a team put together on the fly, late in the season, and all with perhaps the top major league franchise besides the New York Yankees already in the mix.

He knew his guys would have more fun with the SI cover jinx even though they were still playfully exorcising the first. Blake was not surprised in the least when he first heard, then saw with his own eyes that his big affable Mexican lefty was holding court in the clubhouse and entertaining all with his no-holds-barred sense of humor.

Guillen, a devout Roman Catholic, was using his religion to lighten the mood. Proving that it's not what you say that gets you in trouble, but who says it and how you are viewed by others, the hefty lefty was making fun of his church in the context of his baseball team and in such a humorous manner that nobody appeared to be upset with the sometimes touchy subject of religion in a baseball clubhouse.

Miguel was wearing the vocational attire of a priest that he acquired through a good friend at his church, Father John Sheahan. The crusty old priest was an avid baseball fan that possessed a large heart, generous spirit and humor who was never afraid to poke fun at himself or his faith.

Guillen was impersonating a priest exorcising demons from his baseball flock of teammates while Blake stood at a safe distance to witness the comedian in complete control of his audience.

The first up was the losing pitcher from the last contest that temporarily devastated Blake and most of his teammates. Randall Hart's blown save had a very demoralizing effect so it only made spiritual sense to rid him of his demon first.

The goat of the last game came forward, approaching Guillen in reverence, head bowed.

"Father, I'm possessed. Please help me. The devil keeps moving home plate on me."

"Don't worry my son, I can return you to form," replied Guillen as he fought back a smile.

Suddenly, Hart's voice changed as he tried to impersonate Lucifer. He yelled back at Guillen in a veiled reference to a famous line from the Exorcist movie, albeit in baseball jargon.

"Your mother walks leadoff batters in hell," replied Hart playfully in reference to the cardinal sin of gifting the first batter of an inning on base via a free pass.

Guillen was in prime form as he quickly shot back with another reference to the hit movie in altered form again for Blake's baseball squad. "The power of Blake compels you. The power of Blake compels you to possess the Cardinals. The power of Blake Benson compels you to St. Louis! Now get the hell out of here Ryan. You're good, trust me."

Miguel began to call others to his "pulpit." He was clearly enjoying his self-proclaimed pontifical status and kept up the diatribe in preacher-like fashion, exclaiming his powers of salvation.

Ricky Gonzalez came up next, playfully accepting his role as he knew he would be a target after striking out four times in the last game. The outfielder had no problem asking for mercy and a clear spirit, as he truly was feeling guilty for his "baseball sins."

"Padre, I strike out four time last game. I feel shame," he spoke in broken

English, although the Spanish-speaking Gonzalez was actually quite fluent in English.

"Selfish pride entered me through the devil himself. I swing at 3-0 pitch with nobody on base. Feel shame and then I strike out. Boss man Blake cuss me out 'cause I'm no good selfish prick. Please get this no-good slump devil out of me."

Without missing a beat, Guillen repeated the same chant that he used on Ryan and then offered solace to the "suffering" Gonzalez.

"Don't worry too much about it. I take care of you and free you of your evil spirits. Hell, I once crossed up my catcher on purpose with the winning run on second base just to nail the no good sonofabitch in the mask when he got a fast-ball instead of a slider, " replied Miguel, forgetting for a brief moment he was supposed to be a priest and not a pitcher.

The playfulness continued as several more struggling players came forward to be cured of evil spirits by Guillen before third baseman Mike Simons approached. Miguel had a look of surprise as the good-looking Simons inched closer to the makeshift center stage.

"What the hell are you doing here Simons? You are on a hot streak lately and homered last game. I can't disrespect the streak and hurt your chances for today."

"Nah padre, I just want you to give me absolution for lusting in my heart," replied the stud third sacker that had quite the reputation as a ladies' man.

"Ah, I don't think so Simons. Our whole team does that. We're major league baseball players. That's a given. It's God's gift to us to be able to 'undress' those beautiful ladies in the stands."

"Agreed, but this was different Miguel. This sweet thing was your sister who was sitting behind our dugout the other day."

The band of brothers that was assembled all broke out in chorus, laughing at the suddenly peeved Guillen who was very protective of his younger sister and tried in vain to keep her away from his perverted teammates.

"Fuck you Simons. She's just 18. This padre just might put in a word to the man upstairs to sacrifice you to the devil himself, for the good of all humanity."

The tone was changing in an uncomfortable direction when Bartlett suddenly approached to change the topic. The man always was thinking of ways to irritate others, but this was an act of rescue and goodwill this time.

"Take me father, we all know I'm no good," shouted the feisty catcher.

Miguel laughed at the sight of the Rat approaching a man of the cloth and shouted Bartlett down with his hearty laugh.

"Even the devil is afraid of you Bartlett. It won't do any good to offer him to you. Dude wants nothing to do with you man."

Laughter erupted, as even Bartlett's teammates were never too sure which way the feisty catcher was going to turn from one moment to the next and kept a safe distance from him in all manners, mental and physical.

Blake was enjoying the playfulness from a safe distance. Part of him wanted to join in the fun, but he also knew as a manager that it was sometimes best to let his boys blow off steam without the fear of offending the boss. It was a delicate balance for sure, but the new role of player-manager was starting to kick in naturally for Blake rather than hesitation at every trial and tribulation.

Skipper Blake instinctively knew this was the time to step in and start the slow process of preparing for today's game. On this high note, Blake interrupted the playful uproar as he moved closer to the assembled squad.

"Well, I'm glad to see everyone is taking the Sunday loss so hard. Guillen, you're a piece of work my boy. Never has anyone been able to get away with so much with a smile, a paunchy beer belly and an ERA higher than your bloated body weight. It's a good thing you keep this clubhouse loose or you'd be doing standup at some Mexican dive lounge."

"Yeah, you guys would be nothing without me, that's for goddamn sure," retorted Guillen as he began the uniform transformation from clergy to major league ballplayer by ripping off his cassock. The hefty lefty looked very silly with nothing but a jock strap and a white collared black shirt barely covering his protruding waistline.

"Well, if audacity was a virtue, you'd be a saint, big man. It's time to focus a bit on baseball now boys. Let's get the ball rolling our way for a bit now. It's time to make hay while we're at home. Let's get those underworked and overpriced bodies loose. Guillen's taken care of our minds with his shtick. It's all good again."

The manager knew better than to look ahead at his team's schedule, but he knew next week's showdown with the Cards in St. Louis would be on everyone's mind as the road trip was fast approaching. Blake felt it was best to address the elephant in the room rather than avoid it entirely as he spoke his final pregame words.

"You guys have been in pro ball long enough to know that it's tough enough to play this game in the present without looking ahead to series against certain teams a week in advance. Let's concentrate on this series because if we falter here, it won't matter how we do next week or in the future. We've got to win games now, today, and the only way to do that is to focus on the present. Let's look at our game plan for these guys again. There are a few changes since our last advance report."

The team slowly shifted into game mode as the topics became mostly baseball related while players roamed about in various stages of uniform dress. The switch had been turned and it was time to focus on a sport where mental aspects nearly match physical as performance determining factors.

Blake had forgotten about his personal travails as he worked his way onto the field. Without baseball, he knew life would be just that much harder. His love for the game consumed his brain so much that it became all he could think about, and he liked it that way.

It's been said that despite the numerous decisions a manager makes over the course of the season, the difference in wins or defeat amounts to perhaps a handful of games. The game consumes those around it though, and Blake was doggedly determined to pull the right trigger in this last month to gain every tiny edge he could come up with. His former teammates deserved nothing less than full and total commitment to victory.

It was all baseball as Blake strolled around the batting cage, all baseball.

40 — Better Late Than Never

The air felt slightly drier and cooler as fall began to swallow up summer in Chicago as the Phillies came to town. Lake Michigan had started its annual change of disposition with balmy summer breezes from the south sourly switching to predominantly cooler north and east winds, eerily spreading reminders of the foreboding frigid winter.

Major League Baseball had its own seasonal calendar that marked certain changes of direction and ultimately personnel as the baseball year progressed. Generally, few transactions are implemented until past Memorial Day, as the lengthy season requires a significant sample size to make evaluations.

By the All Star break in July, teams usually have a fairly accurate depiction of their postseason possibilities and the rumor mill begins to churn up names on a daily basis. The general managers around the league start to play their marketing games around this juncture to eventually put them in the strongest position to make a one-sided deal in their favor.

The end of July comes and goes, with the trading deadline stabilizing rosters at the end of the month, with the exception of waiver deals like the one that in which Cubs acquired Sanchez from the Padres. Waiver deals tend to be minor in scope, but not always, compared to trades completed before the annual July 31 trading deadline. The final roster moves arrive with the advent of September when MLB allows its big league clubs to call up a handful of prospects from the minors as its season ends earlier. The month long experience prepares prospects for future big league seasons and offers the front office an excellent opportunity to evaluate their prized pupils against top-notch competition.

Teams rarely, if ever, call up anybody but a big league prospect, as maneuvering around MLB's 40-man roster limit requires a deft approach to protect their organization from losing its most valuable players to other organizations.

Unfortunately, there are a handful of very talented career minor leaguers that never get their one chance to prove they belong in the big leagues. Once a player becomes labeled as a career minor leaguer apparently lacking the physical tools to compete against the best, they languish, suffering long bus rides, cheap hotels and meager meal money. They either rot or become so disillusioned that they develop unhealthy chips on their shoulders and become a clubhouse-spoiling cancer on a team.

If the career minor leaguer can somehow keep his sanity after consistently being overlooked and run down, he can make a bit of money and become a name in the smaller communities of minor league baseball. Maintaining a somewhat positive attitude and suffering humiliation in silence can prolong a steady paycheck through a baseball job that often beats the real world.

The Chicago Cubs had one such unfortunate soul in outfielder Larry Hunter. The 33-year-old ballplayer had dominated at the minor league level for over a decade, but became strapped by talent evaluators as insufficient goods. The label was attached to his uniform with adhesive so industrial strong that it never could become unglued from his name.

Larry was a mild-mannered type that outwardly seemed to take everything in stride, but his heart contained a decade's worth of bitterness that was about to become unleashed in a performance fury, because of an event that had nothing to do with Larry Hunter. It was all due to the airline tragedy that struck down 43 human beings who still had so much life in them until that summer's day just outside of St. Louis.

The Cubs organization had become depleted as a result of the terrible accident. Prospects had to be moved up the organizational ladder sooner rather than later as expediency rushed their promotions through without merit in most cases. This ultimately led to the unexpected promotion of Hunter to the big league club on September 1, even though he wasn't considered a big league prospect. There were few other options available without exposing future big leaguers to the availability of acquisition by major league rival executives.

While the Cubs of September were dealing with the day-to-day pressures of a pennant race, Hunter was on cloud nine and loose as a goose at the once-in-a-lifetime chance to personally experience big league baseball.

The first few games on the bench were nothing to write home about for Larry, but he was there in the big leagues and more than willing to sit and stare at his name on the manager's scorecard at the bottom of the list of available players for games.

A smidgen of bitterness began to creep into his uniform after several days as the thrill of daily life in the big leagues began to recede from his psyche. Now he wanted his chance to prove he belonged here years before a tragedy offered him a strange twirl from an opportunistic if not desired twist of fate.

The Phillies were riding high at the moment with a strong 8-3 record in their last 11 contests when they rolled into Chicago to start their three-game series. The pitching rotation for the weekday series appeared to favor the Phillies, with the Cubbies at the bottom of their starting rotation. Philadelphia was throwing their ace in the first game, Travis Oliver, a potential Cy Young candidate himself this season with a 18-6 mark and a minuscule 2.25 ERA. The Phils were deep in starting pitching and the next two contests looked like unfavorable match-ups for the North Siders of Chicago.

Blake's squad was hoping to get off to a fast start and put the recent tough loss to the Mets behind them, but events definitely did not develop as wished for the Cubbies. The team fell behind early 4-0 and the strong pitching of Oliver put a damper on the dugout and in the Wrigley stands, as Philly seemed content to coast with a comfortable 4-0 lead with their ace behind them.

The game slowed to a crawl in the middle innings with the Phillies unconcerned with more offensive production as the Cubs long man, Earl Richards, a seldom-used soft-tossing lefty, held the opponents in check until he wilted a bit and allowed another insurance run to leave Blake's team five runs down after six innings.

Blake had to make a few more managerial moves than desired, but because of the expanded rosters of September, he wasn't too concerned with using every available option in an attempt to get something started in the right direction. The bottom of the seventh inning rolled around without even a whiff of victory this afternoon.

The crowd came to life a bit with another rowdy rendition of "Take me out to the ballgame" that was made famous by legendary Chicago announcer Harry Caray, but the act seemed more like a sideshow than a serious attempt to provide excitement for a comeback.

Blake was going through pinch-hitters and pitchers in whirlwind fashion that seemed to lack any significant strategy, but the manager had credibility now with his players. Nobody batted an eye in the dugout as the game seemed like a lost cause. In a 162-game season there are a handful of games where you simply have to tip your hat to a remarkable pitcher with electric stuff and take the beatdown like a man. This seemed to be such a case as the home team could not get anything started and did not even have one runner in scoring position for the first six innings.

Like many rallies, this one started innocently enough with a hit batter. Then Sanchez flared a bloop down the right field line, just finding a bare spot between three converging fielders as the second baseman, first baseman and the lumbering right fielder couldn't quite catch up to the well-placed batted ball.

Even the Wrigley crowd could not believe in this rally yet as Oliver still looked to be in complete control when Bartlett came to bat. The "Rat" was 0-2 with two strikeouts today and looked overmatched in both plate appearances. Blake stuck with his catcher even though the thought of pinch-hitting came to mind. The manager would have to replace Bartlett with himself and pinch-hit with another. It just did not seem like a baseball wise move, effectively wasting two players for one.

Bartlett was as smart as they come and he could guess with the best of them regarding pitch selection. He purposely lunged over the plate as the first offering came in right down the middle for a called first strike. The cagey veteran was setting up both battery mates as Bartlett correctly assumed the young Philadelphia catcher and Oliver would come back inside with the heat to move

172 – Timothy F. Bouvine

him off the plate. There is nothing like a wounded duck flare down the right field line off a filthy down-and-away slider to get a pitcher concerned that opposing batters are cheating over the plate.

Oliver's exploding fastball came in shoulder high and tight as expected. All Bartlett had to do was turn his back into the pitch with a slight rightward twist and the high heat struck him a glancing blow. Bartlett spun to the ground in Academy Award-winning fashion and just like that the bases were loaded. The overpowering pitcher was suddenly steaming at the clear acting job by the Rat, who was definitely entitled to first base, as the pitching gamble of throwing inside didn't pay off this time.

Philadelphia manager Billy Thompson played right into the uproar by vehemently arguing the call. All he accomplished was further riling up the Wrigley faithful into a consistent roar as the home plate umpire confirmed the beaning, motioned a fallen Bartlett to first base, and tossed Thompson from the game with a violent heave-ho.

Bartlett sprinted to first the moment the ump threw Thompson out, further angering the fuming skipper of the Phillies. All the Rat did was smirk in Thompson's direction as he playfully rubbed his own shoulder as a not-so-gentle reminder of his shenanigans.

Oliver was livid as well and by now it was apparent he was out of control and needed to be pulled from the contest. He fell behind the next batter 3-0 before throwing a fat pitch right down the heart of the plate on the automatic 3-0 offering before the next pitch was lined up the middle. The two-run single narrowed the Phillies' lead to 5-2 with runners still on first and second with nobody out.

Philadelphia had a normally stellar bullpen, but one chink in the armor can turn a reliable bullpen into a mess. Setup men have become very valuable in modern day baseball. However, there's a reason why they are not quite closer material, and today's setup man simply didn't have it.

Charlie Jones had been struggling of late for the Phillies as he was trying to fight through some elbow discomfort late in the season. By the time September rolls around many pitchers are dealing with fatigue, soreness, and ligament inflammation. It goes with the trade. Jones would only be called upon to get a couple of outs before likely being replaced by another setup man in lefty Paul Gibbons, so it didn't appear to be a poor managerial move by the man chosen to replace the ejected skipper Thompson, third base coach Jim Thorn.

A seeing-eye ground ball that just barely rolled into the slightly higher than normal outfield grass between the third baseman and shortstop plated another run to bring the home team within two. The fortunate base hit further electrified the crowd, as the upcoming situation required some pretty nifty managerial decisions with the pitcher's slot coming up next in the batting order.

A pinch-hitter was a no-brainer, but which player to select off the bench would be a gutsy call. Blake had his main lefty swinger Justin Moreland awaiting his call even though it was still only in the seventh inning. The staid baseball book encouraged a manager to save his top stick for a late-in-the-game decisive moment, but most opposing managers knew by now that Blake Benson had thrown his baseball book into the garbage and went by the seat of his pants. The seventh inning was borderline late in the contest, but the more important factor to Blake was his knowledge of the current situation.

Blake knew Charlie Jones firsthand when he caught the Philadelphia reliever earlier when Jones was a Cub. The wise veteran Blake knew Jones continually had problems with his elbow and hated to throw his slider when in pain, as Jones was rumored to be at the present time. If Blake countered with lefty Moreland, Philadelphia would undoubtedly counter with their lefty rookie phenom Paul Gibbons.

All that Blake had left as an option beside Moreland and himself was Larry Hunter, who was a right-handed stick. The book on Hunter was that he could not hit the breaking ball and that continually held him back in the minors. Benson decided that Hunter against Jones was a better match-up than Gibbons versus Moreland, so he called out Hunter's name in a very emphatic manner to encourage some confidence in the oldest newcomer in baseball.

"Larry, come on over here. I've got a hero's recipe in my back pocket for you. Grab your bat and go hit for the pitcher."

"This is exactly what I've been waiting for my whole life Skip. I don't need no recipe, just this weapon in my hands," as he pointed to his solid black bat.

"Just in case, I know exactly what you'll be getting from Jones. He won't throw his slider because he's hurtin' and just how do I know this?"

"Because you guys were teammates before," replied Hunter, who was no wide-eyed knowledge-lacking rookie after spending over a decade in the minors.

"Exactly, he won't do it. He's always afraid of blowing out his elbow. The catcher will signal him for a slider if he gets to a two-strike count on you, but he will continually shake him off until Jones gets the fastball sign. You can bet on it. He might throw a four-seam fastball instead of a two, but it will be nearly the same velocity. Just sit on that speed and you'll rope it somewhere. I'm confident you will hammer it, big guy. I'm calling it right now."

The public address announcer belted out Hunter's name and the crowd politely applauded with a slight hesitation that spoke volumes about their perceived chances with this maneuver. Most fans likely expected the popular Moreland's name to be announced and it felt like a momentary pause was in the Chicago air as the Cubs fans in attendance grasped about for familiarity from a name that was only hesitantly familiar at best.

Hunter even had old school mannerisms as he readied himself for the biggest plate appearance in his professional life. He took his deep rich black bat and smacked its barrel against the instep of both feet to clear his spikes and perhaps steady his nerves. He tugged at both sleeves with his weather worn leathery hands and pulled his jersey toward his shoulders, exposing a pair of massive arms to the crowd.

The conservative old vet didn't believe in batting gloves and he grasped the handle of the bat with his left hand and tapped it on home plate while staring down the pitcher on the mound. He never took his eyes off of Jones as he dug a slight hole in the right hand side of the batter's box with his rear foot, erasing what was left of the chalk line at the back end of the box, ready for battle against Jones.

Larry apprehensively took a called strike as he tried to shrug off his nerves. It looked like a four-seam fastball to him, his eyes still razor sharp after accurately recognizing thousands of pitches during his career. The next pitch came in a bit low and away and again he noted to himself that it was another four-seamer. The next offering from Jones had a bit of different tilt to it and he recognized the pitch as a sinking two-seam fastball with its tumbling rotation. He had failed to account for the heavy sink on Jones' pitch and Larry swung mightily, but fouled it off near his front foot.

Although he was down to his last strike, Hunter was still confident because his manager assured him that Jones would not throw his strikeout pitch given health worries. He dug in looking for a fastball and when he saw the reliever shake off his catcher's sign, he knew what was coming. It would be a hard and hopefully straight four-seam fastball without the sink.

The offering was waist high and over the plate. Clearly, it was a mistake pitch and one which had "belt me" written all over it. Larry's eyes lit up like fireflies before launching himself into the pitch with violent force. He squared up the fat pitch perfectly and sent the baseball well onto Waveland Avenue with a monstrous three-run blast that put the Cubs in the lead 6-5.

The delirious throng at Wrigley began to chant "Laaarrryyy! Laaarrryyy! Laaarrryyy!" as the career minor leaguer rounded the bases in an impromptu mix of jumps and strides like a frolicking rookie ballplayer. He stomped on home plate and high-fived his new teammates waiting for him on the dugout steps as he proudly descended into the dugout like a returning war hero.

The chanting would not cease and in fact became louder as the noise reverberated throughout the surrounding neighborhood affectionately known as "Wrigleyville," until the newest Cubby fan-favorite returned to the playing field for a curtain call. Hunter doffed his cap to the crowd and tears rolled down his cheeks. A decade long of internal frustration had been expelled in one emotional purging.

Nothing makes a group of grown men more uncomfortable than tears. His teammates scattered as Larry returned to the dugout and allowed the emotional Hunter time to compose himself in the walkway to the clubhouse before a sense of normalcy returned to the situation. Two more innings were still required to ensure a happy ending for this moment.

The miraculous moment was preserved as the home team held on for a 6-5 triumph. Guillen came on for a perfect eighth inning and Ryan held off a brief two-out rally that saw the Phillies put two runners in scoring position before a long fly out to the wall in left field was hauled in. The crowd exhaled in relief as the Cubs won another dramatic come-from-behind victory that put them three games up on second-place St. Louis who were stumbling to the last place Astros in Houston.

A surge of adrenalin flowed through the team, propelling them and Hunter throughout the three-game series ending in a Chicago sweep. Blake decided to ride the emotional wave that Hunter ignited by inserting the newcomer into the starting lineup for the remaining two games. The oldest "rookie" in baseball went 4 for 8 in the two games with 3 RBI as Blake strategically placed Hunter in front of the Cubs' hottest slugger, Arnold, to help Larry see more fastballs to his liking.

The pitching more than held their own in the 4-1 and 6-2 victories, but it was difficult to tell if Philadelphia just had cold bats or the pitching was supreme. The dramatic first game had seemingly taken the wind out of the Phillies' sails as well as uplifting the Cubs.

The team was riding high as Philadelphia left town with their tails between their legs. Larry Hunter's dramatic blast had put a different light on the team's fortunes in a once-in-a-lifetime-lightning strike. In the blink of an eye the Cubs had surged to a five-game lead over the Cardinals who had crashed and burned in the Houston heat.

Blake knew danger was lying ahead, even though his team was in their best position since being swept by the Cards in the Cubs' first games back from the disaster in early August. Human nature would now play tricks in the players' heads. The time between this series sweep and the arrival of the Pirates would give them a false sense of security five games up in the standings, but the veteran Blake was keenly aware of how quickly fortunes can change in this sometimes crazy game of baseball.

The sense of actually being in a position to win their division would creep into their collective psyche, which could work against them as well. In the game of baseball it is better to react than think. The Cubs would now begin to think too much and react too cautiously. Some call this human behavioral pattern of tentativeness as the crippling condition of choking, and it was about to rear its ugly head in the Chicago Cubs clubhouse.

176 — Timothy F. Bouvine

41 — What Goes up Must Come Down

Confidence in the baseball world can be momentary, like a woman's seemingly natural right to change her mind. One minute a player or team can be so sure of success that events seem to take on a life of their own, as if a switch can simply be flicked that will magically bring out a desired result. Just as quickly, confidence can wane from downright cockiness to self-defeatism in a matter of several at-bats or a few collective poor performances from a team.

Such was the case of Blake's version of the Chicago Cubs as the Pittsburgh Pirates flew into town. It takes two competing teams to tango and just because one squad is riding high at the moment doesn't mean that the opposing group of ballplayers cannot have a similar swagger about their recent play as well.

The Pirates were red hot themselves with a six-game winning streak. Two streaking performers were carrying the Bucs on their collective backs. Perennial All-Star outfielder Perry Sanderson was having a career season with 40 home runs and 106 RBI with less than 25 games to go in the regular season. He was batting a blazing .500 in the last week with five homers, while the slugger following him in the batting lineup, first baseman Roberto Cuellar, was currently sizzling as well with a .425 BA and 12 RBI over a two-week period.

The national press and local media of Chi-town simply could not get enough of this amazing story. Each player had a good story. It did not seem to matter what else was happening in major league baseball. The Cubs were THE story.

Unfortunately for Blake's team, the mass following and attention shifted the Cubs' focus from a pennant race to celebrity status and its accompanying distractions.

How could a team play with any sense of unity when the national media was clamoring for any type of story angle from any one of the 30 members on its roster? The reporters' pleas for interviews simply became overwhelming to the point where Blake knew he would have to shut it down or at the very least, restrict his players' availability, so his squad could remember what the main goal was here in his clubhouse. Blake was carrying around a huge sense of responsibility on his shoulders for his fallen teammates and their families. He would be forever bound to recalling their accomplishments and the team's proud moments from the past.

It was too bad for the Cubs that it took a disastrous three-game stretch at home before everyone became aware to the damaging aspects of fleeting fame. The Pirates climbed all over the Cubbies, outscoring them 30-8 in the sweep of the weekend series. The Chicago pitching staff had no answer for the dynamic duo of Sanderson and Cuellar who combined for five home runs and 10 runs batted in. The 8-2, 12-3 and 10-3 one-sided contests of the weekend were not even as close as the lopsided scores indicated. The Pirates scored early and often in each game and the Cubbies' offense provided little resiliency themselves never mustering much of an offensive output at any time in the series.

To make matters worse there were numerous mental mistakes that clearly exhibited a lack of focus. The base running was atrocious, with players running the team out of any rallies with unnecessary and unwise daring moves that consistently backfired. The defense was shoddy with seven noted errors and several other mental miscues such as throwing to the wrong base and even forgetting how many outs there were in an inning while playing defense. Remarkably, Desmond Wilson tossed the normal inning-ending baseball souvenir into the crowd… except there were only two outs in the inning.

The weekend was a complete disaster other than the momentary relief that the second-place Cardinals themselves provided by winning only one out of three against the Milwaukee Brewers in St. Louis. The margin of the Cubs' lead was reduced to four games. Blake clearly had a major task ahead of himself in refocusing his team while outwardly showing confidence in their abilities.

Blake was tempted to call a meeting after the final drubbing on Sunday, but he knew the team would be ready for the upcoming series with the Cardinals. What he needed now was to acknowledge what had just transpired over the weekend and to use his vast baseball knowledge and experience to reassure his players that he had seen this type of regression before. The manager would take the blame for this weekend meltdown. He knew this was a possibility and he didn't prepare his squad for it. At least that was his current story and he was sticking to it as he addressed the team post game.

"Well that was sure a butt-kicking weekend boys. It's been awhile since I've seen such a comedy of errors. Forgetting how many fucking outs? Come on. Getting thrown out by 10 feet at third base with nobody out and down by five runs. I know you guys understand this game better than you showed this weekend. If I was still drinking I'd just go out and forget about our lost weekend by downing a quart of whiskey, but I'm now responsible for you bums and I can't do that. At least you guys can. This one was on me, guys. I let you all down by not warning you about the pitfalls of success. We got distracted by fame and fortune. Screw that fortune bit, but you know what I mean. We've got to stay humble and concentrate on each and every moment at hand. It's our only hope. Let's get back to error-free ball and make the other team at least beat us rather than giving it to 'em. We'll get it back starting tomorrow. I know you can beat those damn Cardinals. A month ago I wasn't so sure, but now I damn well know we can beat 'em. I fucking know it! Don't get too down boys, this kind of thing happens to the best of them and believe me, you ain't the best of them."

Blake finished his speech with a smile indicating he was joking about the last reference. He took off his baseball cap and threw it in the garbage. Then he took off his uniform and all of his undergarments and tossed them in the garbage bin as well. He stood there with his bare ass and posed for a moment for all to see as he shouted.

"This weekend was all garbage and I just got rid of my shitty garbage. I suggest you all do the same. We'll have new home uniforms ready when we come back. Tell the fucking equipment men to burn 'em all and make sure they know I said so. We'll see ya at the airport."

Blake strolled ever so slowly to his office for effect while turning around his head to let his boys know he was doing this all in fun. The message was serious if not the method. He closed his manager's office door and plopped his naked body in his chair, all the while shaking his head at what he just did. Blake had no idea where that just came from, but he just went with that impulse. Maybe someone else was talking through him. Just maybe it was someone else who perished before their time a mere 30 days or so ago.

42 — Blake on a Hot Tin Roof

The anxiety built in Blake as he drove northward along Lake Michigan's shore to his home. Any baseball person would understand the importance of the upcoming five-game series with the Cards and Blake knew it could be a defining moment for his squad, one way or another.

Baseball is meant to be played with relaxed intensity. That sounds like an oxymoron, but a baseball player's demeanor says a lot about his confidence level. As the leader of his team, Blake well knew and understood that he must set the emotional tone for his boys. If he looked and acted uptight, it surely would spread to the rest of his teammates and performance would suffer. His players needed to be extremely mentally focused, but comfortable enough to react instinctively, without too much thinking.

Thinking can lead to the slightest amount of hesitation that will put a swing behind a 90-mile-per-hour fastball or put just enough doubt into a pitcher's head on the upcoming pitch to negatively affect the break and liveliness of his pitches.

Blake could feel his increasing uneasiness, but he didn't know how to alter it either, as he got closer to home. He was accustomed to weaning his anxiety level to acceptable levels through several stiff drinks after he pulled into the comfort zone of his house. Worldly anxieties would slowly seep into a separate compartment in his brain. They would always be there for him to deal with on a subconscious level, but for several brief hours he could live in another world free of extreme worry.

That was no longer a viable option, but Blake, in his brief sobriety, couldn't come up with a healthier alternative, at least not yet. He anticipated an evening with Kim at home with irritability, stress, and distractions carrying the tone before the upcoming 11-game road trip.

Baseball had dominated the past week; he'd had very little personal interaction with Kim. The lingering effects of their most recent disagreement had not yet been displaced by the feeling of loneliness that hovers around both husband and wife as reality begins to set in of their time apart associated with every long road trip that baseball has to offer.

Kim had prepared a substantial dinner with several courses in an attempt to fill up the evening with pleasantries and hopefully some meaningful conversation. She could never let go of her instincts to solve problems out in the open and in a direct manner. Blake preferred subtleties and minor adjustments without rocking the boat. He liked to steer the conversational vessel into a safe harbor, waiting out the rough sea until the skies cleared, before he cautiously ventured back into open waters. Kim operated on a rushed schedule that could not, or would not, wait out stormy seas. It was generally full steam ahead with Kim Benson.

It was not yet determined how this night would play out or whose course of action would prevail. Kim knew there were major obstacles to Blake's continued sobriety immediately ahead, while her husband understood his recovery depended solely on the tenacity to remain sober. He wanted to bear his burden alone, while Kim felt the necessity of openness and willingness to accept outside help in the healing process.

Two strong-willed people with clashing styles, each convinced of their own remedy, did not bode well for the evening's hope of relaxation before the stress of the road trip slowly engulfed their respective bodies.

Blake was immediately pleasantly surprised at the ambience Kim had staged for the evening as he entered their immaculate home. The aroma of Italian food filled the house with just the right amount of garlic and herbs sprinkling the invisible air, teasing the senses of upcoming desires.

If first impressions are lasting, this was going to be a surprisingly enjoyable evening, as Blake felt a sudden sense of appreciation for all the effort Kim was showing. There was no way he was going to get a meal like this on the road, no matter how exclusive the restaurant.

Kim sauntered in from the kitchen area knowing her husband had just arrived despite her preoccupation with the dinner preparation. A meal like this was no easy endeavor with strict timetables to ensure the upcoming meal presentation was aligned just perfect for the palate.

"Hello honey, I took it on my own to surprise you with a little treat tonight. How do you like the setup?"

Candles were flickering as if the gentle aromas were teasing the flames, and lights were romantically dimmed, while the dinner table had fresh cut flowers neatly organized.

Blake was stunned, pleasantly so, and he remarked in reverence to Kim at her flair for the romantic this evening.

"Kim, you've no idea how wonderful this has been. This is exactly what we needed tonight. It's magnificent, as are you. "

"Thank you Blake. I think I outdid myself tonight. Now you just sit down and let me entertain you in the fashion you deserve before hitting the road. This is going to take a while, as this isn't a one-course meal. I'll turn on some soft music and get you some water. Or would you like a soda?"

"Hell, let's live it up tonight. No water for me. How 'bout an ice cold Coke?" Blake was obviously enjoying the moment as he playfully accepted his Coke, pretending to sniff and deftly sample the beverage like a fine bottle of wine.

Kim started off the evening's food entertainment with an antipasto salad platter served in a fine pottery bowl. She placed the focaccia bread alongside the platter and returned to the kitchen. She came back with minestrone soup and sat down across from her husband.

"Now don't eat too fast or too much of any one thing. There's so much more to sample, hopefully including me tonight, so don't overdo it. There'll be no dozing off this evening from a full stomach. Let's enjoy a bit of this and I'll bring in the main entrée in a bit."

"You're kidding right Kim? There's more? Geez, you did go all out. It must have taken all day. Good thing we didn't go to extra innings or anything like that. Could've been a disaster with a longer than normal game."

"Sometimes you just have to take chances. Kind of like your recent managerial style, right babe?"

"I suppose, but my chances are coming up blanks recently. I guess that's about to change," replied Blake as he was still in astonishment at the elaborate presentation.

"Yes, this is going to relax you and you'll be raring to go when you hit the ballpark in St. Louis. That and some awesome lovemaking tonight will put a huge smile on your face as you get set to leave town tomorrow."

"Either that or I might be unduly distracted with such pleasant memories," Blake said with a smile to make sure his wife knew he was just joking.

They spent the better part of a half-hour chatting and enjoying the food before Kim got up and returned with the main portion of Blake's going away meal.

There was chicken Parmesan and Blake's favorite, lasagna. He wasn't too surprised with that item as his acute sense of smell recognized the familiar aroma. Blake's eyes widened as he was relishing the dinner delight and his wife's show of affection this evening.

Kim even topped of the dinner portion of the evening with a sumptuous dessert: Chocolate-filled cannoli shells with ricotta cheese, powdered sugar, vanilla, cocoa and toasted pecans, accompanied by a delicious espresso coffee.

There was little or no talk of baseball or life's problems. They held hands and gazed in each other's eyes while reminiscing about their long ago dating period.

Kim suggested a casually paced stroll outside, as it was a beautiful sunny evening with just a hint of cool air on the horizon. They laughed, kissed and had long periods of nothing but silence, buttressed by the human touch of two people in love.

The romantic couple topped off their night in bed with a lovemaking session that seemed so far out of the ordinary that they both felt like the dating couple all over again, at least for this one extremely pleasant and remarkably unexpected evening.

Blake lay awake before falling asleep in his own bed for the last time until he would return a week and a half later. Baseball was the last thing on his mind now, exactly what the doctor ordered. He was still in a state of relaxed bliss, almost unaware of his upcoming crucial road swing, as his night ended.

Tomorrow would bring reality back into play with its personal challenges and tension. Tonight was an unexpected, but timely remedy for the uptight, nervous Blake of a few hours ago. He had been rescued from the hot tin roof by the love of his life. The new manager would need every ounce of energy and willpower to make it through the temptations that accompany the stress of a pennant race road trip.

43 — A Bit too Close for Comfort

Kim drove Blake to Wrigley where the Cubs would be bussing to the airport as a team this clear, crisp morning in Chicago. The mood was somber in the car as it normally was before Blake left on an extended road trip.

Blake was still in a bit of shock over last night's unbelievable surprise and he had no idea where that all came from, but he was so relieved that the night was devoid of tension and arguments. He was even a bit hesitant to bring up the previous night because he just wanted to leave town on a high note for a change.

The silence continued for the whole ride except for gentle music emanating from the Cadillac Escalade's speakers. Kim had become quite the city driver over the years and traffic did not rattle her anymore. She pulled into the manager's designated parking spot and sat quietly while Blake got his luggage from the trunk of her black car.

He casually moved to her driver's side door while Kim got out and gave Blake a long kiss, followed by a momentary hug before she quickly got back in without saying a word. It was obvious she was upset that her husband had to leave for the challenges of the road for what felt like the millionth time.

Blake immediately called out her name, as he could see the pain in her face despite her best effort to shield her agony from her husband.

"Kim, stop for a second," Blake shouted out to her while motioning with his right hand to come towards him as she started to drive away.

Kim braked, but did not respond in any way until her husband finally had to move toward the still vehicle. He walked right up to the driver's side, knocked on the window before his wife finally opened. She turned to Blake and started to cry. He bent over to kiss her again and tried to reassure her that it would all be okay.

"I just wanted to tell you how much I appreciate all you do for us, and last night was something special. Your kindness and affection solidified everything that I have going for me right now. Honey, I won't jeopardize anything while I'm gone. I can promise you that. It's going to be fine. I'll call you from St. Louis after the game tonight."

"I'll be fine too Blake, I just worry too much," Kim replied, trying to stop crying while unsuccessfully attempting to speak in a smooth sentence.

Blake bent over one more time and kissed her on the cheek. He gently wiped away the tears welling from her eyes while offering more reassurances before she collected herself well enough to drive home. They waved goodbye to each other as Kim pulled out onto the street and disappeared into the Chicago landscape.

The loving husband of the moment transformed his soft demeanor into the skipper of his Chicago Cubs as he pulled his luggage toward the waiting charter bus. It was now time to set the tone for the trip and this all-important series. He would have to display confidence and calm to his boys. It was time to flip the switch to the man in charge.

He walked onto the bus with a big smile and turned towards his team. Blake confidently shouted out in an attempt to perk his boys up.

"This is what I'm talking about fellas, the fun begins right now. We're in a pennant race and we get to test ourselves in a meaningful September series. It doesn't get much better than this. St. Louis here we come."

It was a rather subdued bunch of ballplayers the rest of the trip to the "Gateway City." That was disconcerting to the manager. Quietness often reflected a lack of confidence, based on Blake's years of baseball experience.

The four-game lead over the Cards assured nothing at this point. Although somewhat enjoyable to possess, a lead can also make your team less aggressive. There's something to be made of the benefits of being the chaser rather than the chased at this point, but, all things considered, especially the talent discrepancy that favored the Cardinals, being in the lead was far more comforting to the Cubs.

The savvy Blake knew he would have to instill more confidence in his bunch before game time. He also promised himself to be more aggressive in his managerial decisions on the baseball field. He'd weakened in his resolve to throw away that staid baseball book that had been around for a hundred years like a sacred bible, untouched by deviation from baseball disciples too timid to question its relevancy.

Blake's biggest inner fear on this first leg of the trip didn't pertain to booze directly, but rather to the proximity to the crash site that put this whole crazy scenario in place. He knew precisely where the site was, and although he was fairly certain the flight plan would take them close to the scene of impact, he tried to keep this knowledge out of his consciousness as the plane started to make its slight change of altitude indicating the beginning of descent into St. Louis.

Even though he was not on that stricken aircraft, Blake could easily envision the likely scene inside the airplane at the moment of realization they were going down. Blake would be right next to Sandy in the third row of seats behind the coaching staff, invariably in the window seat as Sandy had a genuine fear of flying and wanted no part of visual cues as to their whereabouts.

The younger guys would be making plenty of noise from the rear of the aircraft with their card games and unending trash-talking, rituals of baseballs' down times from professional competition.

A few of the quieter guys would be isolated in their own thoughts or listening to their preferred style of music. Some of the really young were constantly on their electronic devices of varying types doing God knows what. Blake was part of a different era that could not relate to the constant attachment to these devices.

The manager Buck would be sleeping. That's all he ever did on flights. It was probably the only time he could get his mind of his managerial duties and he never failed to take advantage of it.

It was sort of a flashback for Blake even though he was not on that doomed flight. His vast knowledge and recollection of hundreds of flights put Blake on that plane in his mind.

Post-traumatic stress syndrome can take over the brain and torture a person by reliving the moment rather than simply remembering it. Blake was somewhere in between as the September version of the Chicago Cubs were just about to land at Lambert-St. Louis International Airport after their brief 65-minute flight.

Blake never liked to leave his seat belt on while flying. It was mostly psychological, as he did not want to feel in any way hindered if the unthinkable happened. True to form, Blake was staring straight ahead in a half-trance, half-conscious state while visions of the rapid descent of his former teammates played havoc in his brain.

Without a hint of warning, Blake stood up and screamed unintelligibly at the top of his lungs, startling all on board. Everyone was caught off guard by the outburst.

Pitching coach Mark Douglas, next to Blake, immediately got out of his seat and grabbed Blake in a vice hug, afraid that his manager was going to run up the aisle to the cockpit. He squeezed Blake and tried to snap him out of whatever terrifying state he was experiencing.

Just as suddenly as Blake changed from a subdued passenger to an obviously emotionally troubled man, and the skipper returned to his normal self, albeit highly embarrassed. He reassured Douglas that he was fine and returned to his seat. This time he was sure to buckle himself in to allay concerns of another disruptive display.

The whole team was stunned silent, but collectively they had a feel that their manager was reacting to the closeness of the accident site. Teammates looked around at each other and spread quizzical looks, but remained quiet as the plane was moments from landing.

Blake told his coaches that he just freaked out for a moment, but kept silent about his vision of former teammates. He tried to joke away the tension.

"I just saw a Nolan Ryan fastball coming straight at my forehead! Ah, I can't fool you guys. It was an eerie vision of my guys going down right about here. Sorry about that, I'm okay now. Wow that was way too fucking real. It was just my mind playing tricks on me."

Thankfully for Blake, the airplane landing provided a much needed distraction. After a short taxi to their gate, players and coaches went about their business

186 – Timothy F. Bouvine

retrieving their personal items before uncomfortably exiting the plane.

Their manager was still a bit too shook up to explain what had happened to his players. He smiled at his assistant coaches and softly explained that he would deal with his boys about the incident in the visitor's clubhouse at Busch Stadium.

The trip was not off to an auspicious start; the team appeared tense and their manager's behavior was raising eyebrows throughout the squad. The bus ride to Busch had an uncomfortable feel to it and the mood was hesitant as the club went directly to the ballpark. It was several hours to the start of the game with the Cardinals on a clear and cool evening and it appeared nothing could be done to loosen the team this night.

The pennant race was on and the marginally talented Cubs had a feeling they were walking into a hornet's nest in St. Louis. Unfortunately for the first-place squad, their leader was acting a bit stung before the hotly contested series even began.

44 — Man-up to Failure

Blake was struggling to explain his erratic behavior to his teammates and coaches. He knew he had to appear in charge, physically and emotionally, to be an effective leader going into a crucial five-game series incredibly crammed into a mere three days because of the scheduling dilemma created by the Cubs' tragic events.

Everything appeared to be going against the team at this moment. The re-vamped schedule clearly put the Cubs at a huge pitching disadvantage as dou-bleheaders put tremendous strain on pitching staffs. The new Cubs had a makeshift starting rotation at best, plus a bullpen that was currently heavily re-liant on just a few effective hurlers. The September call-ups were marginally talented and incredibly green as all prospects had to be moved up a level after the roster took a beating from the accident.

Coming off a disastrous series against the Pirates, with a shortage of pitching and a skipper who seemed on another planet, an incredibly unprepared bunch faced the Cards.

Blake focused on scouting reports and baseball jargon talking with his team prior to the opening contest. The team seemed to be awaiting some kind of de-tailed explanation to put them at ease regarding their manager's mental status, but "player" Blake overrode "manager" Blake in the clubhouse leading up to game time. He unwisely became obsessed with himself and the demons he was battling. His team rightfully expected their leader to focus on the big picture, but Blake mistakenly retreated to his inner self at exactly the wrong moment and put his team in an unfocused state.

The result of the opening game was predictable. The Cubs fell flat while the aggressive Cardinals and their own rabid fans smelled blood. It was bad from the get-go as the Redbirds plated four runs in the bottom of the first inning after the Cubs had gone down meekly in order to start the game.

Kyle Jacobson was on the mound again, just like the first meeting that started their second season, so to speak. The crafty lefthander appeared to be wiggling out of trouble after the bases were loaded with nobody out, inducing a meek comebacker to the mound to start a 1-2-3 double play, but a rather rou-tine grounder to newly acquired shortstop Sanchez clanked off the heel of his glove and reloaded the bases with two outs.

The gift of an extra out came back to haunt the Cubs as the home team's own new addition, slugging outfielder Tommy Carter, came through with a grand slam homer off the left field foul pole to give the Cards a quick 4-0 lead.

The Busch faithful roared in approval and the Cubs' spirit sank with the grand slam. It set the tone for the whole game as the Cubbies looked and acted

188 – Timothy F. Bouvine

like little boys against big men. Their body language was horrid; the team never mounted any kind of spirited opposition and appeared completely overmatched in all aspects of the game.

Blake wasn't much help this night as he slid deeper into the corner of his dugout and appeared disinterested. His mind was still elsewhere, confounded by his unexpected reaction on the airplane. Troubled by his own apparent lack of understanding, the rookie manager could not break out of his funk until late in the game when a routine play lit his fire again.

The Cubbies seemed to be just going through the motions in the top half of the ninth, anxious to put this game behind them, when a simple ground ball hit by Luis Sanchez provoked a symbolic turnaround.

Sanchez clearly beat the throw to first base as all could plainly see except first base umpire Lou Draper, who signaled Sanchez out. First base coach Billy McGuire and Sanchez argued to no avail before Blake realized his duty was to go out there and protect his player, plus defend his squad.

He may have been a bit slow in reaction, but it was more than made up for with intensity as the exchange between the manager and the umpire spilled over to the Cardinals first baseman.

The words that came out of Blake's mouth that sparked the whole incident were indeed rather ridiculous, given the moment and the last three hours of game time.

The expression of "my guys are out here busting their ass in a pennant race and you're taking plays off" in his argument with the umpire drew laughter and a smirk from first baseman Lenny Charles that Blake caught out of the corner of his eye.

He turned his wrath towards Charles and walked right up to the first baseman's surprised face and poked him in the chest.

"What, you think that's funny Charles? Tell me asshole why you think that's funny?" Blake kept his finger pressed against the 6-foot 5-inch 230-pound Charles, clearly wanting more than a debate out of this exchange.

"Benson, your guys have quit on you this whole game and you don't even realize it. Take a hike old-timer. I don't want to hurt you, but I will if you keep this shit up."

Blake became livid and it took the whole umpiring crew to restrain the manager from further attacking Charles. Blake was immediately ejected from the soon-to-be-ending game the second he put his hands on umpire Draper. The skipper left the playing field in a huff and walked through the runway to the clubhouse seething with anger before he quickly realized that the Cardinals first baseman was exactly right in his analysis. Perhaps that's what hurt Blake the worst and set him off without consciously realizing the truth in Charles' remark at the time.

He sat by himself in the empty clubhouse and gathered his thoughts just in time before his team began slinking in one by one. There was no denying a problem now. He knew he had to address the team and he knew it had to be done immediately before his players started to spread their own thoughts around the dejected room.

He didn't even communicate with his coaching staff before calling everyone together to listen to his mea culpa. The team gathered around their skipper in clear anticipation of what would happen next. Nobody had the gumption to begin to undress as the full team stood around Blake, heads down and shoulders slumped as Blake began to explain himself.

"I blew it guys. This one is on me. I failed you today. Unfortunately, it'll not be the last, but I want you guys to know that as manager of this team, I have to prepare you day in and day out for all our games, and in the biggest game of the season so far, I failed you all."

The team seemed to collectively lift their heads as Blake regained their trust and confidence in his ability to lead.

"It all started with the meltdown on the plane. I'm human and I cared so much about my extended baseball family that perished. We fought, we laughed and we cried many a time over lots of seasons. I lost it momentarily, but I let its effects carry over to the game today and that was wrong. It's understandable perhaps, but definitely wrong."

Coach Paxton started to intercede, but Blake motioned him down.

"Failure is what this crazy game of baseball is all about. It can eat us up individually and as a team if we don't realize and understand that goddamn baseball fact. The good part is that we get to move forward and try to erase past failures for a day or two before they invariably come back. The best teams don't really succeed, they just limit their failures better than the rest."

Now that Blake had their complete undivided attention he got to the meat of his apology.

"I promise to you guys today that I will give it my all, personal issues aside, or I will immediately step down as your manager. But what I want from you guys and will insist on, is that we never go down without a fight like we did today. Losing is one thing, but not caring is unforgivable. We all did that today. That's including me, but it will not happen again," Blake said with passion and conviction in his voice and in his demeanor.

"Now let's get real here. This fucked up series is a bitch. We got screwed. Playing five games in three days with this lousy dealt hand of cards is just not right. But we've got no choice. We'll just give it our all and take it from there. We'll have plenty of opportunities to right our ship regardless of what happens here. Now tomorrow we'll give it to 'em twice as hard. They'll know they've been in a battle. Tomorrow we go back to being the instigator rather than sitting back waiting for the other team to bring it to us."

"Coach, we got your back, it's just one of those things, said Miguel Guillen.

"Things? What things, Chubby? You gone loco?" Bartlett replied with curiosity.

"Things nobody can explain. They just happen. Now can we eat? You're still our leader, coach," philosophized the simple but perhaps accurately astute Guillen.

"Okay, I guess you just wisely summed up our existence, Miguel. It's just things. I'll remember that. Now go ahead and stuff that remarkably ample stomach of yours, but leave just a little bit of room for your brain to continue functioning at such a high level."

Blake assembled his coaches for a private meeting and put it all in perspective.

"I guess Guillen has it right after all. It's just things. Amazing how some people can say so much with so little. There's always gonna be things."

They all left the clubhouse wishing "things" would just go their way tomorrow. With two games, tomorrow would be full of lots of "things" and unfortunately they were still bad "things."

45 — Going Down, but With a Fight

With a three-game lead that appeared very precarious, especially after the drubbing of the day before, Blake's Chicago Cubs came to Busch Stadium on this day feeling somewhat better about themselves, their manager included.

The mentally exhausting day plus the busy playing schedule actually worked in Blake's favor as the night went by smoothly. The day-night doubleheader meant many hours at the ballpark and that was usually a good thing for Blake.

He and his team were up and at 'em early in anticipation of a very important day. Doubleheaders carried a great deal of psychological importance, as nobody wanted to get swept and lose twice the ground in less than half the time. Twin bills just seemed more difficult to sweep or be swept, and a split would be welcome by the front-running Cubs. It would stall the St. Louis momentum and give his Cubs team a bit of confidence, as they were winless in five contests against the Cards so far.

The air had been cleared after yesterday's mentally sagging blowout and the team was markedly more at ease this morning as the clubhouse began to fill up. Blake even found time to make a quick phone call to St. Louis first baseman Lenny Charles and apologize. There wasn't much playfulness, but there was a sense of calm that was lacking yesterday.

Blake tried to pick things up by encouraging his team to get back to some clubhouse silliness once in a while. He didn't want to see his team tighten up so much that they forgot to have fun every now and then. Laughter right after a tough loss would not be acceptable, but dwelling on the past with so much opportunity ahead was counterproductive too.

Blake knew he would have to catch one of the games today to give Bartlett a break, and he would tomorrow as well. His preparation was slightly different when he knew his on-the-field-services would be needed. Blake deferred a bit of authority to his delegated successor, third base coach Lenny Paxton, while Blake lay sprawled out on the trainer's table in anticipation of a lengthy massage to get his achy joints and muscles loose.

He called Bartlett over to the table and spoke in a hushed tone as the two crusty old backstops conspired together. It was not unusual to see the both of them in the trainer's room, so nobody would likely suspect any nefarious activities discussed between the two.

"Bartlett, I'm not going to spell anything out for you today, but keep the spirit in the boys for the rest of the series, if ya know what I mean?" Blake winked at his starting catcher and Bartlett winked back in approval. Nothing more needed to be said to a notorious instigator like the Rat.

Blake was catching the first game today so Bartlett could have a bit of rest after catching last night. His bench activity for this game made it easier for him to scheme while his manager had to deal with pitch calling and the handling of pitchers in game one.

Bartlett made sure everyone heard his clubhouse speech before the team took the field on a damp, dreary September afternoon. Just before the guys left their sanctuary he hollered out to gather round while he secured his teammates' attention.

"Yesterday was a disaster guys. Not the score, but just the way we went about it. We've got to take it to these guys today. Doesn't matter so much whether we win or lose, but just to show 'em we ain't gonna give it to 'em. They're going to have to earn it and we're going to battle them every step of the way. We're going to pitch hard inside, run everything all out on the bases, take out all double-play chances at second and do what we have to in order to get to that home plate. They're gonna respect us. They might get pissed at us, but they're gonna respect us at the end of the day. You know the Rat will be right there the minute it gets rough. Everybody got it?"

There were a few hoots and hollers, but most just shook their head up and down in the affirmative. At least they had a plan today and an attitude to go with it.

Blake went over the pitching game plan with his starter Terry Riley. The 10-year veteran was a junk-baller, plain and simple, but he could keep your team in the game provided he could keep the opposition off balance. The southpaw had a preference to zero in on the outside corner of the plate and entice the batters to chase his rather soft tosses. Blake had seen this approach work, but he knew Riley would have to keep those hitters honest inside to own the outside portion of home plate.

For whatever reason, Riley always seemed uncomfortable throwing inside and keeping those hitters from disregarding the inner half. Blake drilled into him over and over again that he had to pitch inside, and even during warm-up pitches he positioned his catcher's glove right on the inside corner to right-handers that would make up the majority of the Cards lineup today.

The Cubs offered little in the way of offense to open up the game in the top of the first. Blake wanted to start the game off aggressively on the base paths, but as they say, you can't steal first base. There were simply no opportunities; making a statement would have to come on the defensive side today.

The Cardinals led off with second baseman Jeff Dorman, a short, somewhat stocky player, a bit unusual for a middle infielder; he was a very patient switch-hitter that sprayed the ball to all fields, making him an excellent choice to bat first in any lineup.

He was a scrappy ballplayer that one would expect, given his lack of physical stature. He also liked to crowd the plate, which made him the perfect candidate to show the enemy that today was going to be much different than yesterday.

Riley's first pitch was a high and tight fastball that spun the spunky infielder around in surprise. The second pitch was right at his feet and forced him to shuffle out of harm's way. He called for time from yesterday's first base ump that was involved in the fracas, but had moved behind home plate in the normal umpiring rotation.

Dorman looked down at the crouching Blake and smiled uncomfortably, knowing this was a deliberate strategy meant to make a quick point to the home team. Blake didn't say a word, especially with the home plate umpire right behind him always looking for visual and audio clues of intimidating tactics like throwing at a batter. Blake just moved his body real close to the inside portion as if to say, you aren't going to change my pitch selection.

As Riley delivered the pitch Blake shifted to the outside corner and received a knee-high, outside corner strike. This was what big league baseball was all about. The gamesmanship was on. Riley delivered another inside fastball that jammed the right-handed hitting Dorman. His feeble pop-up to the first baseman Arnold made Dorman look every bit the part of a small, powerless batter, for this time anyway.

Unfortunately, as had been Riley's track record, he shied away from pitching inside to the next few batters, missing out over the plate, and the Cardinals batters laced three consecutive solid line-drive base-hits to the outfield. The last one was so solidly struck that the lead runner had little chance to make it home, and was held up wisely by the St. Louis third-base coach.

Blake called time and strolled out to his pitcher, but with an inner disgust that belied his slow gait. He took off his mask, put his catcher's glove over his face to keep the opposition from reading his lips and yelled at his timid hurler.

'Goddamn it Riles, that first batter was perfect and now you're pussy-footin' again. Go back inside," said the player-manager in slow but distinct expression. He walked back to the plate trying not to show emotion that might indicate disapproval of the pitching method. Experienced catchers were so aware of tipping their hand in any fashion.

As luck would have it, or perhaps fate, the next batter was the first baseman Lenny Charles from yesterday's fracas. No matter now, it was time to make a point again.

Riley simply decked Charles with a pitch that whisked right under the big first baseman's chin. He went down like he was shot, but dusted himself off as the home crowd howled in anger. He took a moment to collect himself and dug in as usual in the batter's box, deep and close to the plate.

The next offering from Riley was meant to be low and in, similar to the second pitch to the leadoff batter Dorman. Riley apparently hung onto the pitch a bit too long and it struck the slow moving Charles right on the left ankle. He was writhing in pain, but wanted to get up and charge the mound in retaliation. He yelled at Riley in no understandable words, but the message was clear.

Tensions were high, with the crowd screaming for blood and the Cardinals dugout on the edge of their steps just waiting to respond if the Cubs came out of their own dugout. They were hollering at the home plate umpire and at Blake, before they shifted their wrath toward the pitcher Riley, who had that blank look on his face like a crime suspect hiding their emotions at trial.

The umpire took off his mask and warned both benches and the pitcher Riley in one of major league baseball's stupidest rules. Warning benches, managers, and pitchers, that the next retaliation will result in an automatic ejection, is supposed to prevent further bean-balling attempts, but in reality just rewards the initiator.

Now both managers were pissed. Blake, because he insisted that his pitcher wasn't throwing at Charles, plus if any pitcher on the Cubs came close to a Cardinals player from here on out, both pitcher and manager would be tossed from the game leaving Bartlett as the only catcher left. The Cardinals manager Don Leighton was all charged up because his star player was down on the ground hurt and he couldn't retaliate.

The warning all but eliminated the pitching strategy that Blake wanted to use to send a message. At least the Cardinals were well aware that this Cubs team today would not be a pushover, but now Blake had a bigger problem with the bases still loaded and his squad already behind 1-0.

Charles had to come out of the game with an injured ankle that appeared unbroken, but x-rays were ordered to rule it out. Blake never wanted to see an opposing player hurt and tried to let the husky St. Louis first baseman know it wasn't intentional, but Charles would have none of that explanation.

Everybody knew there would be retaliation at some point. It was now simply a matter of when and how, not if. Leighton was old-school and the Cards' skipper would never let an incident like this one go unpunished. The teams would be on alert from here on out.

All things considered, Blake's boys came out of the inning fairly well as the Cards tacked on only one more run on a sacrifice fly before Riley induced a ground out to end the first inning with the Cubs trailing 2-0. The game could have been out of reach after one inning with an extra-base hit, but the 2-0 deficit seemed almost like a win for the Cubs at this point with Charles out of the game as well.

This time the Cubs came right back at the home team, with more of the type of baseball for which Blake had been receiving national credit from baseball types across the seemingly endless media spectrum these days.

Blake had reinserted newcomer and career minor leaguer Larry Hunter back into the lineup after the outfielder had slowed down some from his hot start. The manager correctly figured if anybody were to appreciate the moment and hustle their buns off, it would be Hunter.

Chicago opened the inning with a lead-off walk to Cubs cleanup hitter Ricardo Sanchez, followed by a hit-and-run single from third baseman Mike Simons, perfectly placed into the hole previously occupied by the Cardinals second baseman Dorman. The Cardinals infielder scampered over to cover second base after the pitch was thrown and vacated his normal fielding position. The well-executed maneuver avoided a double play and allowed Sanchez to safely reach third base. Chicago outfielder Larry Hunter was next up with runners on first and third with still nobody out.

Hunter swung and blooped a hit over the shortstop's glove that settled into no-man's land in shallow left center. Sanchez scored easily, and Simons advanced to third while Hunter surprisingly made a beeline for second base in a daring attempt at a double. The Cards left fielder threw into second in an attempt to nab Hunter, but the scrappy and extremely motivated Hunter slid head-first into second, just beating the throw. He jumped up quickly, asked for time from the umpire near second base and after his request was granted, Hunter pumped his fists into the air as the Cubs bench came alive.

The visiting Cubs had plenty of fan support at Busch, as is the norm between geographically close rivals. The Chicago fans finally had something to cheer about and let their voices be heard before they were drowned out by boos from the far more numerous St. Louis fans.

The Cubbies manufactured two more runs on consecutive sacrifice flies to take a 3-2 lead. Simons tagged up to score on a medium deep fly ball to right field. Hunter continued his daring base running by also tagging and barely beating the throw again, this time to third base. Larry then scored easily, tagging up once more on a deep blast to center that was hauled in by the Cardinals outfielder.

With a bit more spring in their step and a much-needed confidence boost, the Cubs took the field in the bottom half of the inning determined to go toe to toe with the Cardinals. Riley settled into a bit of a groove keeping St. Louis off balance with an assortment of breaking balls, orchestrated masterfully behind the plate by Blake. The veteran pitcher and the experienced catcher had the Cardinals batters talking to themselves in disgust at their inability to drive some very hittable pitches from the crafty southpaw.

The game action calmed down a bit, pausing the inevitable excitement as zeroes mounted up on the huge modern scoreboard that had become the norm at most parks except Wrigley and Fenway Park in Boston.

196 — Timothy F. Bouvine

It was still 3-2 in favor of the Cubs in the top of the sixth when the old seasoned and knowledgeable manager Leighton started to scheme a bit himself. He wanted to get into the Cubs bullpen in the worst way as he astutely analyzed the upcoming situation of back-to-back doubleheaders. If the Cardinals could wear down Blake's limited bullpen options, the remaining games would shift decisively in the Cardinals' favor since their pitching depth far outweighed that of the Cubs.

Leighton ordered his pitcher to throw a couple high and tight pitches to Blake when he came up. He reasoned accurately that the heightened tensions would provoke the rookie manager into losing his cool and putting his team in jeopardy for the rest of the contest with the Cubs' scarcity of available catchers. Blake insisted that he needed more pitching arms than a third catcher, but that made his team susceptible to maneuvers that could backfire.

After the second close pitch, Blake got a little heated with the home plate umpire that had previously warned both benches after the first inning beaning of Charles. The ump was no fan of Blake in the first place after his involvement in the umpire dispute with Dorman yesterday, and he didn't toss the Cardinal pitcher Barkley out of the game, as was his option.

The next pitch from the Cardinals' tall right-hander struck Blake on the thigh as was once again ordered by Leighton. This time the home plate umpire had no choice but to eject the pitcher, Barkley who was conveniently going to be pinch-hit for in the bottom half. The cagey Leighton didn't mind losing his pitcher to ejection and was hoping to entice Blake into charging the mound which would likely lead to his ejection.

Blake fell for the ploy and he raced out to tackle Barkley before the benches emptied. Order was quickly restored, as Blake clumsily missed the pitcher while other Cubs teammates held him back after he fell to the back of the pitching mound on the tackling whiff.

Blake was tossed from the game, as were Barkley and manager Leighton, as the rules mandated after the previous warning. Blake got played and gradually realized the wise, old manager Leighton had put one over on him as he left the playing field, as much angry at himself as the opposition.

Third base coach Lenny Paxton took over managerial duties in Blake's absence, but in reality Blake could still pull his coaching strings from the clubhouse. There were only a few innings left and the rookie manager figured he was still in the clear.

Leighton wasn't called the dean of all managers for nothing. He had the astute ability to find weaknesses in the opposition and exploit them. He pulled up a chair just inside the runway to the home team's clubhouse, out of sight from the umps' wrath, as he was supposedly kicked out of the game.

As Leighton stealthily peered out to the playing field, he knew he had the Cubs by the balls here if he could get Bartlett tossed as well. Even though he respected the storied manager, the two of them had a longstanding feud from Bartlett's days with the Cards when the St. Louis skipper let it be known to the media that the Rat was rapidly losing his baseball skills before they shipped him off to the Mets for basically a bag of balls, i.e., nothing.

Knowing each other as they did, the two of them were a perfect match. Both were highly competitive and would stop at nothing to come out ahead in a game of checkers, much less a major league baseball game.

Leighton let it be known to his teammates that the number one objective for the next few innings was to get under the Rat's skin any way they could. The savvy skipper figured the Cubs would come back at one of their guys with a beanball. If they didn't, Leighton figured that even if one of Riley's pitches were even close to one of his batters, the home plate ump would have to toss Riley from the game as well.

The Cardinals' skipper instructed his batters to spin out of the way of any offering that was even remotely close. However, he told his boys not to go after the pitcher, as is normally the case, but rather start something with Bartlett.

The two sides were both going to extremes here, but every game would be so vital from this contest forward that any move could decide the divisional championship. Each contest was essentially a two-game swing. A Cards win here would put them only two games back, but a loss would put the Cubs' lead up to four games and ensure that they would leave town in first place.

Blake didn't have to tell the veteran pitcher what needed to be done in retaliation. He just forwarded the message to his third base coach Paxton that Riley should use his baseball head and decide when was the right time to respond without putting the game's outcome too much in jeopardy.

With the home team batting in the bottom of the seventh and still trailing 3-2, Riley easily got the first two hitters out. It just so happened that the Cardinals catcher was standing in the batter's box at just the right time to retaliate.

The St. Louis catcher, Paul Evans, was no rookie himself. He had been around and he knew better than to dig in here. In fact, the veteran expected to be plunked and smirked at Riley as if to say, I know what you know before you even think it. The pitch came right at the hitter's rib cage, but Evans was aware enough to turn his back into the pitch. The pain would still be significant, but anything would be better than a shot to the unprotected rib cage.

Evans did exactly as instructed and put a bear hug on Bartlett before tackling him to the ground. The surprise reaction from Evans caught Bartlett so much off guard that Evans actually had to let go of Bartlett to make sure the Cubs' lone remaining regular catcher responded foolishly enough to get tossed.

Evans loosened his grip on Bartlett before launching into a vitriolic tirade against the Chicago catcher, knowing he had to get a response. Most knew enough of Bartlett to understand that he was a hothead who would strike back first and ask questions later. Sure enough, the Rat took the bait and planted his catcher's mask right on Evans' nose, bloodying him for all to see.

It worked to perfection for Leighton, who by now was sitting in the clubhouse laughing at the predictability of his schemes. Bartlett had fallen for the scheme, and the Rat was caught in the trap by his own hot temper.

Bartlett was chased from the contest, as were Evans and Riley, along with acting manager Paxton, as rules dictated.

This put emergency catcher Arnold into the game from first base and presented the Cubs with a serious handicap for the rest of the game. His previous appearance in this role was a disaster. Everyone knew the Cubs were at a huge disadvantage at the most critical juncture of the all-important first game of the day-night doubleheader that would go a long ways to determining the divisional pennant race.

Chicago got out of the last of the seventh without any more damage, as the pinch-runner for the tossed Evans was stranded at first base. The Cubs held a precarious 3-2 lead as the inning rolled over to the eighth.

The stellar St. Louis bullpen was taking over the game and shutting down the opposition Cubs and now it appeared the Cubs pen was going to have to close it out, as base runners were suddenly at a premium in this tight contest.

The Cubs went down in order and as the bottom half of the eighth inning began, Blake sent word to bring in his favorite lefty, Guillen, to shut down the Cards. Not only was the lefty the Cubs' best setup man, but being a southpaw enabled him to keep a closer eye on any potential base stealers from first. Arnold was a definite liability, but if nobody could get on base, it wouldn't matter.

Guillen was pumped like he had never been before, at least as a Cub. The adrenaline rush can work both ways however, especially for a pitcher. Overthrowing as a result of being too amped up can lead to wildness and even take away some much needed movement on pitches if not thrown smoothly.

Miguel walked the leadoff batter in the eighth, a cardinal sin if there ever was one in such an important late-season game. Now he was overly focused on the runner at first. He tugged at the back of his cap with his pitching hand and then wiped the same hand down the side of his pants. The moment was full of suspense and strategy as Guillen came to the stretch with his glove hand and pitching hand resting together. The wise move called for the southpaw to hold the ball for quite some time in a dual effort to freeze the runner at first and to get the St. Louis batter to tip his hand about the possibility of a sacrifice bunt.

The Cardinals batter became impatient and asked for time from the home plate umpire. He stepped out of the box and looked down again to the third base coach for confirmation of the signs he had just seen moments ago while Miguel toed the rubber and squinted at the catcher's brightly coated fingertips for the pitch selection.

Would the Cards bunt here or would they try to steal against the emergency catcher Arnold? The answers were about to come, but nobody could sense for certain what the next move would be, as Guillen paused and momentarily held his front right leg high to hold the runner before he unloaded the first pitch with his powerful left arm whipping past his thick torso and toward home plate.

The St. Louis batter took that pitch right down the middle and the runner stayed close to the bag at first. The pitch was one that any reliever would expect to throw in this likely bunt situation, especially with the bottom of the Cardinals batting order due up. Guillen guessed bunt and offered a belt-high fastball to the batter, but surprisingly nothing was happening on the bases or at the plate.

Perhaps a sign was missed, thought Guillen. Something should be happening here, one way or the other. Arnold called for a pitchout, a smart call with one strike on the batter and the possibility of a steal attempt in order. The pitchout came and nobody was giving away their intentions, as the runner never strayed and the batter simply took the high and outside pitch for a ball.

Blake was as puzzled as the rest as he picked up the game on the clubhouse screen. He simply had no idea what to relay to his team. He sat for a second and got right back up in a very fidgety state.

Guillen caught his breath and stalled a bit as he tossed over to first several times, alternating between his average pickoff move and his best deceptive move to first. The St. Louis crowd booed the tactic incessantly, but Guillen simply didn't care if the St. Louis fans screamed all night at him. This runner and batter were that important.

The third pitch of the sequence would tell the story. St. Louis was certain they could run on emergency catcher Arnold, but the tactic was to see as many of Guillen's pickoff moves as possible first. Guillen obliged with an assortment as wide as the nearby Mississippi River before finally delivering toward home plate.

The fastball came in at the high end of the strike zone, the pitch normally called for in this situation as the toughest to bunt and likewise the easiest for the catcher to come out of his crouch quickly to throw out a potential base stealer.

The Cardinals batter shifted into perfect sacrifice bunting position, knees slightly bent and bat out in front of his body near eye level as the runner took off from first. Just as quickly, the batter pulled the bat back in as the bluff bunt was on. The tactic worked to perfection as the batter got into the vision of the catcher Arnold. As the seldom-used backstop sprang up to get out of his crouch, he lost track of the pitch.

The fastball went right past Arnold's oversized catcher's mitt and all the way to the wall behind home plate. The Cardinals runner moved all the way up to third base on the passed ball as the home crowd screamed in excitement. Now the tying run was 90 feet away with nobody out and the Cubs and Guillen frazzled.

The lefty reliever lost all confidence in his catcher's ability to receive his lively pitches. He lost the fluid motion, and his reluctance to let loose with abandon took its toll on his command. Back-to-back screaming doubles in the left-centerfield gap plated the tying and go-ahead runs and sent the crowd into a frenzy before pitching coach Douglas had to come out to the mound to yank the composure-less Guillen from the game.

A clearly steamed Guillen didn't even wait for his coach to get to the mound as Douglas had already motioned for the right-hander option in the bullpen, a definite player no-no. He flung his glove against the dugout wall and walked right up the runway to the clubhouse in disgust, mumbling all the way in Spanish at a failed attempt to hide his anger directed at the third-string emergency catcher.

Blake stopped Guillen in his tracks and immediately took all the blame, falling for Leighton's scheme. Blake knew he had been outcoached in the biggest game of the year to date. Arnold was simply doing the best he could. It is the manager's responsibility to put his players in spots where they can best accomplish good results.

St. Louis tacked on an insurance run, manufacturing the third run of the inning with a ground out to second, followed by a sacrifice fly to plate the fifth run of the game, and the Cards took a 5-3 lead into the ninth.

The Cubs were beaten before the Cardinals even took the field for the last inning. They knew their chance at eking out a win had disappeared into the cool September air in the bottom of the eighth. Chicago went down meekly in the top of the ninth, displaying none of the fire that they had possessed for most of the game. The home team celebrated a hard-fought victory with high-fives and handshakes galore as the crowd stood and cheered throughout the inning, whooping it up on every strike as the first two batters struck out before a pop-up to short ended the game.

Their lead was down to two full games as the Cubs tried to regroup for the second half of the day-night doubleheader. Thankfully, there was ample time to calm down and return to some semblance of order for the nightcap. The team and Blake would need every minute of it.

46 — Familiarity Breeds Contempt

There was anger in the clubhouse, but for the most part, it was directed at the St. Louis Cardinals and their fans. Blake feared mutiny as a result of his poor managing but, except for Guillen, the team was steaming at the opposition that had now beaten them six times in a row.

The baseball hatred shown against the Cardinals was welcome news for the beleaguered manager. It was diversionary and it also showed his team was really emotionally into this pennant race.

Cubs' teammates were bitching about the Cardinals from their looks to their irritating mannerisms. Six humiliating losses in a row to this arrogant bunch was more than most of them could stomach. St. Louis had gotten into their heads and poisoned their minds with retribution rather than winning each individual match-up throughout the game.

The sting of losing a tight contest was multiplied by the day's events that included plenty of heckling from both Cubs and Cards fans, bean-ball fights and excessive showboating by St. Louis that irked Blake's team even more than the first two grievances.

The skipper let his boys blow off some steam for a short time before reminding them all that another game was coming up in several hours. There was a time and a place for everything before baseball routine would naturally take over.

"We're pretty lucky guys, we get to go right back at the bastards in a few hours. No waiting until tomorrow to get even. You can be sure of one thing. Those guys in the other dugout know they were in a battle today. Emotions are running high on both sides and there are plenty of battle scars to go around today. I've got a few of them myself, including some self-inflicted. There'll be no more emergency catchers. I'm sure Marty is already making a move to get us another catcher. I blew it. I thought two would be enough and I convinced Marty that Bartlett and I could handle it. I fucked up again, but we'll get over this together. I just want to thank Jim Arnold for not bitching and trying his best to help his team. He never once resisted my pleas for him to catch and I'm sure he dreaded it, right Jimbo?"

The big lumbering first baseman stood up and took the blame for the loss on his shoulders, disregarding the opening his manager had politely given him. "Any one of us could've caught that pitch from Miguel. I just missed it. No excuses. That play cost us the game and put an arrow in our lefty's heart. My catching is for the birds, Cardinals I guess," he said with a slight self-mocking laugh at the pun.

Blake immediately stood up for his big man and put any talk of blaming Arnold to rest for this tough loss. The man in charge clasped the baseball cap from his head, squeezed the lid and sent the cap whizzing through the air in frustration.

"Jesus Christ Jim, you're too nice of a guy sometimes. You did what you did for this team and not at all for yourself. We all know you can't catch a lick, but you put your teammates first. I just miscalculated the opposition. That fucking Leighton conned me and I'm not going to forget it. I've got a long baseball memory and his day will come, trust me."

The moment just couldn't go by without the pudgy lefty Guillen throwing in his two cents worth as he stood up and belted out his own apology, not before throwing his glove against the clubhouse wall to get his teammates' undivided attention.

"Aw Christ Arnie, I was just pissed at myself, but I couldn't accept my role in the blown lead. I lost it plain and simple. My composure went right out the goddamn stadium. I've learned that I've got to control myself better. I couldn't ask for a better teammate than you. Everybody respects you Arnie."

Blake couldn't resist and piped in his own retort before Guillen could get another word out of his apologetic mouth. "It's just things Miguel, just things. We've got your back, just like you did for me."

"Yeah, you got me there big fella. I own it. That's it in a nutshell. It's gone now. I just threw it away with the wind of one of Bartlett's annoyingly stinky farts. I'd recognize that brand anywhere."

The team all got a big laugh out of Guillen's joke and seemed to set the tone for the nightcap. Laughter began to slowly reemerge with increasing pace, followed by intensity. The squad had purged their sins, confessed and moved on. It was like a communal penance with Blake leading the prayers.

The next few hours were spent talking about anything but baseball. The pain and the memories were still fresh, but they were suppressed for the time being. The second half of the doubleheader would bring all those facets to the surface when the time came.

Blake indeed received a phone call from the general manager informing him that another catcher would be joining the club, addressing the problem all could see in hindsight. Another pitcher would have to be taken off the roster and Blake was not happy with that move, but he felt in no position to argue against the roster decision given his blunder in the biggest game of the year to date.

Blake's next phone call lit up Blake's antennae. He recognized the phone number. It was coming from the St. Louis manager's office. The crafty old sonofabitch Leighton was probably calling to defend his actions in the fracas today and Blake would have no part of it.

"Let that goddamned phone ring fellas," he instructed the other coaches in his office.

"I know why he's calling and I don't buy his likely regret. He can kiss my Chicago ass. I'll accept an apology after we knock those bastards out of the playoffs."

Blake felt an awful lot of respect toward Leighton after he had called to encourage the frustrated Chicago manager after their first series against the Cards ended so poorly for Blake and his squad. That emotion seemed to be from another galaxy at this moment. This feeling was just short of bodily harm to the old geezer.

The divisional pennant race was definitely on from this day forward. There would be no holds barred from here to the end of the regular season, and perhaps even longer.

47 — Close Only Counts in Horseshoes and Hand Grenades

Emotions had settled down and the pregame routine that ballplayers have been through countless times began to take over the Cubs' preparations as Busch Stadium was filling up once more for the second game of the day-night doubleheader in St. Louis.

There was even a hint of fall in the air in this normally hot, muggy city. The surest sign of cooler weather taking over the fall air is not football season, colored leaves or even longer nights, but rather the switch to baseball jackets again.

What had been a rare sighting of a baseball jacket in summer now became the norm as nights decidedly cooled down in the month of September in most parts of the country, especially the Midwest. While the air was cool, the fever pitch of the fans was white hot. The rabid fans could smell blood as the Chicago lead steadily dwindled. A victory tonight would leave the home team just one full game behind the Cubs.

The consensus from the sports media in St. Louis and indeed, the nation as a whole, was that any margin that was within a game or two would pretty much wrap it up for the Cardinals. Perception prevailed that this ragtag, makeshift Chicago squad could not keep up the pace with the Cards if the margin was close to even for the last two weeks of the season.

Blake was sitting this one out because he wanted to totally concentrate on managing. The game plan was for Bartlett to catch game two. The manager felt comfortable with Bowman starting the nightcap. He envisioned his savvy starter keeping his team in the game. There was the likelihood of several runs scored off Bowman, but not an excessive amount, as he usually didn't beat himself. His superior pitching command and his innate feel for pitching out of tight jams normally made for close contests.

The pitching match-up looked fairly even as St. Louis countered with a back-of-the-rotation guy in left-hander Richard Jeffries. Like Bowman, the southpaw would be more finesse than power. Jeffries didn't walk many batters either, so it looked like both teams would have to earn their offensive output tonight unless either team's fielding fell apart.

The umpires made sure everybody got the message that there would be no shenanigans allowed in game two. There would be no warnings and zero second chances for offending players. Of course, both managers shook their heads up and down in unison, but nobody knows what can trigger a bench-clearing brawl.

St. Louis manager Don Leighton again tried to explain his actions in the opener to Blake, but the Cubs skipper just interrupted Leighton and said now wasn't the time to air things out. There wasn't any smile on either manager's face as the seriousness of the second game was felt by all involved.

The freshly painted white chalk lines around home plate were all set to be erased as the Cubs' leadoff batter stepped into the right-handed batter's box and assertively placed his back foot on the exterior of the chalk line. He dug his cleats into the soft ground, essentially wiping out the line so carefully inscribed moments before.

Home plate umpire Wes Larson bellowed, "Play ball!" and the teams were ready to square off one more time to set the stage for the remaining two and a half weeks of the season.

The respective pitchers both controlled the early innings as home plate ump Larson displayed his usual large strike zone, much to the chagrin of the hitters. Every umpire has his own tendencies, just like the players, and their reputations dictate strategy to be involved in each game.

It was a fast-moving, crisply-played clean game that upheld its pace for the majority of the first four innings. Neither team showed much of an offensive threat so far. Chicago never got a runner past first, and the Cardinals only put one runner in scoring position before Bowman struck out his counterpart Jeffries to get out of a mild jam in the bottom of the second.

Unfortunately for Blake's squad, the roof caved in during the home half of the fifth inning, as an uncharacteristic Bowman leadoff walk, followed up by consecutive Rickey Sanchez errors on routine grounders, left the bases loaded and nobody out.

Blake called out for time and casually strolled to the mound in an effort to calm events down. He had virtually no instruction for his team or Bowman, but simply went out to give his pitcher a break and hopefully slow down some Cardinal momentum.

He smiled upon arrival and declared, "I've got nothing boys. I'm just here to wish you good luck Bowman. Get that at 'em ball going and let's turn two the normal way. Let the run score and let's stay away from the big inning."

The manager must have forgotten his lucky rabbit's foot. The next two batters hit seeing-eye singles through the infield slightly in and shaded toward the middle for the double play. Three runs scored as the St. Louis faithful felt right at home again in the lead against their rival. They tacked on one more run on a sacrifice fly before Bowman finally induced a twin-killing grounder that ended the inning with a 4-0 lead for the Cardinals after five frames.

A temporarily deflated Cubs team, heads down and in an all-too familiar deficit, meandered into the dugout before Blake tried to pick them up.

"This is exactly the type of game that will show these guys that we're in this for the duration of the season boys. Do you want to get their respect or do you want to crawl in your cave and give up?"

Blake knew the answer to that question and he continually encouraged his squad to come right back at them. This time they listened as Bartlett roped a double to start the inning. The screaming line-drive gapper to the left center field wall provided just enough of a spark to restore team confidence.

The elderly big league rookie Larry Hunter moved the runner over to third with a strategically placed stroke to the right side of the infield. Although it produced an out for the home team, Hunter did exactly what a professional hitter should do in that situation, which left his teammates feeling better about their play. Hunter gladly received high-fives from his teammates in the dugout on a job well done as the next batter came to the plate to try to do his job bringing the runner in.

Mike Simons took his opportunity to hit the first fastball he saw from Jeffries and lined it past the outstretched glove of the diving St. Louis third baseman, Jimmy Lucas, a perennial All Star. The ball squirted around the left-field corner of Busch stadium, evading the Cardinals outfielder like a butterfly and allowing plenty of time for Simons to check into second base standing up.

The bottom portion of the Cubs batting order was coming up, putting a bit of a damper on expectations for a big inning. Blake knew he would have to pinch-hit for Bowman and rely on a suspect middle relief bullpen to keep the Cards at bay, but he had to come back with at least a couple of runs here in the top of the sixth to make a game of it again.

Fortunately for Blake and his Cubbies, the pinch-hitter, longtime bench player Willie Evans, came through with a clutch two-out single up the middle after a strikeout threatened to stamp out any further rally. Evans' hit cut the deficit to 4-2, but Desmond Wilson lined out sharply to the shortstop to end the inning. However, the feeling was a bit more optimistic heading toward the bottom half of the sixth.

The game went back and forth for a couple of innings. Single runs by the Cards in the sixth and seventh frames were countered by Chicago singletons as well. It was as if the Cards were playing cat and mouse with the Cubbies as St. Louis seemed to let their fiercest rival get just close enough to taste victory before putting more distance between themselves and the Cubs.

Blake brought in Guillen to keep them within striking distance and the lefty responded in exemplary fashion. He redeemed himself from the poor outing in the first game as he struck out the St. Louis side in the bottom half of the eighth inning. He looked dominant mowing his opponents down with a nice mixture of pitches. The Cubs had just a ray of hope entering their last at-bats, trailing 6-3.

The Cardinals had perhaps the best closer in all of baseball, Jerry Waddell, who confidently strolled in from the bullpen to nail down the victory and bring the Cards to within one game of the Cubs in the National League Central Division.

Waddell threw heat as one would expect from a premier closer, but it was his equally nasty change-up that separated him from the rest of the closer class. The only hope against him was an occasional wild spell, and his own hot temper that bit him in the ass occasionally.

As is often the case in baseball, and sports in general, there seems to be one team that gives a player illogical trouble and for Waddell, the Cubs were just the franchise. It simply didn't matter if the team was particularly good or not in a given year. Maybe it wouldn't matter if this Chicago team was hastily scrambled together and unfamiliar with the oddly unsuccessful history that plagued Waddell. They wore that Cubs uniform and that's all that seemed to matter.

Blake knew about the franchise's success against Waddell and didn't hesitate to let his boys know that, for whatever reason, the future Hall of Famer hated to see the white, red, and blue of the Chicago uniform or, in this case, the road gray color complemented by blue and red.

Blake turned to his bench coach Ronny Williamson and uttered loud enough for those nearby to hear what he had in mind. The skipper picked up a random bat and struck it repeatedly against the dugout railing making an easily audible racket.

"Jerry hates us. We always get under his skin because we are the 'it' team for him. He can't figure us out or we can simply figure him out. The baseball gods don't give us an explanation on these matters, but he's on edge the moment he gets on the mound against us. Spread the word to the rest of the boys and tell them not to be shy about reminding Waddell that we've got his number. Even the replacement Cubs got him. Put on this uni and he's toast."

Sure enough, the troubles immediately began for Waddell as he walked the leadoff batter on five pitches, two of them borderline strikes.

Blake stepped to the top of the dugout steps and hollered in Waddell's direction. "Boy those sure looked like strikes to me Jerry. I guess it's the jinx again."

Bartlett strolled to the on-deck circle, acutely aware of Waddell's past history as his one-time catcher. He had a few choice words for the closer as well.

"I guess it's the same old story Jerry. Here we go again. Nice to be on the other side of it this time," as the hot-tempered closer walked around the mound in disgust, wearing the familiar look of a marked target like a branded steer waiting for slaughter.

One walk wasn't quite enough to light his fuse, but the match was being pulled from the pocket as the hard-throwing righty angrily fell behind 2-0 to the next batter, Jim Arnold. The veteran Waddell knew that Arnold would be taking a strike in this situation, but for all of his fame and fortune, the stellar closer couldn't find the strike zone as he walked Arnie on four pitches.

Bartlett kept his eyes on his St. Louis counterpart as the wily veteran approached the batter's box. He stared at Waddell as if to say, I know you like the back of my hand.

The tying run was at home plate in a drum-tight situation in the form of the Rat, and the Cubs couldn't be happier knowing the familiarity of Bartlett with Waddell.

Bartlett did not even look down to third-base coach Paxson for signs even though the baseball book called for the next batter to take a pitch in such a situation and force the pitcher to throw a strike before even thinking about swinging away. The seasoned vet knew the only chance to get three runs in was to take advantage of the pitcher's weakness at this moment. He couldn't wait for even one strike as the supreme closer would invariably find his rhythm and mow down Bartlett and the Cubs. He would answer to his manager later, whatever the result.

Waddell did just like Bartlett figured and took just a bit off his fastball to throw a much-needed strike. It was standard baseball strategy to force a struggling pitcher to throw a strike first before swinging away. The pitch came in belt-high, dissecting home plate right down the middle. Bartlett could not have asked for a better pitch to drive, even though the offering was still crossing the plate at about 90 miles per hour, but considerably less than Waddell's best mid-90s heat.

The Cubs fans in attendance let out a resounding cheer as the Waddell offering was thunderously turned around. Bartlett got it all, but the flight of the batted ball still did not have enough lift to clear the center field wall. The scorching high-arcing liner struck the bottom third of the wall and ricocheted right past the St. Louis centerfielder as he tracked the blast to the warning track before the sheer power of the batted ball beat him to the fence.

The extra time it took the surprised outfielder to turn around and chase the ball rolling toward the infield allowed even the slow-footed Bartlett to cruise into third base standing up. The noise from the visiting fans in attendance pumped up the excitable catcher even more as he looked into the visitor's dugout and emphatically clapped his hands to fire up his teammates.

Two runs scored, cutting the Cardinal lead to one, and the tying tally was just 90 feet away at third base. Blake was trying to remain calm as he had important decisions to make, but even he was overcome with excitement, exchanging high-fives with the run-scoring teammates and with every other player within slapping distance.

Waddell looked to be really bearing down as the situation certainly called for the utmost intensity. He scowled for a moment as he awaited the announcement of the next batter before climbing the mound. He stared intensely toward home to check the sign from his catcher and came to the stretch position, keeping a close eye on the runner Bartlett at third before violently delivering to the plate.

The Chicago batter, outfielder Ricky Rodriguez, had no chance at the over-powering fastball that sailed past his bat before he could even come close to getting the barrel out in front of this 97 mile-per-hour heater. The Cubs batter had no chance as he had the misfortune of facing a dialed-in Waddell. A laugh-able swing and a miss at Waddell's nasty change sealed Rodriguez' fate as he fell behind in the count. The third pitch was another blazing fastball that painted the outside corner. The towering St. Louis closer, who stood at an imposing 6-foot 5, dispatched Rodriguez to the dugout with an arrogant pistol-shooting motion with his pitching hand. The showboating gesture irked the Cubs as the home plate umpire bellowed out his called strike three to the delight of the home crowd.

Blake had refocused during the at-bat and pondered the situation as Ro-driguez was quickly retired. Bartlett was a slow runner indeed and the Cubs needed the tying run to score in the worst way to continue the contest. A speed-ier runner might fare better on a potential sacrifice fly, but Blake was hesitant to replace Bartlett and be down to one catcher again. The third catcher, Terry Reynolds, called up from the minors by GM Anderson, had not arrived at the ballpark so soon after his promotion just hours earlier.

The rookie skipper hesitated just long enough for the next batter to get to the plate before Blake could make a pinch-running move. The Cubs' Felix Gon-zalez swung at the first offering, flaring a weak pop-up down the right-field line and over the drawn-in St. Louis infield that hoped to cut off the tying run from scoring on a potential ground ball. Waddell had overpowered the Chicago batter with a belt-high inside fastball that avoided the sweet spot of the bat, striking instead toward the handle and resulting in a lazily looped airborne fly down the right-field line.

The Cardinals second baseman, Jeff Dorman, had anticipated a weak pop-up as he picked up the catcher's sign for inside heat. He had seen this result fairly often from his closer and figured there was a decent chance of this play developing as the pitch made its way toward the batter's box. His excellent jump proved to be the deciding play of this tight game.

Dorman sprinted to the area just on the outfield grass about 70 feet out from first base with his back to the infield. He dove for the ball with his outstretched glove, just barely corralling it in the web of his fielder's glove. He rolled over on his grass-stained uniform, lost his cap from the jolting impact and immedi-ately sprang up, realizing the tying run could tag up from third. In whirling fashion, he fired a perfect strike to his catcher Paul Evans. The burly catcher was blocking home plate as Bartlett attempted to sneak in from third on this daring play. The wily veteran Bartlett was hoping to catch the opponent off-guard on a batted ball that was only 150 feet or so from the plate. The momentum from the catch, away from the action of the infield, would certainly make it a difficult play to throw out any runner trying to score. It was a difficult play perhaps, but not unattainable, and the rally was snuffed out by the heady play of the Cardinals second baseman. The tag was firmly applied by the catcher as Bartlett's only chance was to bowl over his counterpart catcher with force in an attempt to dislodge the baseball. The catcher held on, showed the ball to the waiting home plate umpire and the Rat was called out to end the game.

There was no fighting as a result of the play. Both players realized the seriousness of the situation and the hopelessness Bartlett faced as he stared down the waiting catcher, guarding home plate like an armed security guard.

The St. Louis bench erupted in delight at the outcome and raced onto the field to congratulate their second baseman hero and the game-saving catcher. The victors were in no mood to fight after such an amazingly tense, crucial contest. Bartlett and his teammates were stunningly silent, too much in shock at the startling outcome to muster up any hatred for the opposition. The losing team just stared blankly into the cool dark St. Louis night wondering what possibly could go wrong next.

Being on the short end of a 5-4 contest was mind numbing for the moment, but their senses would reappear shortly. There was definite cause for concern as the visitors left the field losers once again. If winning has a thousand fathers and losing an orphan, Blake was feeling all alone at this vulnerable moment.

The lead was down to one full game with a doubleheader tomorrow. The sudden realization that his team could leave the Gateway City of St. Louis out of first place for the first time this season made Blake wonder, once again, if he was worthy of such a responsible position. The beleaguered manager looked at the landmark St. Louis Arch and wondered if he was on a gateway to hell.

The self-doubt was creeping back into his fragile psyche. There was only one way he knew how to deal with the loss of confidence. The false front of artificial stimulation through booze and accompanying sexual trysts could deceive the damaged mind just long enough to make a lousy road trip bearable.

Blake was recalling such moments as he undressed and prepared for the return trip to the hotel. The thoughts were even pleasant at the moment, but the alcoholic mind knew deep down they were more than self-destructive, they were lethal to his club's chances, remote as they seemed at this downtrodden moment.

48 — Second-Guessing First Impressions

Doubt lingered in the clubhouse air as losing one-run games magnifies nearly every decision. Some blame themselves, some blame others, and some blame the head honcho, in this case one Blake Benson.

The manager himself can toss around blame with the best of them. Some lament the talent they have on the field that reflects poorly on the team's general manager. Others throw their players under the bus in the media with subtle, and sometimes, not so subtle, shots at underperforming professional athletes. A top-notch manager will accept blame himself and always use the collective term we instead of naming individuals.

Blake was more than willing to take blame for his mistakes on this day. He knew the decisions made or not made, did not turn out well. He didn't run from it dealing with the press after the nightcap, but reminded members of the media that he told them before, when most of Blake's moves were turning up golden, that the results were bound to change.

He did his best to deflect criticism that was coming his way more frequently from the media with the usual clichés. The arrows slung were stinging because they did not involve specific managerial moves, but rather the inability to use foresight in situations like the ones that developed today. Blake froze on the pinch-runner decision when he should have thought that out beforehand, when the first-game fiasco revealed the dangers of carrying only two catchers.

After the Skipper briefed the media and before the team left for their hotel, Blake knew he had to speak- up and address the situation upfront and directly with his teammates. Word got around that their manager wanted to say a few words as the players huddled in mass outside of Blake's visiting manager's office at Busch Stadium.

The rumblings of second-guessing were cautiously boomeranging around the clubhouse. The players that were so enamored with their fresh and exciting Skipper a mere week ago were now questioning his leadership. The veteran player in Blake knew this would happen, but the rookie manager, barely inscribed in his new role, was uncertain how to proceed. He knew he had to accept blame, but he also needed to remain authoritative. It would be a delicate balancing act as he stepped out of his office dressed in a suit and tie for the short trip to the team hotel.

"Okay guys, listen up. I'll make this brief as it's been a long day and I know you all want to get back to the hotel. We had some things go against us today and I contributed my share as well. I continue to come across situations that I'm not quite used to as a manager. Mistakes all teach us a lesson that hopefully will not be forgotten. I can assure you I won't make the same mistake twice and I'll expect the same from all of you. Tomorrow is another day. You guys gave it your all today and I couldn't be more impressed with your efforts out there. Those bums over there in the other clubhouse know they're in for a battle now every step of the way. We'll give 'em everything we've got tomorrow and take it from there. Get some rest boys, it's another long day tomorrow and don't forget it's the old-fashioned type of doubleheader tomorrow. Its back-to-back games tomorrow afternoon as the league is getting worried about weather post-ponements and the like. They want to allow as much time as possible to get these things in. Let's head out. Keep your heads up because your manager is too, no matter how it turned out today."

Blake did his best to shield his own self-doubt from his players. He figured some probably bought it and some not, but that was okay for today as he had bigger issues on his mind as the bus traversed the city to the hotel.

He was exhausted from the long day, but he had a difficult time pushing his mind in another direction away from the temporary allure of alcohol. The dull ache in his body could be soothed in a heartbeat with a shot of whiskey and a cocktail to wash it down. He knew it would bring instant courage and help him regain the self-confidence he was lacking at this dire moment. The problem in Blake's mind was semi-alleviated by the past self-educated knowledge of that false confidence that spikes, then wanes, and ultimately sets you deeper in self-doubt with every drinking episode. Tempered with that knowledge, the craving to drink tonight was too intense to just disregard.

He had to talk to someone. It was times like this that he deeply wished his parents were still alive. Their fatal traffic accident had robbed him of so much advice and guidance that he craved in moments of despair. He had a couple of uncles on his dad's side that once acted as mentors to him, but that was so long ago. He of course had his wife Kim, but she tended to direct, not discuss. Marty was a logical choice until Blake surmised that the man in charge of his employment might deem him unfit to carry on.

Blake thought of his coaches as his confidants. This was his new family and by God, he was going to bring them into his deep, sometimes troubled, inner world.

It made sense, as they were right there with him. They were with him more than his wife. He knew that he would be there for them in a pinch, so he figured he might as well ask them to come support him tonight. The manager really needed company and distraction.

The dilemma was just how many Blake should involve with his deeper troubles? He pondered for several moments as he took in the nightlife of St. Louis before the bus pulled up at their destination. His blank stare at the outside elements indicated that his mind was elsewhere, even if the eyes said otherwise.

The answer came to Blake just in time as the team was unloading from the bus. The coach that seemed always nearest to Blake wherever they went was Mark Douglas, his pitching coach. For whatever reason, pitching coaches and managers are always tied together. Many teams will often see changes in the coaching staff from year to year, but pitching coaches somehow tie a deeper and longer-lasting bond to managers.

They certainly talked the same lingo with Blake being on the receiving end of countless pitches in his professional life. They looked at baseball situations often in the same analytic manner.

Sure enough, Douglas was right behind Blake as they stepped down off the bus to street level. The manager tapped Mark on the left shoulder and motioned just off to the side of the hotel entrance to the lobby. They silently walked together out of the path of arriving players and sat down on an outdoor bench, attempting to be as inconspicuous as possible.

"What's up Skipper? Have a problem?"

"Mark, you and I are pretty close, right?" Blake hesitated and looked directly into his pitching coach's eyes waiting for a reply.

"Yes, I think so Blake. You're starting to worry me a bit. Just spit it out."

"Well, it's like this. I don't really have any one to turn to when I get some of these cravings to turn to the hooch. That was my MO before, but I can't do that anymore. I need someone to settle me down a bit tonight. I don't want this to sound weird or anything, but can you come to my room after you settle in? I just can't deal with this alone right now. You know, just hang out and watch highlights on ESPN, bullshit a bit just to get my mind off things until I can relax. Would you do that for me tonight and maybe other nights on the road as well?"

"Jesus, is that all? I thought there was a huge problem. That's fine, big guy. I get it. Sure can't be easy dealing with all the pressures of this team and then worrying about your own shit. I'll be up in 15 minutes. Will you be okay until then? Fifteen minutes can be a long time when you're in need."

"Thanks Mark, I really appreciate this. We've all got our own shit to deal with and I'm guessing you have more than your share too. I'll just call Kim to say goodnight and find out what's new at home and I'll meet ya up in my room in 15."

Blake filled his wife in on the day's events although she was aware of most from the tight sports coverage. He did his best to assure Kim that he was doing fine with all the stress, but his shortness with her hinted otherwise to his nearly lifelong companion. Blake played the exhausted angle and let his wife know he would call her in the morning as he slowly paced his walk to the hotel room to account for the quarter-hour time frame.

Blake was so uneasy at the moment that he did not even want to enter his room before Mark got there. There always was something eerie about shutting that hotel door behind you knowing that there was no one else besides you and your incessant thoughts.

His pitching coach arrived right on time. Mark seemed taken aback by Blake's odd appearance standing alone outside of his room. "What's up Blake, did you lose your card?"

"Nope, I was just waiting for you. It's kind of strange huh? Come on in and I'll give you the shortened Blake Benson neurotic guide."

Blake opened the door to the scent of a freshly cleaned hotel room with clean linens and a slightly lower than expected chill from an air conditioner left on too long.

Acting like two normal sports guys, they both fuddled for the remote before Blake spotted it first and clasped it like a valuable lost possession excitedly re-discovered. Both assumed correctly that ESPN would be the channel of choice and Blake did not surprise his visitor when he immediately centered in on the all sports channel.

"Hey, let's watch someone else's problems for a change. I'll flip the channel if they feature our game, okay Mark?"

"You're the boss Blake and it's your room."

"Yep, sometimes I forget that don't I?" The manager smirked as he recalled his inaction today at the crucial game moment.

"You've got to keep your sense of humor Blake, that's good. We all make 'em, it's just yours are there for all to see and second-guess."

"Speaking of second-guessing Mark, do you think we really have any kind of shot here with this group of players? I thought so at first, but maybe I was just a little too giddy from our hot streak."

"We've got a shot Blake, for sure. It's only two weeks. Anything can happen in a two-week stretch. We've got to make the plays though. We didn't today."

"Thanks, I needed that and I needed this respite from my overly obsessive alcoholic mind. Okay, no more ball talks unless it's the other teams' issues."

The two of them watched some highlights, talked a little news and family stuff before Blake stretched out on his bed, fluffed up his pillow and thanked Mark again before asking one last favor. "Markie boy, can you just stick around until I fall asleep and let yourself out when I crash? And about that standing outside the door thing when you arrived, I just get a little freaked out at times when I suddenly realize I'm all alone. It's like I suddenly realize I can do what-ever I want behind closed doors. It's kind of my ultimate inward battle against the booze temptation."

"Sure thing Blake, I'll let myself out when I know you're out. It can't be easy what you're doing and I know you're doing it for all the right reasons. We're a band of brothers, us ballplayers. Get some rest."

Blake fell asleep in under 30 minutes while Mark took a pillow and placed it securely behind his neck while reclining in his chair, staring at the television wondering if his manager was going to make it to the end. He wondered that all night long as he stayed in the chair until near dawn before sneaking out with Blake unaware of his friend's extra effort and selfless good deed.

The last day of the rare five-game series would further cloud the future of this bunch of Chicago Cubs and one Blake Benson. All involved knew this day would be crucial and all knew it would be incredibly taxing, physically and mentally. If only they really knew.

49 — Dugout Dissension

The final day of the all-important series with the Cardinals was here as Blake awoke to the sound of what he guessed must have been hotel workers scurrying about in the hallway. He did not recall much of anything after gabbing with Mark for a bit from the previous evening. It was reassuring and troubling at the same time that he'd slept so well. Not tossing and turning in an uneasy state of mind was indeed a pleasant change from previous sleepless road-trip nights, but the mental and physical fatigue was building up and Blake could feel its toll on body and mind.

It was out of the norm that Blake felt so discouraged about today's double-header. He usually was realistic, but positive nonetheless about his team's chances, provided his players played with passion and baseball smarts.

Today was a different story. The number of makeup games in such a short time frame left Blake without much quality pitching available, while chance had it that the Cardinals had their two top throwers ready to sweep out the series and take over first place.

The message to his boys on this day was going to be one of 'just do your best' as he felt there was no point bullshitting his team about undue expectations. The schedule was for the birds and these Cardinals were all set to take advantage.

Blake spent more time on the phone this morning with Kim. She was very concerned about Blake's discouraged tone of voice and tried to keep his spirits up, but to no avail. Blake felt the unraveling was beginning and in his rare state of defeatism, the rookie skipper was unwittingly contributing to the expected demise of his team's chances and their cohesiveness.

It was no surprise to the coaching staff that the team was down and not particularly happy as the players gathered in the clubhouse this late morning. All involved, including the coaches, were looking forward to getting out of town later today where they might be able to put this discouraging series behind them and live for another day. The schedule watchers knew that the Cubs had a last chance crack at the Cardinals at Wrigley to end the season. The lingering hope today was that the team would still be within striking distance when St. Louis came to town in a couple weeks.

There was nothing unusual about the pregame routine or clubhouse antics. It was difficult to see if that was a good sign or not, as the manager made out his lineup card. Blake was torn between playing or devoting all his time and energy to managing for both games of the double dip now that his third catcher, Terry Reynolds, had joined the team. He always felt more focused and into the game when he was actively involved as a player, but he also realized his squad was at a critical juncture where he wanted to watch all involved very closely to see if he could pick up any signs that needed to be addressed immediately before this whole thing blew up in his face.

He decided to insert Bartlett as the catcher for the first game and deferred the final decision about his own availability until later. The lineup was producing fairly well at the moment so Blake more or less left everything alone, but he had to remind himself to play with some reckless abandon regarding strategy. It felt like he had 16 at the blackjack table and the dealer had an ace showing with the odds of a face card beneath quite high. He did not want to throw caution to the winds, but he did not want to look desperate either. Both extremes could send signals to his squad that the manager was attempting to avoid. The media would jump in either way with their criticism, but Blake was still a bit too sensitive to their crass displays of unwarranted opinion to avoid their influence altogether at this young stage of his managerial career.

Blake had his hands tied with the pitching staff. He was forced to go with spot starter Earl Richards. He was the type that could fill in during an emergency, but was not the preferable option to go against Cardinal ace pitcher Salvador Torres in a September race for first place in the National League Central Division. The hope here was that Richards could keep his team within a couple runs through five or six innings just to give the Cubbies a chance to snare game one.

The normal packed house in perhaps America's best baseball city of St. Louis, on a gorgeous sunny fall day, made for an excellent athletic atmosphere this afternoon. It was gorgeous indeed for the home team and its fans as the Cards scored first and they scored often in a degrading 10-1 loss. The only positive Blake could come up with was that his long relief man ate up all the innings in mop-up duty so the bullpen might have a chance in game two.

However, that surely was not the most significant event from the opener. Blake's team put up a bigger fight amongst each other than against the opposition.

The Cubs were batting in the top of the fourth inning, already trailing 8-0, when an incident sparked a brawl among teammates. Bartlett had just struck out on a disputed check-swing third strike call and had returned to the dugout even more surly than usual. He slammed his bat against the metal railing leading into the dugout and slung his batting helmet violently inside the dugout. This alone made many pissed off at the grouchy catcher, but what was to follow irritated those around him even more. Rickey Sanchez followed Bartlett in the batting order and grounded out weakly to the second baseman, which by itself was a minor occurrence. The notoriously moody Sanchez, newly acquired from the Padres, trotted down to first base unenthusiastically, tossing off his helmet as he jogged toward first base, veering off toward the visitor's dugout well before the first base bag.

Bartlett immediately called out Sanchez for his lack of effort, but many did not feel that the poor behavior just exhibited prior by Bartlett did not make him the best in-house candidate to confront the veteran shortstop Sanchez. It was an egregious display of a lack of passion and commitment, but would likely have been dealt with by Blake in a more discreet fashion than by the Rat.

His Latin American brethren did not care much for the sometimes culturally insensitive Bartlett and although they did not condone Sanchez' lack of effort, they did not want criticism coming from someone that never could relate, much less who was clearly not fault-free himself.

Sanchez hollered back at Bartlett and as Rickey re-entered the dugout the two of them went at each other, pushing and shoving before their teammates could intervene and separate them. The incident did not last long, but it clearly had a demoralizing effect of dissension and, even worse, split the team somewhat along ethnicity and color.

The old-fashioned doubleheader was in place today with near immediate back-to-back games instead of the now common day-night doubleheader that allows for two separate gate attendance counts and boosts revenue. Major League Baseball was already under the gun with makeshift scheduling and wanted to ensure that these games would be completed in a timely fashion and to allow for any weather-related delays. This was also Chicago's last scheduled trip to St. Louis, making completion of both games a necessity.

The lack of time between games created an unsettling non-resolution of the heated conflict between Sanchez and Bartlett. Both would be sitting out this second game, Bartlett by design and Sanchez by necessity. The conflux of games would allow Blake a good excuse for Rickey's absence in the second contest, allowing more time for the issue to be addressed and hopefully resolved before the next leg of the road trip in Cincinnati. Blake kept himself out of the starting lineup for the nightcap to look out for potential powder keg explosions. He wanted to get a close look at his new third catcher Terry Reynolds in this last game that Blake quietly dismissed as an unlikely potential win.

The pitching match-up was very one-sided again in favor of the Cardinals. The Redbirds' number two starter, Phil Terrell, was just behind Torres in stuff, but had a bit better command of his pitches than the St. Louis ace. He would oppose Woody Williams of the Cubs in the nightcap. Williams had been on the 15-day disabled list with a sore right shoulder, but was activated just in time for this trip. The rookie right-hander was the Cubs' top prospect, prepping in Des Moines when the accident took place. He was very raw and would be under a lesser pitch count coming off the DL. He had the stuff to compete with Terrell, but lacked experience in such situations, and nobody knew how the young man would react to the pennant-race pressure.

The late afternoon shadows were slowly creeping toward the pitching mound as game action began. Players are never very fond of such conditions, especially batters, who have to rely on their quick ability to recognize spin coming from the pitched ball. It's that eerie moment when the ball passes from the pitcher's hand, through the daylight, before instantaneously switching to shaded light from the shadows, that puts fear into the batter's box. Reactions are slowed just enough to create a tidbit of doubt from a hitter that needs to recognize and then explode their swing into the trajectory of the pitched ball to create power.

However, as visibility improved with the shadows overtaking the mound, and with the second trip through the batting order, the Cardinals began to figure out Williams. There was no such similar occurrence for the Cubbies though, as their bats remained silent throughout the whole game. St. Louis put up a four spot in the fourth inning, added single insurance tallies in the fifth and sixth innings and coasted to a 6-1 victory that finally put the Redbirds in first place, overcoming the Cubs' significant 10-game lead Chicago inherited following the crash.

As Jim Arnold flew out to the left field wall to end the game, the crowd that was standing the whole ninth inning cheered deliriously at the culmination of a five-game sweep. The Cardinals had rallied from a four-game deficit in the standings beginning the series to a one-game lead over the Cubs, which seemed and felt like a half-dozen game advantage given the talent differential between the two squads.

The slumping Cubs outfit had now lost eight games in a row to drop into second place in the division. The team was never the same after the demoralizing late-game loss in game three. Their spirit was broken and their cohesiveness under internal attack.

There were not any overt disagreements in the dugout in game two, unlike the first contest, but the mood was noticeably awkward, hanging over the dugout like a bad smell for the whole nine innings.

Blake hated impromptu meetings called to clear the air, but he knew he had no choice as the finale wore down. He left it up to his assistant coaches to spread the word as the team, heads held low, dragged their way back into the clubhouse while the manager withdrew to the confines of his private manager's room to gather his thoughts and prepare for the upcoming speech. He knew this could get ugly, but a cathartic release might be the best option at this troublesome team moment.

50 — Airing Dirty Laundry

Blake sat in the visiting manager's office and knew he and his team had hit a crossroads. What was a promising start had turned into a nightmare this past week, and if it did not get turned around soon, the hopes for a potential playoff spot and redemption for Blake would fly out the window of time.

First things first, he thought. If he did not get his players unified right away, success on the baseball diamond would not even be a remote possibility.

He always felt it was best not to set an agenda for these types of emergency meetings. Whether he had been a passive witness or an active participant in past conclaves, he was certain that whatever came up first would be addressed and so on, until everybody felt that their opinions, whether wanted or unwanted, had been heard.

The bus trip to the airport for the next destination on their road trip, a charter flight to Cincinnati, would be put on hold until resolution was accomplished, or at the very least, deeply delved into.

The manager opened his door and looked as stern as anybody had ever seen him before. He calmly shut the door and took off his baseball cap. He proceeded to rub the already unkempt hair he had underneath that cap with his left hand while holding the headgear with his right, and briefly paused for effect. He wanted to express extreme frustration and it showed through loud and clear as he finally spoke to the assembled squad.

"Gentlemen, we are at a crossroads here. We've lost eight in a row but, worse yet, we are fighting ourselves instead of the opposition. Yes, we've lost our lead, but that can be saved. What can't be saved is our team unity unless we hash things out right now, right here. Our plane will wait. I'm going to step aside here and let you guys take the floor and say whatever comes to mind. We've got to get some things settled and behind us before we move on."

There was an uncomfortable pause as is normally the case before someone takes the initiative and gets the emotional juices flowing. It was no surprise that outspoken Miguel Guillen took the floor to air out the team's dirty laundry.

Even the normally playful Guillen was stern in demeanor as he let it be known right away that their skipper had lost his rudder lately. "This is for you, Blake. Are you our teammate here, or our manager? Before I go on I'd like to know which."

The manager looked surprised and confused that he was the initial topic of discussion, but he calmly stepped forward and spoke hesitantly. "I'd like to think this isn't an either or situation, but if you're going to put me in a corner, I'd say right now I should be your manager first."

Miguel hesitated, unsure how his next sentence would be taken, but then suddenly emotionally let go with a dramatic reply. "Well then goddammit Skipper, start acting like it then. You've become hesitant and unsure of yourself, even distant. Take that play the other night when Bartlett got to third with one out. Everybody knew a pinch runner was immediately in order, but you did absolutely squat. Are you trying to lose or what?"

Suddenly Blake felt like a target and he was totally unprepared for the sneak attack. "Whoa buddy, nobody wants to win more than me. The rest of this fucked up season is for my guys that died in the crash."

Blake was confused and had a difficult time believing he had become THE problem. "Do the rest of you guys feel the same way?" Blake sat down and looked for verbal and non-verbal replies. It didn't take long for him to realize the sentiment was universal as heads nodded up and down. "Well then, all of my teammates can't be wrong. Yes, I've had a difficult time lately. Just like many of you when you go through a bad stretch on the field. I'll admit that right here and now."

Nary a noise was evident for about 10 seconds before Blake finally began to act like a manager should when he loudly professed his rededication. "I gotcha loud and clear, you're right and I'm going to change that right now."

Blake walked over to Bartlett who was sitting naked with nothing more than a towel draped over his thighs and spoke authoritatively to the snarly catcher.

"John, I understand your frustration at those who don't put their whole effort on the battlefield. God damn it though, you can't call out your teammate in front of everybody when you just acted like an ass too. That's not what equals do. You put yourself above the team there and we can't let that happen. Do you understand Bartlett?"

The Rat was speechless for a second or two as the manager stuck his finger in Bartlett's chest for emphasis before the veteran catcher nodded his head up and down.

Before anybody else could speak up, Blake immediately walked over to Rickey Sanchez and angrily looked down at him before setting the shortstop straight. "Rickey, if you ever do that again, and I don't need to describe it because you know damn well what you did, you'll be gone and I'll let everyone know that will listen to me that you are a team cancer. That'll cost you right in the pocketbook, young man when you go for a new contract. I don't care if you cheat yourself, but these teammates won't stand for it. Now, you got that?"

The young talented shortstop already was feeling guilty about his action on the field today and was more than willing to man up. He stood in front of his cohorts and apologized. "No excuses today. I was wrong. It won't happen again. I want to win this thing bad, for Blake, for his old teammates and for all of us. I just let my frustrations take over my actions. I apologize."

The manager was satisfied and comforted his infield general with a pat on his shoulder before Blake spoke up again. "Is there anything else out there? Now's the chance to speak your mind if you want it resolved."

Guillen stood up again and spoke from the heart.

"Skip, we all feel for ya. You're doing a great thing here by taking care of us while dealing with a ton of shit yourself. We're gonna get back on track, you'll see. Our manager needs us to stay together, no more finger pointing and no more dividing by the color of our skin. Everybody's gonna be together from here on out. I don't know about the rest of you guys, but I'm getting a big hatred for those guys across the building from us. Let's catch those bastards. I want to rub it in their faces so bad when they come to Wrigley. That's only going to happen if we go all out, get back to the style of play we had before and stay together. Now is everybody in?"

A resounding yes filled the clubhouse air, and voices began to pick up their chatter as everyone could feel a natural and conclusive ending had just taken place.

The manager stood up much more confidently than he did minutes ago and proclaimed the team ready to move on. "I feel much better. We've hit the crossroads and taken the right path. Now let's get the fuck out of this city. I've seen enough for this trip."

It was not a magical elixir, but the damaging mood had been replaced. The possibility was always there for bad vibes to return, but the page had been turned and a new chapter was beginning. Cincinnati could not be any worse, the manager thought to himself. Like everything else in the sporting world, that remained to be seen.

51 — Wifely Reassurance

It was an uneventful flight to Cincinnati and a welcome one at that. There had been enough trying challenges in Blake's life the last few days and he was ready for a quiet, restful evening in Ohio. It was difficult to believe that his demeanor could be somewhat calm and his mood relatively upbeat after the troublesome series and the falling out of first place. The team meeting had cleared the air and lifted some of the burdens beneath the surface, although it came unexpectedly toward the manager, and not his players. Nonetheless, the effect that carried over was positive despite the wave of anger and disappointment flung Blake's way.

The next leg of the road trip had brought about a feeling of a fresh start coming off the drastically disappointing series in St. Louis. Baseball has a way of doing that with its numerous destinations and constant flow of new opponents.

There could be no denying that an eight-game losing streak would have its own lingering effects, though. The streak sat over the Cubs' collective psyche like an elephant that simply could not be pushed out of the way.

Tonight felt like a perfect time to have a lengthy phone conversation with his wife. Blake was surprised at his team's perception of him and he wanted to ask Kim if she had any inkling of Blake's recent display of self-doubt.

After he had settled in for the evening and convinced his newest friend Mark that he was doing just fine tonight and likely would not need his presence, Blake enjoyed a nice room service dinner and comfortably plopped himself on his hotel bed to let the delicious rib eye steak and baked potato digest. For several minutes he browsed through some local tourism pamphlets left in his room, trying to clear his mind of baseball related distractions before he called Kim.

Before the loneliness of the hotel room could seep into his psyche, Blake, somewhat more anxious than usual for his near nightly conversation with Kim, hit the speed dial button on his cell and waited for his wife to answer.

It took Kim a bit longer than normal to answer, but he certainly did not think anything of it as he patiently waited through repeated rings before she answered in a breath-gasping tone.

"Hey there honey, sorry it took me so long to answer. I was just coming in with some groceries."

"Do you want me to call back? I can wait for you to catch your breath and gather yourself too, if that's better," Blake did not like the sound of her rushed demeanor.

"Nope Blake, we're good, it's all put away. I'll catch my breath in just a second. I'm sitting now and feeling better. It sounded like another really tough day. Do you want to talk baseball or just let it go for the night?"

"Actually Kim, for once I kind of want to talk more baseball with you."

"No way, really Blake? That certainly surprises me. Do you need my opinion on who to start tomorrow?" She tried to joke, but immediately realized that her husband was very serious at the moment and apologized. "I'm sorry Blake. I can tell you're not in a joking mood now. Forgive me please. I rushed in with a sarcastic comment without thinking first. This certainly caught me off guard."

"No problem honey. After all these years of me giving you grief for asking about the game, I'd expect you to be shocked."

Kim interjected before Blake could finish his thought. "Now you've got me concerned, what could possibly be an issue where I could help?"

"We had one of those closed-door meetings after the last game today. It was the kind that I always made fun of for their usual insignificance. Anyways, the first issue that comes up is slung at me and I was totally caught off guard."

"How could that be Blake? You're the boss," she inquired.

"That's why I was dumbfounded, but it turns out my behavior both on and off the field has taken its toll on my guys. Kim, do you think that's possible? Could it be I'm just a vulnerable scapegoat at the moment? It's no secret I've been visibly unsettled this past week."

"Well honey, I could tell you've been questioning things in your own mind. You've been distant and apparently unavailable to your own wife based on the few phone calls I've been getting and the time you want to talk. I know you well enough to tell when you are in self-doubting mode. When you're quiet, it normally means you're preoccupied with your internal thoughts. I bet your guys are speaking from the heart. Remember Blake, you're supposed to lead them and set the tone, in case you've forgotten."

Blake became agitated at his wife's directness and responded in kind.

"Of course I know what a manager is supposed to do, but these guys have to want it too. Sometimes I get the feeling they just want the season over with."

Kim jumped at that obvious opening.

"And what about you Blake? Do you just want the season over with too at this point? Seems to me you're the one looking for a scapegoat. There can't be any doubt in your guys unless you show you're not all-in as well."

"God damn it Kim, you're always right. I've been giving them excuses and they're just piling on. I have to do better from here on out for those poor guys that were killed. They did not deserve that and they don't deserve the results they've been getting lately. I don't care how lousy the pitching match-ups or how vicious the schedule is. This is major league ball here. We should never have an eight-game skid."

"Blake, that's right. Have you been thinking too much about your old teammates?"

"What do you mean too much? I think about them all the time. Aren't I supposed to use them for motivation, for my team and myself?"

"That could be the problem Blake. You get in these guilty periods and it affects your moods too much. Everybody has to die someday. It's not up to you or me. Anybody would go crazy trying to figure out why. Jesus, look around the world. Nothing really makes sense to any of us. Do you think it's fair that you were born with major league talent? How many young men would kill to be in the major leagues? You've got to let that guilt go, honey."

"I know you're right Kim, but it just eats away at me. I should have been on that plane too. I should have, but because I screwed up. I'm still alive. Isn't that wrong?"

"First of all Blake, you've got to get it out of your system that your old teammates were somehow saints. You didn't care that much personally for a few of them and they all had major flaws, all of them, including your almighty Sandy. He wasn't always what you thought he was. Others could see it, but I guess you couldn't. Nobody deserves to die when they do. It just happens for reasons currently unknown to us and maybe we never know, based on one's religious beliefs. Let it go Blake. Let it go and just concentrate on being a leader on and off the field. Spread your baseball knowledge and let the rest happen as it may."

"I'll just keep plugging away, just like staying away from the liquor. Thanks for all the pointed words though, Kim. You've definitely hit home with your analysis. I guess I just need to talk to more people to get through all this and somehow make sense of things."

"Blake, that's what I've been telling you all along. You need to figure out the why before you can figure out the lasting remedy. You've got to take the emotion out of it and analyze without guilt, shame, or confusion."

"Okay Kim, I get it," blurted her husband in the tone usually reserved for don't go any further.

"Blake, you should just get a good night's sleep, eat well, and try to concentrate on baseball. You're a natural there. Let it flow unhampered by anything personal. You'll know what to do, when it happens, just on your instincts alone. Let your staff work with them on improvements. Get your boys to believe in you again and the team will improve, you'll see."

"Damn, honey, you sound like you should be wearing my uniform. I guess a lot has rubbed off over the years."

"You got that right Blake. You've picked up many things from me too, whether you want to admit it or not."

"I realize that more and more every day, but thanks for reminding me. I feel so much better after talking to you. Why do I resist your knowledge and understanding so often?"

"That's just another thing for you to figure out Blake. All in due time, all in due time," Kim smoothly reassured her husband in an empathetic tone of voice.

"I'll call you in the morning Kim. I think I'm realizing that I need to communicate with you more often and without fear. Damn that's a toughie for me though, the fear part anyways. Good night babe, I love you and respect your outlook on us."

"Thanks Blake, for the loving words. You're there for me too when I need it. Love you too and we'll talk in the morning."

With that comforting exchange behind him, Blake said goodnight, sprawled across his spacious hotel bed, and let out a big sigh that relieved any tensions left over from the emotional upheaval of the day. The next thing he remembered was waking up several hours later, glancing at the hotel room radio clock before fully undressing and realigning his large athletic frame comfortably beneath the sheets. A nice relaxing sleep was definitely in order and incredibly welcome.

52 — Getting Back to the Lighter Side

The series against the Cardinals was awful in so many ways, but one immediate concern of everyone involved was the lack of just plain having fun. The five games in three days with St. Louis were overwhelming in many regards. Tension throughout and little time away from the stresses of the playing field left the team fried to its core.

After the team meeting and before arriving in Cincinnati, several members of the team put their collective heads together and tried to come up with some shenanigans for the clubhouse to relax everyone and provide a temporary distraction from the division pennant race. The one-game deficit felt huge, like a half-dozen at times so a diversion was definitely in order to get the team's mind back into proper perspective. A one-game deficit with 13 games left was nothing. Any team can outperform another in such a small sample size. It was time for Blake's boys to remember that long-standing unwritten rule that crazy things can happen in baseball in the short term that nobody could ever predict.

While flying to the Queen City it was suggested that something about football season would be a good distraction. Almost all the players enjoyed the sport and had their favorite teams. Some preferred college football but, because of the sheer number of college teams, it was decided that some sort of pool would be set up just to get everyone's mind in another direction, and professional football it was.

As usual, Guillen was in the middle of this idea. He was strutting through the clubhouse the following afternoon, hours before the evening game against the Reds would start the three-game series. "Check this out homeboys. We have a nice pool going here for football. Here are all the games for this week. All you have to do is pick the winner of each game. No spreads involved here. We don't want the Commish to come down on us for that one word nobody wants to hear. I ain't even gonna mumble that dirty word that everybody freaks out about. Thanks Pete Rose, and while we are in his city too. Imagine that.

"No money Senor? That's just un-American. That's right, you wouldn't understand," teased Bartlett never one to shy away from a touchy subject or a jab at minorities.

"But hombre, this is going to be even better. We get to pick the penalty for whoever gets the worst score for the week. Take Simons over there. Mr. Pretty Boy would have to wear grungy old sweats for the week where we go as a team. No custom-tailored suits for that week. Let's take a look at Arnie. He lives and dies with his Green Bay Packers. He gets the worst score and he has to wear all Minnesota Viking garb for a week, head to toe. We can really have some fun with this if we go down the bench and pick a penalty for each guy. We all have to agree and pick something totally opposite of them. Come on, it will be the perfect tonic for an eight-game losing streak. Let's laugh all afternoon and pick the worst possible penalty for each guy."

Blake was just off in the distance reading a newspaper and appeared to be out of the conversation, but he suddenly leapt to his feet from his chair and yelled to Guillen.

"Okay, what about you Chubster? What we gonna do for your sentence? Is there anybody out there with the best possible outcome for Miguel, or should I say the worst? He still thinks football is soccer so we know there's a good chance he'll be the biggest loser. I say we're all in as long as we get the best booby prize for the ringleader."

"That's going to take some serious thinking. We can all take our time and save the best for last. Guillen's last and his has to be unanimous," shouted out the quietest player on the team, big Jim Arnold. The stunned audience all got a kick out of the extremely non-verbal Arnie taking the lead on this one.

"You must want him good Arnie," chortled Bartlett. "If it means that much to Big Jim I am definitely all in," chimed the smart-ass catcher.

With that universal sentiment, the whole team agreed on Guillen's brain-storm and went down the team's roster one by one before they finally had to choose the ringleader's punishment if he came in last as all hoped.

At the end of the line, big Jim Arnold stood up and offered his punishment should Miguel lose. His outspoken demeanor again belied his normal muted self, and shocked his teammates.

"I say Miggy has to let the rest of us feed him the whole week if he loses. And that includes drink. Only nourishment that goes down his throat comes from me and I'll let my teammates decide the menu, but I'll be watching to make sure he don't cheat. We're gonna be roomies for a week. How's that sound Miguel? No alcohol, no beer and nothing but fresh fruit and vegetables for a week. A complete health trip for a whole week for our notorious chow hound and biggest beer belly boy."

"That could be detrimental to the team Arnie," shouted Giullen, resisting the suggestion. "I need my strength and my hydration for the awesome move-ment on my pitches."

"He doth protest too much," shouted back Big Jim. "It must be the ultimate penalty for you, huh Miggy?"

The whole team, including Blake and his coaches, chimed in with universal agreement. It was agreed that if Miguel should lose it would be a health trip for one notoriously overweight and out of shape left-handed flamethrower.

"Hey Miggy, you ever hear the saying be careful what you wish for, you just might get it? Well, at least you unified the whole team. Everybody is pulling for you to lose," joked Blake in response to the surprising level of support for this plan now that Guillen looked to be the most vulnerable.

"Now wouldn't that be something if that was the plan all along, boss man," replied Miguel. "Maybe I not so dumb as I look," he spoke in broken English.

"Nah, that's not possible Miggy. You're definitely as dumb as you look," chided his manager. "But when you're on the mound, you look like gold Miggy, you look like a rare gem."

Miguel smiled at the backhanded compliment from his manager, knowing all along that Blake stood behind him 100 percent.

Now it was Blake's turn to start to get back the respect and admiration he initially received from his whole squad. A new beginning, he thought, as he got back to preparing for the opening pitch of the three-game set, while his team began the mental preparation for the contest as well. It felt good to laugh again, but results are all that matter in the game of professional baseball. It was time to see if the new beginning was real or just an empty expression.

53 — It's Always Darkest Before the Dawn

The new series, a different city, and a return to the lighter side brought a fresh state of mind to Blake's team. He could feel it as they began preparations for the opening game. All the positive energy would mean nothing though, if his squad did not start playing better and winning.

Playing better on a consistent basis was an oft-expressed necessity. His players just did not have enough talent to give anything away. The new Cubs would have to play near errorless ball, mentally and physically, to meet the challenge, and even that might not be enough.

Blake preached to this squad that winning baseball would have to come through solid pitching and clutch, timely hitting. His boys would likely not have an abundance of chances to drive runners in. They would have to take advantage of every opportunity and, of course, luck would have to play its part as well.

The good news was that with the number of games dwindling on a daily basis and the team within striking distance, the better the odds of achieving the impossible dream of five weeks ago. Blake could vividly recall the list of players that were available when he first scanned the names of ballplayers left unprotected by their former teams and his immediate thoughts of despair at the lack of talent.

Now, even after the disastrous five-game sweep by the Cardinals that saw their lead dissipate with alacrity and alarm, the ragtag bunch had a legitimate shot to actually win the division and advance to the postseason. That in itself was a near miracle that Blake himself had somehow forgotten in all the confusion that eight-game losing streaks invariably bring into the clubhouse.

Tonight's game would be played in miserably damp, rainy conditions. It was the kind of evening that an experienced ballplayer recognized as a "must play" game, based on the importance of the contest and the immediacy of approaching playoffs. This type of game would most likely be a rainout if these conditions persisted in May, but not September when options to reschedule become extremely limited. To make matters worse, the forecast offered little in the way of improvement for the remaining three days of this series.

The Cubs handled the difficult playing conditions very well while the Reds did not. Perhaps the significance of the game for the Cubs and the lack thereof for Cincinnati worked in Chicago's favor. The Cubs took advantage of three errors by the home team and a generous six bases on balls from Reds' relievers to coast to a 6-2 win.

The pitching was solid all through the victory. September call-up, Gary Wilkens, started it off with six strong innings, scattering six singles while allowing two runs. The journeyman lefty Wilkens was another one of Blake's emergency starters, but carved his way through two-thirds of the game. The bullpen fell perfectly into place with Miguel Guillen rolling easily through the eighth, and closer Randall Hart striking out the side in the ninth inning in a technically designated non-save situation. Blake's switch to Hart still called for the closer based on importance of this game alone in stopping the eight-game slide.

The streak was over and there was a huge sigh of relief coming from the visitor's managerial office as Blake finally felt like a winner again. It did not matter that the Cardinals also won on this night to keep the deficit at one full game. The team had played like a winner, made no glaring mistakes, and scraped out enough runs on offense to give the Cubbies a comfortable margin that the bullpen made stand up.

The mood was upbeat but cautious after the game. A win is a win, but one victory does not constitute a streak, it just prevented a different kind of skid from continuing in the wrong direction.

Blake had seen his boys go hot and cold before and he was hopeful that his team would take off again in the right direction. As the manager contemplated the rest of the season in his head while sitting in his temporary visiting manager's office, he knew a streak would not cut it anymore. The team absolutely had to play consistently productive baseball for the remaining 13 contests to close out the regular season.

The Friday evening game between the Redlegs and the Cubs turned out to be the pivotal game of the four-game set. The weather improved just enough to create a better style of play, as the temperature was cool by September standards in Cincinnati, but not damp and wet as the night before.

Blake was happy to start his number one pitcher, Kyle Jacobson, after being forced by a cramped schedule to rely on call-ups and not-quite-major-league-quality replacements.

Jacobson was breezing through the Reds batting order that was littered with September call-ups themselves. Baseball can be a crazy, cruel game, but on this night and in these conditions, with this batting lineup, it appeared Jacobson would go the distance and shut the home team down.

The Cubs themselves put up little offense, but had just enough pop in their productive at-bats to put the visitors up 3-0 after six innings. A two-run homer by slugger Jim Arnold in the fourth had opened up a bit of a margin that seemed likely to hold up.

However, a bloop double to lead off the bottom of the seventh started a downward spiral that put the lead in jeopardy. A hit batter and a swinging bunt that somehow was perfectly placed down the third base line loaded the bases with nobody out.

Blake was sitting this game out as a catcher and paced in the dugout wondering if he should go to the bullpen. He preferred to leave the eighth inning for Guillen to start out with a clean slate and nobody on base, but he was pressed by the importance of this late-season contest to warm up Miguel in the seventh. The manager asked for time from the home plate umpire as he sprang out from the dugout as soon as the Reds batter was announced. He took his time to reach the mound so Guillen could get some extra pitches in to warm up.

There was little said on the mound as Blake told his starting pitcher he would be staying in, but the manager wanted to stall, and he just stood there chewing his gum and looking straight into Jacobson's eyes as if he was talking to him. It was all a regularly rehearsed act that fooled nobody, but there was not anything the umpires could do to prevent the planned delay. Usually, the home plate umpire walks out to the mound, which forces a decision one way or another. As tonight's arbiter pulled even at the mound, Blake clapped his hands and barked out some encouragement to Jacobson before returning to the dugout. Hopefully for the Cubs, building momentum would be slowed and their starting pitcher could catch his breath in anticipation of a crucial at-bat.

The Cincinnati batter stepped into the batter's box and dug in, scraping his back foot several inches into the dirt for a solid base to explode into the thrown pitch. As is often the case in September when teams are out of contention like the Reds, this batter was a call-up prospect, with little advance scouting available to adequately prepare Chicago pitchers. Blake and his staff did have some background on the kid, but it was spotty.

The Cubs infield was at double-play depth, willing to sacrifice a run for two outs. The hope was for just one run to come of this rally, or better yet none at all, but maintaining a lead was critical.

The first pitch was put into play as the batter flared a Jacobson offering into shallow left center. The runner on third held, as is proper, to see if the ball would be caught. He would score easily if it fell in uncaught, but would be in line to tag up if the fielder caught the shallow ball in a compromising position.

The other two Cincinnati runners were sort of caught in no-man's land as they more or less had to go halfway between bases to be able to quickly adapt to either, scamper ahead a base if the ball fell in, or retreat to their occupied base if the ball was caught.

Cubs shortstop Rickey Sanchez turned toward the outfield and sprinted to where he thought the batted ball might land without turning back to visualize the baseball. That would have slowed him down just enough to let the ball fall in play. At just the last moment, Sanchez turned around and spotted the falling sphere before fully stretching out to make an unbelievable catch. The base umpires were a bit slow to recognize the ball was caught and there was no visible signal from any of the arbiters dressed in dark blue to assist the runners.

Sanchez hid the baseball by pulling his fielder's glove towards him and underneath his body in a deceptive roll before leaping up with the baseball in hand. Cubs second baseman Petey Arroyo scurried to the second base bag, and with both Cincinnati runners in a vulnerable position, Sanchez quickly snapped the ball to Petey, who stepped on second before the Reds runner could return in time for out number two. The runner on first simply froze wondering what the call was going to be and never left his tracks in the baseline between first and second. As the stunned Cincy runner looked at the umpires for direction, Arroyo ran over with the ball in his glove and tagged out the runner for an amazing triple play that allowed Chicago to escape a game-threatening situation.

The umpires finally made a visible out sign, but it was too little, too late for the home team. The Cincinnati manager was irate at the non-call that left his runners without any clues to properly run the bases in this situation. It was a tough break for the Reds, but the umpires had to wait to see for sure if Sanchez had caught the ball. The sparse couple thousand fans in attendance at this late season game littered the field with anything they could find at their disposal, but the call stood. The Cincy manager was tossed from the game and the Cubs went on to shut out the Reds 3-0 behind a complete-game effort from Jacobson.

The momentum and spirit that were lifted by this rare play allowed the Cubs to feel they were destined to win rather than hoping for such results. The team was riding high and the Cubbies followed up this turnaround game with a resounding 10-2 victory the following afternoon. The bats were hot, led by Sanchez, Bartlett and Rodriguez with a home run from each and six RBI in total from the three. Bowman was solid on the mound and Cincinnati appeared lifeless for the whole game. The few fans left in attendance at the end of the contest were mostly boisterous Chicago fans that whooped it up for the visitors on a cloudy, cool afternoon that was sunny in the eyes of all who cheered for the Cubs.

They now had a streak, three victorious games in succession that pulled them even with St. Louis for first place for 24 hours until Cincinnati salvaged the last game of the four-game weekend series behind a spectacular pitching outing from their ace pitcher Jose Alvarez. The 2-0 shutout defeat, coupled with a Cardinals win, returned the deficit to a full game after the weekend results.

There were no excuses; Blake's team played a solid defensive game, but simply could not solve the pitching repertoire of Alvarez. There was no shame involved here, as the dominant Reds right-hander was a leading candidate for the National League's Cy Young Award. His 19-5 record with a 2.30 ERA left many teams shaking their heads in frustration. It was simply an outstanding effort from a spectacular player, and all the Cubs could do was tip their hat in appreciation of their opponent this afternoon.

Blake's team was back on track and playing consistent baseball. That was all he could ask for from his players. It was now on to Pittsburgh to complete the road trip. The deficit in the standings was only one while the number of games left had shrunk to 10.

Ten whole games were all that stood in the way of an unlikely Chicago post-season appearance. Anything can happen in a 10-game stretch, thought Blake, as he stared out the window of the charter plane at nothing in particular while he heard the aircraft's landing gear pull up into the belly of the Boeing jet. This flight was just beginning, but the journey of this bizarre season was starting to wind down.

Ten games would decide the fate of this Chicago squad and would likely define the legacy of both Chicago Cubs teams of this season. The pre-accident Cubs and the makeshift Cubs that were forced by fate into a prominent national role would likely be remembered by whatever happened in these 10 measly baseball games. Many years from now historians and baseball aficionados would recall the legacy of these grown men throwing a ball around a diamond; adults playing a child's game that can be decided by the smallest minute happenstance ever imagined.

It could be a gust of wind, a funny bounce, an argument with a wife by a prominent player that affects his performance. Any quirk of fate, just like the one that put Blake Benson here in the first place when he missed that doomed flight. Any tiny factor could decide the legacy of this unique situation. The irony was not lost by one Blake Charles Benson as his eyes fixated on the diminishing terrain of Cincinnati without his mind registering anything at all that he was visualizing.

Before he knew it, the plane began its descent into Pittsburgh. Blake could not begin to know what would happen in the next 10 days.

54 — Fighting the Battle Alone No More

The team mood was noticeably calmer, more confident and collected as Blake's boys reached Pittsburgh for the final road destination of the season for the Chicago Cubs. However, this bunch did not have the feel of a normal squad reaching its 162-game limit.

The abbreviated mini-season for the hastily arranged roster of "emergency" Cubs minus one made for a strange feel. This haphazard bunch had played together for slightly over a month and the newness of the squad actually prevented the players from feeling some of that mental fatigue that sets in over such a lengthy season.

The baseball year starts in February and continues with only scattered single days off except for the five day All-Star break in July, on through the dog days of August, before it finally reaches the season end in the beginning of October, a total of nearly eight months.

The life of a major league ballplayer is indeed glamorous and the pay is unbelievable, but the physical and mental challenges of such a long season take their toll. Not only does the length of the baseball year have its professional liabilities, the personal effect of traveling and being away from one's family carries with it plenty of personal risks as well.

The team becomes your family and, like most, they fight, love and dislike, perhaps even hate, when together for extended periods of time. Bonds develop with some while others keep to themselves, but the unity is undeniable. Some squads develop unity better than others, but it's always there in varying degree.

Even this aspect of brotherhood was profoundly less developed based on time alone, but coming from so many different organizations where the mundane and the specific varied greatly, it was to be expected that this band of brothers would be more like orphans for the rest of their season. Their abbreviated season consisting of August and September, perhaps October if miracles do indeed happen, simply made togetherness a physical element only, without the emotional aspect that truly needed to be developed over time to have significance.

Blake was generally a fairly social guy with his teammates past, but this time it was so different, mostly due to brevity and the authority of managing. He had been keeping to himself for the most part to remain capable of making tough personnel decisions and, of course, there was the drinking element that had to be addressed.

Most players drank at least some alcohol, some more than others, just like any other workplace. This group was often confined in close quarters and the drinking became a male bonding event that, despite its potential harms, made alcohol the preferred social mixer.

Obviously, Blake had to avoid this potential trigger that could lead him down the destructive path which started this whole scenario developing in the first place. It seemed natural when Blake holed up somewhere on the road and just waited out temptation until the next game rolled around.

Blake was beginning to see the light after his recent mild setbacks. His original game plan had obvious pitfalls that he could not have envisioned or even felt at the initial time of decision. Toughing it out was usually a man's first thought on virtually every problem that comes up in life, albeit physical or emotional.

However, the continued struggles, particularly on the road, forced Blake to reexamine his initial game plan. It had finally caught up to him after the last incident where it was necessary for Mark Douglas to physically spend time with Blake in his hotel room. The sound sleep that prevailed that night provided a clearer head to the troubled manager. At that point he began to realize an important fact. Dealing with his alcohol problem alone simply would not cut it any longer.

His last, rather lengthy phone call to his wife offered some immediate comfort, and provided a separate, but profound impetus to a newfound outlook. Blake often resisted Kim's advice, out of male pride he guessed. However, he knew deep down that she was often right. Kim had known all along that dealing with it alone would not last, but she also knew her spouse well enough to know Blake had to run out of possible options before his ego would finally and reluctantly give in.

The time between the team's arrival in Pittsburgh on a Sunday evening and the next scheduled game the following night meant there was going to be more idle time than Blake desired. He knew by now that the time he had previously spent in similar situations on the road by himself would not work any longer, as if it really ever did. He just endured the constant thoughts of drinking, barely hanging on by a thread to his sobriety.

"Allergy to the body and obsession of the mind" was very accurate in describing drinking excessively, as well as the seemingly non-stop processing from the brain regarding any and all issues brought back to remembrance by the slightest association to alcohol from the past. He had to communicate with others to find some solace in his daily ordeal.

Blake was now at that point where he needed his wife's advice on how to proceed. Blake had an idea he wanted to run past Kim, and he was fairly certain she would be on board, but he also had come to realize that his perceptions of her desired outcomes had been wrong too many times in the past. He best get her verbal approval via the phone before he proceeded with his next step in the alcoholic healing process.

On a Monday morning after a fairly restful night in his hotel bed, Blake knew that his mind would begin to obsess with too much time to kill before arriving at PNC Park in downtown Pittsburgh. He showered after starting his day with coffee and perusing the complimentary USA Today. Now, with a towel wrapped around his waist, he leaned on his non-throwing side and hit the speed dial for his wife's phone.

"Good morning Blake," Kim answered quickly before he could greet his wife first.

"Good morning honey," replied Blake in earnest, as he was determined to get right at the point of his morning call.

"Sorry to be so blunt this early in the call, but I need to get your help on something. I've got to talk to someone about the things buzzing about in my brain that just won't quit. There's a phone number in the bedroom drawer right by my reading lamp. It's the counselor that spoke at the AA meeting I was at. I'm going to call him and see if he can help ease my mind some before we head to the ballpark. I was pretty sure you'd be happy to hear I'm calling him today and since I didn't bring the card it was written on, I figured you'd be more than willing to relay his number. This should be a good thing, right? I mean this is what you've always wanted me to do, isn't it Kim?"

"Yes, Blake, but this should ideally be in a group setting. It's a good start though. Hold on, I'll see if I can find the number."

Blake was patiently waiting while he listened to his wife walking up the stairs at home. He could hear the footsteps and her heavier breathing the higher up she ascended.

"Kim, maybe you need to start working out again babe? I can hear your panting. Did you find the number yet? It should be right on top of all the papers." He grew more impatient by the second listening to her fiddling around in the drawer.

"I found it Blake. What was that you said about me being out of breath? Well, if we didn't have such a nice house with as many steps to climb, I suppose it would be easier. You won't catch me complaining about a big house though."

"You know I'm just teasing. At least it shows I am in a better state of mind than I have been lately. I'm ready now, what's the number? I forgot his name also, but it's on the card. Please give me that too."

Kim relayed the information to her husband, but before she finished it came to her suddenly that this might not be the best approach, at least as far as the order of Blake's impending action.

"Hold on a second Blake. Don't you think it would be better to run this by your boss? He's also your friend and since he was with you that night and introduced you to the man, he probably has a right to know what you're contemplating."

There was several seconds of awkward silence before Blake finally chimed in.

"I see your point Kim, but I don't want to unnecessarily worry Marty. He might be questioning my capacity to lead this team if he hears about it. Do you really think I should let on that I'm having troubles?"

"There you go again Blake. Always wanting to do everything on your own and your way, isn't this why you are supposedly going ahead with this? Don't be afraid to reach out for help. Marty brought you there for this exact reason and to get it through your thick skull that reaching out is a good thing and not a sign of weakness. Go ahead and do what you want, you always do anyway."

Again there was a noticeable pause after Kim expressed her frustration with her husband before Blake finally responded.

"I said to myself and to you that I'd start to reach out and open up. You're right, Kim. The man has a right to know and he is so supportive. He will likely understand. No more secrets with the people doing their best to help me out with this daily battle. I'll call him right now before I go ahead and call the counselor."

Kim had calmed down in response to Blake's reinforced admission for help and began to speak very supportively to her husband.

"This is the right way Blake, you'll see. You never fail when you put your mind to something and open up to others that care for you. I'm damn proud of you honey for taking this next step and doing it in the right way."

"Okay, enough with the love fest here. I've got work to do, but seriously Kim, thank you for pushing me in the right direction even though my stubbornness makes everything tougher for us both in the long run. Maybe someday I'll learn to trust right out of the gate and not have to knock myself silly first before I realize you were right all along. Wish me and the team well tonight. It's sure looking like we might just hang with those damn Cardinals right until the hopefully not bitter end."

"Yes, Blake, go get 'em. This city is really behind you guys and they're starting to believe in miracles around here. I'll be here whenever you need me, but don't wait until tomorrow to call me. Just a quick message to hear your voice does wonders for me too, you know."

"Gotcha. Later Kim. I promise to call you tonight win or lose. Bye for now and thanks again honey."

The phone conversation ended and the man inside still wanted to go it alone, but the manager in him knew it would be best to call and let Marty know what was going on with his daily battle. Why do I have to be so doggone stubborn? He contemplated that thought for a minute or two before he sat down in his chair, facing the mirror in his hotel room and, shaking his head at the reflection of such a stubborn, prideful man, finally called his boss Marty.

55 — It Takes One to Know One

Blake quickly punched in Marty's number before he could change his mind and revert back to "one-man Blake" who never could admit that his own way could be fallible. Never needing another person made him feel in control, even though the reality was as far from being in control as possible.

Naturally, Marty recognized the number and initiated the conversation with a boisterous greeting.

"Blake my man, how's tricks? It sure is nice to see you guys moving in the right direction again." The general manager spoke with apparent delight and conviction with his upbeat tone of voice.

"Hello Marty. Aren't you in the least surprised to hear from me today? I'm not one for initiating phone calls."

"Why, now that you mention it, I suppose it's a bit out of your norm, but I kind of expected a call from you fairly soon," replied the wise old man, who drew on so many of his own life experiences to anticipate one step ahead of others.

"Marty, remember that meeting that you took me to and that fellow, the counselor that you introduced me to?"

"Of course I do Blake. Most things in life I do for a purpose now days so these things stick in my mind a bit better. We've all got battles to fight and it's not much fun getting old. The memory can get the better of me at times these days."

"Well, I've been bothered lately by some thoughts and you know these road trips are a never-ending challenge to my sobriety. I just feel the need to open up and talk about some concerns I have to other people that I know can help me. To be honest, I was a bit apprehensive about calling you first before phoning the counselor. I didn't want you to think I couldn't handle this responsibility."

"Blake, I've been doing this job for a long time now, probably too long, but I've got eyes and ears you know, and I've got connections you never even knew about. I've got a pretty good understanding of what's going on in your mind these days. Did you forget that I was in the same boat as you're in now? Actually, I stand corrected. We are still in this daily battle together each and every day. It doesn't matter how long we've been sober. I sometimes feel I know you better than you know yourself, at least at this point in your recovery. I try to stay a step ahead of you to anticipate how I can help you out."

"Christ Marty, I can be so stupid sometimes. I should know better. I know you're behind me and that you stuck your neck out for me."

"That's right. I did Blake and I did it because I know you can do this. That doesn't mean we don't all have daily challenges. I'm here to help and to make sure you realize what's in this never-ending process of staying sober. I've been there. I'm there now."

"Jesus, it's finally getting through to me Marty. It's a baby step here, a baby step there, but I'm starting to get it, bit by bit."

"I'm so glad," Marty said. "Now go call Mark Jamison and ask him whatever you want. Spill your guts to him. He's heard it all and he will reassure you that all of these thoughts are normal. He'll probably set you up with a sponsor that you can call whenever needed. These concerns of yours can come up anytime, at the oddest hours even. Trust me, I know."

"Yes, those middle of the night waking up and can't get back to sleep moments in a hotel room all alone can sure cause the mind to wander into unprotected areas. Suddenly you feel so vulnerable to the temptation when you were just fine a few hours ago. It's all very strange. And those drinking dreams are so real that when I wake up I have to think a few moments before I realize I really haven't been drinking. Do you get those?"

"Why Blake, I think just about everyone does. I know of a guy who swears he'd wake up feeling drunk. There are a lot of varieties, but most involve the same incessant conduct."

"That's good to know. Well, I won't bother you anymore Marty. I'll call Mark and bug him for a while."

"Come on now Blake, you've got to get over that guilt. You're never bothering anybody when you're talking to a fellow ex-boozer. That's another step you'll have to get over. People want to help and are definitely not bothered by lengthy talks. But hey, as long as I've got you here, let's talk shop for a bit. How's the team's overall demeanor these days? Are they tight?"

"Well, we all hit a rough patch in St. Louis. We cleared the air a bit and it's been better since the meeting at the end of the last game in St. Louis. Aw, heck, I might as well tell you, the team was bothered by my decision-making or lack thereof, and my own demeanor. For whatever reason, I got very hesitant all of a sudden and was distant and indecisive. Thanks to my own players, it got straightened out quickly. I'm okay now Marty, I really am."

"Blake, for the last time, you should know that I find out what's going on. It's my responsibility to know how my team is faring on the field and in the clubhouse, and on the road for that matter. I knew 95 percent of the shenanigans you pulled on the road and you were far better than most at hiding some of your dalliances."

"Jesus Marty, how did you ever not kick me off your team?"

"It's probably because you guys are ballplayers, not saints. You still had value to the team and the organization, but you got too close to the sun at the end. You were done this time except for the bizarre circumstances."

"Well, that, and because I had a believer in me, thank you Marty for everything. I had, and still have, a lot to prove. We'll give it our best shot down the stretch."

"That's all you can do Blake, that's all you guys can do. We'll all be forever grateful to you and your boys if you just do that for the remainder. Now take care of yourself first and then get the team ready for another big series. And before you go Blake, just remember I may be an old curmudgeon, but I do know my business and I do know my team, and that includes you. There's no need to try and hide shit, I'll find out about it eventually. The reason why I give you some latitude is because I know how badly you want to pull this out for your old teammates. By the way, Sandy would be proud of the way you've conducted yourself since the accident. I know how much he meant to you."

"Thanks boss. I better go before I start to cry. Thanks again. See you back home in three days Marty. Goodbye."

The conversation ended and Blake felt a big weight off his shoulders. Now it was on to another phone call before he could turn his complete attention to his team. This one sure could be interesting if he totally revealed all of his troubling thoughts of the last two months. Today was a good day to start anew.

56 — Lessons Learned While Turning the Corner

Effective coaching takes time, but that was one more thing this ragtag, quickly assembled bunch did not have. There was no spring training with this coaching staff for the makeshift Cubs except for a prospect or two that had been at the Chicago camp in Arizona this past March.

Blake's keen eye for talent allowed him to pick several underachievers in the player dispersal draft right after the accident. He knew several of them had the physical skills to succeed at the major league level, but for whatever reason they had come up short so far in production.

The two outfielders plucked from the Marlins organization had raw power in their bats, but the offensive hitting philosophy preferred by Miami was based on an approach that emphasized contact and hitting behind runners to manufacture runs rather than sitting back and waiting for home run bombs to score in bunches. Felix Gonzalez and Ricky Rodriguez could put the ball into the seats with the best of them with a bit of coaching from batting coach Henry Hanson. He was simply known as Hank to all in the game of baseball. Hank was a power hitting slugger back in his day with the Boston Red Sox. He spent years developing his righty stroke to take advantage of the Big Green Monster in left field at Fenway Park in Beantown. His ability to select pitches that he could easily pull into left field to take advantage of the short distance from home plate to the Monster was a key part of his major league success. The six-time All Star and twice home run champion would be the perfect fit to fine tune the power development of these two raw outfielders.

It was no secret in the game of major league baseball that center fielder Desmond Wilson could run as fast as the speediest base running threats in the big leagues. The old saying that, "you can't steal first base," was the prevailing derogatory definition of Desmond's game so far in his young career. He had a bit of pop in his bat, just enough to convince himself that he could jack the ball into the stands at a pace that would make him more money down the line in contract negotiations. The problem that developed which halted his progress at this level was his stubborn insistence on lifting the ball rather than taking advantage of his world-class speed by hitting the ball on the ground. Wilson had struggled in his first three seasons with the Dodgers, producing a paltry .230 batting average. He simply did not get on base enough to take advantage of his speed. Time after time he would fly out to the warning track, convincing him he was oh so close to being a legitimate power threat, even though all his coaches in LA knew his game required him to slap at the ball more and forget the long ball. Blake was determined to change Desmond's approach to hitting to get the most out of his ability. Third base coach Lenny Paxton, a superior base stealer in his day, would work with Desmond on base running to give the Cubs a legitimate speed game.

As game time approached during an Indian summer evening in the Steel City, Blake felt a resurgence of inner strength after baring his soul to his counselor from the AA meeting. The deeply distressed, newly recovering alcoholic, still coming to grips with his disease and all that it entailed, had finally learned to let loose with his thoughts and emotions. Blake more or less went down the list of disturbing experiences and worrying thoughts that had plagued him from day one of his sobriety.

There was not much the counselor could say except these were very normal feelings and part of the healing process. All Blake really needed was for someone else to understand what he had been going through. There were no easy answers or magic bullets to put an end to worrisome thoughts, but the sheer effect of letting it all go and knowing he wasn't alone made all the difference in Blake's attitude.

He now had another number to call when things got rough, or even when they did not, but just having an ear for his concerns would have a soothing effect from here to the end of the season. He promised his new sponsor, Terry Parsons, that he would call him daily just to keep on a level keel.

The positive vibes emanating from Blake seemed to inspire his players as they continued to play errorless baseball. It was now up to five games without an error and the pitching improved as well, with fewer base runners. The Chicago bats were efficient, if not overly productive in the first game 5-2 triumph over the Pirates.

Desmond Wilson had three hits, two of them the infield variety, as he finally began taking advantage of his speed. Wilson stole a pair of bases and scored two runs as well.

Felix Gonzalez took advantage of the green light from his manager on a 3-0 count and blasted a solo homer on a "get me over" fastball that put the Cubs on top early, and they cruised to victory without much of an effort from the hometown Pirates.

Terry Riley again crafted his way through five innings without giving up a run, and earned the victory. The pitching staff and the defense were on board limiting freebies like bases on balls and infield errors. It had sunk in that the team just had to play mistake-free ball and make the other team beat them rather than giving their opponents extra outs and more scoring chances than they deserved.

The middle game of the series was played once more under ideal fall weather in Pittsburgh. The Cubs stretched their errorless streak again with superb defense, and this time outfielder Ricky Rodriguez stole the show with a pair of two-run homers in a 4-1 victory. The muscular Rodriguez had worked the count both times in his favor and capitalized on a 3-1 count for his first shot. The enigmatic player that showed tremendous power in batting practice, but seldom in games, sat on an inside, belt-high fastball to arc his blast well over the left field fence in the second inning. In the fifth he did much the same before taking a knee-high fastball deep over the center field wall on a 2-1, hitter's friendly count with a man on first.

Baseball can seem like such a simple game when it's going your way. Success can be very illuminating after players buy in to the simple approach of limiting freebies like walks or allowing runners via errors. Scoring first helps set the stage for success as well. Playing with a lead relaxes your players; constantly battling from behind has a troubling mental effect that leads to undue pressure to make up the difference with one at-bat.

Unfortunately the St. Louis Cardinals were not giving an inch in their play-off push with the Cubs. The Cards maintained their one-game lead with a pair of victories on the road in Cincinnati.

The Cubs felt pretty confident in themselves with a 5-1 mark in their last six contests, all played under playoff pressure. Their manager was loose, very decisive and more upbeat than his players had seen him since the first two weeks on the job as player-manager for this restructured Cubbies outfit.

However, just like the last series in Cincinnati, the Cubs could not complete the sweep in Pittsburgh and fell to the Bucs 4-2. The Cardinals were losing as well to the Reds to keep the deficit at one game, with now only a mere seven games left in the regular season. There was no more "later" or "we'll get them next game." This was it. The team was in the final stretch.

If the Cubs were media darlings before with their Sports Illustrated feature, and felt extremely appreciated by their own home fans prior to this road trip, they were in for a pleasant surprise now that all seemed to believe in the impossible. The pandemonium was just beginning.

It would be playoff baseball atmosphere the rest of the way in Chicago as the Milwaukee Brewers were next in line to come to Wrigley before the regular campaign would end with the hated rivals from St. Louis invading the Windy City to try and nail down the division championship on Chicago soil.

The fall temperatures were dropping daily, but the heat would definitely be felt throughout the city for the next eight days after a brief one day off for the Cubbies before starting the series against the Brew Crew from Suds City.

A much-needed respite from the pressures of pennant-race baseball was in order for Blake and his boys. It was time to shore up some loose ends for Blake as he looked forward to competing head-to-head with the Cardinals down the stretch. Winning baseball had made the rookie manager cautiously optimistic and he began to believe his boys could keep this winning stretch going for at least one more week.

If it is true that the underdogs feel little or no pressure, then the Cubs should feel none at all, as nobody expected this ragtag bunch to be in the position they were with a week left. The Cardinals would be the team everybody would expect to win and win handily.

"That's why they play the games," is a timeworn expression to explain how one inferior-seeming team on paper can play with, or even defeat, a supremely talented group. It was put up or shut up time and the Cubs and their fans were ready like they had been waiting for this all their lives.

57 — Calm Before the Storm
in the Windy City

Blake was still riding his natural high from the recent success of his club and the overall improvement in his emotional state when the team arrived back in Chicago Wednesday evening.

The whole team was pleasantly surprised and deeply appreciative of a group of about 100 rabid fans that greeted them upon arrival at the airport. If they weren't aware of the building excitement for this week's action, they were beginning to sense the anticipation as they witnessed the excitable fans firsthand.

Everyone was looking forward to the day off tomorrow and a return to their own beds tonight. The pennant race was never far from anyone's mind as the last two weeks unfolded, but at least a temporary diversion would be in order.

Blake made sure his boys understood that it was important to relax and get completely away from the game on an off day this late in the season. He wanted them to turn off all media and at least try to not hear the team's name mentioned once on their day off. He implored them to refrain from even talking about baseball to girlfriends and wives. It was to be a day of total ease of mind and body.

Unfortunately, an excited Blake forgot a dose of his own medicine, as he wanted to call in all of his coaches to plan ahead for the coming week that would decide their playoff fate. However, Marty Anderson got wind of it, as he seemed to do regarding anything team-related, and ordered Blake to follow his own advice.

Things were looking up on the home front as well and Blake was eager to spend some quality time with his wife. Kim was pleased at Blake's openness and apparent progress in his recovery approach. There did not seem to be any tension building as he returned home just in time for the dinner his wife had prepared for the two of them. The plan was for nothing but togetherness between the married couple and the whole night came off without a hitch.

It had been a while, it seemed to Blake, since both he and his wife were both actually eagerly awaiting their reunion. When one was happy, the other one was not, and vice-versa. The lack of conflict between them made for a spectacular evening in the dining room and the bedroom.

Surprisingly, it was Blake who suggested the two of them take their seldom used, but spectacular yacht for a ride the following day on Lake Michigan. The expensive toy was moored in the Chicago Harbor. It was easily their most extravagant luxury purchase, and mostly sat idle while draining their pocketbook. The weather forecast looked splendid and the change of pace piqued both of their interests.

On a cool but very calm and sunny Thursday mid-morning, the happy couple motored out with no sails onto the unusually still and serene waters of Lake Michigan. Neither Blake nor Kim wanted to venture far away from shore, just enough to find solitude for the afternoon.

It was an ideal setting for a getaway from baseball afternoon. To be unrecognized and to distance themselves from any mention by media outlets was to be in heaven at this moment in time.

The two commented on nature and all of its beautiful surroundings. They outwardly admired the deep blue waters, the radiant sunshine that sparkled on the surface of the vast body of water, and all the waterfowl that they came across. None of nature's delights went unnoticed as the couple duly noted and marveled at the tiniest of splendid detail they were blessed to be a part of this glorious day.

As the powerful engine subsided at a place that was nowhere and everywhere special at the same time, Blake began to open up to his wife, whose hair was shining brilliantly in nature's serene elements of this day.

"Honey, I just wanted to find a quiet spot where we could just talk about you. It's not right that we talk about me and my worries and concerns all the time. It's my fault for not making you the primary focus of our relationship. You've always been the glue and I've always needed putty to patch things up for me. Why don't we spend the afternoon talking entirely about you? We can talk about your aspirations, your feelings and your concerns for once. I have to remind myself to make more of an effort to focus on my beautiful wife more often."

"Why, thank you, Blake. That warms my heart. Where should I begin? This is a wonderful idea, all of this. You've outdone yourself this time, my dear."

Blake reacted with pride from Kim's display of appreciation. He felt better about himself as the conversation continued.

"Kim, let's face it. I'm coming to the end of my baseball career here pretty soon. This next decade should be about where you want to go from here. Maybe you want to delve into something 100 percent and have your husband support your endeavor instead of the other way around? Have you ever thought of what you'd like to personally accomplish before we retire and sail off into the sunset? Maybe you just want to totally focus on us? I don't know your thoughts and I'm sorry I've never asked you before."

"Wow, this new Blake is exciting. Where've you been hiding?"

"First in a bottle of pity and then in an obsession of recovery I guess. I don't really know for sure at this moment, but it's about time I figure it out," said Blake.

"I've thought about my future quite a bit lately. You've accomplished so much in your baseball career. I'd like to accomplish something for myself. I was thinking of getting my law degree like my father. What do you think?"

"That's awesome Kim. You should definitely do it. After your degree, what would you like to do with your license to practice? Knowing you as I do, I'm pretty sure you've already mapped out that itinerary."

"I've only considered it in a general sense. Definitely some aspect of women's rights is where I'd like to head. Now that you've brought all this up, I do have another wish?"

"Anything Kim, it's about time I put you first. Just go ahead and tell me what you're thinking."

"Are you sure Blake? It's kind of a big one for the moment. Maybe one direction is all we should head for right now?"

"Nope, now's the time Kim, I'm tired of putting you on the back burner. Spit it out honey."

"Okay, you asked for it. I want us to adopt a child. I want to be a parent, a mom."

"Wow Kim, are you sure? What about your law aspirations?"

"I know I can handle both responsibilities and the thing is, I would have my husband home to help out. Are you willing to help out now that you've already said your baseball career is just about over?"

"The timing is right, that's for sure. I think we're onto something here. I'm concerned, but I'm also excited. Isn't that what parenting is all about?"

"Oh thank you Blake. This day is one of the best days in my life."

"Well, I couldn't agree more honey. I couldn't agree more," said Blake.

The reenergized couple stood up together and embraced for minutes on end without a word until Blake broke the ice.

"Okay babe, how about we talk about your family for a bit. You haven't told me how everybody has been lately. I think we've hit the hard stuff enough already. Just fill me in on the latest while I get us something to eat."

The rest of the afternoon was lighthearted and the mood was certainly established early on this gorgeous fall day. As they headed back toward shore, Kim had just one thing to say about baseball and hoped it would lift the mental load on Blake's shoulders for the final week of the regular season.

"Blake, this was such a great day. I hope you realize that the pressure is off you now. It should be all gravy from here on out. Your team has made great strides and you've hung in there all the way personally. Nobody can say you or your boys blew it."

"Well, I knew this couldn't go on forever. That's where you're wrong, my dear. The pressure's just beginning. Baseball's about winning and we're this close," said Blake as he held his thumb and index finger of his right hand a smidgeon apart. Blake continued without stopping to let his wife voice her opinion. "This could be epic Kim. This could be the story of the baseball century. We're the goddamn Cubs after all. We never win and we're on the cusp of baseball history. Heck, make that American history. We could sustain the legacy of my old teammates forever. Now that would be a fitting tribute to Sandy and the boys."

Kim just smiled and shook her head gently while staring intently at her husband. Some things about him she would just never understand. Why did he continue to set himself up for failure?

Even their divergent opinions on the next week could not change the overall mood for the day. This was a day off from baseball worth remembering. The driving question from here on out would be whether this final week would be worth remembering. That's why they play the games. Nobody ever knows for sure.

58 — Raucous, Reverent, and oh so Ready

If the Chicago fans were appreciative of, and enthusiastic for, the efforts of the newest Cubs after the tragic loss of numerous lives, they were absolutely giddy toward these athletic heroes now that the team had acquitted itself so admirably to this point.

It was considered a minor miracle, especially after falling behind the Cardinals in the standings, to be only one game back with seven to go. Never mind the 10-game lead this bunch was handed to them; the squad had fought tooth and nail since that first week back after the catastrophe. Since that first series against the Cards whittled the lead to six games right away, the resilient Cubbies had stayed in this race to the bitter end, no matter what happened from here on out.

Perhaps it was the lunacy of it all that gave the Cubs faithful such a fanatic rush of enthusiasm. The notorious, loveable losers from the North Side of the Windy City were expected to lose despite coming tantalizingly close over the decades. It was the tease that was their modus operandi, the normal routine of annual disappointment that both plagued and blessed the team at the same time.

Would this be the ultimate payback for years and years of disappointment? Was this some kind of divine intervention to explain past failures and to honor fans' continued loyalty? The 1969 Miracle Mets would have nothing on this bunch if this team could somehow pull off an upset and keep on playing in October.

The national media descended on Chicago right after the team arrived home from Pittsburgh. The last legs of the road trip had cemented the importance of late-season contests. The final series against the Cardinals would feel like a World Series atmosphere if the Cubbies were still within realistic striking distance. Anything short of a three-game lead for the Cards going into the four-game series would satisfy nearly the whole baseball world that an upset was indeed possible, if not likely.

It would be the ultimate underdog scenario, a David and Goliath setting in one of the nation's biggest television markets. Only the pesky Milwaukee Brewers stood in the way of a nationally televised sporting event that could rivet the country for the length of the series.

The current Cubbies were a bit more cautious after experiencing intense media attention right before they hit the disastrous eight-game skid that started at the end of their last home stand. They vowed to never again fall prey to the distracting elements of media darling status. However, they did not foresee its return so quickly, multiplied with at least a double dose of national attention.

They were enjoying the attention as the series began with Milwaukee, but collectively realized how fleeting fame could be in the game of baseball. There was a time and a place for the public part of the job, but when that first pitch is thrown, the focus had to be fully on the field and not on the airwaves of idolatry.

Miguel Guillen had become a media darling based on his wit and extravagant displays of personal style through his daily apparel. He had the knack of saying something funny and interesting at the same time, even if he was not entirely clear in his English language skills. The outgoing bullpen pitcher had become something of a team spokesman based on his desire to be seen and heard. Many players were very glad to defer to Miggy as it lightened the media load on them.

John Bartlett was also an unlikely source for useful quotes. Despite his cantankerous on-the-field demeanor, the veteran catcher was eager to play Mr. Nice Guy with the press. Perhaps both sides knew they were being played as Bartlett and the press interacted, but neither side apparently cared as long as their professional objectives were met.

Blake had reluctantly acquiesced his valuable time to the media as he was well aware his own legacy was developing right before their very eyes. After all, he was determined to achieve some sort of redemption for his previous, morally wandering ways. He knew the media would love to play along with that narrative, so he fed them his story without holding back the scurrilous details of his past. He would always finish the interview by recognizing his fallen teammates and praising his new players while emphasizing he was a new man or, at the very least, had returned to the honorable roots of his parental upbringing.

Blake had begun the practice of gathering his players after each postgame media session had played itself out. He took the initiative this time and buttressed his increasing managerial credibility by reminding his team what had happened the last time the press went nuts over this new Cubbies squad. There was to be no losing focus this time. The prize was continually on their mind and they now knew that attention would come as long as they produced on the field.

As the team got ready for Friday afternoon's game they were once again smiling in amazement during warm-ups. The ballpark was nearly filled and game time was still an hour away. The crowd was cheering their every move and the Cubbies had a difficult time staying focused on their pregame routines. The Wrigley faithful were already in first-pitch mode, chanting for the home team in near ecstasy.

This was a whole new ballgame from the fan perspective. It was going to be one raucous party all day long. Pennant fever had taken hold in Chicago and the national media was stoking the virus with constant attention.

A manager's job is to worry about every possible threat to his team. Blake never thought he would have to be concerned with his team being too wound up to play effectively, but after witnessing firsthand the outright enthusiasm for his players and the ear-splitting noise reverberating throughout the ballpark, he quickly turned his focus to this problem.

He gathered his coaches and spread the word about keeping his boys relaxed. This would be a monumental task, but Blake and his coaches had experienced something similar to this in their own playing careers. The job at hand was to somehow convince his players to relax and just enjoy the moment.

The coaching staff and the rest of America was about to find out if this bunch had the mettle to handle this delirious crowd and play a simple game in the best possible manner, while understanding that each and every play from here on out could decide their fate.

"Play ball!" shouted the home plate umpire. The leadoff man for the Milwaukee Brewers was about to step in the batter's box as manager Blake Benson sat in his usual home dugout spot shaking his head in disbelief. This was a whole new ballgame for sure, unbelievably totally new.

59 — Veteran's Day to Show the Way

The excitement was undeniable throughout Wrigley Field on this cool, but sunny mid-afternoon game with playoff ramifications. A slight breeze blew toward home plate from straight away center field and off the chilly waters of Lake Michigan.

There would be nerves all around today, as one would expect given the importance of this first game of a three-game weekend set with the neighborly Milwaukee squad, who traveled a mere 90 miles or so to the cozy confines of Wrigley Field.

Blake and John Bartlett were two veterans that had been in more than their share of similar contests. Blake's time with the Cubs had seen him on the cusp of playoffs before, only to be denied by the curse, or the simple fact that other teams were better. Bartlett had seen playoff time and even had World Series experience with the St. Louis Cardinals, but had never won it all either. They both were much more comfortable in today's setting than the rest of their inexperienced teammates.

All would feel that sense of nervous excitement today. If a ballplayer did not feel this emotion, there was no sense for him to be even playing this kid's game for a profession. The difference was that Blake and Bartlett, like other veterans in this position, were able to shake off the nerves as the game wore on, while the inexperienced had a much more difficult time shaking the pangs of distraction.

The rookie manager in Blake knew this would happen and he was not surprised that his team played very tight in the first half of this critical game. Fortunately for the Cubbies, the Brew Crew from Milwaukee seemed to have the opposite malady of indifference as the teams played to a scoreless tie through five innings.

Both of today's starting pitchers were of the finesse type that probably fared better under these circumstances. The Milwaukee starting hurler was Richard Welsh, a lefty with marginal big-league stuff, but definitely major league smarts on the mound. He was taking advantage of the Chicago squad's anxiousness by living just enough out of the strike zone to entice the overly eager Cubs hitters to chase tosses that were designed to keep batters from squaring up the ball on the barrel of the bat.

The Cubs had Kyle Jacobson on the bump to similarly mix up his variety of pitches to stifle the Milwaukee bats. Finesse pitchers often have to rely on an old adage from craftsmen of the past that describes their pitching style as one that, "Makes your strike look like a ball to the batter and make your ball look like a strike to the hitter," as the pitch approaches home plate.

Jacobson took advantage of Milwaukee's apparent disinterest as their team looked like they were just up there at the plate hacking away without any offensive strategy, a normal reaction to indifference.

While Welsh had the Chicago batters swinging and missing at balls dropping just out of the strike zone or keeping the thrown ball off the sweet spot of the bat, resulting in weak grounders and lazy fly balls, the Brewers batters were more or less getting themselves out with a lack of concentration.

The Wrigley crowd was getting a little impatient at the lack of any offensive threat developing and the Chicago bench could feel the nervousness spreading throughout the ballpark. There was a sense of something starting to give in one direction or the other as the game rolled into the top of the sixth inning still in a scoreless tie.

The Wrigley faithful grew even more apprehensive as Jacobson had a rare wild spell to open the sixth and walked the first two batters to put the home team in a perilous position as the game slowly crept into the later innings. Bartlett asked for time from the home plate umpire and slowly removed his mask and tucked it under his arm as he met Jacobson on the rubber to check on the pitcher's status.

"C'mon Jake, we can't be giving these guys anything. Throw the goddamn ball over the plate," he yelled at his pitcher over the constant buzz of the home crowd.

"Jesus, what do ya think I'm trying to do?" replied a clearly agitated Jacobson.

"Goddamn it I know Kyle, but bear down here."

"Get back behind the plate and I'll take care of this," shot back the veteran pitcher, more than aware of the significance of the moment.

Bartlett turned his back to Jacobson and walked rather slowly back to the plate before crouching down and giving his pitcher the fastball sign, as it appeared to all to be a bunting situation.

Kyle let loose with a high fastball that is the preferred pitcher's pitch in such a sacrifice bunting situation. The Brewer batter popped up the bunt down the third base line, but the sacrifice attempt was just out of the reach of both third baseman Simons and pitcher Jacobson. The bunted ball stayed fair, nestling in between the grass of the infield and the chalk of the third base line. Simons was forced to handle the bunt and threw to first base to get the safe out where second baseman Petey Arroyo had correctly scampered over to cover the first base bag as Jim Arnold crept toward home to cover a possible sacrifice attempt.

The threat was real now with two men in scoring position for Milwaukee as the Brewers got nearer to the bottom of their batting order with the seventh man coming up to bat. Strategy would definitely be coming into play with the pitcher or a pinch-hitter up soon.

The first order of business was getting this seventh-in-the-order batter out without allowing the go-ahead runner to score. The infield moved in to the edge of the grass in preparation for cutting off the lead runner from scoring on a grounder, as Jacobson leaned in to get the sign from Bartlett. The lefty came to the stretch position, but was at a disadvantage keeping an eye on the runner at third because his southpaw status forced his back to the runner.

Kyle let loose with another high fastball. His purpose was to try to get the batter to harmlessly pop out to the infield or to make his pitch a difficult toss to bunt in the likelihood of an attempted suicide squeeze.

The first pitch sailed high and away from the right-handed Milwaukee batter for ball one. There was no hint of a bunt here as the Brewers were very deceptive regarding their plans.

The next pitch was repeated in virtually the same pattern as the first, except the Milwaukee runner at third came barreling toward home just as Jacobson was letting go of his pitch.

Third baseman Simons and first baseman Arnold both hollered out "squeeze" at the top of their lungs to alert the pitcher and catcher of the charging runner, but it didn't do any good, and the Brewer batter was able to get the bunt down despite the high and away fastball that made it an awkward, but successful squeeze play.

Jacobson had no choice but to throw to Petey covering first base again, and the go-ahead run scored while the Cubs recorded the second out of the inning at first.

It was an ideal time to pull off that play and veteran Milwaukee manager Billy Curran was able to have his cake and eat it too with the clever maneuver. With the successful squeeze, the manager was able to both take the lead and find a way to keep his starting pitcher in the game. Now he would not have to pull his pitcher, who was clearly on the top of his game today, as the Cubs and Blake chose to intentionally walk the eighth batter to bring the pitcher's spot in the order up to the plate.

Welsh struck out to end the inning, leaving runners at first and third, but the Brewers now carried the lead as the home team came up in the bottom of the sixth trailing for the first time in the critical contest.

John Bartlett led off the inning for the home team as the crowd began chanting in earnest for the Cubs to get their offense rolling. Blake walked over to his catcher as Bartlett was just grabbing his bat and helmet in preparation for the turn at the plate.

"Let's get something started Rat Man," yelled Blake.

"Yep, we've got to get smarter with our at-bats. This guy's got zilch, but he's killing us with soft stuff away and out of the zone. I'm not swinging until I either have two strikes on me or he's forced to throw me something hittable.

Enough of this shit. I know you and I are smarter than this, Blakester. We've got to reach these kids somehow," Bartlett said.

"You got that right big fella, I'm getting my stick ready in case I'm needed. I've been watching this guy close. The only time he comes inside is either to try and get a called third strike or to brush back on an 0-2 count. I'm ready for his good-for-nothing soft shit myself if the time is right for me to pinch-hit. Glad we've got that third catcher now just in case," said Blake.

Bartlett just nodded his head and turned toward the batter's box. He strapped on a protective shin guard for his left leg as he had a tendency to foul off pitches on his front left foot facing toward the pitcher. He pulled his batting gloves over both hands, tapped the top of his batting helmet to secure it and to get a bit of pine tar for good grip, and stared at the pitcher Welsh the whole time as he neared the plate.

The wily veteran catcher possessed a career .276 batting average with almost 200 homers in his 14-year stint in the major leagues. He could jack a homer with the right conditions and a favorable pitch. He was looking for a pitch to drive as he ground his spikes into the soft dirt in the once clearly drawn batter's box that had been obliterated by constant use this day,

The afternoon was slipping away. A light fog swooped in from Lake Michigan to make for an eerie setting as the last half of the sixth began. The ballpark lights had been switched on after the top of the inning and were just beginning to take effect.

Bartlett himself had been fooled by Welsh on his first two plate appearances. He struck out in his first appearance when he chased a ball clearly out of the strike zone, and hit a comebacker to the mound in his second at-bat when Welsh had him lunging for a pitch on a 3-2 count.

Bartlett was determined to work the count this time as he stepped in, ready to deliver, as a veteran should in these situations.

Bartlett held off two tantalizingly close outside pitches for a hitter's friendly 2-0 count as the Milwaukee pitcher stared in at the home plate umpire in disbelief at the borderline calls that went against him this time.

No pitcher wants to walk the leadoff hitter of an inning, especially after just taking the lead. Bartlett correctly figured Welsh would challenge him with a fastball here. The Brewer pitcher clearly felt the effects of a shrinking strike zone. He felt pressure to get a bit more of the plate this time to get a strike call.

The Rat took a mighty cut at the ball and squared the pitch up perfectly, depositing the fat pitch into the left-field bleachers to tie the game at 1-1. The crowd went crazy and stood on their feet until Bartlett came out of the dugout to acknowledge the fans after he circled the bases. Bartlett doffed his batting helmet in appreciation and returned to the dugout with more slaps and high-fives from his rejuvenated teammates.

"That's what I'm talking about guys. That's what I'm talking about," repeated Blake as he pointed toward his catcher in appreciation.

"Work the count and then make him pay. Let's follow Bartlett and knock this guy out."

The nerves had dissipated and were replaced by exhilaration as Mike Simons stepped up to the plate. Welsh felt the umpire was squeezing him; the close calls went to the Cubs batter and not the pitcher. This time Welsh did not give in and walked Simons rather than floating up another fat one to a batter clearly ahead in the count.

The crowd could smell blood. Welsh clearly became agitated and the momentum was all on the Chicago side at the moment.

The rally was stifled for a moment as Felix Gonzalez got a bit overanxious one more time and flew out on the first pitch from Welsh. It clearly ticked off Blake after the manager had advised all to follow Bartlett's lead.

That would bring up light-hitting second baseman Petey Arroyo in the eighth spot, but before the scrappy second sacker stepped up to the plate, the manager called him back to the dugout and Blake told Petey that he was going to pinch-hit for him. That decision was not surprising, but the announcement of Blake as the pinch-hitter stunned most media members and likely a fair number of fans as well.

The crowd was deafening as Blake strolled up to the plate. The Cubs manager figured this was a good spot to use his experience and knowledge at the plate. With the pitcher coming up behind him, Blake was fairly sure he would get something good to hit. The baseball book that Blake hated dictated that no batter should be intentionally walked to put the go-ahead run in scoring position with only one out. However, this unorthodox maneuver could force Blake's hand somewhat. The manager would have to ponder whether to leave a poor-swinging Jacobson in the game to hit or pull him in favor of another pinch-hitter off the bench.

Blake also was well aware that he had hit Welsh well throughout his career and, given the pitcher's druthers, he strategically might just pitch around Blake in any other situation. The batting student in Blake knew Welsh would like to pitch him away early in the count, but Blake also correctly figured that Welsh knew Blake would not chase pitches in this situation.

He had seen Welsh throw a get-me-over curveball to start off the batter when the pitcher surmised that the prospective hitter would not chase borderline pitches early in the count. Welsh's game was all predicated on the lefty's ability to get ahead in the count where he had batters in the palm of his hands.

Now, the get-me-over curveball, as the name implies, is not a terribly tough pitch to hit. It works to get ahead in the count because it's so rarely thrown that batters normally just take the toss. It is almost always thrown on the first pitch when hitters are not in any immediate danger.

Blake had convinced himself that Welsh would do just that as he eyeballed the Brewers hurler from his position at the rear of the batter's box, in his normal position well off the plate.

The pitcher shook off his catcher twice, further convincing Blake that this pitch was coming. As a catcher himself he knew it would be highly unlikely for the catcher to call for such a seldom-used pitch. Blake readied himself as Welsh nodded his head in agreement at the third signal from the catcher. He knew he would get just one chance at a fat pitch and he had to take advantage.

Blake reminded himself to keep his weight back as he immediately picked up the ball's rotation as it left the pitcher's hand, as is often the case when a batter has had success against a pitcher before. The baseball was spinning right to left as it left the southpaw's throwing hand, signaling curve ball. Blake coiled his aging body and swung with such powerful torque that his bat propelled the baseball to a prodigious height and distance onto Sheffield Avenue and the crowd roared in disbelief at the magnitude of the blast.

The veteran Blake rounded the bases like a star-struck rookie after his first homer. This was no ordinary home run and it showed as Blake clapped his hands together all the way from the moment he realized the ball had cleared the fence until the time he jumped on home plate in an emphatic display of emotion.

His teammates were out of the dugout to greet him as he neared the steps. Smiles were all around as the team seemed to forget there were still three innings left to play and their club only had a precarious 3-1 lead.

Maybe they knew something the rest of the audience didn't, as the resounding significance of the moment and its subsequent emotional carryover propelled the Cubs the rest of the way in the final 3-1 score.

Miguel Guillen was allowed to go two full innings instead of one, further proof of the critical need to come out on top in this game. He cruised through his stint without allowing a single base-runner for the statistical hold for the game, and closer Randall Hart withstood a one-out ninth-inning walk to get the save and close out the victory.

The stands were rocking as the fans were out of their seats and stomping the whole last inning, while the fog thickened to create a surreal scene at Wrigley.

The Cardinals did not play until nighttime and they eventually won to keep the deficit still at a single game. However, of more immediate importance was the continued building of self-confidence coming from this bunch of guys that shared little or no bond just two months ago.

Everything appeared to be rolling in the right direction as the weekend took hold in Chicago. Saturday would provide another opportunity to build, or to stall out the sails of the Cubs. Blake liked his team's chances as he undressed in the clubhouse, but he had seen these ups and downs unfold before. Only time would tell in the crazy unpredictable world of baseball.

60 — Double Vision Derailing

Game two of the weekend series was sure to bring more of the same thrilling excitement that the opener produced in the Cubs' 3-1 victory. The Chicago players more or less expected the same enthusiasm from the crowd for the remainder of the season as long as the team still had a chance to catch the Cardinals.

There was little else in the name of surprises coming from the players' perspective, except of course for the ultimate question yet to be answered. Only the final outcome of the race was hanging in the balance now that Blake and his boys had seen firsthand how the Chicago faithful and the media were responding to their final push to make the playoffs.

The team was enjoying the newfound energy emanating from repeated successes of the past week. Gone were the doubting Thomases that brought the Cubs clubhouse down in enthusiasm and self-doubt. The clubhouse was jovial and extremely interactive.

In today's electronic world it is very easy to slip into isolation and aloofness when team chemistry goes south. The pattern that had started to take over the team when the losing streak climbed to eight games had been reversed through winning again. Everybody was a fair target when the going was good and it was easy to throw out insults when one knew it would come right back at them in playful fashion. The clubhouse had a completely different feel to it this weekend; winning had dulled the sharp objects thrown at each other into harmless bantering between less sensitive players.

The crowd was arriving early once more on this very cool day. It felt more like football weather as the cool wind had increased in intensity off Lake Michigan, but at least there was abundant sunshine and warming electricity from the rabid fans.

The joint was jumping as the Cubs took the field for the opening pitch. The mood was so high that the fans were cheering at just about anything that seemed amusing to the crowd. As simple a ritual as the manager bringing the lineup card to the umpires around the home plate area brought fans to their feet. Blake was their hero, worthy of adulation just for presenting the team's lineup on this day.

The Cubs were playing with confidence and it showed in all aspects of the game. The team had committed only one error in the last eight games and, better yet, played consistently sound, fundamental, defensive baseball. Throwing to the correct base from the outfield, hitting the cutoff men, holding runners close to the bases, and executing defensive plays from fielding sacrifice bunts to short, quick rundowns. It was all there lately and the trust level between fielders was rock solid.

This contributed to the rate of effective pitching as well, with less pitches being thrown and limiting the opposing team to three outs instead of giving them four or five an inning. One extra out from a poor defensive play, be it an actual physical fielding error or not, can lead to numerous extra runs scored that never should have happened and can lead to pitchers placing an undue emphasis on striking batters out themselves. It all falls into place one way or the other and fortunately for the Cubbies, it was flowing in a positive direction for them.

The momentum from yesterday's game carried over from the get-go as the Cubs took an early lead on a Desmond Wilson triple into the right-field corner leading off the bottom of the first frame. That was followed by a one-out Jim Arnold towering fly home run just into the cage that separates the fence from the bleachers throughout the outfield. The blast down the left-field line got caught up in the crosshairs of the wind blowing in today, but had just enough carry to give the home team a quick 2-0 lead.

TJ Bowman was cruising against the Brewers, allowing only three harmless singles through five innings as the Cubbies maintained that early two-run cushion into the latter stages of the game.

A funny thing was happening in the crowd at Wrigley as the home fans began cheering at odd moments of their own baseball game. The overconfident crowd had begun to tune out the game in front of them to follow the first-place Cardinals' game, where the Redbirds were taking on the Pittsburgh Pirates in St. Louis.

There were scoreboard watchers, and ever-present technology nerds that could follow the game in St. Louis on their own electronic devices. The events from out of town began to overshadow the game right in front of their own eyes as either cheers or groans could be heard throughout the stands reflecting good or bad news coming from Busch Stadium.

The Wrigley scoreboard showed the Cardinals trailing 4-0 in the fifth and the crowd was sensing a tie in the standings from a Cubs win and a Cardinals loss. There were no secrets anymore as even the home team was keeping one eye on the diamond and the other on the scoreboard.

Blake became unusually tense, perched in his regular dugout position. He knew it was the time of the year when it was inevitable that his team would be watching the scoreboard. However, it required a delicate balance of intense focus on your own contest, with just infrequent glances at the out-of-town scoreboard at Wrigley that was still extremely unique in its antiquated style of changing scores manually.

The manager spoke up in the dugout as his team was preparing to bat in the last half of the fifth.

"We can't sit on our lead boys, and lose concentration. Don't let the St. Louis game creep in and take away our focus. This game ain't over by any means and we can't control out-of-town events, so let's get the bats started again," Blake said to his complacent team.

Unfortunately the words of advice seemed to fall on deaf ears as the Cubs stalled out at two runs in their own game, while the Cardinals slowly began creeping up on the Pirates in St. Louis and only trailed 4-3 after the sixth inning.

There continued to be a disconnection between the Wrigley fans and the game playing out right out in front of them. The crowd lost their boundless enthusiasm for their own players as the game in Chicago seemed well in control despite the meager two-run lead.

The Cubs were still cruising starting the eighth inning, but starting pitcher Bowman had reached his pitch limit, and then some, with 105 pitches. Blake knew Guillen was unavailable today from his two-inning stint the day before and tried to get a few more pitches out of TJ, but the move backfired as the Brewers reached Bowman for two solid singles to start the inning before Blake was forced to go to his bullpen.

The manager decided he would try to get two outs from two different relievers before bringing in his closer Randall Hart for a rare two-inning performance or, to be precise, one and a third innings to nail down this critical game.

Without the stellar Guillen, Blake knew his pen was vulnerable, but he was optimistic his relievers could get two simple outs before turning the game over to Hart, their closer.

Blake brought in left-hander Earl Richards to match up with lefty-swinging Joe Mason of the Brew Crew. The crowd suddenly became anxious and apprehensive and the changing mood was eerily overhanging Wrigley. One could sense the uneasiness floating around the ballpark as the Cubs reliever quickly fell behind two balls and no strikes in the count.

Catcher Bartlett asked for time and walked briskly out to the mound to get his point across in person to start throwing strikes or this game and possibly the season could be lost. Unfortunately, the pitcher Richards took his words too literally and grooved the next pitch right down the middle, and expectedly, Mason drove it over the center field fence over 410 feet from home. The three-run blast defied the steady wind blowing in and easily cleared the 400 foot sign in center to put the visiting Milwaukee squad up 3-2 with only two more cracks at the Brewers bullpen remaining for the Cubs to mount their own rally.

The Wrigley crowd became silent for several minutes while Blake came out to pull his unsuccessful pitcher while the organist played music in the background.

While the new Chicago pitcher was warming up, a discernible collective groan spread through the ballpark like an approaching tidal wave. The Cardinals had just put up a four spot in their game in St. Louis with one big swat as their slugger Lenny Charles belted a grand slam to put his team up 7-4 in their half of the eighth inning at Busch.

The double whammy hit hard as moments ago it appeared the race would be tied. Now the Cubs were in danger of dropping a full two games behind St. Louis with only five games left after today. The mood turned somber even though the Cubs were still only down by a run.

The Chicago bullpen stiffened, and the home team came to bat in the bottom of the eighth with hopes of a rally, but the collective damper in the air possessed a bad omen. The Cubs went meekly down in order as the tension grew in the Chicago dugout.

Blake decided to buck conventional wisdom and brought in his closer Hart for the ninth, even though his team was down. This move turned out much better than the manager's last inning maneuver, as Hart easily retired the Brewers in order, stemming the tide and bringing a bit of life back into the stadium.

The crowd tried to reignite the team with a standing ovation as their Cubbies came to bat, although the noise emanating from the stands was noticeably more subdued than earlier in the contest when things were going their way.

The players in the dugout went into full rally-cap mode with their caps folded inside out with the lids placed backwards on their heads in a good luck superstition ritual universal to baseball.

The excitement built as leadoff hitter Rickey Sanchez lined a solid single up the middle to get the crowd even more involved, but the rally fizzled when the Cubs could not execute a sacrifice bunt. The Milwaukee infield was able to force out Sanchez at second when a Mike Simons bunt was directed too firmly at the charging infielders.

Blake gave it his best bench shot by calling up his two best pinch-hitting options. A fly out to the warning track in left by Justin Moreland created a hopeful cheer from the crowd, but came up just short, and a line-out to the Milwaukee shortstop by Willie Evans ended the game and took the air out of the rally balloon as the crowd suddenly shifted to deafening silence.

The 3-2 loss and the turnaround win by the Cardinals created a pall over Wrigleyville as the fans moped while filing out in subdued fashion on this crushing September Saturday.

The Cubs players were equally subdued and seemed to be in a bit of shock as the team returned to their own clubhouse in relative silence.

This one hurt big-time and the players knew they were definitely behind the eight ball after they choked this crucial game away. The players and Blake's coaches said all the right things to the media after the game to indicate they were still very hopeful of catching the first-place Cards, but their unenthusiastic demeanor belied their words.

There was not much for Blake to say to his team today after this devastating loss. The team dispersed to their temporary residences in the Chicago area, vowing to fight until the bitter end.

Blake just sat in his office and contemplated what he could have done differently before realizing this loss was mostly a result of inexperience in this type of situation. These growing pains had come at a terrible time. Hopefully the lesson was learned to take care of their own battles first before relying on another team, totally out of their control, to help them out in a pennant race.

61 — Hanging by a Thread

The Saturday afternoon loss created a ripple effect throughout team head-quarters. Marty called Blake to see if both the team and his manager were okay after the double whammy hit like a ton of bricks. Marty's voice and message, although positive in words, lacked the convincing tone to carry any weight with the manager.

Unbridled enthusiasm throughout the city was replaced by the dampening realization that there weren't enough games to be played to catch the Cardinals. If they could somehow maintain the deficit at two full games going into the season's four-game finale with St. Louis, there would still be an outside chance to tie the Cards by winning a challenging, but not impossible to believe, three out of four games against the Redbirds.

Hanging over the team's collective head was the glaring number of nine consecutive defeats at the hands of their rival; nary one victory against the first-place team with this hastily assembled bunch. To visualize a three-wins-out-of-four scenario required a gigantic leap of faith. Not impossible, but a near miracle. And of course, that unlikely scenario would just put the Cubbies in a tie, prompting a one-game playoff to decide the division winner.

Blake calmly and wisely decided to just keep repeating the remedial chain of daily practices of late that seemed to keep him relaxed and focused without too much fear of failure. He checked in with his sponsor and openly discussed the pain of losing and the greater possibility of coming up just short in their pennant chase. Blake talked without hesitation to his wife, which kept him from the debilitating effects of emotional isolation. Marty and Blake communicated often throughout the evening, keeping hope alive with tales of historical come-backs that were once deemed near impossible.

Sunday's contest would ultimately decide the importance of the upcoming series. A three-game deficit would be an emotional killer and mathematically remote.

Those damn Cardinals just would not lose, making deficit reduction more of a fantasy than a palpable goal. However, the lesson was learned the hard way that taking care of your own business is always the best approach. The Cubs had won five out of six before and a repeat scenario here would put them on top.

It was another football weather type day, but even the Bears playing at Sol-dier Field against the Minnesota Vikings this afternoon could not match the at-tention this Chicago Cubs team was garnering. It might be a Bears town, but baseball was the word of the day as an historic sports achievement was still within the city's grasp, barely hanging by a thread as events now stood on a September Sunday.

The assembled crowd was electric despite the growing odds against the home team. Perhaps it was the ultimate appreciation for the totality of their cause, but it felt genuine, and that's all that mattered for Blake as he doffed his cap to the Wrigley crowd in appreciation before the first pitch was thrown.

A new day had taken over and it could not have been more welcomed as the Cubs turned their attention to the task at hand. They had learned their lesson about distracting elements yesterday. Blake could only ponder in his own mind what might have been. These past weeks had produced so many firsts for his boys that had to be experienced before the full tale could be told and understood. Unfortunately, the inexperienced, green team had blown several games in its educational growth. The manager surmised the Cubs would at least be even in the standings if his young team had learned lessons without the accompanying losses, but it seemed, growth and maturity from his squad could only be gained through heartbreak and defeat.

The damp, cloudy morning was hijacked by the warm sun, and stole the Chicago show for the rest of the dwindling daylight hours of late September. The ivy-covered outfield walls barely held on to their annual green shade, desperately refusing to succumb to winter's dull brown takeover just yet. The shadows were longer, but the afternoon sun held out for good fortune as the Cubbies longed for an auspicious turn of events in the series finale.

Blake's pitching wish was for starter Shane Anderson to give him seven solid innings before turning over the eighth to prodigious set-up man Guillen and the ninth to the recently stellar closer Randall Hart. The manager felt if he could get seven efficient innings from any of his starters, he would always take his chances against any opponent with the likes of Guillen and Hart on his side.

The Wrigley faithful were buzzing early as slugging first baseman Jim Arnold hit a towering fly ball that dropped just over the left-field wall for an early 1-0 Cubs lead. The crowd was on its feet again in the bottom of the second frame when light-hitting second baseman Petey Arroyo flipped a hanging curve ball from Milwaukee starting pitcher Frank Wilson down the left-field chalk line, somehow clearing the fence just inches on the good side of the foul pole for a 2-0 lead.

Anderson was cruising on the pitching mound, retiring the Brewers in order for the first three innings, before Milwaukee leadoff batter Paul Mortenson banged a triple to right center field before plating the first Brewers run on a one-out sacrifice fly that cut the Chicago lead in half.

The scoring went on hiatus for the next few innings until the Cubs broke open the contest with a bases-clearing double by John Bartlett that sent a crescendo throughout the ballpark. The deafening roar signaled a likely Chicago win this gorgeous afternoon and the home team hiked its lead to 5-1 in the bottom of the sixth inning.

This time the Cubs and the crowd would not let up in their intensity. The St. Louis Cardinals' game looked clearly in the bag for the Redbirds once again as they were cruising 7-1 themselves at Busch Stadium. The focus remained in Wrigley as the crowd cheered every Milwaukee out as if they were about to clinch the pennant this afternoon.

Shane Anderson was given a standing ovation as he left the mound with one out in the top of the eighth and a runner on first that was stopped dead in his tracks when Miguel Guillen quickly squelched the Brewers' hopes for a rally with back-to-back strikeouts to end the inning. The hyper Guillen was ever so demonstrative after retiring the opposition and repeatedly pumped his left fist in his glove as he jumped up and down in response to the crowd while making his way into the Chicago dugout.

The ecstatic fans were roaring on every pitch from here on out to end the game. Randall Hart breezed through his ninth inning while every out increased the deafening roar until the last lazy fly ball was gathered in by center fielder Desmond Wilson to finish the contest. The Cubs had prevailed 5-1, and while the Cardinals also came out victorious on this day, the current two-game deficit ensured that the series against the Cards would be relevant to the bitter end.

The clubhouse was rocking as the team felt a sense of accomplishment in getting this far despite all the setbacks that created doubt, confusion, and even anger at the predicament major league baseball had put them in to finish out this season in relative professional limbo. This Cubs team might not advance to the playoffs, but nobody could say they quit or did not give it their all.

"Bring on the Cardinals, bring on the Redbirds," shouted the boisterous Bartlett. The whole team joined the chant in unison.

The team was itching to make amends for the untimely matchups that put the Cubs at a huge disadvantage against St. Louis in their two-series, nine-game set and left the Cards with a lopsided nine games to zero record against their nearest rival. The first series was the inaugural performance from the new Cubs, only days removed from the terrible accident. The second five-game set came at the absolute worst time for the Chicago pitching staff as the make-up games piled up in rapid succession. There would be no excuses this time. It was put up or shut up time. And the Cubs absolutely had to win three out of the next four to force a one-game playoff.

David, meet Goliath!

62 — Taking a Deep Breath

Blake was high as a kite, naturally this time, as he dined with his wife this Sunday evening. The defining moment had finally come for Blake and his team. His pride was perhaps a bit premature, but the finality of the regular season, coming up in just four days with his squad assured of a meaningful ending, gave the rookie manager cause for comfort.

Kim had prepared a bountiful meal with exquisite taste, knowing full well that her husband would be happy and in need of good nutrition for the upcoming nerve-wracking series. She designed a dinner with a wide range of foods for Blake: salad, freshly-baked homemade bread, prime rib and baked potatoes. She topped off the meal with a delicious chocolate cake that her husband loved, but he could barely fit a small slice in his overstuffed stomach this evening.

The conversation was continuous and light-hearted for most of the evening before Blake got a bit sentimental. He reflected on the nearly six-week ordeal that began with him pleading for his job without much hope for any chance at some kind of personal redemption this season. All of this, after narrowly bypassing death through drunkenness, of all things. Somehow the loving concern of his best friend Sandy safely guarded his newfound path to sobriety.

Here he was about to lead his troops onto the professional sports battlefield. He would be acting as an honorable general after starting this journey as a renegade private hell-bent on personal self-destruction. He wondered whether this accomplishment would be enough to adequately honor his fallen teammates as he continued the conversation with Kim.

Kim suggested they step outside and relax by the pool on this clear, cool, and now dark evening. Blake grabbed a sweater while Kim threw on her gray Cubs sweatshirt and flipped the hood over her head. They talked in depth about the fate of the next few decisive days. Blake clearly was in the mood to talk and his wife welcomed the chance to share emotions this night.

"Kim, do you think I've done enough? If we come in a competitive, close second, is that good enough to at least clear my conscience that I've done about all I can to make sense of this whole awful mess?"

"Honey, I'm not the one who can answer that." She paused several seconds for effect, hoping Blake would get the message that only he could internally determine that outcome, before continuing on. "Blake, perhaps you've been looking at this all wrong. Maybe this is to honor you, instead of your teammates that died. Did you ever think of that?"

"I just can't see how one life like mine can somehow add up to the 35 that died that day. Maybe it could be both, but I certainly can't see me as the desired honoree. I'm a professional athlete, a major league baseball player, and we're all about winning. It's the only way we honor our accomplishments on the field."

"But Blake, maybe that's where you've had it all wrong for all of your adult life. This baseball crap distorts so much of what's really important in life. You put our marriage second behind baseball, your physical and emotional well-being behind baseball, and we never had a family with kids because all you could think about was baseball."

"You could be right Kim. But is it wrong to deny who and what you are? Where much of your passion is in life? I'll be the first to admit I lost some desire to play the game, but I'll never admit that baseball isn't why I was put on this earth. I feel I was born to be a player, a student of the game, and an ambassador of baseball to others. It's who I am, but that doesn't mean I don't want you to share in its glory with me."

"Well, you know how I've always felt Blake. It hurts sometimes that I obviously come in second," Kim's voice trailed off slowly in disappointment as she told her husband for at least the thousandth time that his obsession with baseball left her emotionally scarred.

"That's not true Kim, that's not true. I've felt like both you and I experienced all of this together."

"But my feelings for the game aren't nearly as deep as yours Blake. How can I feel an equal part in all of this if it doesn't give me the same fulfillment as you?"

"I don't have an answer for that, Kim. Maybe that's where I'm headed. Maybe I'll go out in a blaze of glory here and we can put baseball in its right place for good."

"I'll believe that when I see it. It's too addicting for you."

"Well, I've been doing okay kicking one habit. Maybe another one's on the way. I'm certainly learning that addiction in any form isn't healthy. In fact, I'm learning that it's detrimental. You most definitely deserve credit for making me realize that stopping drinking is a multi-faceted ordeal and that balance is necessary to comfortably move ahead in life."

"Speaking of balance Blake, how are you going to tamp down the excitement of your players so they can perform at their best this series? You've always preached that baseball has to be played with relaxed confidence and that anxiety is a ballplayer's worst enemy."

"That's a very good question honey. I'll sleep on it tonight. At least I've licked this booze thing for now. I'm feeling pretty good about that at the moment."

"Blake, I'm surprised at you. Have you forgotten all of the baseball lessons you've taught me over the years? One day at a time. One day at a time has always been your baseball motto and it certainly applies with alcohol recovery. Heck, that saying originated with AA. Now, don't you go looking down the road and forgetting today. Make sure you tell your team that too. Just win the game in front of you and, Blake Benson, just don't drink today. Keep it that way."

"What would I do without you, Kim? I surely get ahead of myself don't I? Lesson learned my dear, and I'll apply it to my boys too. Thanks for keeping me grounded. This whole series and all the excitement brewing had my brain a bit unsettled. Jesus, it's easy to get sidetracked. I didn't even realize my obvious contradictions. Another lesson learned. It sure is funny how my misguided thoughts apply to our situation. I'll be sure to point out that my wife realized the error of my ways and was instrumental in setting the proper demeanor for our team the next several days."

Kim felt a sense of pride in her observations and boldly suggested a new role for herself.

"Maybe I should put on a uniform and stand beside you in the dugout? I can scratch and spit with the best of them!"

"That's what I'm afraid of my dear. That's what I'm afraid of. I don't want you becoming one of us. This baseball bunch has guts and character, but they'd have you with more bad habits than you could shake a stick at. Trust me on this one, you don't want to become like us. This bunch would turn in their grandma to the police if it would help them win. We need at least one honorable Benson in the family."

"I suppose Blake. I'll just keep you and the team focused from afar."

"Works for me honey. Did I tell you we get a $65,000 share if we come in first? It's yours when we win, but I wouldn't start spending it just yet," Blake answered with a smile. "One day and one game at a time, right Kim?"

His wife nodded her head and smiled at her newly relaxed and confident husband. His team might not win, but damn, he was certainly back to his old self-assured demeanor and that was a sight for sore eyes.

63 — No Hocus-Pocus, Just Plain Focus

The still inexperienced manager woke up this highly anticipated morning with the realization that he would have to address his players to properly prepare them for the season-defining four-game series starting this afternoon.

The thrill of accomplishment at making this series with the Cardinals the determining factor in the division race was slowly being overridden by the knowledge that only on-the-field performance would dictate how the games and their legacy would be remembered.

Most fans and neutral observers, like the overwhelming media covering this baseball and enthralling human-interest event, would likely historically reference this season's Cubs from the result of this upcoming critical series.

The players would undoubtedly have heretofore unfelt nerves to deal with. How the players reacted to this expected human condition, given the importance and attention this series entailed, would likely have an effect on the game's outcome.

Of course, a few players, like Blake and John Bartlett, had dealt with this potential problem before, and they would be followed closely for guidance. It was one thing to verbally address the possible problem, but entirely another to lead by example.

Blake had the nerves today as well, but he knew from experience they would dissipate from the opening pitch when the game developed its own flow.

He cunningly avoided the collective media throng outside Wrigley Field by surreptitiously following a predetermined, seldom-used, and secretive path to the clubhouse. Blake sat in his office, anxiously fidgeting in his favorite chair while staring at the Cubs team photo from spring training this past March in Arizona. He was searching for guidance from the memories of his now deceased teammates as he followed the photo lineup one by one, row by row. He hoped that thoughts of inspirational words would somehow transfer from the players of the past to the players of the present through Blake's mouth, as the inexperienced bunch would have to deal with the uncertainty of the moment, living these circumstances for the first time.

Nothing originally came to mind as he continued to gaze at the team photo, which was unkempt and slightly crooked on the wall. Blake would just have to trust his instincts and recall how past managers dealt with this type of situation. Many years of experience had provided Blake with a catalog of information that he either discarded as flawed, or stored in his brain for future use when he agreed with the approach.

Blake could sense the quietness of the clubhouse as he searched for words to help out his boys. He could not even hear the normally playful Guillen pouncing and peacocking around this day.

The manager sensed enough was enough as the quietness indicated too much tension hanging over his clubhouse. He quickly leapt out of his chair and opened his door, letting out a big belch as he tried to loosen up the mood of the clubhouse with some crass behavior.

"Jesus, did you guys forget that this is only a game out there today?"

Blake belched again and complained about the clubhouse food he ingested.

"Anybody else feel like you swallowed an elephant? Food just goes down differently before a big series. Did I ever tell you guys about Billy Jensen, God rest his soul? He'd barf and nearly shit his pants before a big game, until our manager Buck told him he'd have to do that every game after he went 4-4 with 5 RBI in a crucial contest. It sure was funny how Buck cured him. The point is, everybody gets nervous. Those guys over in the Cardinal clubhouse are nervous too."

Bartlett jumped into the conversation, recalling how a current member of the Cardinals used to deal with the nerves when the Rat was poisoning from the other side.

"Their center fielder Jones sits on the throne for an hour or longer just staring at the stall's door with his headphones on. You better not disturb him either or he'll swear up a storm at ya."

"How do you know this Bartlett? You wouldn't have punked him would ya? I could see you throwing a snake in there just to piss Jones off," Guillen said in jest.

"Oh, word must've gotten around. That's just what I did to the poor bastard. He barely made it out to his center field position in time for the first pitch. He was scared shitless. Hey, it worked, didn't it?" Bartlett was reveling in the moment as he recalled pranks from his glory days.

Blake raised his hands after several seconds of laughter and motioned for quiet so he could continue with his words of wisdom speech.

"You'll feel strange for the first few batters, but trust me, it goes away. Of course it comes back again in tight situations, but all you have to do is focus intently on the baseball training you've received and practiced thousands of times. The mound is 60 feet 6 inches away as always and you already know to closely examine the pitcher's release point and pick up the rotation. Pitchers already know that you focus sharply on the catcher's mitt and rely on the catcher to take some of the pressure off you by letting him call the game. Fielders just follow the ball off the bat as always and look for certain pitches from the catcher's signs to anticipate the direction the ball might be hit. It's all the same guys. Let your muscle memory take over by being in that relaxed, but intense state. We'll try to keep the bench loose by looking through the stands for hot women. God knows I don't have to worry about you bullpen guys. You could sleep through a tornado, playing your silly games and lounging out there in your chairs. Seriously though, anticipate whom you likely will be called in to face and have a plan of action. Preparation will help calm the nerves too. Stay in your normal routine and follow it like always. Repetition is another stress reliever. Just try to enjoy the moment. We've come a long way in a short time and I'm proud of you guys for sticking together when things looked rough. This is your reward. Now go enjoy it and hopefully there'll be more to come."

The manager did not want to add to the mental burden by bringing up his former teammates. Not at this point, and probably not until they had several games of this type under their belts. He let his players go before suddenly re-calling his wife's advice from the night prior.

"Hey guys, one minute. I just wanted to let you know that even an old horse's ass like me forgets this stuff from time to time. My wife had to remind me last night as I got a bit out of focus myself. She wisely reminded me what I've always preached, that in baseball you have to take it one game at a time. I forgot because I got carried away in the moment. So you guys help each other get back into the right frame of mind, as I know you'll stray for a bit. She also reminded me, you can't win playing safe. You'll know when to take a chance from your years of baseball experience. Just let instinct take over. Don't be afraid to lose or we can't win. Wives and family members keep us all grounded. Listen to 'em."

Blake waved them off, indicating it was time for them to resume their pregame routine. Hopefully his words would have some positive effect. The player-manager also felt that this game would be the perfect time for him to play in the crucial series. He had good batting numbers against the Cardinals starting pitcher and he wanted to lead by example today to help alleviate any nerves his younger guys might face.

The Cubs would counter the Cardinals starter, Jonathan Perry, with rookie Woody Williams. The promising prospect had been out with injury until re-cently, when he pitched out of the bullpen for a bit to get back in game shape. Williams had been the organization's top pitching hope in the minors and by chance and good fortune for the young man, the front office wanted to give him more seasoning at triple A Des Moines, despite being more than ready to throw in the majors. Otherwise, his career and young life would have vanished in the team tragedy.

Blake felt this kid was ready to live up to his potential. The tall right-hander had the major league stuff to balance out the pitching matchup with the oppo-sition today. At least that was the hope as the fire-balling pitcher warmed up with Blake before taking the mound to throw out the first pitch.

It was another Indian summer day with warm, but not hot, temperatures as the Cubbies took the field. The weather conditions were once again ideal. Wrigley was howling from the warm-ups on, as fans felt they could give their team the edge they needed to stop the nine-game losing streak to the Cards.

Blake was basking in the sun moments before Williams strolled in from the pen, simply enjoying the moment, when he caught a glimpse of something strange out of the corner of his left eye. He abruptly turned to face the Wrigley crowd and confirmed what he thought he saw. Kim was sitting in the stands behind the Cubs dugout with several of his teammates' wives. Kim never liked to be subject to the vicious comments coming from obnoxious fans and had long ago decided to not attend home games. It warmed Blake's heart to see his wife participating in today's huge event. He whistled and waved to get her attention. When Kim noticed that Blake had spotted her, she smiled from ear to ear at her husband, who responded in kind with the same ecstatic smile.

Her presence in the stands just confirmed what Blake had felt from the moment he took the field today. It felt like the whole city was behind his team in support and appreciation. It was no longer just his boys against the St. Louis Cardinals, but the whole city against 25 opposing players. The emotional awareness of complete togetherness gave the manager a whopping sense of community that had to be some kind of intangible edge today and perhaps the rest of the year.

The youthful Cubs took the field in the top of the first looking more like a football team running out of the tunnel with their emotions at a fever pitch, than a baseball squad that operated under relaxed intensity most of the time.

The crowd never sat down after rising for the national anthem. The boisterous throng clapped in unison, chanting, "Let's go Cubs," over and over until Williams completed his warm-up tosses on the mound and Blake sent a practice throw right on target to second base before getting the game started on a sunsoaked Wrigley afternoon.

Unfortunately, it was a matter of minutes before events began to go against Chicago and the enthusiasm of the fans was quickly transformed into collective groans from the crowd, mixed in with a smattering of boos as Woody Williams' nerves got the best of him. Despite Blake's repeated trips to the mound to calm down the overeager young pitcher, the rookie Williams walked the bases loaded with nobody out.

The slugging Cardinals cleanup batter, Lenny Charles, took the ballpark's mood from bad to worse as he cleared the bases with a line drive gapper that rolled all the way to the right center-field wall. Charles coasted in to second base with a standup double that turned a scattering of boos into a resounding and lengthy howl, as the boo-birds were now out in full force and there wasn't even a single out recorded.

Blake's first managerial move of the critical series backfired in a big way early, but even the rookie manager in Blake knew things could change on a dime in this game if a pitcher got into a groove. The highly touted prospect settled down some and escaped the rest of the inning unscathed, but still smarting from a three-run uprising to end the top of the first down 3-0.

Cheers returned to the ballpark as the Cubs took their turn at the plate in the bottom of the inning. However, nary a base runner in the initial frame for the Cubbies dropped the decibel level several notches as the team went down meekly, giving the Wrigley crowd an uneasy foreboding of failure.

Their premonition was spot-on, unfortunately for the home team, as the Cards put up another crooked number this time, matching their first-inning total of three runs to bolt out to a comfortable 6-0 lead before the Cubs could even get their second at-bats. Blake was just about ready to pull the young pitcher from the game when Williams suddenly found his rhythm and began putting up zeroes on the Wrigley scoreboard.

The St. Louis hurler Perry was cruising along with a commanding 6-0 lead, looking very relaxed like he was talking a walk in the park as the game reached its halfway point, while the crowd's intensity waned to a respectful lukewarm cheer for their players. There simply were not enough base runners to get the fans jump-started and possibly ignite a much-needed rally.

Blake added to his playing and managing status on this day by taking on the role as head cheerleader too. He tried his best to keep his boys from getting too down while maintaining their self-confidence of late. He instinctively knew that one spark could light a raging rally inferno once the crowd got a sniff of smoldering smoke.

Truer words were never spoken, as the prophetic Blake saw his vision come true in the bottom of the sixth inning. The old baseball saying of a bleeder, a bloop, and a blast came true as slugger Jim Arnold deposited a three-run homer into the left field bleachers after a couple of seeing-eye singles set the table for Big Jim.

Just like that, in the blink of a baseball eye, the Cardinals' lead was cut in half to 6-3, and almost as importantly, the crowd started believing in miracles again. Hope had vanished somewhere in the ballpark but magically reappeared after the three-run homer. The constant roar of an excited crowd foretold good results coming the Cubs' way, but it had to be maintained. That was no easy task considering the talented opposition.

Despite flaming out in the sixth after Arnie's homer, the fans dispatched the momentary disappointment and reveled in the rapid change of events that made this contest competitive again.

Blake continued to ride his young pitcher. Despite being within a pitch or two of being replaced in the second inning, Williams hung on and kept the Cards stuck in neutral after the disappointing start. Blake's confidence in the young man was rewarded as Williams breezed through the seventh inning, clearly keeping the momentum on the Cubbies' side.

The last of the seventh held promise for the Cubs before an inning-ending 6-4-3 double play snuffed out another attempted rally. The short to second to first twin killing sent a huge sigh of disappointment into the warm fall air as the crowd seemingly exhaled in unison when Petey Arroyo struck the first base bag with his left foot just a split second after the relay throw beat him to first. Petey threw up his arms and kicked the dirt portion of the infield with his right foot in disgust before regaining his composure as fellow infielder Rickey Sanchez brought Petey his cap and fielder's glove to get ready quickly for the next inning.

Suddenly the wind that had been swirling throughout the ballpark felt just a bit colder as the innings disappeared into the descending fall sun.

Blake was pleased he got seven innings from Williams after such a rough start and felt good about bringing in Miguel Guillen to pitch the eighth. Not only was the electric lefty a superb pitcher, he always brought excitement to the crowd as they fed off his emotional reactions. If ever there was a time to keep the fans up for the last few innings, now was the critical moment after the double play letdown.

If the start of the game did not go well with Blake's initial managerial situation with Williams, the skipper redeemed himself with the insertion of Guillen. Normally, a team and its crowd rallies when they are at the plate, but this time the defensive side brought renewed life to the team and the rowdies in attendance with Miggy's dominant eighth inning performance. The hefty lefty struck out the side in order with typical Guillen-like demonstrative demeanor. He pumped his fists and pounded his glove while talking to himself in ecstasy after each strikeout. The Wrigley faithful ate it up and encouraged the southpaw to yuck it up even more. Guillen was not hesitant about adding anything to his showmanship arsenal. He used a pistol-like charade to shoot down the last batter of the inning before blowing out the smoke in his six-shooter and stuffing the weapon into his holster just as he began his sprint to the dugout.

Blake and the coaches were determined to keep the momentum going as the team got ready to take their hacks in the bottom of the inning. The manager shed his catching gear and shouted out for all to hear. "I can feel a rally in these old catching bones. The crowd's into it, we've got the meat of our order coming up and I think this relief pitcher is raw meat. Let's get 'em!"

As if on cue, Rickey Sanchez lined a single over the Cardinal shortstop's outstretched glove and his leap was inches short of snaring the batted ball. Big

Jim Arnold confidently approached the batter's box as if he was rightfully claiming his own territory. His confidence was high from his previous at-bat, a three-run dinger, and the Cardinals were clearly affected by the demeanor of and confidence exuded by the Cubs first baseman.

The St. Louis approach to Big Jim suddenly shifted to nothing but breaking balls as their pitcher and catcher desperately wanted to not give Arnie another fastball to smoke out of the park. Arnold caught on quickly and held off chasing these tantalizingly slow pitches that screamed 'hit me' as they approached the plate, but always suckered the hitter to swing in a feeble manner at the suddenly out of the strike zone pitch. Down by three runs and not two, the slugger gladly took the walk, bringing the tying run to the plate in the person of third baseman Mike Simons.

The Cardinals' approach was clearly flawed, at least by the traditional baseball book that strongly discouraged pitching around a batter to bring the tying run to the plate late in a crucial ballgame.

Blake was astutely watching the action from his on-deck perch when St. Louis pitching coach Paul Jurgens asked for time from the home plate umpire after leaping out of the dugout, obviously disgusted with the flawed pitching strategy. Jurgens then strolled to the mound in a veiled attempt to slow down the Chicago momentum that was building pitch by pitch, and to get the pitcher and catcher straightened out regarding their odd pitch selection.

Of course, all the participants on the mound were hiding their words with their gloves to avoid nefarious lip-reading attempts, but Blake was keenly aware of the message Jurgens was likely to be expressing. Blake's long catching career had cataloged many tidbits on players and coaches and they were about to come in handy in this critical situation.

Blake tried to get Simons' attention as the third baseman was in the batter's box, eager to get a crack at a struggling pitcher. Blake had to creep closer to the plate and whistle to get Simons' attention to come back to his manager for a bit of advice. Now it was the Cubs' turn to turn away from the action to secretly pass on some information.

"Bartlett filled me in on his old coach Jurgens. The old fart practically has a stroke when his pitchers won't challenge batters. He lets his temper get the best of him sometimes. Throwing nothing but junk to Arnie when he wasn't even the tying run must've put his undies in a bundle. Look for heat until he gets two strikes on you anyways. I'm sure they will pitch you away with heat. You can bet on it Mike."

The bit of a dilemma plaguing the situation was Blake's on-deck status. It was near impossible to display signs to the third base coach Paxson while Blake was out in the open for all to see. Wisely, the rookie manager had anticipated this situation beforehand, and had a provisional sign ready to flash to his main on-the-field coach, who was peering in at Blake from his usual position of the coach's box, straddling the borders of the chalk line, hands on his hips in a knee-flexed position. A simple tying of Blake's shoe indicated that Paxson had the ultimate say in this strategic position.

Blake had to swallow hard as his third base coach gave Simons the hit-and-run sign at this critical moment. That was clearly out of the baseball norm given the situation, but Blake had long since told his staff to be aggressive, throwing caution, and convention, to the wind. The baseball gods clearly owed them more than one lucky favor after going 0 for 9 against the Cards, but this was quite the daring gamble, letting the runners from first and second take off with nobody out. They weren't even the tying runs, designating them sort of insignificant in a baseball strategy maneuver. Paxson was clearly counting on a fastball too in this scenario, making it easier for Simons to put the ball in play.

In another out-of-the ordinary move, the Cardinals were strangely wary of a bunt in this situation and held the lumbering Arnold closely at first base before they would take a step or two toward home in defense of a sacrifice bunt attempt. This odd move clearly left the right side of the infield vulnerable to a ground ball given all the available space created in defense of an unlikely maneuver, but all opponents now were all too well aware of Blake's unusual strategic moves.

As the pitch was delivered home, veteran second baseman Jeff Dorman of the Cards was as surprised as anybody in the ballpark when big Jim Arnold took off from first base on the back end of a hit-and-run play. Lead runner Sanchez took off from second. Dorman quickly shifted toward the second base bag, instinctively realizing that the slow-footed Arnold would be a dead duck if the Cardinals catcher threw down to second instead of third.

Fortunately for the Cubs, Simons lined the pitch through the right side of the infield, right where Dorman had vacated to cover second. All that stood between an inning-ending rare triple play was the few feet that Dorman had shifted as he was attempting to dart to the second base bag. What could have been a triple play was now a run-scoring single that also advanced Arnie to third with still nobody out and the Cubs within two runs at 6-4.

The knowledgeable Chicago fans knew that Blake's team had dodged a kill-shot bullet by pure gambling and roared in approval of the daring, but successful maneuver.

The feeling of fortuitous fate had the Wrigley crowd in a gleeful state of mind as if nothing could stop the Cubs now, as Blake stepped to the plate with a hero's welcome. The savvy and experienced Blake realized his team had the Cards reeling at the moment and paused in the batter's box as if to create more doubt in the opposing pitcher's mind, while the crowd never allowed even a decibel's drop in noise to try and rattle St. Louis.

Blake worked the count in his favor at 2-1 before crushing a fastball to the left center field warning track. Unfortunately this time, the blast had a bit too much loft and not quite enough carry. The ball was caught several feet from the wall, easily enough distance for even the pokey Arnold to cruise into home without a throw from the center fielder. The fundamentally sound St. Louis squad knew they had to keep Simons at first and wisely threw the ball to second as Arnie crossed the plate cutting the lead to a single run at 6-5.

The Cubs were tantalizingly close, but still desperately in need of at least tallying the tying run. Even though Blake's sacrifice fly brought the Cubbies closer, it had the subtle effect of slightly slowing down the momentum with Simons still at first and one out. The subtlety turned readily apparent as the rally fizzled, with Simons stranded at first to end the eighth inning.

The tension was building throughout the damp fall air as the late afternoon sun fell victim to patchy fog drifting in from the shores of a cooling Lake Michigan. There was no damper in the crowd however, as the importance of this next inning was obvious to all in the ballpark.

Blake was showing a bit of desperation as well, with another do-or-die move. He was risking the possible availability of his best set-up pitcher by stretching Guillen out another inning to open the ninth. Blake knew he absolutely had to keep the Cardinals' lead at one and somehow pull out this game, or the season would be done for all practical purposes.

Miguel was thrilled to keep slinging bullets up to home plate for another inning and he was determined to keep the score unchanged while flaming the fans even more in preparation for a last-gasp effort in the bottom of the ninth.

Guillen took over right where he left off as he struck out the first two Cardinal batters of the inning, bringing his streak of consecutive strikeouts to five before the third and final out of the ninth was recorded on a lazy fly ball to center fielder Desmond Wilson.

The moment of truth had come. It was now or never to produce at least the tying run to extend the game into extra innings. There was no doubt about the significance of what was about to happen next and the fiery Guillen did all he could to bring pandemonium to Wrigley for the decisive ninth. Miggy pumped both his arms as he sprung off the mound before signaling to the Cubs fans that it was time for them to get up and on their feet for the ninth. No ifs ands or buts, this game just had to go Chicago's way or bust.

The Cardinals super closer Jerry Waddell entered the field of play, cockily strolling in from the bullpen amidst a chorus of deep boos from the Cubs faithful. Most closers relish the vitriol spewed at them from rambunctious rowdies in the stands, and Waddell was no different. He seemed to spit at their collective faces while entering the combative arena, wearing a symbolic smirk the whole time.

The Cardinals closer glared into the bellowing bastion of Cubs fans, the perennial All-Star certain of their impending doom. Stoppers like Waddell lived for the moment when he could shut the door on dreams. It was his nature, his calling to be an onerous ogre to opposing fans.

Waddell was good and he knew it. The pitching mound was his home, his territory to ward off attackers with pitching bullets. He stomped around on the elevated dirt with a white rubber slab as his doorstep and he was not going to let anybody in his house. He had an intimidating stare that he utilized at this crucial moment as pinch-hitter deluxe, Willie Evans of the Cubs, was called upon to start the bottom of the ninth, and hopefully save the season. Waddell always got ready to pitch by lowering the bill of his cap so all one could see at the plate was his menacing eyes. Evans just focused on the closer's anticipated release point and refused to be intimidated as he dug his spikes into the game-worn dirt of the batter's box.

Evans took several pitches without offering a hint of a swing; this was his norm coming off the bench cold. He had an uncanny knack for gauging the differing speeds of the pitcher, by observation only, until he became comfortable with the timing and rhythm of his current nemesis on the mound. Evans had a count of two balls and one strike before he pounced on the second fastball he saw. The perfectly timed swing squared up on the baseball as he lined the pitch up the middle and the crowd howled with glee. The fans could smell victory in the damp late afternoon Chicago air.

Leadoff batter Desmond Wilson stepped up to the plate and the strategy really began to heat up. The baseball book had written in stone that the second batter of the inning, after the previous hitter reached first, must sacrifice bunt in this situation unless a power hitter was at the plate. Desmond liked to think of himself as a slugger, but that approach often got the speedy Wilson in trouble, and his coaches always preached slapping the ball on the ground to take advantage of his speed.

The roar from the crowd was nonstop, elevating in intensity and decibel level after each thrown pitch, then subsiding just enough between pitches to be noticeable and beginning the upward crescendo again as the next pitch became imminent.

A bunt seemed in order from the St. Louis perspective, as Waddell went into the stretch pitching motion to keep the tying runner close to the first base bag. The Cardinals catcher had given his infielders a flurry of signs that likely would set the infielders in motion, preparing for a likely bunt as the pitch came to home plate.

However, Blake had different plans for this situation. He knew Waddell struggled, for whatever weird reason, against the Cubbies. He also knew his bullpen could not match up with the Cardinals' in depth or talent if the game went into extra innings. His baseball instincts talked to him just as the speedy Wilson began his batting routine. Wilson had one foot in the box and the other just outside the line as he held up his hand to the umpire to indicate that he wasn't quite ready to step into the box yet. Blake flashed his signs to third base coach Paxson. After a slight pause, Paxson then went through a laundry list of body motions to alert the runner and the batter of the strategy their manager wanted for each and every pitch.

Desmond dropped his hand and set both feet inside the batter's box, indicating to the pitcher and umpire that he was ready. The Cardinals catcher then flashed signs to his pitcher as he crouched behind home plate and just in front of the home plate umpire. The catcher hid his signals from the opposition by using his glove as a shield, while his geared up legs also provided a visual obstacle as he crouched with his legs shoulder-width apart.

The guessing game was on as Wilson squared around as if to bunt while the infielders charged the plate in response. Desmond pulled the bat back at the last moment, letting this high fastball go by for ball one. A new set of signs from all possible connections was then set in motion one more time.

Waddell's second pitch came in just below the letters of the hitter's uniform and the fastball split the plate in half coming right down the middle. However, this time Wilson never squared around as if to bunt. With eyes as big as beach balls at the sight of a fat pitch coming toward him, the Cubs centerfielder let loose with a mighty cut that centered the sweet spot of his bat. The normal crack of a well-struck baseball was drowned out by the mighty roar of the crowd, but the trajectory of this batted ball was visible for all to see.

The Cardinals right fielder turned his shoulders and ran backward to the wall in right, but the rocket sailed over his head as he turned the wrong way losing sight of the baseball. The deafening noise added another confusing element to the equation, as the puzzled outfielder struggled to find the ball in the ivy-coated walls of Wrigley. He ran toward where he thought the ball had hit the wall, but he could not find it.

The well-struck baseball ricocheted off something on the wall, perhaps some hardened ivy. The ball rolled toward the right-field corner before any St. Louis player could alert their puzzled outfielder where the ball was hiding.

There was mass confusion, as only a handful of players on the field knew exactly where the ball had caromed. By the time the Cardinals tracked down the baseball nestled in the right field corner 340 feet away from home plate, Evans had turned the corner at third base and was cruising home with the tying run.

Desmond Wilson was finally using his top-notch speed in peak performance as he ran right out from under his batting helmet, flying around second base before turning toward third at just about the time the Cardinals right-fielder picked the baseball off the ground and into his glove. The outfielder quickly spun around and unleashed a strong throw toward third that was cut off by the second baseman lined up as a relay man.

The crowd could do nothing but scream in approval, sensing the dramatic moment of victory near, as Wilson raced toward third base focusing on his third base coach Paxson for the stop or go sign to check in with a triple or possibly even attempt an inside the park home run if Paxson waved his arms in windmill fashion.

Lenny was halfway down the third base line toward home when he finally put the stop signal up for Desmond after originally waving him on in as Wilson rounded third and was streaking down the third base line several feet in foul territory after niftily cornering the third base bag.

It was the prudent move by the third base coach as the tying run had already scored and there was still nobody out with the meat of the order coming up. The prudent move flew right out of the ballpark as Wilson had a full head of steam going and attempted to score. The heat of the moment took over, as Wilson knew speed was his game and had a flawed sense of confidence that could not be halted.

The Cardinals second baseman Dorman, a knowledgeable and seasoned veteran, caught the throw from the outfielder chest high and in perfect position to make an accurate relay throw. The problem for Dorman was that he spun to his left and prepared to look toward third, not realizing above all the pandemonium that Wilson had run through his third base coach's stop sign.

The slightest shift of bodily momentum threw off Dorman's balance as he quickly realized he had to throw home, but his shoulders and hips had not yet squared around in proper fashion to make an accurate throw. In his haste to get rid of the ball, his throw to home was off-line and toward third base, up the line about 10 feet instead of an on target throw at the plate.

The Cardinals star catcher Paul Evans still had a shot at tagging Wilson out, even with the off-line relay as he corralled the errant throw ahead of Wilson's body blazing toward home plate with the possible winning run.

With the play right in front of him, Desmond was able to slide inside of the chalk line running from home plate to third, toward the infield grass, to avoid the lunging Evans attempting valiantly to tag out the evading runner. However, because Wilson had slid so soon to avoid the tag, he came up just short of the plate, inches from touching home. Desmond quickly lunged forward and touched the plate with his right hand just before Evans' tag struck Wilson on the right shoulder.

The Cubs had pulled off their most dramatic win of the season, sparing them near-certain elimination for at least the next two days. The noise emanating from the victorious Wrigley crowd was deafening. The dugout was already empty of players even before Wilson plated the winning run, and it took no more than a few seconds for him to be mobbed by his jubilant teammates.

Surprisingly, Blake just stood there several feet from the dugout, admiring the victorious scene from relatively afar. He glanced back in Kim's direction and caught her attention with a resounding fist pump into the air. He could see and feel the unbridled joy in her face as Kim whooped it up with the rest of the fans. Blake blew her a kiss and turned around to resume watching the pandemonium on the field. He had to fight back tears, as the emotional moment had struck in him a different note than the rest of his team.

He felt a rush of pride fill his soul as the boys continued their unscripted and wild celebration. He and his boys had done well. His former teammates would have been proud of their resilient efforts today. And they would have been extremely proud of Blake. The rookie manager had come to grips with their sense of mystic association with these scrappy players that now made up the Chicago Cubs team.

Blake felt in his heart that all the players of this year's Cubs were united in their passion to pull this extremely unlikely divisional championship out of a fairy tale book and into miraculous reality. It was now both fallen teammates and makeshift roster as one. The inspired manager could feel it in his soul as he watched his players slowly move toward the dugout and up the runway to the clubhouse, victors knocking on the doorsteps of the Cardinals' lead now at the scant margin of one.

64 — Daydream Believers

With one swing of the bat and a speedy circumnavigation of the bases, the prevailing mood of players and Chicago fans alike went from I think we can to I know we can.

The city was alive with passion for their Cubbies. Nobody thought they could win it all, but a division championship over their fiercest rivals from nearby St. Louis, given all the obstacles these players had to overcome, would be miraculous in its own right.

Blake had gone from an underachieving has-been that had lost respect from teammates and fans, to a heroic figure of redemption, in a matter of seven weeks. The rejuvenated player-manager was now bigger than life itself. He represented a human quality that all people of this world could relate to, the dogged determination to fight back at life's biggest challenges.

The Chicago area loved their vagabond Cubbies, but their passion was fixated on the lone remnant of the team that had been assembled in March, performed wondrously in the first four months of the season, but had perished in a ball of flame in August.

This was Blake's team and Blake's town. It would be his story that captivated the country during a time when professional football normally stole the sports show from baseball. Football might hold its own against Blake's plight in the sports pages, but his was also a very inspiring human-interest play where the final act was still to be determined.

The drama was building to a climax that could go in a variety of directions, from good to bad or from bad to worse, if Blake succumbed to devilish temptations. At the moment it looked like good was a distinct possibility, but a train wreck could also draw a huge number of gawkers worldwide. Either way guaranteed a media circus at this point.

Blake's agent was already fielding numerous pitches for endorsements, but he was only seven weeks into sobriety and a relapse was still entirely possible. Yet he and the team had come a long way. People were starting to believe in him, but nothing the newly sober Blake had accomplished so far had stood the appropriate test of time for such delicate matters.

Perhaps Blake was just the newest star of the television reality show stage with massive followers watching and waiting to see which side would win out. Would he withstand temptation and the pressures of intense scrutiny? Or would he implode in dramatic fashion? It was all to be determined, as the focus shifted from the dramatic come-from-behind win to the upcoming contest that could put both teams in a mathematical tie for first with only two games left.

Blake arrived early at the ballpark the following day for the Cubs nighttime contest against the Cardinals, the second game of the four-game series. He was eager to get the game started, but he was even more anxious to find out how his boys would react coming off the emotional win the day prior.

The manager in Blake wanted to make sure his players were loose. The sudden realization that they could be tied with the Cards as a result of a victory tonight might cause a nervous tension that hardly ever brought out good results in baseball.

Most of Blake's players shared his desire to get to the park early. The clubhouse was often the players' sanctuary from professional and personal distractions. Interacting with fellow comrades that shared so many daily events only a professional baseball player could understand and appreciate created a common bond between disparate ethnicities that otherwise would be strangers to their personal plight. The lengthy schedule a major league baseball team endures, rather than fully enjoys, only adds to the need of the players to escape for several hours from daily stress.

Blake was relieved to see a large contingent of his boys mixing it up this afternoon in a very playful manner only hours from the next "most important" game of the season. As usual, Miguel Guillen was leading the banter. Today's target was the hero of yesterday's game, speedy centerfielder Desmond Wilson.

Blake partially closed the door to his office and stayed out of view, but he was listening intently. He knew this was going to be entertaining so he rolled up his chair and put his legs up on the manager's desk to enjoy the fun.

"Dezzie, I think I've got a new nickname for you after the slick maneuver you pulled off yesterday on your inside-the-park homer," said Miggy.

Wilson knew this wasn't going to be pleasant, but he played along to amuse the assembled group. If nothing else, the boys would get a kick out of Miguel's take. They always did.

"Pray tell, Miggy. What possible insight could you provide to your minions that they don't already know about me? You do know that most of your nicknames never stick, big guy? It seems that you're the only one who ever likes them. Just like your stale comedy routine. You need new material dude."

"You may be right Dezzie and thank God we've got teammates like you that give us plenty of ammunition. I've got to give you credit though. We're going to pull this thing out because you are as you are. Blakester lets Dezzy be Dezzy and they both come out smelling like a rose."

"It's called baseball instincts my boy," said Desmond. "You pitchers don't know nothing about that though. You flamethrowers just rear back and fire the ball. Doesn't take much to shake your head up and down when you get the catcher's sign and fire away. It's just a God-given gift from your Mommy and Daddy. A damn robot could do that just fine. I've got to smell out the situation

286 – Timothy F. Bouvine

and go with the flow, my man. My vibes tell me what to do. That takes talent. If you've got it, you've got it, Chubster."

"Dezzy dude, you're like that kid in Little League that just keeps on running until he either gets tagged out or somehow scores. There's no stop in Dezzy. Coach Lenny put the brakes on you, but you just kept on going. So therefore I, Miguel Guillen, the prince of pet names, now pronounce you, 'Go Go Wilson'."

"Hot damn Miguel, I think I actually like that one. Go Go Wilson. That's not too shabby. I'll see if the uniform guys will let me put just Go Go on my jersey."

"How's about we just proclaim to the media that there's no stop in Go Go?"

Wilson stood proudly, walked right up to the always-playful Guillen, and gave him a big hug before anointing his teammate as a proud partner. "Miggy, I just made you my promotional advisor. Anybody that can turn a phrase like that can't be no robot. You got talent too. There's no stop in Go Go. Let's take it one step farther, my man. Instead of using the word stop, why don't we just use a stop sign to replace the written word with a sign? You're a goddamn genius fat boy. I take back all the bad words about you being a dumb Mexican."

"Okay, Desmond, it's truce time. I'll quit calling you an ignorant black man, at least until we sign a contract. Then you're stuck with this wetback no matter what."

They both broke out in laughter, erasing any possible tension at the slurs, and bumped chests for good measure. The rest of the team that had gathered around followed on cue. The slightest hesitation at the awkward moment when Guillen and Wilson threw racial and ethnic barbs at each other was suddenly overridden with laughter, relieving all in attendance of the possible sensitivities of the topic.

Blake had laughed along in relative silence behind the partially closed office door with a huge blue Cubs insignia. The playful banter had gone on long enough to loosen everybody up for the big game. Blake instinctively felt it was time for him to enter the fray and keep the subject matter on a straighter line, now that the laughter had eased the uncertainty of possible touchy subjects.

The manager let out a big laugh and shut the door behind him as he immediately made himself the center of attention with his authoritative voice. "Okay boys, now that we've settled on a new brand name for our up-and-coming star, why don't we try to rebrand these damn Cardinals into anything other than perennial champs? I don't know about you guys, but the possible sight of those guys celebrating a division championship on our turf makes me sick to my stomach. Let's tie this thing up today and put those guys on notice that we aren't going away."

There was an immediately loud reaction to their manager's words. Most players were outspoken in their disdain for the Cardinals and wanted to knock the Redbirds out of the playoff picture in the worst way. Plenty of hoots and hollers filled the clubhouse as the team prepared for the night game.

Before the manager retreated to his office, he had just a few words for his heroic game-winning base runner, Desmond Wilson. Blake did not want to embarrass his player in front of the rest of the team, but the Cubs leader had to make sure Wilson did not get carried away with his daring ways that, more often than not, failed at their intended goal.

"Hey Desmond, yesterday is over. You can only hit on an inside straight so often. I think you used up your card playing magic for the season yesterday. Go Go will be gone if he doesn't put his glasses on and follow the team signs. No more trying to win it all by yourself. But hey, Dezzie, that was one helluva play. Just thank your lucky stars it worked out this time. I think we had some help from above on that one from one of my old teammates, but just remember there are ex-Cardinals in heaven too."

"You got it Skipper. We're just playing along here for dramatic effect. You know I just want us to win," said Desmond in true sincere fashion.

"Well let's cut the drama for a bit guys. I know I'd appreciate a nice lead tonight instead of the heart-stopping do-or-die rallies, but hey, if that's the way it's got to be, so be it. Just win baby."

Blake retreated to his private refuge and started the deliberate process of game day strategy. No changes were needed in the batting order. Yesterday was full of offense and mostly productive at-bats, so why change a good thing? He often contemplated upcoming game-day moves by playing a bit of garbage can basketball in his office. Anything to get his mind off other stresses in life as he crumpled up sheets of paper, whirled around in his chair and pretended he was Michael Jordan while pondering personnel and in-game maneuvers.

This relaxed the often-anxious Blake and made him focus solely on his players while he fixated on the garbage can/basketball hoop.

He had already determined, in consultation with his pitching coach and new-found friend Mark Douglas, he would skip over his back-of-the rotation pitchers and go with his top three starting pitchers to end the regular season. There was no reason to hold back at this point and his pitchers were all in agreement that they would do what was necessary to pull this thing out.

Obviously there would be consequences if the Cubbies somehow managed to win the division and advance with an overused, arm-tired staff facing off against well-rested opponents. It just did not matter at this point. Full steam ahead, with later matters be damned at this juncture.

Kyle Jacobson would take the mound and attempt to give his club a chance to win tonight. He normally kept his team in the game, but he also rarely shut down the opposition completely as his pitching stuff was just a bit above average. His pitching moxie usually kept opponents off-balance enough to limit the damage to several runs per seven innings, an acceptable production, but one that could put his squad in jeopardy if they went against a top-notch ace capable of shutting down hitters completely.

That was exactly the case tonight, as St. Louis would counter with their ace pitcher, Salvador Torres. The Cardinals manager Don Leighton had moved up his own starter a day early in what Blake thought was somewhat of an arrogant move. Leighton was already looking ahead to the playoffs, lining up his star pitcher for the opening contest of the National League postseason.

Blake knew he had his own issues to worry about so he tried to disengage from anger at this point. Leighton had his own team to worry about and would have to live with his own choices if the he arrogantly looked too far ahead.

Blake wanted desperately to scratch out any kind of lead against Torres and the Cards, putting pressure on the St. Louis manager to consider removing his ace prematurely for a pinch-hitter if it came to that.

Blake himself realized that he was also falling into that trap as well. One can never look too far ahead with baseball; it seems to always come back to bite you in the ass. Still, a lead of any kind would be a welcome sight indeed on this cold, damp night at Wrigley Field.

The air was cool, but the mood was hot as the Chicago players took the field for the opening pitch. The fans instinctively felt that their incessant loud cheering would give the Cubs the confidence they needed tonight to tie this pennant race up. It felt like just another uphill challenge for a team that had already overcome numerous hurdles of their own to get to this point.

Blake could see and feel the increased self-confidence his team was showing just by their body language taking the field. The manager stood proudly in the dugout as he watched in awe at the scene developing before his eyes. He gave himself one minute to just sit back and reflect on the surreal scene before switching to game mode.

Just as his starting pitcher Kyle Jacobson was finishing up his warm-up tosses, Blake stood on the top step of the dugout and twisted his neck around to confirm his wife's presence once again. He was aware of her desire to be there again tonight, but he just wanted to see it with his very own eyes to feel the sense of participation his wife's presence brought to him. It was definitely reassuring for Blake to see her in the same section as yesterday.

Blake returned to his favorite spot in the dugout that, coincidentally, was the warmest, wind-protected area that sheltered him from the cold. He tugged at his cap to secure it to his skull before watching the leadoff hitter for the Cardinals occupy the batter's box in preparation for the game's opening pitch.

Jacobson tossed a perfect top of the first, easily retiring the St. Louis batters on three separate groundouts to get the Cubs off in the right direction. Blake could sense his team still had the momentum in their favor, a carryover effect from yesterday's dramatic win.

The manager's sense of intuition turned to gold as his boys struck early. The longstanding baseball theory of the need to get to a dominant pitcher early in the game before he got into his groove set the stage for Chicago's urgency to get off on the right foot from the get-go.

Desmond Wilson picked up right where he left off with a ground ball single through the right side of the infield to lead off the inning. The speedster promptly stole second on the first pitch and the team could definitely feel itself off and running.

Wilson advanced to third on a wild pitch before plating the game's first run on a routine groundout to short with the Cardinals infield playing back, conceding the run so early in the contest. The 1-0 lead did not stay that way very long as shortstop Rickey Sanchez lined a screamer that cut through the stiff Lake Michigan wind blowing straight in tonight. The rocket found the first row of the bleachers in left just 15 feet or so inside the left field foul pole for a home run that had the Wrigley crowd in a delirious state. The fans clamored for a curtain call before they would settle back down into their seats, and Sanchez obliged with a rise to the top step of the dugout and a tip of his cap to the ecstatic crowd.

The Cubs took the field in the top of the second already in the lead 2-0 and those few daydream believers that had faith in their club at the start of the day suddenly became part of a rapidly developing bandwagon of dreamers that could now envision the team in a tie for first place at the end of this night.

Not only did the Cubs hold on to the lead for the first half of the game, they even tacked on another run via the perfect example of small ball. Petey Arroyo coaxed a 10-pitch walk out of Torres to lead off the third inning, advanced to second on a well-executed sacrifice bunt from the pitcher Jacobson, before advancing to third with two outs on a Wilson groundout to second.

Ricky Rodriguez beat out an infield hit on a dribbler up the middle that just evaded the pitcher Torres. The weakly hit grounder slowed just enough in the damp, thick Wrigley infield grass forcing the shortstop to try a barehanded pickup and throw to first all in one motion. Fortunately for the Cubs and Rodriguez, the shortstop was unable to pick up the baseball cleanly, and Ricky raced past the first base bag excitedly clapping his hands as Wilson crossed the plate to push the lead to 3-0.

Jacobson was cruising through the game, keeping the opposition hitters off balance the whole time. The veteran pitcher even dusted off an old pitch he had abandoned years earlier in a crafty attempt to confuse the Cardinals hitters even more. Jacobson already possessed a vast repertoire of pitches, but his renewed acquaintance with a screwball obviously caught the Cards off guard.

The line-up that lefty Jacobson had to face a lineup strategically assembled by Cardinals manager Don Leighton. The St. Louis skipper filled his batting order with a predominantly right-hand hitting lineup, as is the preferred norm against southpaw pitchers. However, the screwball pitch is unusual in its trajectory as an offering that breaks away from righties; most breaking pitches from a left-hander break toward the right-handed batter, making contact easier. The in-game adjustment threw off Leighton's strategy in Jacobson's favor.

No advance scout could have seen this coming, and in fact Jacobson only improvised with this old friend, screwball, as a long shot gamble. Kyle had developed elbow issues from the repeated oddball pitch, but in his search for something else to confuse the Cardinals, he figured it was worth a shot on this critical night. With his elbow fresh, without any pain, Jacobson found a perfect pitch at just the right time to shut down the St. Louis offense.

The Cardinals finally broke through on the scoreboard with a single tally in the sixth inning, scratching out their run on a leadoff walk, a hit-and-run single that put runners on first and third with nobody out before a sacrifice fly plated the lone score of the inning. The 3-1 lead still felt fairly solid, as Jacobson seemed in command.

However, St. Louis got to within one run in the top of the eighth and knocked Jacobson out of the game with a solo homer. Blake jumped out of the dugout and raised his left arm to the bullpen to summon an arm-weary Miguel Guillen to the mound to replace Jacobson.

Blake held out his right hand for the game ball from Kyle and patted the star of the game on his non-throwing shoulder to indicate his appreciation for the outstanding effort. The Wrigley faithful rose to their feet and thunderously applauded Jacobson's performance as the fatigued pitcher made his way to the dugout. His teammates were up on the top steps of the dugout to greet Jacobson and congratulate him on his stellar performance, but everyone knew there was more work to be done to seal the deal tonight.

Guillen was told earlier that he would only be asked to face one batter in a pinch, and with the tying run coming to the plate with two outs, Blake felt the urgency to have his top lefty stopper in the bullpen matchup against St. Louis' power hitting outfielder Jorge Cruz. The left-handed swinging Cruz was a solid hitter against anybody, but his power numbers were significantly reduced against southpaws.

Miguel did not like his stuff warming up, but he gutted out a seven-pitch at-bat against Cruz before the outfielder flied out to medium deep center field to end the inning with the Cubbies precariously holding on to a 3-2 lead.

All that stood between the Cubs and a tie in the standings was one more at-bat by the Cardinals in the ninth after the Cubs went down meekly in their half of the eighth inning.

Blake held true to his promise and replaced Guillen with closer Randall Hart to start the ninth. The tension was eerily present to all in the stands, as the in-experienced Hart would be called upon to close out the crucial game. He had never been in a save situation with this much on the line before, and the appre-hension of the crowd could be felt in the nervous applause that greeted him to the mound to begin the last stanza.

There was even a smattering of boos emanating from the crowd after Hart, clearly battling nerves, walked the leadoff batter on four pitches.

Now the strategy would really begin as St. Louis manager Leighton faced a tricky situation. The century-old baseball book strongly suggested a manager should play for the win on the road in such a scenario and resist the temptation to sacrifice bunt, but it wasn't a hard and fast rule. The theory being that the visiting team has to hold off the home team for two innings to pull out a win if they play for a tie. Indeed, the home team held a solid edge in extra-innings games with the last at-bats.

Leighton shunned the bunt and went by the book with his player swinging away. The first pitch from Hart was lined into left, fielded on one hop, and im-mediately thrown back into the infield by Chicago left-fielder Gonzales, but not before both runners were safely stationed at first and second with no outs.

Hart and the Cubs were now in a heap of trouble with the tying and potential go-ahead runners on base. The crowd was fidgeting in their seats at the night-marish thought of shattering their dreams of a tie in the standings.

It was a near certainty now that St. Louis would sacrifice bunt the two run-ners over, especially with the pitcher's spot in the batting order due up. Al-though most pitchers practice bunting all season long, the odds favored a pinch-hitter here to advance the runners with a batter adept at handling the bat.

Leighton sent up a light-hitting middle infielder, further signaling the like-lihood of a sacrifice. Blake hollered at the home plate umpire for time and walked confidently toward Hart, joined by the catcher Bartlett for a mound meeting. Hart was still standing on the pitching rubber and looking like a kid waiting for his dad to scold him.

"Randall, I got your back. This is how the rest of the game is gonna play out. Just follow my advice and it's game over big guy. Trust me, I've seen this scenario happen over and over, too many times to not know what will happen."

"Skipper, how in the hell do I get out of this? Why did I walk the leadoff guy?"

Blake just gently put his right arm on Hart's shoulder and tried to comfort his closer while at the same time giving him a shot of much-needed confidence.

"Take a deep breath, big guy and look at me and Bartlett there. We've seen more games and situations like this than you can even imagine. We absolutely know how this is going to play out. Listen to us, follow Bartlett's signs and trust your stuff. You throw heat better than 99.9 % of people on this planet. And, by the way, just about every kid that's ever played this game would love to be in your shoes right now. So fucking enjoy this," said Blake with an impish smile.

"Listen up quick, ump's gonna hurry us up. They're gonna bunt for sure. Just take the free out. Walk the next guy to load the bases. I know Hairston like the back of my hand," Blake said in reference to the following scheduled batter.

"Just throw him low and away fastballs. Nothing else, I guarantee he'll roll over on it and ground it to short. Guaranteed, its 6-4-3 DP, ballgame. Infielders take the conventional DP and we'll go home tied tonight," Blake said, apparently forgetting that he was the only player to make his home in Chi-town.

"Got it Bartlett? Got it Hart?" Blake quickly glanced at each player for acknowledgement. They both nodded their heads and Blake just smiled and walked away, certain of the results in his head, just as the home plate umpire reached the mound.

Now, Blake was as experienced as they come, but he knew nothing was guaranteed in baseball. He ducked inside the dugout and stood in the corner all by himself. He just shook his head and prayed to God that he was a good enough actor to convince Hart and his players that he was dead serious.

The sacrifice bunt was a near certainty and that played out just as he envisioned. Hart picked up the bunt about 10 feet straight out from home plate and never thought of anything else other than throwing to first to get the giveaway out. The two runners advanced and first base was now open.

Bartlett stood rose from his crouch as the next batter stepped in the box. The crowd was hesitant. What was going to happen next? Bartlett held out his left glove hand signaling for the intentional walk as the crowd buzzed.

The bases were loaded with one out and the Cubs protecting a precarious 3-2 lead in a must-win situation with an inexperienced closer and a makeshift squad. Would they react with poise? Could the players on the field trust the teammates next to them in a critical situation? Uncertainty was everywhere except in Randall Hart's mind. Blake's acting job had been worthy of an Oscar in a leading role. Hart had put all of his trust in his manager's experience and expertise.

Bartlett shifted his weight ever so slightly to the outside portion of the plate as the right-handed swinging Jeremy Hairston planted himself in the batter's box. The catcher framed the low and away target for Hart and flashed down a set of signals that were totally disingenuous to the Cardinal runner on second, who was peeking to try and steal a sign to possibly alert the batter Hairston what pitch was coming. It was to be all fastballs as Blake had directed. The key was to hit Bartlett's glove target and not so much to confuse the batter as to what pitch might be thrown next.

Blake had indeed felt very confident that Hairston would try to pull the ball as he always seemed to. The Cubs manager was counting on Jeremy's stubborn refusal to adapt to the situation. Blake knew all about the Cardinal outfielder's insistence that only he knew what was best for hitting. Hopefully, this was not the time for the stubbornness to give way to manager Leighton's constant bickering for him to hit the pitched ball toward right field once in a while.

Hart missed to the outside of the plate on his first pitch, at least missing in the right direction as a ball misplaced over the middle of the plate could be disastrous in the situation at present. The crowd became restless and pleaded for Hart to throw strikes, but Hart again missed away, to fall behind 2-0 in the count.

Blake was edgy in his dugout as well, but the silver lining in this potentially dark, ominous cloud was the aggressive mood this count was sure to create in Hairston's mind. The Cubs manager was begging internally for the kid pitcher to hit his spot this time, and Blake chewed his gum even more intensely with the huge pitch coming up.

Hart religiously followed his orders and delivered a perfectly place two-seamed fastball on the low and away corner. Hairston could not resist and took a mighty swing, but the pitch was too "heavy" to lift with a pulling batting swing, and, just as Doctor Blake had ordered, the Cardinals outfielder hit a well-struck grounder to the shortstop Sanchez.

The Cub shortstop was in perfect double play position, fielded the hard grounder securely, and quickly flipped the ball in a sidearm motion to second baseman Arroyo, who was slowly moving toward second to catch the ball thrown from Sanchez, timed perfectly for the moment he arrived at the base. Petey caught the ball and unloaded a super-quick relay throw to Jim Arnold at first, making a flawless pivot at second to avoid the oncoming base runner all in one continuous motion. Arroyo delivered a perfect chest-high throw to first just as he was up-ended by the charging runner. The play could not have been executed any better from the Cubbies perspective. It went 6-4-3 double play, game over. Cubs win. Cubs win. Cubs win. And now tied with St. Louis in the standings.

It all happened so quickly that it took a second to sink in before the whole Chicago bench stormed the field and mobbed Hart, Sanchez, and Arroyo for a raucous display of unbridled emotion. The Wrigley Field crowd was as loud as Blake had ever heard it in a coordinated roar of affection and appreciation for a remarkable accomplishment.

True to form as a manager, Blake stayed away from the celebration and let

294 – Timothy F. Bouvine

his players be the focus. He was forced to sit down by the nearly overwhelming relief he felt at this unbelievable moment. An exhausted Blake looked upward to the heavens and thanked who or what decided the manager's vision would come true. Whether it was the fallen Chicago players, the deceased legendary Cubs announcer Harry Caray, or God above that made this happen, Blake was going to be eternally grateful.

It had been a long, winding road back to a tie in the standings, but there were still at least two more games to be played. Heaven help us all Blake thought, unable to envision a more excruciatingly exciting moment than this.

65 — Two Steps Forward and One Step Back

Giddy was an understatement for the mood in the Chicago clubhouse after the 3-2 victory marking the culmination of a month-long climb in the standings to get even with the Cardinals.

About the only thing missing was the champagne shower associated with clinching the title. Various players were hugging each other and talking big-time smack about their opponents. The amped up music intensified the victorious mood, and virtually all were celebrating in some form or fashion until the veteran John Bartlett stepped in to make a dramatic point.

He shook his head in disgust as he walked over to the source of the music and angrily hit the power button, silencing the celebratory mood with a loud whistle. He did not have to feign anger as he shouted out to his teammates. "What the hell is going on here? Did I just come out of a coma and realize we won the division? Or just won the Series? Jesus, I know we've got a young team, but you guys can't be this stupid. We haven't done Jack squat yet. Surest way to screw this up is to start celebrating now when we still have to win two more games against these old pros."

The rest of the team looked stunned at Bartlett's outburst. Nobody had the guts to confront him, but there was obvious disdain for his actions. Third baseman Mike Simons, a seven-year vet himself, looked the Rat in the eyes and tried to downplay the emotion that was on vivid display moments earlier with a remark of his own.

"C'mon Bartlett, these guys deserve a half-hour or so of pride in what they've accomplished. They've been around a bit too, you know. Give 'em a bit of respect."

Bartlett was clearly agitated at Simons' comeback and returned a verbal shot back at him harder than his first outcry. "Simons, haven't you learned anything in your time in professional baseball? That's correct, I forgot you haven't won anything so you don't have a clue. We celebrate when we've finished something and not a moment before that. Surest way to fuck this up is to think we've actually done something worth celebrating. I've been on championship teams. I've seen what it takes. I've seen how veteran pros handle themselves, and by God, this ain't it."

Just then Blake came out of his own office. His curiosity was piqued by the sudden silence before Bartlett's rants became audibly unavoidable. The manager was half-dressed and clearly confused as he examined the scene in front of him.

"What the hell's going on Bartlett? If I didn't know better, I'd think we just lost the biggest game of the year instead of won. What in God's name could possibly be the problem? Tell your manager just what the fuck you're doing, please. Before these teammates of yours rip you to shreds."

"Jesus Blake, you should have my back. I'm trying to do these neophytes a favor here. We can't get too carried away over this game, there's still way too much to do. They're celebrating like there's no tomorrow and by God, there will be a huge tomorrow and the day after and maybe the day after that too. I won't be satisfied until we win the whole goddamn thing and we're weeks away from that. Tell 'em Blake. You know I'm right."

"Bartlett, I hear you and you are right for 99.9 percent of teams. This ain't one of them 99%. This whole fucking thing is unprecedented." Blake paused, hitched up his pants and continued. "Now guys, Bartlett's right, you know we've got more work to do, but by God we're going to celebrate this achievement even if it's only worthy of the 30 or so guys in this room. This ain't real life John, this ain't life or death. This ain't even a real baseball team. We're orphans, bastards if you will. We can't put ourselves in the same position as other teams. It's all too new and unique to follow some historical baseball-code precedent. Now turn up the volume on that sonofabitch and let's boogie."

A loud cheer erupted and the music resumed, but the Rat just sulked in his own corner shaking his head before Blake asked him to step in his office for a moment.

"Sit down next to me John. I just want to make sure you've got no hard feelings toward me. You were right and I do know you were definitely helping the team with words of advice from an experienced vet like yourself. It's just that this is all so different, John. Part of this whole process for me is to understand that there's more to life than baseball. We've given a huge effort down the stretch and I couldn't ask for anything more from these guys. I hope you'll understand. Trust me, I'll let them know you were giving them sage advice and that there's nobody out there with more knowledge about the game than you." Blake sat silent and still for a moment waiting for any visible reaction from his temperamental catcher. When none was forthcoming the manager just put his left hand on Bartlett's shoulder and offered more encouragement.

"John, I know you've done more for this team than anybody, and sacrificed so much for these guys. I couldn't have asked for a better leader for this team than you. For all the years we battled and were professional enemies, you've done more in these past eight weeks to overcome any bitterness we might have felt for each other. I know why you've always been in demand as a catcher, John. You are a winner and a champion. Thanks for teaching these guys every day what it means to be a professional."

This time Bartlett opened up and reacted positively to his manager's kind words. "Blake. You're still a sonofabitch, but now you're my sonofabitch. After all our battles I never thought you'd go soft on me, but I get it. Thanks for the butt-kissing too. I like compliments as much as the next guy."

Blake stood up with a smile on his face and playfully asked the normally snarly Bartlett a question. "Do you think we've got those guys worried over there? Because I think they're scared to death to lose to a bunch of rejects like us."

"Blake, you have no idea. They are one cocky bunch that always talks a lot of shit. They're playing scared and I can easily see that. Now the fun begins though. They'll be ready from here on out, that's for goddamned sure. That's what I was trying to convey to the guys because the Cards will be a different team starting tomorrow. I hope they know that."

"They will know, John, because I'll make sure you tell 'em before the game tomorrow. Go out there and joke around with these guys. You can dish it out as well as take it so just stick your neck in there and enjoy the bullshit."

"You don't have to worry about that Blake. I'm pretty good at defending myself, verbally and physically if I have to."

"Now, now John, too much of a good thing can be bad for you. Save the fisticuffs for the Cardinals."

"You never have to worry about me, Skipper," said Bartlett with a wry smile.

"Exactly, that's my problem. You're too damned good at this ruffling feathers shit. Just piss off the other guys for the rest of the season Bartlett. I've got too many other things to worry about without any internal bullshit."

"Loud and clear Skipper, I got your back. For this season anyway."

"That may be all I have to concern myself with. This could be it for me Bartlett. I just want to go out on a high note so badly. For my former teammates, for my new guys, and goddamn it, for me too."

"Jesus, Blake, you're gonna make me cry and that's not good for my reputation. We'll give it our best shot, I promise that."

"Thanks John, that's all I can ask for."

The two former combatants and now respectful teammates looked at each other and nodded in agreement. It was time to move on and get mentally ready for tomorrow's most-important game of the year, strung together at least four games by now. Every game from here on out would surpass the previous one in importance. Such is the case in any pennant run.

Blake enjoyed another peaceful night at home with Kim. The mood was so light even his wife seemed concerned that Blake and his team might be a bit too complacent with his team finally catching the Cards.

The two of them were enjoying a late-night drink with Blake choosing a warming hot chocolate and Kim sipping a warm tea. The after effects of several hours in the damp cool air of Chicago in the early fall still chilled their bones despite the warming of a dramatic victory.

The conversation was light and pleasant with little mention of the game or the team. Normally Blake's thoughts about the pennant race would nearly fill the whole communication. Kim leaned back in her favorite chaise lounge with the cup of tea gently cradled in both her hands, and wondered if she dare broach the subject. Her curiosity eventually got the best of her and she lightly approached the topic with a casual tone of voice. "Blake, are you satisfied with catching St. Louis in the standings? I can't help but notice your very calm, relaxed demeanor tonight. Usually, after a game, you're still wound up in excitement, worry, or downright depression, depending on the outcome. Care to express any thoughts to your wife?"

Blake was also very relaxed in his own favorite lounging chair. He seemed to be in his own world at the moment staring out the window on this slightly moonlit night. He looked to be barely grasping his cup of hot chocolate as it lay dangerously close to spilling on the armchair, tipping at a near 90-degree angle. He snapped out of his trance just in time to hear his wife's question.

"I guess I feel somewhat vindicated at the moment. It's been a long tough road for the team and for me too. I feel like I've answered the critics that questioned my managerial ability and my newfound sober lifestyle. Am I wrong to just enjoy the moment and the comforting feeling that comes with it?"

"Well of course not Blake. But you've been a winner all your life and I've never seen you satisfied or even remotely happy with anything but first place before. Heck, you even get moody when you lose to me in cards or come in second to any of your friends in a game or contest."

"Yes, losing has always bothered me more than enjoying the thrill that comes with winning. Somehow, I feel like I've won already though, but I know what you're saying. Even Bartlett warned me today about enjoying this moment too much. Maybe you're both right. Don't worry, the next loss will bother me just as much, whenever it comes, that I can assure you. Now let's go upstairs while I'm still in my pacified mood. Hopefully it will lead to a good night's sleep. Biggest game of the year tomorrow you know. Haven't heard that much lately have you honey? I know, it gets old to me too, but it's the truth."

The night and into the morning went as smoothly and comfortably as possible. Every minute of life seemed to be enjoyable for Blake as he ate a delicious hot breakfast of pancakes and bacon, lovingly prepared by his good-luck charm wife. The superstitious manager just had to make sure his wife was coming to the game again this afternoon to keep her two-game winning streak intact.

"Don't forget to sit in the same seat too honey. You're definitely coming I hope?"

"Yes, Blake. I'll be there, don't you fret. Now, how about a thank-you for your meal?"

"I'm sorry Kim. Where are my manners? Thanks honey, it's perfect. I just hope it's a victor's meal and not a consolation prize."

"Well, that's more like the Blake I adore. It's winning above everything else. You better get rid of the melancholy mood from last night. It's going to be one hell of a battle."

Kim herself was quite the competitor, and her love of sports nearly matched her husband's intensity at times. Any wife of a professional athlete will speak from experience that life with her husband is more pleasant in a winning season. It can be very difficult to isolate one's self from a magnitude of critical comments from fans and media alike. It always felt very redeeming to her when Blake answered the critics with exceptional play. She would be the Cubs' and Blake's biggest supporter today in the Wrigley Field seats.

Wednesday afternoon at historic Wrigley Field would be another humdinger of a baseball game, or so was the prevailing theory going into the critical contest.

The joint was jumping and the weather was perfect for the third game of the four-game set to decide the National League Central Division championship. The crowd was bellowing from the moment the Cubs hopped on the playing field. Pregame preparations or live game action, it just did not matter to the Chicago faithful. Their players were now heroes. Every movement was acknowledged by loud cheers.

Unfortunately, Bartlett's, and even Kim's, fear of a letdown seeped into the Chicago players' psyche and the team looked lost, in love with themselves for simply catching the Cardinals in the standings. A tie was simply not enough, the team needed to realize a lead in the standings was the goal, not a tie.

Right from the first batter of the game there were immediate signs of a lack of concentration. Center fielder Desmond Wilson failed to pick up a routine fly ball that was lost in the sun, despite his securely attached sunglasses that should have made the play as easy as they come.

With the St. Louis leadoff batter on second and nobody out, the next batter sacrificed the runner to third, but nobody covered first base and suddenly the threat of a much bigger inning muted the exuberant crowd as an apprehensive hush took over.

The hush turned to boos as the next batter smacked a three-run homer to left. The Cardinals had indeed come out with a deeper sense of urgency, just as Bartlett feared. Their team was on a mission today and it was immediately apparent.

If the Cubs had gradually developed a sense of secure self-confidence from their recent near-perfect play, the Cardinals knew that their team could erase, or at the very least, severely diminish that confidence with a resounding win today. The always cocky Cardinals did not just want to win today; they wanted to destroy the Cubs and put that self-doubt right back into their minds.

Self-doubt had to creep into the Cubs' minds after they displayed terrible base running in the early part of the game. Rickey Sanchez apparently missed a hit-and-run sign and Desmond Wilson was an easy tag at second, as Sanchez never took the bat off his shoulders to protect the runner. The second inning provided another deflating moment as outfielder Felix Gonzalez got caught up in the heat of the moment and tried to stretch a leadoff double into a triple. Baseball's golden unwritten rule was to never make the first or last out of the inning at third base, but Felix heard the roar of the crowd and could not stop himself from running. The relay from second baseman Dorman easily beat Gonzalez to the bag and he was out by five feet.

The Chicago defense once again did its part in the sudden demise of fundamental play with infield errors from first baseman Jim Arnold and third baseman Simons. Both corner infielders saw grounders clank off their gloves in the fourth inning, leading to a pair of unearned runs that stretched the St. Louis lead to 5-0.

It soon became painfully obvious to everyone that the Cubs somehow were not focused and ready to play this game today. There was no momentum carried over from the first two Chicago victories of the series plus, if anything, the third contest exhibited the kind of resolve one would expect from the championship caliber Cardinals. As one longtime major league manager had duly noted before, momentum only lasts as far as the next day's starting pitcher allows. In this case, the Cubs' starting pitcher left momentum behind in the bullpen warm-up.

The middle innings cemented the victory and secured a one-game lead for St. Louis as they piled on five more runs to take a commanding 10-0 lead into the later innings. The crowd began to disperse after the second home run of the game from Cardinals slugging first baseman Lenny Charles stretched the lead into double digits.

By the time the dejected fans filed quietly out of the ballpark, the 13-0 final tally displayed on the scoreboard looked more like a football shutout than a baseball game between two apparently equal squads, or so the standings implied despite the unique circumstances of the season.

The whimpering and psychologically wounded Chicago Cubs left the dugout with heads drooping low. It was quite the contrast to less than 24 hours earlier when Blake and his team felt on top of the world with their fleeting accomplishment.

Blake was limping along the runway to the clubhouse, partly as a result of physical pain, but mostly from the deep wound he felt in his heart for not listening to his veteran catcher and to his alter ego, Kim, who had learned so much about baseball over the years from her husband. Blinded by his own jubilation, Blake had ignored much of what he had preached to others countless times.

The rookie manager felt like punching the wise old catcher's face, his own face that foolishly wore a figuratively shielding mask to keep him feeling naively proud. There was no other explanation for Blake's reluctance to use his numerous years of baseball experience at the most important juncture of this disjointed season. Did he really want to win? Or was he mired in his history of self-sabotage? The questions lingered in his troubled mind for the remainder of the day.

Blake's toughest postgame moment came as he walked past John Bartlett. The two of them locked eyes, but only one of them had the guts to keep fixated on the other. Blake's sorrowful set of eyes remorsefully began dropping downward in self-doubt. He knew he had hurt his team by letting his guard down for even one jubilant victorious moment.

Bartlett caught up to his manager seconds later and reassured Blake that he and his team unconditionally believed in him at this point and forward. They all had come too far not to dismiss mistakes made from all sides, even from the supposedly above-it-all manager. Bartlett smiled as only he could do with that devilish smirk and quietly mouthed a sarcastic comment after the supportive words. "When God speaks next time, listen to me okay? Or we might have to duke it out one last time."

Bartlett pointed to his chest as if Blake needed a refresher on the arrogance of one John Bartlett. Blake knew however, that Bartlett was indeed calling himself God. It was not out of character in the least.

Blake's competitive spirit reawakened and he shot back at Bartlett with vigor. "Don't worry about me, you slimy bastard. I'll kick your ass any day of the week. Hell, I'll even come back next year and track you down someplace to get another piece of you Bartlett. One Blake Benson can be a surly sonofabitch too."

Bartlett smiled once more at Blake and toyed with him again with another snarly comment. "Jesus, I can play you like a piano, Blake. That's the Blake Benson I want to see tomorrow and the rest of the way. Lead the boys into battle tomorrow. Got it?"

"Christ, you're good Bartlett. How in the hell you're still in one piece after all these years amazes me. You can piss off Jesus Christ himself. Let's just hope you still have a smidgeon of goodwill coming your way from the real big guy up in the heavens."

'It's all good, my man. Confession is good for the soul as they say. I spend most of my night's asking for forgiveness and repenting. I think the Big Guy upstairs has taken a close eye on this sinner."

"Well, ask for some forgiveness for me. I blew it today."

"Don't worry Blake. He understands baseball quite well. Every game is a day of redemption in baseball. You know that, I'm sure."

"I can't argue with you there, John. Tomorrow is indeed another day."

Nothing more needed to be said as the two went their separate ways and began to mentally prepare for the next day. It was a simple equation now. Win tomorrow or go home, but first Blake had to return to his own Chicago home tonight to eat some more humble pie, dished out by his wife.

Kim was extremely kind and understanding when her dejected husband arrived home. She knew from his sour expression that she did not have to say 'I told you so' to an already humbled Blake.

"Don't worry Blake, win tomorrow and this game will be forgiven and forgotten. As my grandmother used to preach to me, live and learn. You'll be a better manager from this experience."

"That's exactly where my anguish is coming from. It's live and learn, not live and relearn. I should've known better. Hell, I think I did know better, but I just wanted to bask in the moment for as long as we could. It looks pretty foolish now after today's debacle. Well, I've always seemed to have a preference for doing things the hard way. I might as well keep up that tradition. We better win tomorrow or I'll be second-guessing myself the rest of my life. We just better win."

"You're right Blake. That's all it ever takes. Just win and all else will be forgiven. I'm not sure about forgotten though. This game today will be a long-standing part of this story no matter what the eventual outcome. It's over with, Blake. My God, we certainly know you can't take back the horrible events in life. This is just a baseball game though; a very important one, but still just a game. Two months ago was a horrible life-changing event, this was just a game."

"Everybody is making so much sense today. I guess it's true that one learns more from losing than from winning. I just wish it didn't have to crush my thick skull with such vengeance. Let's not mention this game anymore tonight. Lesson learned. I just want to relax for a few hours. Find us a feel-good movie for tonight Kim. I sure could use it."

The two of them cuddled in bed watching an old Alfred Hitchcock movie from a director they both admired, but Kim could sense Blake was entirely elsewhere throughout the whole show. She truly did not expect anything else from her husband. He always had such a difficult time letting go and with the final countdown ending perhaps tomorrow, she would have been shocked if he had somehow escaped baseball's all-encompassing shadow, especially with such a personal stake dangling with the eventual outcome.

66 — The Final Countdown

Blake slept so soundly that when he awoke the following morning it took him several seconds to come to grips with his surroundings and the fact that today would be the final day of the regular season. If he was relaxed during the night, he definitely became excited upon awakening.

It was a good excitement, the kind that makes one feel very alive at the great possibilities that could play out right in front of them in their relatively short Earthly existence. The sound sleep had revitalized Blake and allowed him to put some perspective behind yesterday's loss.

Sure, it was a mistake-filled day, but not that much different than many days on this planet. It sunk in overnight that every day is filled with errors, misjudgments, and often self-inflicted harm.

He was sober despite the kind of day that would have previously led him right to the bottle for false comfort. He had a chance to make today a better day, while many others, like his former teammates, did not.

He was going to stay positive all day and leave nothing of himself in the dugout of life. This might be his last day of a boyhood dream plenty of others scoffed at the long-shot possibility while Blake was growing up. If he was too placid yesterday, he was bound and determined to compete to his highest capacity all day long.

Blake suddenly recalled a vivid dream he had experienced last night. Perhaps this might be his competitive resurgence this morning, he thought as he recalled the dream. His former Cub teammates that perished were vehemently arguing over one of their regularly held highly competitive card games. These players were teammates and friends for the most part, but they were arguing amongst themselves over a silly card game. He dreamt his teammates were extremely disgusted with each other and had near physical confrontations. This was indeed the team that Blake fondly remembered for their extreme competitiveness at anything in life. The baseball diamond was just another extension of a group mentality that often carried this year's team to new heights in the standings before the crash took it all away in a few moments of fear and despair.

There was shortstop Johnny Gilliam, who had an irrational fear of losing. A few games in a row on the short end of the scoreboard could send the highly competitive Gilliam into a deep funk. He hated to lose with a passion and his notorious outbursts of temper could set the team mood for days until the Cubs won again.

Third baseman Paul Fregin would take pride in his devious deceptions and sometimes downright illegal tactics to win. He felt there was not any situation on the baseball field that could not be overcome with trickery, and he felt no guilt at all no matter what tactics he used to come out ahead in a baseball contest.

There was right fielder Casey Tedin, who would brazenly boast that there was not any family member he would not run over to score, even his grandmother. He would rationalize this disturbing thought by declaring that dear old grandma would understand if he told her after the fact that it was necessary to win.

Even Blake's dear friend Sandy, despite his genteel demeanor off the field, would stop at little to come out ahead on the baseball diamond. There were many a time where opponents and even unsuspecting teammates were surprised at the sometimes vicious displays of competitiveness shown by Sandy that were completely opposite the norm of the usually quiet and stoic off-the-field gentleman.

Blake had a subdued smile on his face as he sprawled in bed covered by layers of blankets to stay warm and comfy this cool fall morning. He was recalling pleasant memories as he prepared himself psychologically for the managerial demeanor he insisted on exhibiting today to his boys. Blake could feel the outright anguish of his former teammates if they finished one or two games back in the standings. He had to convey that same emotion today and remind his players that in order to honor his former teammates' memory, his current players had to hate to lose just as much as the team that built the once-huge lead in the standings.

He certainly did not have to remind his current players of the large financial reward that was tantalizingly close in front of their greedy eyes, but he did have to point out once again that their manager held his former teammates' legacy close in his heart and soul. The current Cubbies had held up their end of the bargain so far and Blake was extremely grateful, but he knew in his heart that only a divisional championship would prolong their legacy into infinite baseball history and lore.

With a much more positive spring in his step this bright morning, Blake showered and met Kim downstairs for breakfast. The mood was light, even carefree as they bandied about small talk for several minutes while enjoying their ham and cheese omelets whipped up in a hurry by Kim. The tone of the conversation changed, however, as soon as Blake started discussing baseball and impending future decisions that he just began to share with his wife.

"It's a wonderful morning honey and I feel great today, but I can't stop thinking that it could all be over after today's game. Sometimes I don't know if I subconsciously want to lose so it will all be over. At least I could walk out with my head held high, unless I really screw up big-time today. You know Kim, I've been thinking pretty seriously about hanging up the spikes and retiring after this season."

Kim stiffened her spine and glared at Blake, who recognized what was coming next. He interjected immediately.

"Honey, don't get mad now. I was going to discuss it with you first. I know you want to be included in all decision-making. I am telling you now so you can be involved. I don't know for sure what we should do." Blake coyly threw in the collective reference to hopefully appease his wife's concerns, but he was surprised to hear her quick and intense reply.

"Stop it Blake. You guys are going to win today. I will hear none of that retiring talk until the time when a decision is necessary. Right now you have to motivate and inspire your guys to win. You get that right out of your mind this minute. Your teammates will pick up on your own lack of game focus if you continue down this path."

For once it was Kim who wanted to limit a conversation, not her procrastinating and often indecisive husband who would cut off their discussions when the topic became unsettling. Blake was pleasantly surprised at her reaction that focused more on the team than him. He never liked the focus on himself, especially when it came to his wife's often none-too-subtle advice.

Blake was inwardly conflicted and becoming more aware of his contrasting emotions. In the end, it all came back to the respect he had for his deceased teammates. He had to give it his all for them. This had to be about them and not him. He would not be able to live with himself if he gave anything less than his full effort. His recovery was about self-respect. To risk losing that would bring even more temptation for him to return to alcohol.

Leaving well enough alone, he decided to eat quickly and depart for Wrigley for what could be his last day in a major league uniform. Blake had already decided that he would lead by example and play today. Plus, he wanted to ensure himself at least one more meaningful playing day in a baseball lifetime of so many mundane and unimportant games with a franchise riddled with failures.

The positive feeling was following him around everywhere he went this morning. It was now time to check out the mood in the clubhouse on the day that would define their season.

He pleasantly kissed Kim goodbye and walked out the door, hesitating just for a moment outside his home to look up at the bright sunny sky and inhale all the fresh air he could take in his robust athletic lungs before exhaling in calming fashion. He realized it could all change in a minute once the game started, but he felt relaxed and confident as he entered today's choice of vehicle, his one-month-old navy blue Range Rover.

Zipping along the always hectic Chicago roadways, without nearly as much tension as one might expect on the last day of the regular season in a pennant race, Blake was either feeling the weight on his shoulders being lifted with his brief managerial stint soon ending, or he was simply enjoying the ultra-competitive moment in front of him today. It did not seem to matter at this point where the anxiety had fled to, only that it was absent from his mind.

Further brightening his day was the upbeat mood he immediately sensed emanating from the Chicago clubhouse. There was no tension lingering over the room, and laughter was abundant this morning. Perhaps it was just too far away from game time to accurately gauge the collective team psyche, but the player in Blake knew that it always was liberating to chase another team in the standings rather than protect a lead. Even a tie, as was the case before yesterday's game, had a tightening effect for many. It was back to being the hunter and not the hunted, and Blake's players were definitely enjoying the clubhouse safari at the moment.

As usual, Miguel Guillen was court jester as Blake stopped to analyze the give and take common in clubhouse comedy. The resounding laughter suddenly turned to clubhouse commotion as all the players in attendance at this scene began to shout at Miguel. It was too disorganized to ascertain their various loudly uttered words, but Blake could tell it was something about tomorrow and tee times at the local country club, which seemed bizarre given the team hopefully would be playing a one-game playoff with the Cardinals to determine the division championship. Of course, the Cubbies had to win today first. There was no way his boys could want to lose today.

Blake moved closer to the scene and immediately his players recognized their manager's presence. Suddenly the mood changed to utter silence as Blake's players lowered their heads in apparent shame. Blake took the bait and fell for the trap.

"What the hell are you guys doing? Did I really just catch you guys planning for tomorrow at the golf course? There should be no doubt in your minds we're gonna win today. Jesus Christ Miguel. Did you organize this?"

"Skipper, it's just a contingency plan. We're gonna give it our all today to win and force a playoff, but hey, just in case, we figured why not? Most of us aren't gonna be back here next year anyway so we wanted to tentatively schedule one last outing together for old time's sake. It's not like you're gonna be in charge of us anymore old man, after the next few days. You're what we call a lame duck manager and I mean real lame."

The startling comment forced a collective laugh as the players all let their beloved manager in on the joke. Nothing was said for several seconds as the pranksters just continued to laugh and howl at Blake's gullibility.

"We're just messin' with ya Blakester. We had a lookout who saw you coming and alerted us. Just trying to keep everybody loose, ya know."

"You guys just think you're so smart don't ya? I knew all along about your games. There's fucking cameras in here you know. It's always on with a direct connection to yours truly, your commander-in-chief that knows all. That camera up there behind the television is equipped with audio, and nothing gets by me."

All his unsuspecting boys glanced back at the big screen where the team followed the ESPN stream constantly. They quickly realized there was not any camera there, but before anybody could retort back at Blake, he jumped in first. "Now just look who's gullible? Cameras in the privacy of the clubhouse where you guys haul your naked fat asses around all day? C'mon guys, let's get real. Wise up."

Blake was the one with the last laugh, but then he let on to his true reaction.

"You guys actually had me though. I've got to give credit where credit is due. You bums are good actors and better actors than ballplayers for sure."

Their manager immediately laughed at his suggestion and began to pat several of his nearby players on their shoulders before continuing his remarks.

"My turn to just mess with ya. You all know I think the world of you as ballplayers and as men too. There's absolutely no reason why we can't sink that listing ship across the dugout from us today. All we've gotta do is play hard and play smart. A little luck from the baseball gods wouldn't hurt either, but hey, that's always the case."

Miguel once again spoke for the rest of the team, as his emotions were clearly visible when he expressed their desire to win this for their manager.

"Skipper, we're not going down without an epic fight. We know we can win, but if we don't it won't be from lack of effort. It won't be from a lack of sincere desire from your boys to let the baseball world know how much we think of you and all you've done for us."

Now their playful manager was beginning to melt with appreciation, but before Blake could begin to let that happen, he cut off his emotions in time to keep his focus on today's outcome. This was not yet the time for team reflection and recognition. He snapped back into pure managerial mode with inspirational words to his assembled outfit.

"Go out there today and give it your all, but just take a minute or two to remember that we're not only playing for ourselves, but for our predecessors that I knew all too well. By God, they hated to lose, especially to these guys. Remember them, their families and this city that has taken you all under their wings as one of their own. You've been an inspiration to many in this city, me included. Just play baseball the best you know how, that's all I'll ever ask. Now get back to your shenanigans on some other poor sucker. I'm going into my office to prepare myself for the biggest game of my life. I suggest you do the same."

Blake quickly turned away from his players and walked directly toward his office, but not before the sound of a single clap from Miguel Guillen began to spread to a chorus of clapping hands from Blake's teammates. As he shut the door behind him, Blake began to weep uncontrollably, but somehow managed to keep his overwhelming emotions silent from his teammates with the aid of cupped hands over his mouth and a wooden door between them. The heartfelt moment was sure to be followed by many more today. He had to stay in control to keep his baseball mind sharp. He had done what was necessary to focus his players on this moment, on this game alone. Behind closed doors, he just hoped he had said enough.

67 — It's Now or Never

Blake's team would have to win today. There were no ifs, ands, or buts. Baseball parlance indicated some very unusual maneuvers would be in store today. What normally would be seen as a bizarre managerial move today would be accepted from a team that simply has no tomorrow. Anything goes in such a scenario and creativity is looked upon favorably, unlike any other day in baseball when, a preferred course of action is to be followed in blind sacred custom.

The lineup card for the season finale looked very ordinary, except that manager Blake had inserted player Blake into the lineup and even moved him up to fifth spot in the batting order. His sense of confidence and positivity today carried over to his pregame ritual.

He was determined to soak it all in as he stood in the plush outfield grass at Wrigley Field. He constantly gazed around the ballpark in between a constant stream of batting practice tosses coming from third base coach Lenny Paxson at the moment.

The air was fresh this late morning in early October and the sun was shining brightly as high noon approached. The tantalizing aroma of ballpark food had a bit extra bite in it on this critical season-ending day, with light breezes gently stirring the whetting appetite brought on by the smell of sizzling meats on the grill.

One could easily spot the horde of media begging for interviews around the batting cage, while already exuberant fans were beginning to take over the now nearly empty seats. Before long there would be rousing cheers emanating from the crowd in an attempt to be part of the action themselves, but for now all Blake could hear was the repeated crack of crisply struck leather-wound spheres from powerfully swung wooden baseball bats.

There were the catcalls of occasional early-to-the-ballpark stragglers, but for the most part the sound was all baseball with rawhide smacking wood and leather. If this was indeed Blake's last game he wanted the sights and sounds from this day to last forever in his baseball brain. As a longtime backstop behind the plate he loved the popping sound of a blazing fastball striking the pocket of a catcher's mitt. He would forever recognize that sound and he could hear it in the background at the moment. Somebody must be having a throwing session in the bullpen and he glanced over his shoulder to see which pitcher was throwing that heat-seeking missile. It was an unmistakable sound.

Blake peered up to see the rooftop seats of adjacent apartment buildings that set up shop on every Chicago Cubs game day at Wrigley. This old ballpark had such charm that could not be replicated in any other city. At this moment he felt very fortunate to call this ballpark and the city of Chicago his longtime home. It was rare in this era of free-agency baseball for a player to be a lifetime fixture in one uniform. The huge centerfield scoreboard was anything but modern and that was a huge part of its appeal. The scores were changed manually, just like in a bygone era when baseball was indeed America's pastime.

Just as Blake was beginning to lose himself in recollection and admiration for days gone by, he caught himself. He knew he had to immediately snap out of this softer, reflective mood to get hungry for the present rather than glorifying the past. That time would come, but as Kim said earlier this morning, it was for another day.

Wrigley Field transformed from a serene practice field to a raucous three-ring circus as the daughter of deceased Cub Casey Tedin belted out the national anthem.

The Cubbies took the field with a battery of TJ Bowman on the mound and old-timer Blake Benson behind the plate. From day one Blake had instilled confidence in Bowman, as the manager had trusted baseball people in the know that said this pitcher was much more productive than his pitching stuff might indicate. There would be no better test of this appraisal than today's contest with so much on the line. Blake had felt his own managerial body of work was at stake today as well, and felt a sense of personal responsibility to call the game behind the plate today with his protégé.

The only issue that the player-manager was concerned with would be addressed as a result of Blake's conversation with another longtime veteran catcher and teammate, John Bartlett. Blake wanted to make sure he did not miss any detail of importance as the game progressed. He gave his first-string catcher the responsibility of game day management along with Blake. If the cagey Bartlett saw anything from his former teammates that could help beat these guys today, Blake wanted to hear about it no matter how insignificant it might seem. There could be no stone left unturned today.

Blake stood up after receiving Bowman's warm-up pitches and peeked into the stands just to make sure his wife was indeed there. He could not tell for sure, but he thought she made eye contact with him as he took his mask off. It did not matter at this point. He felt reassured knowing Kim was indeed there at his biggest moment. If it would be his last game, she would be a part of it too.

The crowd, just like Blake, had clearly gotten over yesterday's disappointment. The noise was deafening and it was constant. It was a new day and it felt like something special was about to happen. This could all disappear in a matter of minutes if things did not go Chicago's way once it all became real and not just wishful thinking, but at this moment Blake, his team, and the fans felt invincible.

The game progressed rapidly and without scoring for the first time through each team's batting order. In fact, neither Bowman nor Cardinals starting pitcher

Terry Ryan had allowed a single base runner through the first three innings. The scoreless tie perhaps indicated tightness from both teams, but in any event, the pitchers stole the show from the get-go.

The middle innings saw a bit of a crack in both pitchers' dominance with base-runners in scoring positions several times, but neither squad could come up with a clutch hit and left the runners stranded. The closest either team came to a run was in Chicago's half of the fifth inning when the Cubbies had a runner on third with one out, but back-to-back strikeouts left the Wrigley crowd groaning in disappointment.

By the top of the seventh both sides knew even one run was going to be crucial in this game. It just had the feel of a 1-0 contest, but which team would break through?

Much to the dismay of the home crowd, the Cardinals finally plated a run in the seventh on a smartly executed small-ball string of plays. An infield hit followed by a perfectly placed sacrifice bunt put a St. Louis runner on second with one out.

Blake pondered intentionally walking slugging first baseman Lenny Charles, but passed in favor of attempting to coax Charles into chasing a bad ball, but the strategy did not work. Charles walked, resisting several close breaking balls that fleetingly failed to entice the slugger.

After a trip to the mound to discuss the next batter, Blake crouched behind home plate and put down an array of signals to Bowman that were jumbled to disguise the pitch so the runner on second wouldn't be able to tip off the batter on which pitch was coming. The runner at second, Lonnie Jackson, was not looking for the pitch selection to relay to the batter, but to try and steal third base. Whether it was a lucky guess or a tipped-off signal, Jackson stole third without a throw. The curveball Bowman delivered bounced in front of home plate and all Blake could do was shift to block the errant pitch with his chest protector. There would be no throw to third as the ball struck Blake's padding, which kept the pitch slightly in front of him, and kept the other runner from advancing from first.

The aggressive and daring successful attempt immediately paid off. A long fly ball off the bat of Cardinals outfielder George Sanderson that was hauled in by Desmond Wilson in center easily allowed Jackson to tag up and score the game's first run. The damage was limited as Bowman struck out the next batter to end the inning, but this one tally looked awfully big at the moment. The Cubs were down to nine outs left in their amazing season if they could not rally.

The Cubs continued to go down meekly in their half of the next two innings as the crowd continued to interchange loud inspirational cheers with collective groans of frustration that signaled the season's end might be near.

Blake was pulling out all the stops with pinch-hitters and pitching changes. The bullpen held up its end of the bargain with scoreless innings. Miguel Guillen did his best cheerleading while on the mound for his scoreless ninth inning. His perfect half was followed by repeated motions for the crowd to get up out of their seats and spur the team to victory.

In came the intimidating Cardinal closer Waddell to start the last half of the ninth. The Cubs had always been his nemesis, but the All-Star closer was the best the National League had to offer at nailing down games for St. Louis and manager Don Leighton.

While the cocky Waddell strutted around the mound like he owned the important piece of real estate, and stared at the Wrigley crowd in utter contempt, John Bartlett called Blake over in a last-ditch effort to somehow rattle the combustible Waddell into losing his composure.

Bartlett smirked at Blake and spilled the beans on Waddell.

"You know there's that unwritten code pitchers and catchers shouldn't disclose some tricks of the trade Blake. I know you know it and I've almost always followed it, but goddamn it I want to win the game for this city and for you. Not always on every pitch, but Jerry scuffs the ball with sandpaper that he hides in his glove, just under one of his fingers, usually his index finger. If you see something crazy out there with ridiculous movement on his upper 90s fastball, ask for time from the ump and demand to see his glove. If nothing else, it'll rile him up. Hell, I know our guys do it too, but it's now or never for us. Just remember you didn't hear it from me."

Blake did not even verbally respond. He just nodded his head, perhaps unsure himself if he should resort to this last-gasp desperation tactic if needed.

The Wrigley faithful exploded in an even louder roar after leadoff batter Mike Simons lined the first pitch from Waddell into center field. The baseball book emphatically dictated that one should sacrifice bunt here, but it just happened that Blake was at bat and he had good career numbers against the Cardinal closer. Blake never was much of a bunter either. He still had a couple of options on the bench and he thought for a split second about another player taking over his spot in the order, but rejected that option. This could be his last game of big league baseball and by God he was not going to come out of it for any reason.

Blake rearranged the strap on his batting glove and settled in to face Waddell. He expected nothing but heat from the All-Star closer, as it was well-known Blake had lost some speed off his once lightning-quick batting stroke. It was power against the "once-power" of Blake as he took two fastballs from Waddell. The first one missed up and in, another weak spot for the older Blake. The next one split the middle of the plate, but Blake hesitated just long enough for a swing to be completely out of the question against the heat of Waddell's pitches.

Blake stepped out and shook his head in disgust. Perhaps the cagey, experienced Blake should have known better than to indicate his frustration at pulling the trigger on the swing, but the emotion of the moment overtook his thought process.

The opposition clearly saw the telling look of frustration in Blake's demeanor, and both pitcher and catcher were determined to throw Blake nothing but letter-high heat. The scouting report and everything in their experienced baseball minds taught them there was little chance of Blake getting his hands on top of the baseball with the slower bat speed of a has-been.

As luck would have it, Waddell's next fastball came in lower than the pitcher wanted. It was down in the strike zone that normally was a good pitcher's pitch, but in this instance it was a clear mistake. Blake still had enough moxie and quickness to recognize the hittable pitch that came in around his knees and right over the plate.

Blake swung mightily and squared up the pitch perfectly on the barrel of the bat. The batting stroke plus the speed of Waddell's pitch gave the ball plenty of energy as it left the sweet spot of his 34-inch, 31-ounce Louisville Slugger stick. Fortunately for the Cubs and the city of Chicago, the batted ball was perfectly placed between outfielders in center and right. The ball scooted through the outfield grass and rolled all the way to the wall before the Cardinals outfielder could catch up to it and relay the ball in to the infield.

It was easily a stand up double for Blake and the tying run in Simons held up at third with nobody out. It was debatable whether third base coach Lenny Paxson should have waved the runner Simons in, but with nobody out, discretion was the better part of valor.

As Blake stood on second base with the composed look of someone that had been there before, the Wrigley faithful were ready to bow in reverence to their hero. It was pandemonium in the stands, but calmness on the bases and in the Cubs dugout, as there was still plenty of work to be done. Once more, Blake thought about replacing himself, this time with a speedier runner, as he possessed the potential game-winning run at second. He may have been composed, but he was still stubborn old Blake who rejected the thought of replacing himself in what could be his last game.

Amidst all the anticipated noise of victory, St. Louis manager Leighton walked to the mound much like one would expect a 75-year-old man to move to discuss strategy. It seemed to take Leighton a minute to walk the 100 feet or so to the mound from his dugout, but perhaps it was by design and not necessity. There were options to think about, but by the time Leighton met Waddell, the crusty old manager had made up his mind what to do next.

They would walk the bases loaded as the next batter's run did not mean a thing and the maneuver would set up a force at any base, especially at home to cut off the tying run. The Cubs were definitely not home free and they knew it. Waddell was a premier strikeout pitcher. A strikeout and a double play grounder and it would all be over, tantalizingly close to victory, but still, oh so far away in the sometimes cruel world of baseball.

The thrill of anticipated victory flowing confidently from the crowd suddenly became much more cautious as second baseman Petey Arroyo struck out on three pitches. Waddell had his mojo back and was confidently controlling the mound again. Blake kicked the infield dirt in disgust at second after the called third strike. He had a pinch-hitter left and he considered using it here, but decided to hold off. He who hesitates is lost, in life, and apparently, in baseball as well.

Due to a double switch earlier in the game, the pitcher's spot that was normally up in the ninth spot of the order was presently occupied by outfielder Larry Hunter. The career-long minor leaguer who so desperately wanted to prove he belonged in the majors was now going to get the ultimate test against one of the best closers in the game, if not the best.

Blake stood several feet off second base in a safe lead and once again considered a pinch-hitter, but resisted. He had only one bullet left in Willie Evans. Blake was very tempted, but he believed in Larry. What could be a more redeeming spot to be in than this? The moment seemed to be made for Hunter so Blake went with his gut instinct, even if it was a bit emotional and not based on reason.

The tension was building to an expected climax here shortly, one way or another. Some fans were standing and some were sitting in their seats with hands over eyes in fear of what might happen. Some were like Kim, nervously biting their nails and on the edge of their seats in anticipation.

Hunter seemed confident in the batter's box, but the confidence drained from his face as he took two called strikes on the first two pitches. Somehow, he held up on the next three pitches that were borderline strikes. Waddell was extremely frustrated at not getting the strikeout call from the home plate umpire and he glared at the ump for several seconds after the last non-strikeout call.

Now every fan in attendance rose to rile up Waddell even more. The next pitch would spell out the season. Waddell peered in for the sign, came to the stretch position, hesitated for a second or two and then delivered the nastiest pitch Blake had ever seen. The pitch came in knee high at nearly 100 mph on the ballpark's radar gun and suddenly dove out and away from the left-handed swinging Hunter, who unsuccessfully flailed away at the unhittable pitch, striking out and silencing the crowd.

Blake had the best seat in the house and he was convinced the minute he saw the pitch dive that Waddell had indeed scuffed the ball in that slight hesitation before he delivered the filthy pitch.

"Time! Time out!" he yelled immediately and time was indeed granted by the second base umpire.

Blake walked straight to the home plate umpire and requested that the crew chief inspect that ball. The St. Louis catcher Paul Evans immediately dropped the ball in the dirt, a giveaway if there ever was one. He tried to smear the ball in the dirt, but the umpire bent over quickly and examined the ball. There was indeed a clear scuff in the cover of the baseball that had actually slightly frayed the skin.

Blake could see the umpire closely examining the ball in question and he yelled out for Waddell to hear.

"Check the pitcher. I think he's got something in that glove of his. I saw him from my vantage point at second. He clearly made a motion that looked to me like it was to deface the baseball. Check him out! You've got to keep the integrity of this game intact. There's too much at stake Billy."

Blake was pleading with home plate umpire and crew chief Billy Thompson, a big burly man with a professional reputation for no-nonsense and strict interpretation of baseball rules.

It appeared as if Thompson noticed something strange on the baseball and he slowly walked toward Waddell in an apparent confrontational mode. St. Louis manager Leighton suddenly found youth in his old legs and sprinted to put himself directly between his pitcher and the crew chief. If Waddell was guilty, his manager wanted to give him a bit of time to dispose of any incriminating evidence before Thompson took the pitcher's glove to examine.

Fortunately for the Cubs and Blake, one eagle-eyed spy in John Bartlett knew better than to take his eyes off of Waddell for any reason whatsoever. Bartlett stood on the top step of the Cubs dugout and watched the pitcher intently, like a Chicago police detective waiting for incriminating evidence to appear.

While many in attendance and those directly involved in the action were focusing on the confrontation between the Cardinals manager and the home plate umpire, Bartlett keenly observed Waddell shaking his glove down around the pitcher's left hip even while Waddell himself was screaming at the umpire.

There it was, Bartlett observed. He could see a couple of pieces of something fall harmlessly to the ground. Waddell had colored the sandpaper to look the exact same shade as the infield and mound dirt in a further attempt to hide any incriminating evidence, but there was no way Bartlett was going to take his eye off that spot. He was riveted on the evidence gathering, and knew exactly where the foreign object was. He was not going to be distracted by anything else.

Bartlett hollered out to Blake in an excited squeal. "I got him Blake, I got him. Look down at the dirt on the first base side of the mound. It's there. I saw it drop."

Now the whole bench was picking up on the impending investigation. Everyone was motioning and hollering for Blake and the home plate ump to check the incriminating spot while Waddell was cleverly rubbing his spikes over the evidence in an attempt to hide or shred the evidence.

The other umpires heard the clamoring and walked over to the area in question. They looked like a group of men sifting through the dirt for a lost contact lens and not some material that could be used to deface a baseball and give the pitcher a distinct edge.

The crowd was hollering and booing even though many, if not most of them, did not know exactly why they were booing the scene unfolding in front of their eyes.

Home plate umpire Thompson finally made his way to Waddell and motioned for him to hand over his pitching glove. The Cardinals pitcher just smiled and put out his hands in an exculpatory motion that indicated his innocence after handing over the glove. Thompson first looked over Waddell's fingers and hands and apparently did not find a thing. The other umpires were scrounging through the dirt, but could not be sure what they saw on the ground was a substance or foreign object. Waddell had a smug look on his mug until Thompson pulled out a small square of sandpaper that apparently stayed stuck in the pitcher's glove even after he tried to shake it all loose. Waddell could not look at the ground while he was trying to get rid of the evidence for fear of incriminating himself, but he thought he felt the two small squares of sandpaper that he had in the fingers of his glove fall harmlessly to the ground. Obviously he was mistaken; the evidence was clear and convincing and Thompson gave the demonstrative heave-ho motion indicating Waddell had been kicked out of the game.

Even though the Cubs were now down to their last out with the season hanging in the balance, the Wrigley crowd howled in approval as the bombastic Waddell had gotten his comeuppance. There was not much Waddell could do except walk off the field as he was caught red-handed. This time, the reliever never made eye contact with the fans as he sauntered into the dugout and disappeared from view.

The St. Louis manager Leighton was a completely different story. He was old school and stuck to timeworn customs and baseball's unwritten rules. He was livid at Blake for pulling out this desperation move at such an important moment.

Blake just sheepishly looked the other way, displaying a revealing smirk that undoubtedly pissed off Leighton even more. The crowd loved the fiery response from the Cardinals manager and egged him on with continued chants.

The Cardinals manager could not even get tossed from the game, as he had no beef with the umpires, just the opposing manager. He finally huffed his way back to his dugout, but not before signaling for Waddell's replacement from the pen. The riled up Skipper was so peeved that he did not take a strategic pause to consider his next pitching move. He immediately signaled for his lefty Jose Paulina, as the hard-throwing southpaw was undoubtedly his best available pitcher.

However, just as Paulina was taking the mound, Leighton finally recalled that the Cubs' top pinch-hitter, Willie Evans, who was still available on the bench, had absolutely owned Paulina over his lifetime with an unbelievable .620 career batting average. Leighton stomped out to the home plate umpire in a desperation attempt to change his mind about the pitching change. There was nothing the umpires could do however, as Paulina had already been announced as the replacement for Waddell and he was required by rule to pitch to at least one batter.

Blake just laughed at the boneheaded and impulsive maneuver by Leighton. He now had the Cardinals and their manager right where he wanted them. The bases were full and there was nothing the Cards could do except pitch to Evans.

Anything could still happen, as there are no guarantees in baseball. Evans could hit the ball square on the nose and still make an out, but there was something in Blake's mind that felt otherwise as Evans stepped into the batter's box. This wild turn of events seemed to display matters that were out of everyone's hands, as if this was somehow magically predetermined.

The crowd was not aware of the odds in Chicago's favor, but they were keenly aware that an out here would put a crushing end to what, minutes ago, looked like a storybook ending. They were giving it their all too, standing and screaming at the top of their lungs with every pitch.

Paulina was obviously aware of his unsuccessful past against Evans as he came nowhere near the strike zone with his first two pitches. Evans waited patiently in the box in the catbird's seat, as there was nothing worse from a pitcher's standpoint than to walk in the tying run in such a critical situation. Willie knew a fastball was coming and he was determined to make this one pitch the crushing blow to St. Louis.

The fastball came in just a bit off the middle of the plate, tailing right into Willie's sweet stroke. The decisive moment was here and the ball was lined into left field for a solid single. With two outs on the board the runners could take off with the sound of the bat. The tying run was a given, but would Blake have enough speed to outrun the throw in from left?

Blake's baseball instincts took over and he correctly rounded third base in proper form to limit the amount of real estate he would have to cover scampering home. Third base coach Paxson was wheeling Blake on home, but it did not matter, as Blake had already made up his mind that he was going to try and end it here.

Left-fielder Sanderson gloved the solidly struck ball on one hop and with perfect form as his momentum carried him right toward the plate to give his throw the maximum force available from his body. Generally, left fielders have the weakest arm in the outfield, and this was no exception. Sanderson's throw was on line, but the speed stalled out like a sputtering car.

Blake did not have much speed himself at this point in his career, but he had just enough to beat the throw home by a split second as the throw took two bounces to reach the Cardinals catcher Paul Evans. There was an attempt by the St. Louis catcher to block the plate with his shin guard and spikes between Blake and home, but the force of Blake's slide pushed the obstacles out of his way. His left foot grazed across the plate as the crowd went into a delirious state of happiness at the dramatic win.

Blake lifted his arms in glee as he slid across home plate and the umpire immediately signaled safe, setting off a dramatic celebration with Blake's team-mates piling on top of the weary baserunner. The whole team jumped on the pile, each player following the other like trained pets following the lead.

Somewhere beneath the massive pile, Blake had nothing but a sweet smile on his face despite barely being able to breathe. Recognizing they might be in-flicting harm on their manager after the spontaneous celebration clouded their judgment, the players frantically began pulling one another off their hero.

The last player was lifted off their leader and Blake just lay there motionless, but with a huge grin beaming from ear to ear. A couple of teammates lifted Blake up and asked him if he was okay. He nodded his head and the players took that as a sign they could pick him up and put him on their shoulders. They paraded around Wrigley with Blake on their shoulders as the manager waved to the deliri-ous crowd, and the posse made a complete pass around the ballpark.

The unbelievable come-from-behind 2-1 victory culminated the regular sea-son in fanatic fashion. After 162 games, two completely separate squads, and too numerous to count travails and tribulations from their lone troubled player remaining from the start of the season, the two combatants were tied in the standings. A one-game playoff would be necessary to decide the divisional championship. As luck would have it, due to a previously flipped coin the Cubs would host the deciding contest.

Blake had nothing left physically or emotionally as he sat in his office chair, devoid of any kind of feeling except redemption. Karma was indeed a bitch. It had bitten St. Louis manager Leighton in the ass. His glaring mistake came back to haunt him and the faux pas made up for Blake's earlier similar managerial miscalculation when he was goaded into a catcher-less situation weeks ago by Leighton.

What better way could there be for Blake and his boys to claim honor for the deceased Chicago players? A one-game battle to prove that they belonged here, that they belonged to baseball history. Tomorrow could not come soon enough as Blake did nothing but blankly stare at the team photo taken during spring training this past March hanging from his office wall. This would be for them. God bless 'em!

68 — Teardrops From Heaven

The clubhouse scene was surreal, with players hugging each other like long-lost friends, a far cry from the reality of only two months together as a hastily assembled roster. These teammates had little in common back then other than shared membership in an elite fraternal group known as major league baseball players and their own players' union.

The thrill of victory was short-lived this time. Blake was very cognizant of his most recent managerial failure, the excessive celebration of one win, no matter how exciting or critical it was, in a lengthy 162-game season that would now be stretched to 163 with the one-game playoff.

After a few minutes of self-reflection in his own managerial enclave, his private office, Blake interrupted the celebratory scene to ensure that his team would now begin to focus on the immediacy of the one-game playoff. He had to convince his boys that the next game would be the prize, and that the just completed dramatic win was simply an appetizer to be digested appropriately before the main entrée was served up tomorrow.

"I hate to be the one to spoil all this fun, but I screwed up last time we went through a raucous victory dance like this only to be followed with a horrible performance. My main man Bartlett was right, we enjoy the moment, but we have to move on quickly. We'll have plenty of time to gloat about this win when it's all said and done. The playoff tomorrow is the prize to shoot for now, not to mention that gaudy winner's share that we've been promised when we prevail."

Bartlett moved closer to his manager and asked to be heard. Blake was more than delighted to give the floor to Bartlett in this leadership moment.

"I know you guys think I'm a hard-ass that can't be happy about anything," shouted the Rat, who was quickly interrupted by Miguel Guillen.

"Nah, we don't think that amigo," said Miguel in a sarcastic tone of voice while laughing and shaking his head. The whole clubhouse erupted in laughter at Miguel's clever retort. Guillen's sly response was undoubtedly shared by most, if not all of his teammates.

"I suppose you might be right fat man, but the point is, championships are all that matters. It's only a start, but a win tomorrow would at least give us a division championship. I'll be the first one to uncork a bottle of bubbly tomorrow when we win, but not a moment beforehand. And I know who's going to be sprayed first amigo. I might as well shoot for the biggest target to practice up for the rest of the guys Miggy."

The laughter was widespread and effusive once more before Blake again put a damper on the delight, bringing his boys back to reality.

"Well, it looks like rain tomorrow and I mean lots of it. Don't go celebrating tonight like school kids expecting a snow day. We won't know for a bit, but the rain, wind and cold looks imminent. For now, just go about your normal routine expecting a game tomorrow. You'll be the first to know if our game is postponed. Oh, and one more thing. That was one hell of a game today and you guys made it happen. Let's visualize success for our playoff and make it happen once more. Cheers to Willie on the clutch hit. That one will go down in history big fella. We'll see you all tomorrow unless Mother Nature wants to keep the baseball world in suspense one more day."

The proud manager waited in his office until all the players and coaches had left the building before heading home himself. He just wanted some isolation to process the day's events. The thoughts of pregame excitement, the near-defeat that gave him just an inkling of what his emotions might be like when it was all over, and the indescribable sheer sense of satisfaction as he slid across home plate with the winning run.

He could only imagine what the feelings might be like tomorrow or whenever the playoff game was played. It all seemed so overwhelming at times, but the ultimate goal of a World Series berth, unlikely as that appeared, would entail so many more emotional days like the past two. The nagging inner self-doubts just would never cease, as Blake could not simply enjoy the moment himself. He long ago realized that much of his anxiety was self-imposed, but he was still deeply concerned about being able to fulfill all of his responsibilities to his team, the organization, and even to himself.

The reflection of the past two months provided him with plenty of examples where he had held strong. He decided he would look backward for confidence in the upcoming weeks and not speculate on what might be. He had handled all of life's sober struggles to date, even though there were moments of doubt and hesitation. He had followed through on his goals and objectives so far and there did not seem to be any reason or circumstance on the horizon that could derail a determined Blake. A more confident man now left the office to begin his drive home in spite of a history that showed he seldom stayed that self-confident for long.

The drive continued his reflective state of mind. He could not get baseball out of his head. He tried to listen to his favorite radio station for music, but all it seemed to do was momentarily distract him from his compulsive inner thoughts. He was searching for resolution deep in his soul. Blake had to go through this process almost daily to keep in emotional balance. It was if he needed constant reaffirmation from his own soul to feel confident and strong in his sobriety. When he felt confident in his destiny, he was able to project and expand that confidence to his teammates. Without it, he was a liability and not an asset to his Cubs team.

Blake would seek reassurance from his wife. He pulled into the driveway anxious to hear her thoughts about the dramatic game. He had spoken briefly to her on the phone, but as was her norm, she preferred to leave her husband alone with his players after a game and let Blake unwind in his own thoughts for a few hours before he arrived home.

As his night with Kim wore on, a different form of anxiety replaced the nervous energy that was eating at Blake regarding the playoff game. Major League Baseball and the Cubs had already postponed the deciding game until Saturday because of the near certainty of impending bad weather. The evening took on an unsettling tone with the postponement of the important one-game playoff with the Cardinals until the day after tomorrow. The prevailing excitement and uncertainty dominated every aspect of Blake and Kim's life; the dual role of player-manager doubled the risk and reward for the married couple.

It was not only Blake that felt a sense of responsibility for the team and the city's shared emotional interest in the outcome, Kim knew that anything her husband did reflected on her as well, a point the alcohol-absorbed Blake of recent past could never fully grasp.

The dinner was enjoyable and the conversation on the day's events was filled with fond recollections. There was even some good-natured ribbing from Kim about Blake's lack of speed on the base path as he trudged home with the winning run. Blake played along by claiming he already was out of breath before his teammates piled on him at home plate and could barely breathe, which was partially true.

However, as soon as word was passed along that tomorrow would be an unscheduled off-day before such a climactic game, there seemed to be a huge void in the conversation. It was now small talk at its finest. The bad weather, and what to do with all the extra time, suddenly became the topics, but lacked the intensity of championship baseball. It was if the anxiety of the upcoming deciding game had formed a bond between husband and wife. There was an emotional letdown in losing that sense of immediacy. Without any agreement on a possible plan, they reluctantly decided they would both do their own thing tomorrow and go their separate ways to fill out the "dead" time between now and Saturday.

The night was uneventful despite the sheer joy that both of them had experienced firsthand today. That feeling had come and gone with the postponement. Baseball had to be put on the back shelf for the time being or both would go crazy obsessing about the eventual outcome of a game nearly 48 hours away.

Friday morning began for Blake with the pattering of raindrops on the bedroom windows. He could hear the whipping wind, which was no surprise, but the reality of the weather elements put even more of a damper on his yet unfilled day.

Blake was extremely fidgety at breakfast, and the two of them discussed what they were likely to do today to occupy their time. Blake knew he would be bombarded with media requests and he would relinquish some of his free time to do several interviews for local media connections, but he had to put his foot down somewhere to protect his sanity.

Kim mentioned chores she could do to stay somewhat productive and perhaps a trip to the grocery store before they reconnected back home for dinner. Blake pondered heading in to Wrigley and team headquarters, but he decided against such a routine move, instead determining that quiet time at home would not be so bad after all. It might be a nice change of pace from the hectic schedule of a player-manager in a pennant race.

The two of them went their separate ways. Blake cozied up to a new book he had lukewarm interest in reading. He went into oblivion mode in his own den, a blanket draped over his near horizontal body. He fluffed up his pillow and placed his chilled feet into his own Chicago Cubs slippers while the fireplace crackled with fresh wood nearby.

It seemed like a perfect way to calm his nerves, but the questions that continued to plague his weary brain put up stiff resistance to the desire for inner peace at this moment and eventually wore down the wish to relax. He was back to daydreaming about Sandy and his former teammates, still trying, to this day, to understand why he was spared death and not his fellow players. It still made no sense, especially since it started out like such a dream season with a World Series win a distinct possibility.

He just could not get the answers anywhere no matter how hard he tried. Yes, he had stayed sober to this point and his new teammates had accomplished far more than any reasonable baseball analyst could have ever expected. Yes, he had been their leader and deserved some respect for their collective results so far, but that simply did not seem like enough.

The city of Chicago had been drawn together by the tragedy, but he knew that would be fleeting. What was this all about? Perhaps he would never know the answer, he thought to himself, as he tossed down the barely read book and walked upstairs to get ready for his baseball interviews. At least they would be conducted in the comforts of home over his cell phone.

These were accomplished with ease; Blake meant no disrespect as he trotted out cliché after cliché during the interviews. It was a necessary evil and served a purpose for the media. Some fans would be thrilled to hear their player-manager spew out such drivel and it was part of the job as a manager. Blake was relieved that they were done for the day, but now he just had too much time on his hands and too much going on inside of his head. He simply had to do something else, but he was still at a loss for his next step. Blake grabbed the keys to his Range Rover and walked out in the rain with a Titleist golf cap and a black Under Armour hoodie for protection from wetness. He sat in his vehicle and stared blankly out the windshield at the raindrops splashing in the numerous puddles of his driveway before turning the key in the car's ignition and began driving to nowhere in particular. He was searching for inspiration in some sign on the road or from recollection in his brain as he drove about aimlessly around the Chicago area.

A stop along a local lake where Blake once again stared out the window searching for anything that might lead him to a further understanding of his dilemma provided useless. He decided on a quick lunch at a fast food stop, drove incognito through the drive-through with his hoodie pulled over his head as discreetly possible, and munched away at his cheeseburger and fries as he continued his drive to nowhere.

A sign along the road he was navigating finally gave him some inspiration on this dark, gloomy, and wet afternoon. It came from an unlikely source, a sign indicating the cemetery ahead where his best friend ever, Sandy, was buried. Several teammates' remains were buried at this cemetery, but it was Sandy's final earthly resting spot that was going to be the focal point for some deep internal thoughts, perhaps fitting on a gloomy day.

Sandy had become Mr. Chicago during his time in the Windy City and it was not any real surprise that his family chose Chicago for his burial site, where whatever remains could be found and identified from such a horrific accident would be entombed in eternity.

It was a macabre site indeed, but Blake had remembered how therapeutic it was to visit his parents' place of burial. The physical proximity to human remains of loved ones seemed to open up the soul to old and new thoughts that proved insightful when other places near and dear to the heart had failed.

Winding through the muddied dirt road past countless headstones that proudly displayed family surnames quickly provided instantaneous thoughts from recognizable names. Blake struggled a bit to recall where Sandy's site was before remembering the solemn ceremony that laid his final remains to rest. The sad recollection refreshed his memory and he made a sharp right turn following the path the hearse took that dreadful day.

As one might expect on such a miserable day, there were very few people around. Blake could barely make out a figure in the distance that appeared to be near Sandy's burial place and he could see a lone worker about 50 yards in front of him that seemed to be occupied doing nothing but getting drenched by the rain.

As he drove closer he was shocked to recognize the figure in the distance by the color and style of the raincoat. Further convincing Blake that he knew who was standing there was an accompanying open umbrella in full shielding form that he had indeed purchased for his wife. It was Kim for sure, but Blake was unsure of what to do next until he caught the attention of the cemetery caretaker soaking in the rain.

Blake drove up closer to the worker and opened his driver's side window with the flick of his finger. He apologized to the caretaker for disturbing him, but he wanted to ask the man a question.

"Excuse me, can I ask you a question? Say, do you want to sit in here for a minute to get out of the rain. I'll even turn on the heated seat for ya. Just a quick question, please."

The caretaker nodded his head up and down and walked over to the passenger side of Blake's vehicle.

"Thanks man, it's brutal out there today. What can I do for you? Do you need information on the sites? That I can't do or I could get fired."

"No, that's okay. I just want to ask you about that person up there by that grave. Do you see her around here very often?"

"Well, I suppose I can answer that as long as you've been kind enough to let me in out of the rain. That lady has been coming here every Friday at about this time for I guess, about two months now. Seems kind of strange, but we learn quick around here not to question people's grieving. We just leave 'em alone."

Blake was stunned by the revelation and simply stared at the middle-aged man with several days of growth in his beard, beaded up glasses from the rain, and what Blake thought was snot dripping from his nose.

The caretaker became a bit concerned at Blake's demeanor and questioned him.

"Are you okay man? I take it that you know that woman."

Blake did not answer the question and simply motioned for the man to leave now with a hand gesture.

"Thank you," was all Blake could answer and the caretaker simply opened up the door getting ready to leave before he paused slightly. He looked back at Blake and asked him a personal question this time.

"Say, are you that ballplayer from the Cubs? I think I recognize you, and of course, we all know that the grave over there is one of the ballplayers that died in that crash. You're Blake Benson, aren't you?"

Blake was clearly agitated and motioned for the caretaker to leave again, but not before he reached in his wallet and gave the man a fifty-dollar bill.

"Nah, I get that all the time. Must be a look-alike or something like that. Here's a little something for your help. Please leave now."

The man was a bit agitated himself, now he knew that was Blake.

"Whatever man. Thanks for the cash."

The caretaker just walked away and returned to his job of standing in the rain, shaking his head as he stuffed the fifty-dollar bill in his front left pocket to keep it dry.

Blake was dreading his next move, but he knew he had to go find out just what in the hell was going on here. He drover closer to Sandy's site before the woman in question turned around and immediately recognized the familiar vehicle. Kim immediately walked toward Blake and the Range Rover before her husband jumped out of the car abruptly.

"Just what in the hell are you doing here Kim? And in this god-awful weather too."

"Me? What about you Blake? Why are you here?"

"Just forget about me. Sandy was my teammate, not yours. He was my best friend, not yours."

"What? Can't I visit the grave of a friend once in a while too? I was visiting my aunt's grave and I just stopped by here."

"Stop the bullshit Kim. I know you've been coming here every Friday for two months now, which is as long as he's been buried."

Blake was inundated with moisture by now. His sweatshirt was soaked through and his cap was dripping from its brim, but he was oblivious and his anger was building.

Kim was speechless and she just stared at Blake not knowing what or how to say what was coming next. It was difficult to figure out if she was crying or if the rain was just piling up on her too, as she just did not seem to care if the rain pelted her now. The umbrella was held at her side instead of as a shield over her head. She began to scream at her husband now as if her soul was going to open up just like the skies had done with the soaking rain.

"Yes, I've been coming here every Friday. You're either at Wrigley or out of town at this time. Today was different and I guess I just forgot or didn't imagine you'd be out here too. Sandy was more than just a friend to me. We were lovers and I miss him so much. I can't hold this in any longer Blake. I'm so sorry. I never wanted you to find out. I didn't want to hurt you. I knew how much you admired him. I didn't want to hurt you Blake. I'm sorry."

Blake's initial reaction was denial.

"There's no way Sandy would've ever done this to me. No way. He was my best friend."

"Blake, you have no idea how this ate him up too. He was your best friend, but he couldn't stand how you mistreated me all those years. It bothered him so much more than he let on that you would constantly cheat on me as if I didn't matter to you one bit. He consoled me often before we both finally couldn't resist our desire for each other."

Blake still could not believe what he was hearing. His disbelief was carried even further by Sandy's obvious love for his own wife and family.

"But what about Lisa? And the kids? He could never do that to them. He would've told me something was wrong in his marriage. He told me everything."

"Obviously he didn't, Blake. He was too afraid you'd find out about us. We didn't want to hurt you. You were in such dire straits already. He was afraid you'd do something even more drastic. Hell, I was afraid too. He loved his wife, but he found out she was unfaithful to him and it killed him. It doesn't matter now Blake. He's dead and we stopped it all two years ago. I should say your fucking GM Marty stopped it. He threatened to ship Sandy out of town in a trade if he didn't stop our brief affair right then and there."

Blake became even more distressed at the inclusion of Marty in this mess. His whole world was turning upside down. How could he handle another disturbing revelation?

"You mean Marty knew about this all along? Fuck, who didn't know? Jesus Christ, you made me look so much like a fool Kim. And Marty? That sonofabitch. He's supposed to be my friend as well as my boss. At least that's what he's been bullshitting me with lately. Everything feels like a lie right now. I gotta get away Kim. I can't believe this. I just can't fucking believe this."

Blake turned around and walked away with his head down, the sorrow in his movements obvious as he slowly made his way to the vehicle despite the drenching rain. Kim thought about chasing him down, but she knew Blake was gone, in spirit and in flesh. It would not do any good to try and stop him now. He was going to mourn in solitude as he always did. Nothing would ever change that.

Blake sped away in a fit of rage that suddenly overtook the sorrow he was experiencing seconds before. Mud and debris were sprayed from the back of his vehicle as he left the troubled scene as quickly as possible without any idea of where he was going. He just had to get away from it all.

His mind was racing along with his Range Rover as he left the cemetery road and entered the highway. A police squad car observed off in the distance redirected Blake's thoughts to a somewhat calmer pace, and he immediately slowed down and started to think a bit more clearly.

Blake was in full-fledged anger mode as he drove away from Chicago toward any place that would possess more isolation than the city allowed. He pounded his fists repeatedly on his steering wheel, bringing up his best friend's name one minute, followed by his wife's name the next, before finally including Marty in his anger taken out on the closest available inanimate object.

The betrayal stung like no other feeling he had ever experienced in his lifetime. The hurt he felt at the moment was decidedly clouding his judgment. He still was very aware of his managerial and player responsibilities, but tomorrow seemed so far away at the moment. He knew he would have to get his thoughts and feelings together by then, but for now he just had to deal with the hurt and pain that could overwhelm anybody, especially a man still recovering from alcohol addiction.

If Blake's subconscious was waiting for an excuse that could push him back toward booze, it was developing now front and center. Who could blame him for needing artificial comfort to deal with this crushing blow?

Alcohol was biding its time, patiently waiting for just the right moment to push Blake over the edge. The urge to drink was never too far from Blake's presence; it hung over him like a dark cloud. The perfect storm would be needed to stir up just the right ingredients for a cloudburst of temptation.

It just so happened that all the stars were aligned. Anger, hurt, betrayal, time, opportunity, and a liquor store in clear view equaled the perfect storm.

Blake was driving along and dealing unsuccessfully with a ton of hurt when he spotted the sign that always caught his attention. The neon lights of a liquor store flashed before him and Blake reacted impulsively, making a quick turn into the parking lot.

He was well aware of the impending decision and its consequences, but he rationalized them away with an often-used excuse. He would just have a few to calm down and get his wits back before he would have to return to either home or Wrigley. Nobody would ever know about this little slipup and he could easily get himself back in shape in time for the big game tomorrow.

Fortunately Blake always carried large amounts of cash. His ordinary apparel and the hoodie covering most of his facial features worked in his favor to purchase a bottle of whiskey on the sly. He walked inside casually and without any sign of distress, picked up his favorite brand of whiskey, Jack Daniels. The clerk rang up the transaction and handed the time bomb to just another rainy Friday afternoon customer.

With his prized possession in tow he opened the back of his black Range Rover and neatly set the bottle in a secure place. Driving along, Blake looked for an out-of-the-way motel to gather himself and his thoughts with some artificial assistance. He now could recall that out of control feeling that often badgered his brain before he would start drinking once more. He knew he was playing with fire here, but he was just getting a wee bit of kindling to commence a singular flame, although deep down he recognized the despair of denial.

It did not take more than 15 minutes of driving to find a bland motel to hide out for the evening. He filled out the registration card with a fake name before the desk clerk asked for identification. Blake calmly resisted, explaining he was trying to find some solitude from an angry wife, while at the same time waving a fifty-dollar bill in his hands as an obvious bribe. The cash was gladly taken with a wink and a nod by the graying 50-something man who certainly looked like he could use a bit of extra ka-ching in his pocket.

The beleaguered Blake grabbed his brown bag and walked briskly into the hallways of the motel, looking for an ice machine before finding his room nestled in the corner of the first floor of the two-story building. He opened the door and was immediately overwhelmed with the stale air of a seldom-used room. It did not matter much to an obviously distracted man simply interested in closed doors, a bottle of whiskey, and a container full of ice. After venturing out in the hallway once more to gather ice in his bucket, Blake returned to his temporary home where he had all three items of necessity.

The door was closed and bolted shut. Blake set the bottle on the bed, grabbed a cheap plastic cup, ripped off the protective covering and filled the cup with ice. He fluffed two pillows behind his head, lay back on the bed, kicked off his shoes and contemplated his next moves. The first decision would be the one that would set all other future actions in motion, in one direction or the other. The ultimate choice was to drink or not drink. Everything would flow from this critical choice in the next few minutes. Blake could feel the tension in his gut, as even he did not know which way he would turn next.

The consequences were mighty, but the temptation was profound, as if coming from a force so powerful that even reason stood no chance against its weight. Blake sat up and looked straight ahead in the mirror directly across from him on the wall and he recoiled in recognition of a man he had rightly abandoned two months earlier. The moment came and went with a flash of remembrance that stopped Blake right in his tracks. That pitiful face was not the one Blake wanted others to remember him by. There was a different Blake that he wanted to leave as a legacy, the real Blake that had existed in his youth under the guidance of proud parents. The Blake that was decent to the core and a good man to all others. This Blake had resurfaced just in time to thwart the temptation of self-destruction, but this Blake still was dealing with a world of hurt.

Now he had to reconcile his newly exposed emotions. He was not out of the woods yet, even though he had chosen the right path of continued sobriety. It was time for some real deep reflection. At least he still had the benefit of time to work through his deepest wounds so far. The scars would always linger, but Blake's soul would have to heal and heal quickly in order to reassume his managerial duties in less than 24 hours.

69 — Self-Reconciliation

The sting of betrayal from the two people closest to Blake's heart, Kim and Sandy, was still too fresh for forgiveness, but the time lapse between that hurtful moment of truth and the solitude of his motel room had sharpened his own inner focus. Blake had calmed down some as he stretched out on his lumpy bed, stared at the water stained ceiling above him, and began to survey his flawed lifestyle of recent years.

The irony of it all was beginning to settle in, and the guilt-ridden Blake wondered if karma was leaving its payback to him for all the misdeeds of his past. He was consumed by betrayal until he realized Kim was doing exactly what Blake had done all those years on the road. He was puzzled by his own failure to recognize the obvious hurt he must have left for Kim to deal with through his many marital indiscretions. How could he be so callous to disregard the pain and suffering he had inflicted on her for all those years? Did it really take similar circumstances dumped on him before he could understand and relate to the emotional turmoil his previous actions had caused?

The answers were becoming clearer to Blake even if his own pain was numb to this inner discovery. He distinctly felt he was in no position to judge or criticize anyone, much less loved ones that he had damaged so much without a concern beyond a perfunctory apology that always lacked sincerity.

His admiration for Sandy never stopped Blake from repeated lies to his best friend. There were countless empty promises to Sandy that had already passed the point of believability even well before the final hours spent together at the airport that fateful morning when Blake went back on his word to Sandy for the last time. In retrospect, with clear and sober mind, Blake could now understand his best friend's anger and resentment toward him. Sandy did not have any justification for infidelity, but perhaps there was justification for any lack of remorse for his actions when Blake was disrespecting Kim on an almost daily basis.

Blake's male pride was deflated by Kim's confession, while his dignity was damaged by ignorance of the situation when others like Marty knew about his wife's affair. His anger toward Marty was defused by the realization that his boss had kept quiet all those years when he obviously was cognizant of Blake's continuing alcohol-fed affairs of his own. Still, it hurt him that the husband seemed to be the last of the inner circle to know about Kim and Sandy's brief affair.

As Blake continued to sprawl out on his motel room bed, staring up at the ceiling as if the answers would come from above, he was at least thankful for one thing at the moment. His sober mind allowed him to think with clarity, pushing emotional overrule to the back edge of his immediate concerns.

The upcoming game began to dominate his thinking, but he still was too troubled to return home to Kim. Blake knew she would be very worried about his state of mind so he sent her a text message explaining he was okay, but he just could not deal with being in the same house with her tonight. He had to work through some things first. Blake emphasized there was no need to worry about him not being in any condition to manage tomorrow. He pleaded for her to keep everything under wraps for now and he would hopefully see her at the game tomorrow.

A brief response from Kim expressed concern for Blake's health, but she understood the hurt he felt at the moment and was in agreement on him not coming home tonight.

However, Kim just could not be sure and she felt an obligation to let general manager Marty Anderson know that there could possibly be a troubling situation for tomorrow's all-important game. A quick phone call to Marty put in place a contingency plan that the general manager felt was necessary to employ if matters got out of hand. He was puzzled at the turn of events, but Kim explained what had happened. It was always their biggest fear that Blake would eventually know the truth. The contingency plan called for third base coach Lenny Paxson to assume managerial responsibilities if Blake had any kind of setback. Paxson agreed to keep this agreement secret between Marty and himself, and the general manager immediately called Lenny to inform him he would be in charge until further notice. Paxson was told not to infer anything from this action, as nobody could be sure of Blake's condition, only that there was some concern that had to be addressed with this touchy executive directive.

While Blake contemplated the decisions of tomorrow's game from the confines of his temporary home, he was unaware of Marty's action that stripped him of those managerial maneuvers. Out of concern for Blake's fragile state of mind, Marty had not even attempted a phone call to Blake, as he did not want to tip off his tentative decision at this point. Marty also knew from previous personal experience that if Blake was using alcohol he could not trust the words coming out of his mouth anyway. Marty felt it was best to wait it out and see if Blake showed up tomorrow, when he could personally analyze his condition firsthand.

Once again, Blake would be out of the informational loop and he would undoubtedly be angry when he found out, but the ramifications of a Blake slip-up could not be ignored at this critical point. The unaware player-manager had temporarily been reduced to player-only status, but his brain was operating as if he was still in charge while he contemplated game-day strategies from his bed.

Blake felt as if his overall condition was coming around. He had gone through the process of self-reconciliation and became very aware of his own detrimental contributions to the disturbing revelation of earlier today. His best friend Sandy had not deserted him even though he had every right to, based on Blake's numerous lies. His loving wife had not abandoned her husband despite his extremely cruel and insensitive behaviors. They'd stuck with him, loved him, and repeatedly tried, mostly in vain, to change his wicked ways. The same was true with Marty. Blake would never have had the chance to be in this position today if it was not for his general manager's belief in him.

It all seemed to be resolving itself, as Blake felt more confident in his resiliency to the nearly devastating revelation. Once again Blake had responded to the emotional challenge, or so he thought, as he was devising a plan of action for tomorrow.

He placed an order for a pizza to be delivered to his room, quickly devoured a few slices and turned in for the night. He flipped the switch to turn off the room's lights as if to just put this troubled day behind him with a flick of his finger. The day and the game ahead would be one of the biggest of his life. He now felt ready for it as he looked at the still unopened bottle of whiskey several feet away. There was no temptation now and he stared at the bottle as if he was standing over a defeated foe, demonstrating his power over the conquest. He had prevailed under the toughest of circumstances, at least for this day. Tomorrow, as always, would provide plenty of challenges, but he felt a sense of self-empowerment at the victorious moment of another sober bedtime, and gave himself a figurative pat on the back.

70 — Dousing the Doubts

If Blake expected to walk into Wrigley as if nothing happened, he was going to be in for a rude awakening. There were security guards on the lookout for Blake at every entrance. It may have seemed like overkill, but Marty and the rest of the higher-ups were concerned that a drunken, angry Blake might cause a bit of embarrassment for the team and for the manager. The situation seemed to call for extra precautions just to be on the safe side. Security was simply to escort Blake up to Marty's office and insist the general manager had to see him in person ASAP. Only if he vehemently resisted would any type of force be allowed. Fortunately, there would be very few people at the ballpark that early.

The player-manager had an eerie feeling as he drove to the ballpark. It was as if it was almost too quiet these last 24 hours. His antennae were up as he pulled into his reserved parking spot. He had known just how close he had come to a relapse and he sensed that others were probably aware of that, as he neared his normal entrance on this bright sunny morning.

His intuition was about to be proven accurate as he immediately noticed the difference at the entrance. The security guards stood out like a sore thumb. Blake hesitantly walked toward them before the biggest guard, all 6-foot-6, 300 hundred pounds of chiseled stone, motioned to him.

"I'm sorry sir. We've got to take you to Mr. Anderson right away. He's instructed us to take you to him immediately upon arrival."

Blake knew right away that word had gotten out. Kim most likely, but it did not matter much now who informed Marty, only that he would have to plead his case once more, just like at the beginning. He was fairly certain Marty would believe him if he gave him his word. An upheaval like this on the day of the biggest game could scramble the whole team. Blake just figured a man as intelligent as his boss would only take drastic action if he had no other alternative. He was too smart of a baseball man not to realize that Blake's removal from the team would likely doom today's chances at baseball immortality. This was too big to fail from an internal decision.

"Makes sense to me guys. There's no problem on this end. It's probably a sensitive personnel situation that Marty wants me to discreetly take care of."

As they walked briskly to the front office, Blake in the middle surrounded by a handful of large men as if protecting a president, the soon-to-be-confronted manager knew he was about to get an earful from his boss, but he did not want to let on to the guards.

"Either that, or he's about to fire me. What's your guess? Maybe he doesn't realize that we're in the playoffs when we win today? You guys have any strategy for me? Now's your chance to be a big hero today if you make the right call."

Blake was full of nervous energy, playing along only to distract from what was his inner fear. He felt so helpless being escorted to the "warden's office" without any hope for a reprieve from the governor.

The largest guard once again took the lead as he spoke softly, but firmly into a microphone that was attached to his body. He notified the general manager's office that Blake was right outside.

A solemn-looking Marty opened his door and thanked the guards before motioning Blake into his office without uttering a word to his manager. The door was quietly shut as if nothing was out of the ordinary despite the very unusual escort.

The mood changed drastically as Marty did not even wait for Blake to sit down before he lashed at his AWOL manager.

"Jesus Blake. Of all the times to go off the deep end, did you really need to sabotage our whole season with a last game bender? The whole city is going crazy over us and you just about put yourself on the front page with your reckless actions. Those damn liquor stores have security cameras. Thank God the liquor store owner kept a lid on it for me. A friend in the media tipped me off or your face would be all over the country by now. What was I ever thinking when I gave you this chance? I should be put in front of a firing squad and be shot for treason, or for stupidity, or whatever!"

Blake sat down before Marty was even finished with his diatribe, sat back in his chair and somehow offered up a smile despite his inner disappointment in his superior. As soon as the general manager finished, Blake pulled himself up to the edge of his seat and fired back.

"Marty, did you ever take a moment to consider I didn't do anything wrong? I'm pretty sure Kim told you what happened, but what if I told you I got really upset, angry, and hurt, but I didn't drink? Goddamn I came close. I even bought a bottle of whiskey as you know, but I promise you I never drank an ounce. I don't have to tell you where I park my ass every night, do I?"

Marty rose out of his black leather chair and stood over Blake like an angry parent looking down at his choice of manager, fighting back words of anger before finally giving in to frustration.

"Blake, you can't shit a shitter. I told you from that first day, right here in this same office and the same chairs, that I had been where you are. I know what you're thinking before you even realize it. I know where we instinctively reach for immediate comfort from pain. Booze becomes the answer before our conscious minds even react to the anguish. I'm not saying I don't believe you Blake. It's the reaction that pisses me off. The first thing you did was run and hide. That has to set off alarm bells in my head. I can't wait for you to come stumbling in to the ballpark. I've set something in motion that I didn't have to do, and it will likely have consequences."

Blake stood up to match Marty's anger toe to toe before firing back.

"But I'm here now and I'm sober. I came in really early to prepare. What could be the problem?"

Now Marty was feeling a bit sheepish about what he was going to say next. He backed off and sat down in his chair, leaned back and paused before filling in Blake on Marty's always present provisionary recourse if there appeared to be a setback for his manager.

"I always had to be prepared for this possible moment Blake. I couldn't logically do otherwise than prepare for the worst, but hope for the best. I have a provisional plan to replace you with Paxson. He didn't want to be in on it, but I forced him. It was only to be utilized if you had a setback. With the stakes at hand I couldn't wait and I felt it was necessary to put this plan in action late last night after nobody knew where you were. I'm sorry Blake. It had to be done."

"Well then take it back again, I'm here now and it'll be chaos if this all gets out. You might as well kiss any hopes of a divisional title goodbye Marty. It's going to take a supreme effort to win today and any distraction would be lethal to our chances. You gotta know that Marty."

"Jesus Blake. You know how hard it is to keep secrets in this city, in this profession. I'm afraid the word is probably already out."

"Well, it sure will be if you wait any longer. Stop it right now. I'll piss in a bottle for you right now. Blood test, whatever, you name it, you got it."

"Blake, you should know me well enough by now that I've already prepared for that possible outcome. I've got medical staff next door just waiting to verify your claim. I'll notify them right now that you'll be in shortly."

"Goddamn, call them right fucking now Marty. There's no doubt I'll pass. I got close enough to sniff it, but I didn't touch it, I swear."

The general manager flipped on the intercom switch and directed his office assistant to prepare immediately for drug and alcohol testing of Blake before Marty had a few more words of wisdom to profess to his protégé, on and off the field.

"Just one minute Blake, before I send you in there and put a tentative stop on the provisional plan pending the final evidence of your claim. This sobriety is a way of life that's much easier if you stop trying to slay the dragon by yourself. I'm disappointed you didn't trust me. You should've called me. Now I know you'd be pissed at me for keeping the secret from you, but it was a condition of terms. They'd stop seeing each other and I would hold off on a trade, but you couldn't be told. It's not as if I didn't keep many secrets of yours over the years Blake, especially from your wife."

Blake was very edgy and anxious to get his test behind him, but could not resist one final jab at Marty.

"But how could you know and I couldn't? That's what pisses me off most."

"Blake, I'm trained to know everything that goes on in this organization. Paid quite handsomely too, I see things that others don't because I'm unattached and afar just enough to see things in an unfettered way. And you were too self-absorbed in a lot of ways that clouded your judgments and perceptions. God-damn booze will do that to you."

"Yes, so much has become clearer in this sober state of mind, both outward and inward. I'm more at peace with myself and with the actions of others now. This one just took everything I could muster up in opposition to resist the bottle. Hell, I had it all coming. I've got nobody to blame but myself. Not Kim, not Sandy, and definitely not you Marty. It's a fucking process, I'm getting better and I'll take your advice from here on out. I've got lots of work to do, but today's work is about winning this game Marty. Let me piss in a bottle and let's get this party started. We can do this today boss, but I've got some 'splaining to do to the boys first. So, I've got the reins again when I pass this test Marty?"

"Yes, Blake you've got the title back as player-manager, but there's a different title I want today: Chicago Cubs Central Division Champions. That's what I want to hear at the end of the day. Now go give me your proof and then you can head down to the clubhouse. I'll call Paxson and let him know. I'm sure he'd rather have it this way anyhow. Give it all you've got today Blake. We've got so many people behind us and a great bunch of guys in heaven cheering us on."

The two of them hugged briefly before Blake initiated the pullback. There was too much to do and Blake was eager to get started. Marty patted his manager on the back and opened the office room door, letting the caged animal out of his pen to enjoy freedom once more.

71 — Win One for the Skipper

It only took minutes for Blake to prove he was clean. One could almost tell from his brashness that the result would be a mere formality. The medical staff gave Marty the good news and Blake was immediately off to the clubhouse with still several hours before batting practice.

There would be no use avoiding the elephant in the room. Blake was sure the boys would be aware of the situation that had developed overnight. Blake even thought he might make use of it to inspire his team even more. After all, wasn't overcoming intense obstacles the moral of their abbreviated season as teammates? This could be just another example of fortitude and determination that the team had displayed up until this final regular season game, albeit an extra 163rd contest.

He could feel anxious eyes upon him as he made his way to the managerial office. Blake felt a bit giddy at the moment, but he knew contrition and an attempt at inspiration would be needed before this issue could be put behind them. He still could not resist an awkward attempt at humor in front of his boys as he struggled with the silence of watchful eyes and ears.

"You guys look like you've seen a ghost. I guess this ghost has nine lives. I'm here and I've never been more excited for a game in my life. You guys didn't really think I'd miss this chance for the world, did ya? On second thought, don't answer that. Did you guys ever stare down the devil before and not blink first? Well, I stared down that bastard overnight and the sonofabitch blinked way before me, and now I feel on top of the world. You guys want to join me up here or wail away in uncertainty and disbelief?"

It should have come as no surprise that Miguel Guillen was the first to speak up. He boldly walked right up to his manager, put his hand on Blake's shoulder and put everyone at ease with his usual straightforward comedic manner.

"Did they test you for LSD Skipper? It seems you might be hallucinating? It's just one more of those things to the top of the mountain, right guys?"

Miguel motioned to his teammates literally and figuratively with his question. The tense mood was lifted with a resounding cheer for their manager. The air was clear of doubt with the arrival of a sober Blake.

Blake was relieved at the response and played along with Guillen for a moment before settling in with his mea culpa.

"I don't know Miggy. Maybe those docs missed something. That devil guy looked remarkably just like you. Okay, enough of the joking guys. Now let me get serious for a bit. I was down to my last strike and last out, but I fouled off a couple of really nasty pitches and hung in there until I began to recognize some of those pitches a bit more clearly. Suddenly, what looked so overwhelmingly filthy became like a pitch sitting right on top of a batting tee, without any movement or speed to blow by me. Now I could suddenly see every stitch of the baseball and it all became clear. I fought back and hung in there just like you all have from day one here. I persevered last night despite some troublesome personal news. We've all persevered through some difficult times these last two months, but it's made us all stronger. This squad two months ago couldn't handle the pressures of a game like this today, but the tough times that we've overcome have made us more than capable of handling anything that comes our way today for as long as it takes to beat those Redbirds. It's just one more obstacle to overcome, no matter what the baseball gods throw our way this afternoon. Hang in there, foul off the tough breaks and persevere long enough to outlast the other team. Make them blink first. Our will can't be denied. Now let's get ready to kick the devil's ass today. There's not a doubt in my mind of our resolve to win. It's got to be stronger than the Cardinals' and it will be. We've proven it so far and we've got one more day to prove it to the baseball world. Get ready and enjoy the ride. It's gonna be a blast fellas."

It was all baseball from here on out in the clubhouse, and that would be carried to the dugout in a few short hours. The distractions were behind them and baseball ruled their minds for the next six hours. With their minds intact, it would be much easier to let their physical attributes naturally take over.

The team certainly had a cohesiveness going into the game today that probably could not have been attained without jumping over the obstacles in place. For bad or for good, for better or for worse, Blake's troublesome rainy day had shaped the theme for an historic baseball day in Chicago. Nine innings of baseball would decide whether it was a winning rallying cry.

72 — Drama King

The sense of relief that overtook Blake after he addressed the team about the resolution of the most recent issue was quickly cast aside by the next important managerial task. He instinctively realized that the season would likely be defined simply by whether or not they could knock off the defending champions today. Distractions dispersed, Blake had to lock in on his game day strategy.

If close only counts in hand grenades and horseshoes, then a near-miracle season on the cusp of a divisional championship, only to fall tantalizingly short of realizing that goal, would be nothing more than a "could have been." History would likely record "close, but not quite," in definition of this year's Chicago Cubs team, and close does not cut it for competitive athletes.

The rookie manager was trying to stay positive, but realistic too, as he mentally approached this game back in the comfy confines of his managerial office. He had to think logically and without bias as he debated the game day strategy in his head.

He was forced to go back in time to the beginning of this whole bizarre scenario. Blake always knew the Cardinals would be their roadblock to a divisional championship despite the Cubs' 10-game head start in the standings. To hold off the defending World Series champions with a team comprised mostly of organizational rejects with marginal big-league talent would indeed be miraculous. Throw in a few out of the norm characters with extreme individual focus, counterproductive to team sports, and you have the perfect recipe for a three-ring-circus-like baseball squad.

They were immediately thrown to the wolves with little or no team preparation, a makeshift schedule that exposed their weaknesses even more with tightly bunched games and a player-manager that was only days removed from a drunken stupor. Blake sat in his chair and shook his head in amazement at the audacity of it all. Even in his reality-challenged, drunken, and semi-conscious state, Blake would never have imagined anything more irrational than what was about to take place at baseball's historic Wrigley Field.

What could be more fitting than having to overcome the pitching talents of arguably major league baseball's best starting hurler, Salvador Torres? Blake was becoming more comfortable with the situation about to unfold and figured appropriately enough that his team should have it no other way than seemingly impossible to achieve.

Blake realized his team would have to play near perfect error-free ball to have a chance. The Cardinals would have to earn everything they got with no freebie walks or extra outs in an inning. To top it all off, the baseball gods would have to look favorably upon this fairy-tale squad. Hard hit balls from the opposition would have to be directed right at Chicago players. Bloop hits or seeing-eye singles by St. Louis would have to be held up in the heavens by baseball angels in the sky for another place and time. And it would not hurt if those same angels wore Cubs attire today and sprinkled Wrigley with well-placed Chicago batted balls. Luck had played a part in more games than Blake could shake his baseball bat at over the years. Today would likely be no different. Only the beneficiaries had yet to be determined as the manager pulled out his lineup card and began to pencil in his pregame thoughts.

Blake had been procrastinating as usual in resuming communications with Kim, but before he could fully concentrate on the lineup card he would have to let her know that the situation had been corrected. He did not want to get into too many details, so he just sent her a text message indicating that he was cleared to manage and that he sincerely hoped she would be present at Wrigley on this historic day. There would be no time for deep marital discussions this morning. No reply was forthcoming at the moment, but Blake had at least reached out to his wife. It was now baseball, all baseball, for the rest of today.

Clear in mind, body, and soul, Blake began to play out today's contest in his head. Of course, there are no guarantees in baseball, but the 15-year veteran had plenty of experience to draw upon regarding likely scenarios developing from an intense, high-drama, one-game playoff.

Blake knew he did not have any pitcher that could match up with Torres for an extended length of time, none that could go perhaps seven, eight or nine innings. It would be an unorthodox approach, but the rookie manager had already shown a strong willingness to go out on a limb and challenge baseball's long held unwritten rules. He would break up his pitching rotation today in three separate three-inning stints. He might have to improvise if one of them struggled, but it would be Kyle Jacobson, TJ Bowman, and finally, Miguel Guillen to finish. The first two were more finesse types so defense would have to prevail along with very strategic fielder positioning. With the advance scouting reports and the numerous recent games between them, both teams had a very strong feel for what the opposition would do. It would be more about execution than strategy today, although every game has one or two very intense moments where all the stops are pulled out to try and gain advantage.

If he could get to Guillen tied or even down by one run, Blake felt he at least had a 50-50 chance of knocking these Cardinals out and claiming first place in the National League Central for his Chicago Cubs.

This event in the Windy City was turning into the biggest story of the last decade in Chicago. Everybody loves an underdog and these guys were even under the underdog in terms of improbability. The national media could not have had more presence if today's contest was the seventh game of the World Series. It was that big and Blake was beginning to feel it, as the noisy surroundings became noteworthy as game time approached. The venerable old ballpark was beginning to shake, rattle, and roll with excitable fans filling the park much earlier than normal.

It was one of those events that fans desperately wanted to be a part of. How else could one feel more like a participating player than arriving to Wrigley early? It sometimes is not enough to watch and enjoy. Games like this had to be emotionally invested. The die-hard fan wants to be a part of the whole game-day process, the slow, steady buildup of emotion as the first pitch nears, the devastating punches of failure, and that one-time thrill of the pleasure that comes from finishing on top. This would be just one step toward the World Series and ultimate pleasure, but to accomplish what was within the Cubbies' grasp this afternoon would be near impossible to top.

As Blake finished up his starting lineup card without writing down his own name today, he looked upward toward the ceiling from his favorite chair. He was not a religious man, but he was a believer, and he so wanted to believe that this whole bizarre and sometimes nightmarish ordeal had a divine ending.

Blake felt as though he had survived the demons, just barely at times, but survived nonetheless, and the dreamer in him wanted to be rewarded for his accomplishment. He knew that was not the way the real world worked, but can't, just for once, a dream come true?

In a very strange moment of spiritual connectivity, whether real or imagined, Blake felt he was living out a dream that had already been played out. It was if he felt the ending today was certainly going to be positive. It did not mean his team would win or that he would somehow be the star, but rather the emotions that had plagued him since the plane crash would be released forever, and he would come to know what God or some supreme being meant for him to discover in life from all this craziness.

When all of Blake and his staff's pregame preparations were finished and strategy had run its course of usefulness, the manager and coaches knew it was time to take the field. There was nothing more they could do to give their team its best chance of winning. It would now be up to the players between the lines. Blake thanked each and every one of his staff personally for all they had done for him and their team. The rookie manager would be forever grateful for their support in his times of need the past two months.

"This is it guys. We've done all we can. Whether the season ends today or we move on to the next round, I just want you to know that some strange circumstances put us all together, but nothing can ever pull us apart. Now let's go out there and act relaxed even though we all are just as nervous as our players inside. You can't play this game of baseball tight. We all know that. Those guys in the other dugout are the ones that should be tight-assed today. To think our boys could beat them in this all-or-nothing game must be tearing them apart."

The coaching staff walked in unison through the clubhouse and into the tunnel that led them to their dugout. When they all stepped out on to the field of play they were simply amazed at the reception they received from the fans on this cool, sunny afternoon.

Blake and his staff all tipped their caps to the crowd in appreciation, a long-time baseball tradition. The coaches were beginning to feel a bit embarrassed, as the crowd would not let up in applause. All coaches are keenly aware that the game is about the players and don't like to take the spotlight away from the true performers.

Blake motioned with his right arm to his coaches to return to the dugout while waving his cap to the crowd with his left hand at the same time. He figured this would be the only way for the crowd to stop their cheers. As they all moved back toward their sheltered dugout, the crowd erupted in chants of "Blake, Blake, Blake."

It was a good thing the dugout was a mere 20 feet from the assembled coaches because Blake was totally overcome with emotion at the chant. He just made it into the confines of his dugout before erupting in tears. He immediately did the only truly acceptable thing a player-manager could do under these circumstances. He lowered his head with his cap pulled down tightly to hide the tears as he walked back up the runway to collect himself.

"Damn sun. Sure is bright out there today." Blake tried to brush off the possibility of teardrops by blaming it on the sun, but the players nearby were not fooled by their manager's poor acting. In fact, they did not want to be fooled. This was their manager's moment and their emotions matched those exhibited by the fans.

Emotions would be openly displayed throughout the pregame ceremonies. There was not a dry eye in the house as the emcee, Cubs television announcer Charley Zuber, reflected on high points of the season including many thrilling moments before the plane crash overshadowed most of what had been accomplished during the season

Many of the families that lost their brother, father, or husband in the crash were honored as well during opening ceremonies. The victims' families were respectfully paraded around the infield as they waved to the many weeping fans in attendance in appreciation of their support. Some of the smallest children had little idea of what was going on in honor of their fathers, but the mere sight of the now fatherless kids brought a stark reality to the devastating effects of the accident that left no survivors from the plane, but many mourning at home.

Sandy's family had a large contingent of relatives that had made the trip from Mexico, along with his immediate family that lived in Chicago. Blake stood in line with his coaches, straddling the chalk of the base path on the first base side and greeted the survivors as they passed him by. When Sandy's family approached the coaching staff, Blake took the baseball cap from his head, signed a heartwarming note on the bill of his cap, and presented it to Sandy's oldest son. Tears were flowing and hugs were in abundant supply as Sandy's immediate family embraced Blake as the only remaining link to their own fallen hero.

The ceremonies ended with Sandy's wife, Lisa, throwing out the first pitch to Cubs starting catcher John Bartlett. Blake was relieved that he did not have to do that task today, as he was still unable to get his best friend Sandy's marital indiscretion with Kim out of his mind. The pain was still too fresh to know exactly what Blake would actually do or say to Sandy's wife if he had a moment alone with her.

The national anthem was again brilliantly sung by Casey Tedin's talented daughter. This time, the courageous performer was overcome by her own emotions just as she finished the final climatic note and had to be helped from the field by several Chicago players as she sobbed in remembrance.

It was now time to begin the deciding game and not a moment too soon, as the emotional wrangling of the honoring ceremonies was becoming a concern to Blake. There was only so much emotion and energy untapped in every player. Reach that limit too early and the team will be spent before the most crucial innings begin to unfold. Not to mention the added pressure felt by Blake as he witnessed firsthand the still too fresh pain and suffering exhibited by the survivors. It only added to Blake's never-ending angst over if he could ever do enough to honor his former teammates and their families. There were times when Blake felt even a near impossible World Series title would not be enough, much less the division championship that was dangling in front of the Cubs today. Blake could not help but feel that winning today's game was the bare minimum necessary to claim noteworthy honor for the deceased.

The manager began his walk to home plate to meet with the umpires and exchange lineup cards per usual at any game. The weather was undecided as the sun peeked out intermittently from behind the clouds, alternating between comfortable in the sunlight and cool in the shade, as is often the case on a Chicago October afternoon. Blake had started his walk without a jacket, but returned to the dugout to retrieve his blue Cubs jacket as a result of the fall chill.

Blake could see his managerial counterpart approaching home plate, and the umpires as well. Their eyes connected and the two nodded to each other before starting up a gentlemanly conversation huddled up with the umpires.

"Good luck Don. May the best team win today," said Blake as he extended his gloved right hand to shake with Leighton before realizing he should pull off his glove before shaking his hand.

"Yes, Blake. Good luck to you and your guys too. You've done a helluva job with them."

"Thanks Don. You and your team have always represented baseball well. Defending World Series champs and right back in it again."

"It sure was quite the scene here before the game. Must've been tough for you," said the elder statesman Leighton, as the two of them chatted while the umps routinely went over the ground rules, the managers ignoring the arbiters like passengers brushing off flight attendants going over safety features before a flight.

"Yes, big man. It just doesn't seem to get any easier, but at least we have a few hours of battle to engage our brilliant baseball minds with," remarked Blake with a smile indicating his sarcasm.

"Blake, whatever the result, you've done baseball well, good luck once again," replied Leighton as the umpires finished up their conference and the two managerial combatants parted ways and returned to their respective dugouts.

The husband in Blake could not resist a quick glimpse into the stands to see if Kim had indeed shown up today. He did not want to make eye contact with his wife, but rather just note her presence. He immediately recognized her flowing blond hair even from a peripheral glance, and settled in his usual managerial position in the dugout comforted by Kim's continued support in this difficult time for both of them.

The butterflies were busy darting around inside the stomachs of all participants today as well as the fans as first pitch neared. The Cubs took the field in unison to a now expected roar every time the home team moved a muscle.

The scene was set and the drama was about to begin. From here on out, the manager could only alter strategy. The rest would be up to the players unless some unforeseen scenario developed where Blake would have to perform double duty today. There was more than enough on his managerial plate this afternoon. Playing in the game himself seemed too much of a physical and emotional stretch for Blake. He was already feeling the strain and the game had not even started.

The first inning would indeed set the tone for the rest of the game. Blake was praying that his boys would stand up to the initial pressure as Kyle Jacobson threw the game's first pitch right down the middle for a called strike one as the fans settled in their seats after another lengthy standing ovation.

So much was at stake today. The crowd had expectations of a postgame celebration and this makeshift Chicago Cubs team was now the whole nation's destiny darlings. Most everybody outside of Missouri wanted to see the Cubs prevail. The support was very much welcome, but it also added to the pressure. To disappoint so many people would be a crushing blow to these Chicago players. A poor performance would be a huge national letdown.

If Blake was praying to God for a clean start to this game, he might as well have saved his plea for another day. The first two St. Louis batters reached on solid singles and the crowd was already showing signs of apprehension. The Wrigley fans were suddenly silent as if they were now expecting the tidal wave to come ashore and dash the hopes of a playoff win before they could even finish their first hot dog and beer.

Blake hollered to Bartlett to get him to walk to the mound and calm Kyle down. The fidgety pitcher looked rattled at the inauspicious start, but the savvy Bartlett knew he could reassure Jacobson that he was only one good pitch away from putting out the fire. Of course, Bartlett did not care to stress the painfully obvious alternative that the Chicago pitcher was also only one pitch away from burying his team before they even came to the plate in the bottom half of the inning.

This time the baseball gods were dressed in Chicago Cubs colors as the first pitch to St. Louis slugger Lenny Charles was roped on a line to shortstop Rickey Sanchez, conveniently placed right behind the leadoff runner Lonnie Jackson about 15 feet from second base. All Sanchez had to do was snare the hard liner that was targeting the shortstop like a sniper's bullet to the chest. It was tailor-made for an easy double play as Sanchez caught the ball and flipped it to Petey Arroyo covering second base. Petey stepped on the bag and just like that there were two outs in the inning with a runner on first.

The crowd exhaled in relief, but not before Jacobson did likewise, and the lucky break calmed down every Chicago player and fan alike. Jacobson settled in and found the composure needed for success today as he retired the next Cardinals batter on a routine fly to center to end the inning unscathed.

It did not matter that the Cubs went down meekly in their half of the first. They had withstood that initial fear of immediate failure and were locked in, and the game started to flow like any of the other 162 games played already this season.

Jacobson was just crafty enough through the first three innings to keep St. Louis off the scoreboard. The Redbirds had a few runners, but could not get that clutch hit to get the game's first run through three.

The Cubs were simply overmatched by the wicked repertoire of the league's elite starting pitcher Salvador Torres, who had more than his usual days of rest between starts. The layoff seemed to refresh Torres and he looked more dominant than ever, retiring the Cubbies in order, nine up and nine down through three.

Blake stuck to his guns and removed Jacobson in favor of TJ Bowman. The move was met with skepticism by the media in attendance and no doubt a few of the many second-guessers in the stands. It was unique strategy, but the sports-writers and broadcasters had come to expect the unexpected with Blake Benson. It would only be flawed strategy if it did not work.

Bowman had his sinker going early and the Cards pounded three grounders into the thick, damp fall infield grass in the fourth inning, resulting in three routine outs. The easy half-inning was just as the doctor ordered and the Cubs' quick return to their dugout seemed to lift their confidence.

There was a hint of optimism as leadoff batter Desmond Wilson coaxed a walk, followed by a seeing-eye infield single off the bat of outfielder Ricky Rodriguez. The bleeder luckily dribbled just past the pitcher Torres' out-stretched glove before the baseball stopped dead in its tracks in the plush grass. All the charging Cardinals shortstop could do was pick up the ball and flip it back to Torres without any chance of throwing out the batter at first.

The hint of optimism collectively felt by the crowd had grown into an ex-pectation of a serious threat now that the Cubs had the first two batters of the inning on base and the meat of the order coming up to the plate. This opportu-nity would give Blake his first real chance of executing managerial strategy in this decisive contest. It was only the fourth inning and not a likely bunting sit-uation with his three best hitters coming up in succession. However, Blake des-perately wanted the game's first run to take the pressure off his team and perhaps throw that heavy-weighted elephant onto the Cardinals shoulders.

Ricky Sanchez was at the plate and Blake knew the often temperamental shortstop did not like to bunt, but he went ahead anyway and flashed the sacrifice bunt sign to third base coach Lenny Paxson. The reaction from Sanchez could be a telling signal as Paxson went through a series of deceptive hand motions be-fore flashing the one true indicator of a bunt attempt. If Ricky was all in today he would not hesitate to bunt. If Sanchez showed any irritated body language at giv-ing up himself in order to advance the base runners, all of his teammates would take notice, perhaps dividing the team instead of uniting the squad.

There was not a speck of discontent in Rickey as he laid down a splendid sacrifice bunt on the first pitch from Torres. The bunt was deadened perfectly and all Torres could do was routinely pick up the baseball and toss it to first as Wilson moved to third and Rodriguez to second with still only one out.

All of Sanchez' teammates jumped to the top of the dugout steps in unison and excitedly congratulated their shortstop on his unselfish play. It was just the unifying moment that Blake had in mind when he decided on a bunt attempt even though he had some trepidation that Rickey might not share the manager's enthusiasm.

Blake's team was confident and unified and there was a sense in the dugout that something positive was going to happen. Just as bad play snowballs and leads to more unforced errors, good play tends to lead to better results as a continuation of confidence.

Big Jim Arnold stepped to the plate uncertain if the Cardinals would pitch to him with first base open. From the opposition's perspective, big Jim offered a high-risk, high-reward possible outcome. The beefy slugger struck out often, well over 150 times this season, but when he made contact the results could be dramatic, as his power stroke paid off in force, if not in frequency. Torres was the games' premier strikeout pitcher so it was not too surprising that the power pitcher went right after Arnold in an obvious attempt to strand the runners on base with a strikeout in this situation.

Manager Leighton positioned the infielders halfway in. It was not a given that the fielders would come home with a grounder in an attempt to keep the game scoreless. Arnold's extreme power forced the infielders on the left side of the diamond to play back just a bit, based on the speed of the batted ball off of Big Jim's stroke. It would all depend on quick instinctive reactions from the third baseman or shortstop whether to come home or throw to first and allow the game's first run to score. After all, it was still the first half of the contest.

Torres started Big Jim off with a nasty slider that took advantage of Arnold's anxiousness in this situation. The slugger salivated at the sight of what looked like a hittable fastball right down the middle of the plate until the pitch quickly darted out of the strike zone, but not before he started his hands in motion and went around for a swinging strike, even though he attempted in vain to check his swing. The next pitch was a high heater, the type of pitch that looks great to hit, but seldom is struck solidly as it is near impossible to get your hands on top of the ball to drive it. As is the norm, Jim fouled the pitch back for strike two and the crowd groaned in fear of an impending strikeout.

In baseball, there is thinking and sometimes over-thinking. The pitcher with perhaps the best stuff in baseball wanted to throw a curveball next. Not his 95 plus fastball or his nearly unhittable slider, but a curveball that Torres was sure would freeze Big Jim in his tracks and break over the plate for strike three.

To be sure, Big Jim was not expecting the next offering to be a curveball, but a hanging curveball just seems to sit there, pausing over the middle of the plate belt-high and screaming, "Hit me!" Arnie was indeed fooled, but he had just enough time to stop his hands from moving through the hitting zone, although his weight had mostly shifted to his front foot, draining some of the massive power from his torso. He had enough oomph left in his stroke to flick his huge hands through the zone, striking the baseball solidly and on a high arc to left center. The St. Louis outfielders converged on the fly ball, sauntering back to the warning track before the center fielder called off his teammate and hauled in the deeply struck baseball.

348 – Timothy F. Bouvine

Desmond Wilson tagged up at third base and easily scored the game's first run on the sacrifice fly from Jim Arnold. It was not a dramatic blow like one of Big Jim's mammoth home run blasts, but breaking through first against one of the best pitchers in baseball had a unifying effect on Blake's team.

Torres did not normally make too many mistakes in a game, but he went with his third-best pitch in a best pitch scenario this time and it cost him. One run might not have seemed like a significant deficit in a mid-July regular season game, but for the underdog Cubbies it played a big role in the team's psyche.

Torres kept the deficit at a single run by striking out Felix Gonzalez to strand Ricky Rodriguez at second base, ending the fourth inning with the Chicago Cubs up 1-0 on the defending World Series champion and hated rival St. Louis squad. The crowd was slowly starting to believe this scrappy Cubs team could actually come out on top today. The confidence was growing steadily throughout Wrigley Field, and the Chicago players and home team spectators could sense the impending fairy-tale ending, while at the same time the tension ratcheted up as well.

The visiting Cardinals just could not come up with a clutch hit, stranding a pair of runners against Bowman in the top of the fifth as the sun began to descend behind the upper confines of the fabled field. The shadows would be a complicating factor for the batters and it was beginning to feel like runs would be at a premium today, as is often the case in playoff baseball.

Just as Blake's dream scenario was looking like it would take hold, with his top pitcher Miguel Guillen closing out the last three innings of today's game with a lead, the Cardinals scraped out a run against Bowman and the Cubbies in the top of the sixth to tie the game. There was little Blake and his team could do to counter the perfectly planned hit-and-run St. Louis neatly executed to put runners on first and third with one out. The Cubs and Bowman held the runner at first closely and the infielders held their positions to the last moment before Cardinals second sacker Jeff Dorman grounded a ball right where Chicago's Petey Arroyo was standing before he had to scamper to second to cover the base as the runner was moving. A tip of the hat to Dorman was in order as the Cubs were helpless against the deftly executed maneuver. The next Cardinals batter chopped a high one-hopper over the pitcher Bowman's head. All the shortstop Rickey Sanchez could do was hastily grab the softly hit ball with his bare hand, throwing across his body in one swift motion to barely beat the runner to first base with his throw for the second out. The St. Louis runner from third was able to scamper in with the tying run, knotting the game at one run apiece.

The crowd moaned even as Sanchez' outstanding play prevented a bigger rally. The game was back to even and if tie goes to the runner in baseball, a tie in this situation would go to the defending world champions with their ace on the mound as the game neared its critical stage.

Bowman kept the game tied with another one of his ground ball outs to end the inning, but the team jogged in from the field to their dugout with just a bit less spring in their steps as the task ahead took on a slightly different tone. The Cubs manager immediately took note of the subtle shift.

Blake stepped out of the dugout and on to the grass in foul territory just several feet from the railing, hollering at his boys as they neared the dugout.

"C'mon now boys, nobody ever promised you this was going to be easy. These guys are defending champs and they're good, but we're gonna be better today."

Blake backslapped his players as they entered the dugout encouraging them all the way in, a pat here and a more forceful, prodding flip of the hand there, but always in support. The uplifting positive approach by Blake was reinforced by none other than the normally cantankerous Bartlett, but with a much different tone.

"You guys better buck up right now. We've got to earn this. Those hard-nosed competitive pricks over there aren't gonna give it to us. Keep our heads up and meet their challenges head-on. This is baseball, not war, but we're gonna battle them until they retreat or surrender. It's a battle of wills now."

The good-cop, bad-cop routine was just what the team needed to get back its edge. There was hollering and cheering from many of the teammates sitting in the dugout now. They were so close they could taste it, but the rewards of winning could be pulled back, replaced, never to come again if they simply did not take advantage of every opportunity presented to them in these last few innings.

Blake motioned for his pitching coach Mark Douglas to meet him just up the runway outside of the noisy dugout scene. Douglas already knew of his manager's pitching schedule that would put Guillen on the mound in the seventh, so he was a bit perplexed at Blake's wish to speak to him. The pitching coach had a binder that he always kept with him, folded neatly shut to open at a moment's notice for any changes. He began to open the folder before Blake brushed back with an emphatic don't bother hand motion.

"Mark, you just get on that bullpen phone and tell Miguel it's up to him to bring us home. Just tell him there's nobody in baseball I'd rather have finish up this game than him. Oh, and tell him he's got a lifelong free bar tab from me when he pulls this off."

"Blake, you're a great manager and I never would disobey an order, but I think this should come from you. Tell the man yourself and it will mean that much more to Miggy."

"By George, I think you're right. Just come and show me how to use the damn thing. I've never been on the calling end of this contraption before."

"It's only got one connection Blake. Pick up the damn thing and it rings in the pen. We baseball men aren't too smart you know. They keep it at a third-grade level," said Douglas with a wry smile.

Blake immediately walked back to the dugout and placed the call. There was not much time for chitchat with the half inning starting shortly.

"This is Blake. Get Miggy on the phone," said the eager manager as his bullpen coach answered the ring.

"Damn, you guys got my order wrong again. I said no pepperoni on my pizza amigo." The wisecracking Guillen never failed to take advantage of a comedic moment although he was unaware it was his boss on the other end.

"Miggy, this is Blake. I thought I told you no more goddamn pizza during the game. Aw, shit, never mind. Get your million-dollar arm loose, Miggy. I'm riding you the rest of the way. It's up to you to bring us to our promised land. You know your promised land, that one with free booze and free food the whole time. Seriously Miguel, before you take the mound next inning I just wanted to tell you that there's nobody better in baseball than you to bring us home. I've caught them all, big guy, and you've got the stuff to match them all. You are one helluva fighter on the hill. Now get loose and show them bastards who is THE man."

"Thanks Blake. I won't let you down. I won't let the team down. I got this. Gotta run Skipper. The nerves are jumping now. Oh boy, I've got to shit something fierce.."

Blake hung up the phone and just shook his head. His favorite pitcher held a soft spot in his heart even though Blake thought the man was half-crazy. The manager resumed his perch in the dugout and contemplated the next moves as the Cubs' first batter of the inning stepped in the box.

It did not really matter, as there was little Blake could offer in strategy against Salvador Torres. The powerful righty was cruising along, sharp as ever, mixing his pitches with supreme command. The world belonged to young Salvador and the opposition Cubs were putty in his hands. Torres was just blowing them away at this point, retiring 11 batters in a row now, six of them set down by strikeout. The superstar pitcher was well rested and it looked like he could pitch until sundown the way he was rolling along. The only question was how long manager Don Leighton would leave his ace in the game. Torres stood at a respectable 75 pitches through six innings. Most managers will not let their pitchers throw much more than 110 pitches, 120 plus max, in extreme circumstances.

As the seventh inning commenced, Miguel Guillen gave everybody in attendance a spark with his demonstrative reactions to his pitches. The Wrigley faithful were further delighted by his perfect inning, striking out the last two opposition batters to end the inning. While the crowd was rising to sing the traditional seventh-inning "Take Me Out to the Ballgame," Blake was scratching his head for possible pinch-hitting substitutions or strategic maneuvers that could somehow, some way scratch out a run against Torres.

Unfortunately, if nobody even reaches first base, a manager is left twiddling his thumbs. Blake had no answer for the nasty pitches from the pitching ace Torres. He set down the side in order once more, extending his consecutive streak of not allowing a runner to 14 straight batters. The only consolation this inning was that Torres was up to 95 overall pitches and 20 for the inning, as the Cubbies were at least providing lengthy at-bats.

Another scoreless inning went by and the tension continued to build. The weather and lighting conditions were changing as the day's sunlight was just beginning to dim. The lights were turned on and the chill of impending darkness started to take hold of the scene, just as the course of the game was heating up nearing its likely finish.

The scene was set for a dramatic finish, with only the heroes and goats to be determined, as the excitable Miguel Guillen started the ninth inning, the frame in which most games end but which, in today's tight contest, looked like a prelude to an extra-inning battle.

A quick glance in any direction would show high anxiety from those in attendance. There would be several extremely nervous fans on the edge of their seats and biting their fingernails in one row. In another row there would be several fans that enjoyed actively participating on every pitch, jumping up and shouting either in favor or disgust, depending on the pitch's result. In another area there would be some so nervous that they would be frozen in place. There might even be a few that simply enjoyed the anticipation of sport, not living and dying with every play, but rather just living in the moment, appreciative of the ultimate reality show, an extremely intense athletic event.

All shared the same feeling though, that sooner, rather than later, something was going to give in determining a victor. There was anticipation of a climactic ending that would send millions of people in opposite mood directions. One side would be ecstatic beyond belief and the other would wallow in the wounded spirit of defeat.

The top of the ninth started favorably for the home team. Guillen retired the first two batters of the inning on routine ground ball outs, but the third batter of the inning, catcher Paul Evans, provided the breakthrough moment that immediately turned the contest into a strategic chess match. The veteran catcher roped a Guillen pitch down the left-field line, past a diving Ricky Rodriguez. The smart play would have called for admitting he had no chance at making the spectacular catch and simply playing the ball on a bounce or, at worst, chasing the ball into the corner, but limiting the damage to a double. Rodriguez got caught up in the emotion of the play, gambled on the spectacular and lost with predictable result. Evans cruised into third with a triple before Rodriguez finally righted himself and tracked down the baseball. He fired the ball to the infield, disgusted at himself, while the crowd added insult to injury with catcalls and boos emanating loudly from the bleachers.

The Cubs and Guillen were now in a pickle and Blake knew it. Still, there were two outs and Guillen had the odds in his favor. The best hitters in baseball only reach base about three out of 10 times so there was no need to panic. It didn't take long for the 15 years of major league baseball experience in Blake to kick in. He realized immediately what he had to do, but it was risky. There was no need to discuss this with his coaches, so he jumped out onto the field and asked for time.

This would be the riskiest maneuver yet for the player-manager Blake Benson...and he had attempted quite a few in his short tenure. Some worked and some didn't, but he never hesitated to trust his instincts and take a baseball educated chance.

Bartlett joined in the impromptu conference on the mound and asked Blake what he had in mind. Blake just smiled at Bartlett and motioned for him to come closer while the three of them, Guillen, Bartlett and Blake, played bandits with their hands and baseball gloves. They covered up their faces so the opposition could not read their lips and discussed the strategy.

"This is what we're gonna do Miggy. It's risky, but it's smart too. It will speed up the end result of the game one way or another. You have two more batters to face before you get to the pitcher's spot. You're gonna intentionally walk the next two batters as we have bases open. This will put Leighton on the spot. He'll almost have to pinch-hit for Torres given the circumstances. We'll get that nasty hombre out of the game, but you'll have to face their best pinch-hitter in Walker and of course, you can't walk in the go-ahead run. Now Walker is tough, but you're tougher, Miggy. Just listen to Bartlett and he'll get you through the report on Walker. I'm going back to the dugout and pray that this triple plays out in our favor. Walk the next two and do what you do big guy."

There was no response from either Bartlett or Guillen. They both knew the stakes and the rationale behind the move. It made sense like all baseball moves do in theory, but in practice can have a way of backfiring.

The crowd was a bit perplexed by the first intentional walk, but the strategy soon became evident to most knowledgeable baseball fans the minute Bartlett stuck out his glove hand indicating another intentional walk. Leighton would have to make his move now. He could leave his star pitcher in the game with the likely result of an out by Torres, or he could pinch-hit with his best and try to win it here. The odds favored a Leighton response of pinch-hitting and he followed true to form, bringing out Tommy Walker to pinch-hit.

Walker was a career .300 hitter in his prime, but now was called upon in spot duty like this to deliver. He had been a very solid pinch-hitter, no ifs, ands, or buts. The strategic wheels were in motion and it was now time to see if this initial move would pay off or backfire on Blake.

Guillen took a deep breath on the mound, shook his head slightly up and down acknowledging the catcher Bartlett's sign for a first pitch fastball, came to the set, and quickly looked at the runner at second before delivering the 93-miles-per-hour fastball right down the middle of the plate. Guillen cringed just a bit after he let the pitch go, as he immediately realized a location mistake.

Walker's eyes lit up like Christmas tree bulbs as he immediately recognized the spin of a four-seamed fastball coming right into his sweet spot. His hands were not as quick as they once were, but his recognition skills had plenty of life left in him. He swung mightily, centered the bat on the ball and lined the pitch right back up the middle.

Guillen reacted like a hockey goalie, instinctively sticking out his glove just before the baseball smacked right into his webbing and stayed there for the third out. It was pure luck, but it did not matter, and Guillen jumped up and down at the fortunate result before heading triumphantly into the dugout.

All that strategy and counter-strategy, and all that mattered was a lucky break from the baseball gods to decide the biggest play of the game. Such is the game of baseball that knows no right or wrong, nor blame or excuse. An out is an out no matter how it comes about.

That feel-good vibe of destiny was back in the Chicago dugout and in the stands as the bottom of the ninth was about to begin. Could it really be moments away from happening?

The Cubs had the advantage now, two at-bats for every one by the Cardinals, as extra innings generally favor the home team, but Blake knew the advantage only lasted for a brief few minutes if the team did not produce a run. The Chicago manager was in a stressed mood himself, as he knew Guillen did not have much left in him, and the rest of his pitching staff did not match up well with St. Louis.

"Hey Miggy, nice at 'em ball there. Do they play hockey somewhere in Mexico that I'm not aware of?"

The usually comedic Guillen was running on fumes and could not even come up with a wisecrack answer this time due to his fatigue.

"Nope." The straightforward and unusually brief answer was highly indicative of his exhaustion. Blake had just one more favor.

"Can you give me just one more? Just one more, Miggy? I gotta have it."

"Yep, one more. Only one more," was all that he could mutter this time.

The tension was now bordering on the excessive as the Cubs took their turn

354 – Timothy F. Bouvine

at bat. They had forced Leighton's hand and he dealt the Cubs at least a pair of kings to start the inning. No more Torres, but no slouch either in left-handed set-up man Chucky Willis, a hard-throwing country boy who looked like he came off the farm fields of Missouri to pitch for the Cards. There was no mistaking his country boy image for niceness, however. Chucky was known as "Old Chuck and duck," because he was not afraid to knock the opposing batters off the plate.

The bottom end of the order was coming up for the Cubbies, but Blake had confidence in his bench as well. The old veteran himself began to loosen up his aging joints as the thought of pinch-hitting himself was entering his mind now that the team was carrying three catchers.

The inning started off harmless enough with a strikeout by third baseman Mike Simons before John Bartlett stepped to the plate with his chance to be a hero and get some revenge for the Cardinals trading him to New York. Bartlett had a decent stroke, but like most catchers he was primarily known for his defense and game-calling skills. He could be a dangerous hitter if the circumstances were right. The Rat could also dial long distance on occasion with homer totals usually in the double digits throughout his many major league seasons.

The crowd was hoping for the same outcome; not a long-shot desperation play, but maybe a one-in-40-at-bats proposition based on his career numbers. There was not a doubt in Bartlett's mind that he was going to go all out in hopes of ending the game now. This was his once-in-a-lifetime chance to be the ultimate hero, and he was not going to punch one the opposite way here. He was thinking long ball all the way.

He worked the count in his favor by laying off a couple of sliders from Willis before taking an outside corner fastball that he had little chance to drive. The next two balls and one strike pitch set off a chain of events that would live on in baseball lore forever.

Bartlett was looking fastball all the way again and zeroing in on the inside half of the plate in anticipation of a drivable offering from Willis. Christmas came early for one John Bartlett as the pitch came in just left of center of the plate and thigh-high. This mistake pitch would be his one chance at eternal baseball glory. The veteran catcher got it all with one mighty cut, sending the ball skyward and down the left-field line.

The crowd jumped out of their seats in anticipation of the greatest upset perhaps in the history of the game of baseball. Bartlett did his best imitation of Red Sox catcher Carlton Fisk who jumped up and down and provided the most famous instance of baseball body language in its history during the 1975 World Series. Fisk waved, prodded, and begged for the ball to stay fair and it followed his command as the ball struck the foul pole, providing the game-winning homerun in Game Six of that Series.

Bartlett was repeating that motion and although he was uncertain of the trajectory of the batted ball, the umpire racing down the left-field line signaled home run and the place went berserk with glee. Bartlett was clapping his hands and jumping up and down at the same time as he crossed first base. The crowd was hollering in sheer ecstasy while the whole Chicago Cubs team ran onto the field to celebrate while waiting for their hero to cross home plate.

The St. Louis pitcher Willis was walking with his head down in disappointment towards his losing dugout when Cardinals manager Don Leighton raced onto the field demonstrably declaring that the batted ball was foul and not a game-winning home run. He pleaded with the umpires to look at the replay while the crowd continued its celebration. Some overly excited fans had even made their way onto the Wrigley Field playing surface and were mingling with the winning members of the apparent Central Division champion Chicago Cubs.

The celebratory mood stopped on a dime when the umpires converged and discussed the play before retreating to the camera room inside the premises to review whether or not the ball was a home run or a foul ball. Blake had run out to the umpires huddling behind the pitcher's mound insisting there was no way they would be able to overturn the call, but the umps had already made their consensus opinion that a replay review was in order. Given the stakes of the outcome, how could there not be a review to be certain?

It was a very odd scene this late Saturday afternoon in Chicago with both teams and the fans mingling about, uncertain of the ruling that could either declare Chicago's Cubs the winner or instruct the players to continue the deciding game still tied at one apiece. The longer the delay went on, the quieter Wrigley became, as the mood had a feel of reversal.

The umpires came out onto the field with suspense of utmost importance hanging throughout the cool, Chicago air. The crew chief immediately signaled no home run and ordered the players back onto the field to resume the game. The crowd was livid, Blake was outraged and John Bartlett was beside himself in a fit of anger at the decision. It took a lengthy delay of 15 minutes after the decision to clear the field of fans, get the players back to their positions and restore some sense of order to the bizarre situation.

The crowd and Blake could holler all they wanted, but the verdict was foul ball and that was not going to change. In reality, television cameras confirmed that the ball was indeed foul. Not by much, but by a discerning distance. The umpire crew was certain in its ruling.

Both Blake and Bartlett were fortunate they were not tossed by the umpiring crew that showed remarkable restraint, most likely as a professional courtesy for the gravity of the moment. It was understandable they were upset, but in the umpires' eyes it was only important to get the call right.

After all the commotion and dangling suspense had ceased, for the moment at least, the game resumed with one out in the bottom of the ninth and a two-ball, two-strike count on Chicago catcher John Bartlett with the bases empty.

It is a difficult emotion to overcome when the anticipation of victory is snatched away. Blake had always sensed this troublesome emotion after a closer failed to hold a lead late in the game. It is hard to win a game twice in your mind. The best remedy is to never assume a win until you are certain, but human nature is difficult to ignore or reject. It is somewhat natural to sense a victory that appears so close, but to have that taken away makes it hard to regain that confident feeling again.

The Cubs would have to overcome just another one of seemingly countless obstacles in their way, but this one hurt inside. The victory was already there, they felt it and reacted as one would expect, flying around like little kids discovering their favorite toy under the Christmas tree. This time, Scrooge had taken the gift back, much to the dismay of the players.

The crowd was now subdued unlike any other time today, as John Bartlett stepped into the batter's box, put his feet back right in the indentations from his last swing, and muttered something inaudible as he lifted the bat off his shoulders in preparation for the next pitch. It was fairly obvious to all that Bartlett was still incensed and certainly not focused at the moment. It came as no surprise that the unfocused catcher took a called strike three to end his at-bat on the first pitch. The crowd came out of its shocked status enough to fill the air with resounding boos at the umpire's third strike call, even though the pitch from Willis was right down the middle of the plate and comfortably above the knees.

Bartlett walked back to the dugout, still mumbling under his breath but thankfully inaudible to the home plate umpire that just called him out. The Rat turned his head back to face the umpire and just stared at him before hiding his anger in the dugout, where he took his baseball bat and broke it against the wall.

Bartlett had lost his composure and the rest of his teammates were not too far behind. The Chicago bench could not resist hollering in the direction of the umpire who had finally reached his boiling point. The long-time and well-respected crew chief Paul Abbott removed his mask and hollered back into the dugout before he walked briskly over to the Chicago bench to warn Blake's players for the last time. The next utterance would deserve an ejection. The Cubs manager did what any good field boss would do and took up the conversation with Abbott himself in an attempt to shield his players from trouble.

Blake got a few words in edgewise before he announced to Abbott that he was going to pinch-hit himself here for Petey Arroyo. Blake went back to the dugout and grabbed his bat, rubbed the pine tar rag on his own personalized weapon, and strolled toward home plate. This time the crowd reacted positively and gave their manager a standing ovation as his name was belted out over the loudspeakers.

The mood from the crowd had changed from bitter to appreciative with Blake's personal insertion into the contest. The crowd was in love with Blake Benson, this Blake Benson, not the one that was wallowing about in self-pity two months earlier, merely a shadow of his once star-studded status.

Blake took his time preparing himself mentally for this at-bat. He knew he needed to regain focus and get a game plan set in his mind for this turn at the plate. The old baseball saying professes that nobody ever hits a home run while they are actually trying for it, but Blake knew that not to be true in reality. Some sluggers go up to the plate with nothing else on their mind. Blake was going to do the same, although he could not recall ever going up to the plate with this narrow goal beforehand. It was an all-or-nothing moment for the new and re-furbished Blake Benson.

The cat-and-mouse game was about to begin. Blake was well aware of the baseball book on him at age 35. The scouting reports all said his bat speed was down and Blake himself knew that to be true as well. Opposing pitchers would throw him heat inside or up in the zone where a batter has the toughest time catching up to or adjusting his hands closer to the body to keep his swing inside the ball. The information was correct, but the pitcher still had to execute. Blake had to look for that one mistake and jump on it.

The 15-year major league veteran was now in the proper frame of mind to take on the hard-throwing Willis. Blake tugged on his batting gloves and fidgeted with his uniform sleeves to loosen the feel. He adjusted his helmet, planted his feet in the box and addressed the pitcher in his slightly open stance with hands held letter-high, holding the baseball bat ever so loosely to take the tension out of his swing.

Willis was one batter away from doing his job in the bottom of the ninth as he glared in to take the sign from catcher Evans. The relief pitcher always threw from the stretch as most pitchers out of the bullpen do, regardless of base-runners or not. Willis came to the set, took the sign for an inside fastball and let loose with a nasty two-seam fastball that ran inside on Blake's hands. Blake's slower bat speed prevented him from getting a handle on this pitch and his swing resulted in a very weak foul ball off the handle of the bat. The baseball traveled meekly down the first base line, foul by several feet and embarrassingly futile.

As Blake stepped in the batter's box again, he saw no reason why Willis and Evans would speed up Blake's bat by offering him a slower pitch. The catcher in him knew what his counterpart Evans would call for, but if there was

358 - Timothy F. Bouvine

one thing Blake had learned in his many years of baseball, it was that pitchers don't always throw the ball where they want to. Blake was hoping Willis would miss out over the plate and not further inside where a crafty pitcher knows it is okay to miss.

Blake knew he had to cheat a bit here, so he lowered his hands just a smidgeon and moved them slightly closer to his body in preparation for an inside fastball. He was quite familiar with Willis and Blake knew right where to look for his release point. He had fairly good history with the Cardinals pitcher, Blake forgot to look up his own stats against the hard thrower, but he knew he hit him pretty well. The Chicago player-manager looked for the high three-quarter release point, adjusted his eyes to the dimming afternoon light as the Wrigley lights were just starting to take effect, and prepared to take the biggest cut he could muster up in his advancing age.

The crowd had come back to life with their hero Blake at bat and had risen after the first pitch to give him an extended standing ovation. There was that momentary split-second lull from the steady outburst of affection as the pitch came in to home plate in anticipation of something dramatic about to happen.

Blake recognized the spin on the fastball from Willis, as this time he had decided to throw a higher velocity four-seam fastball up and in no doubt, except this time the St. Louis pitcher held on to the seams just a fraction too long. The resulting location of the pitch was off by several inches, bringing the pitch closer to the center of the plate than Willis wanted. He had failed to miss inside, but rather missed out over the plate where his fastball would be much more hittable. It was the biggest mistake of Willis' career as Blake met the velocity of the pitched ball slightly out in front of the plate where the aging, but still powerful Cubs catcher could mightily drive the baseball.

Blake centered the ball, immediately realizing the thrill of perfect contact with little feel of impact as the ball carried off the sweet spot of the Louisville Slugger Blake Benson, maple wood bat. The hard maple made a sound that Blake would recall for the rest of his life as the ball rose on a majestic arc to straightway left field. That ball was not coming down in the ballpark and Blake knew it was a game-winning, division-clinching, walk-off home run before he even took a step toward first base.

This time there was no doubt about the validity of the homer, as the ball landed halfway up the bleachers in left field where a lucky Cubs fan snared the memento with his baseball glove. The scene was reminiscent of moments ago, but this time it was cemented in baseball history with a walk-off 2-1 victory for the Cubbies. Blake would eventually get possession of his dramatic home run ball for a king's ransom to the lucky fan, but for now that was the last thing on Blake's mind as he nearly tripped over first base in excitement. It was perhaps the longest home run trek around the bases on record as Blake jumped up and down as much as he put his excited feet forward. It was not until he nearly reached third that he displayed anything resembling a home run trot. He slapped the hands of third base coach Lenny Paxson in jubilant fashion before making his way homeward to his eagerly awaiting teammates.

Blake was mobbed by his fellow players the second he stomped on home plate in exhilaration. He was always their hero although he disappointed his players on occasion, but now he was their savior as well. The storybook ending could not have played out any better. Blake's teammates hoisted him on their shoulders and paraded around the ballpark to worshipping subjects that displayed sheer unbridled joy, mixed in with a few tears of happiness from more sentimental fans.

This time security was ready after Bartlett's overruled homer incident that saw fans overrun the established boundaries of the playing field. It was a Chicago Cubs star production as it should be, not some unruly fans' freak show. The players bounced up and down propelling their victorious manager about, still on their shoulders, but shuffled around like a tossed salad.

After one victory lap with their hero and leader still hoisted in the air, Blake emphatically motioned for his players to let him off near the home team dugout. The players were puzzled, but nobody was going to deny any request from their king. Blake got his bearings on the ground after being six feet up in the air for an extended period of time. He looked left and then he looked right, before he noticed his wife Kim actually straight ahead in front of him on the top of the dugout. She desperately wanted to share the moment with Blake,

Blake jumped into the stands and atop the dugout, made a beeline straight for Kim and gave her the biggest hug and kiss he had given her since God knows when. He pulled back and shocked his wife with a sincere and deeply felt apology.

"Kim, I'm so sorry. I'm truly sorry. I love you. I love you so much."

"You're sorry, what do you mean you're sorry? I'm the one who broke your heart."

"I'm sorry because until I felt the pain myself that I had caused you so many times in the past, I couldn't know the depth of hurt my thoughtless actions caused. All I know is right now I'm the happiest man on this planet and that I love you with all my heart and soul Kim. Please forgive me."

"We're starting over from this point forward, Blake. It's a clean slate. Now come here you marvelous hero. You did it, Blake. You really did it. This city loves you. Look at them. You could run for mayor, for God's sake."

The crowd indeed did love Blake Benson and, as always, the city of Chicago had a special place in its heart for the Cubs. The drama king hero and his wife waved to the crowd while dancing up a storm on the roof of the dugout.

Music was blaring from the ballpark loudspeakers, as most of the crowd created their own unique victory dance celebration while singing the band Queen's, "We are the champions." The often-used sports song reverberated into the crowd. Nobody was in any hurry to leave the party. The fans simply continued to enjoy the victorious moment.

Most of the Chicago players were still on the field, while the Cardinals players had long since departed with their tails between their legs in disappointment. The victorious players continuously moved around the ballpark interacting with giddy fans leaning over the railings separating them from the playing field.

While Kim and Blake continued their dancing spree, joined by several coaches and their wives atop the dugout, a few pranksters led of course by Miguel Guillen, planned their devious, but fun, victory ritual of Gatorade dousing of the head coach. The trio of Guillen, Desmond Wilson and notorious bad boy John Bartlett snuck towards the unsuspecting manager who was too busy playing the part of crowd hero to notice the shenanigans coming his way. Pitching coach Douglas noticed the imminent surprise attack and whisked Kim away from her husband while the dousing came upon a stunned Blake. He immediately spun around and his initial reaction was to give a little back in return to the troublesome trio. Blake took a couple steps toward Guillen and appeared ready for revenge, but instead suddenly opened his arms for a hug from his victorious pitcher who had played such a huge part in the team's late-season resurgence.

Guillen, moments ago uncharacteristically out of words with fatigue, now possessed the adrenaline of victory in full fashion. He ran toward his manager and friend, opened up his weary arms, and gave Blake a big bear hug before suddenly erupting in tears of joy.

Blake was deeply moved by Guillen's show of emotion toward him and whispered in his ear, just loud enough to overcome the buzz of the crowd, to express his own deep appreciation.

"Miguel, it was you and the guys, all of the guys, from coaches, players and the front office, that gave me the undying strength to continue on through all of our adversity. I owe you all big time for sticking with me and winning this division to honor my former teammates and their families. This moment can never be taken away from us, Miguel. You're one helluva pitcher and an even better human being."

"Coach, we're not even done yet. Look at us, look at the fans. We believe. Now we can take on whatever team we face without any doubt or fear. Bring on the Giants. We'll kick their asses too before we keep knocking them all down to get to the Series."

"Miggy, just enjoy the moment. We'll tackle the next round tomorrow. This day is for Chicago and for us. Just promise me one thing Miggy?"

"Sure Blake, whatever you want man. You're the greatest."

"Don't eat and drink so much tonight that you can't pitch again in two days."

The notorious pleasure glutton looked puzzled at his manager's request before finally nodding his head up and down in approval.

"I suppose I could take it down a notch or two from my usual party mode. I'll just drink beer, no hard stuff and I'll just eat enough to keep the beer from coming up in revolt."

Blake once again had his wife in his arms and they were twirling together like a dance team, but the manager was listening intently to Guillen's pledge, and the elevated whispers became shouts due to the distance between them.

"Screw it Miggy, eat and drink like there's no tomorrow. Life's too short not to enjoy memories like this to its fullest. Tomorrow may never come, days like today should never end."

73 — Seeing the Light

It is the coldest night of the winter and Blake and Kim scurry to get inside the posh New York City hotel where Major League Baseball is hosting their annual postseason awards ceremony. If it weren't for all the familiar faces of baseball executives, media types, and a few of the game's top stars in attendance, baseball would be the last thing on anybody's mind in the depths of winter.

Blake was still a focus of media frenzy for his remarkable stretch to end the season with his personal and professional triumphs. It did not matter to anyone in attendance this evening that Blake's Chicago Cubs team was swept in the first round of the National League playoffs by the eventual World Series champion San Francisco Giants, three games to none.

What mattered this frigid New York night was a story that had so many personal levels, combined with the excitement of America's pastime, and had riveted the sports world several months earlier. Blake was the face of the amazing story, the epitome of overcoming personal and professional challenges. Everywhere he turned this evening he was greeted by well-wishers, admirers, and appreciative professional colleagues. It was getting to the point of embarrassment for Blake, but he understood well his role in the promotion of a sport that he'd the pleasure of being part of for so many years.

After what seemed like an endless length of time enduring attention and fanfare before finishing an exquisite dinner, the main event for tonight's gathering was commencing. There would be several awards given to players and managers who had shined above all others this past season. The debating of potential winners was intense as usual except for the highly anticipated selection of Blake Benson as Comeback Player of the Year. It was not a perfectly fitting tribute to Blake, as he had, in fact, only been productive the last two months of the year and had acted as both player and manager. This unorthodox role made categorizing his accomplishments very difficult, as the statistics he compiled during this stretch on a personal level were not spectacular in the least, but his role as manager in this remarkable story had to be honored in some form or fashion. There seemed to be a consensus building in the media that Comeback Player would be the appropriate category.

Commissioner of Major League Baseball, Jonathan Franklin, turned over the microphone to tonight's awards presenter, the play-by-play announcer of the national network's sole postseason television source, one affable Paul White, who began the evening's tributes with a moment of silence for the members of the Chicago Cubs organization that had perished in that awful plane crash.

Blake felt all eyes upon him as once more he was the face of the tragedy and would be perhaps forever. He just bowed his head and prayed for their families as he had done so many times previously. He clasped Kim's hand and held on even after the moment of silence had passed. She was his strength, always had been, but Blake had become much more aware of his wife's positive effects on him during these past several months.

The tension was building in Blake and Kim as the award for Comeback Player was up next. It seemed a given he would win, but one learns in sports at an early age that nothing can be taken for granted regarding any game that possessed a human element. Voting often had been notoriously tainted by a number of personal factors that sometimes got in the way of professional accomplishments.

Blake did not want to presume an award, but he had to be prepared nonetheless. He did not prepare a speech per se, but he had indeed written down a few subjects the wanted to address. The hope was that he would speak from the heart when his time came. The emotions expressed would be stronger if he was not simply reading off a prepared text, but rather sharing a feeling deep down in his soul at that particular moment that could be snatched from within.

"And now, this season's Comeback Player of the Year Award goes to Blake Benson, the player-manager of the Chicago Cubs."

It was as if the crowd had anticipated this announcement, and they were up and out of their seats before Blake's name was completely finished. The standing ovation lasted well beyond Blake's acceptance of the award at the podium. He just stood there, smiling broadly, acknowledging the people in attendance with a symbolic clap of his hands and a slight bow of the head. Blake motioned for the crowd to stop so he could begin his acceptance speech, but they simply were not ready yet to quit their applause. Finally, Blake just started speaking over the noise and eventually they sat back down to listen to the award winner.

"Thank you all. Thank you all. It's an honor to be here tonight with so many of the game's great ambassadors."

The crowd was now back in their seats and the silence made Blake uneasy for a moment before he continued on in appreciation. The pause created a sense of awkwardness, for Blake was never too keen on public speaking, and the intensity of the moment caught him briefly off guard.

"I never wanted to be considered for this award because it obviously means you were awful for an extended period of time. Standing here at this moment, as the winner, definitely has changed my opinion. It's difficult for me to express how much this recognition means to me. There are only a handful of people here that totally understand the depths of my uphill climb out of a deep, dark hole. I'd like to recognize two of them tonight. First, I want to thank my wife Kim for staying beside me through my darker moments and providing me with the strength and courage to not only endure, but to overcome. Kim, will you please stand for a minute? This woman has the strength of a whole baseball team put together. She's the reason I'm here tonight accepting this award."

Kim rose sheepishly and acknowledged her husband's kind remarks with a hand-waved kiss to her husband. The crowd politely applauded while Kim sat down quickly to deflect any praise coming her way.

"Secondly, I want to thank my boss Marty Anderson. Being a general manager isn't all about contracts and player acquisitions. It's about belief, belief in the ability of men to change for the better. I doubt there was more than a handful, if that, who would have been willing to give me another shot at redemption after using up more than my share of get-out-of-jail-free cards. This brave man took one hell of a chance on me and I'll never forget the moment he indicated that he would allow me to continue playing for the Cubs, much less offering me the managerial post. It takes courage, conviction, and compassion to be a great general manager and friend at the same time. I thank you with all my heart, Mr. Anderson. Would you please stand up for me? It wouldn't be the first time, and I'll make darn sure it's not my last either. Thank you Marty."

The longtime Chicago general manager was recognizably visible to all as a veteran of many off-season award ceremonies. He stood proudly and waved back at Blake in his own appreciation before quickly realizing his own place and sitting back down. It was to be Blake's show.

"These two people have had a huge impact on my life for many years, but now I want to thank a group of guys that I've only had the pleasure of really knowing for less than six months, but boy, what a six months it was. To all my teammates, coaching staff and players, this award is a reflection of our team effort. None of this, including me standing here accepting this award, could've been possible without the strength and character of the team that was so hastily put together, but so preciously assembled. You won't find a better group of young men in any organization. What they went through this past summer was unprecedented in major league baseball. Trust me, it wasn't all peaches and cream. We had our issues, but we stuck together and made our place in baseball history. It is my pleasure to be forever associated with them. Thank you all."

Blake knew what was coming next and he hesitated once again in apprehension. He grabbed a glass of water that was handed to him earlier and swallowed hard. This part was not going to be easy.

"Now most, if not all, of you know that I was the sole survivor of the initial Chicago Cubs squad of this past year. That awful day saved my life and changed so much in my life's direction, and it was due to the extreme circumstances of my destructive lifestyle that had taken over my mind and body to the extent that I was sent home early from our road trip for rehabilitation. I can't stand here tonight and accept this award without thanking and remembering all of my teammates that died in that plane crash. Their lives were taken way too young. It was because of their memory that I was able to prevail during difficult times. I was bound and determined to do everything in my power to recognize their lives in an honorable fashion. I hope that we were able to accomplish that. I believe we did."

The crowd clapped at the tribute and acknowledged with their applause that they indeed agreed with Blake's assertion. He had the audience in the palm of his hands. They were gripped with his story, his emotion, and his own appreciation for others. Blake could sense that he had their devout attention, so he continued on with a disclaimer.

"Now I know most of you, myself included, don't care too much for lengthy speeches, but I feel I have a story and a life lesson here that needs to be heard. So, please bear with me as I continue on for a few more moments. It's important for me too. I want to be heard."

There was a steady round of applause that Blake took to mean his audience was very receptive to his continuing.

"Thank you for that. I'll try to make this as short as I can."

This would again require deep emotion that Blake could only hope that he could accurately convey with meaning.

"When I somehow was diverted from that plane crash by being a rotten human being, I struggled to comprehend why this all happened as it did. It made zero sense for me to live while my teammates died. Zero sense. The guilt was immense, but somehow I figured this would have to make sense someday even if that seemed nearly impossible at the moment. After many days of soul searching and dealing with the shock of losing my baseball family, I began to put a few pieces back together in my mind. What was God telling me? Was there a God? Why would He spare me? My life had been pretty much all baseball up to that point. I loved my wife, but I'll admit I didn't put her first and that was wrong. I began to think that it was only through baseball that I could redeem myself, and I vowed to remain sober and pleaded with Mr. Anderson for a second, third, fourth, or whatever chance I was on. This had to be a part of the plan that God or some supreme being had for me. Mr. Anderson believed in me and suddenly I felt on the right path again. The trouble was I had made a conscious decision to change, but I didn't know how to change properly.

It was through the process of learning with all its ups and downs that I came to understand what was planned for me and what was needed. Oh, I came close to drinking again, as crazy as that sounds. The power of the demon is greater than you can ever imagine. But in the end I didn't and I learned along the way that I didn't have to do this alone. I didn't have to carry the weight of the world on my shoulders. I felt such extreme pressure to honor my deceased teammates in the right way that I lost sight of the bigger picture which is that, as great as this game of baseball is, it will not ever take precedence over family. I had gone astray from my roots. Baseball had spoiled me. I was worshipped, cared for, richly rewarded financially, and became my own worst enemy with my personal destructive behavior. I lived for the moment without any consequences for my actions and how they affected others. It cost me my friends, my wife, and my own self-respect. I lost perspective and that is now what I have regained. I had lost my sense of community and love for others and that's what I've regained. The achievement of our season isn't to be diminished. It was the greatest overall team effort that I've experienced, but more importantly, I learned to love others again. I learned to not think only of myself, or by myself. It's good to ask for help. It's good to let go of your pride and acknowledge that others may know more than you about something other than baseball."

Blake paused again to reach for more water before resuming his speech. He knew it was getting long, but he could not stop now. It was, after all, his moment.

"I resisted going to treatment at first and I indeed made it through the season staying sober, but that wasn't the right way to do it. I am learning more about myself every day now that I've gone through treatment and am continuing on a path to sobriety. I realize now that I am not at all unique. Everybody has problems. It's how you deal with them that's important. I've learned that you can't put anybody on a pedestal, because we're all human and that means we all make mistakes. I learned that one life can affect so many others in positive ways. The last two months of the season and the reactions of thousands of fans at Wrigley proved that to me. The story that I lived, that our team lived and that I'm continuing to tell today is one that can have a positive effect on thousands of others. My life was spared, but my old lifestyle died along with my fallen teammates and I was given another opportunity to affect so many others in this world. And I'm still learning, that's the best part. The answers that come our way are never completely the final answer. We search constantly for answers. That's just life. We do make our own choices, though. We don't get to choose life or death, but we make choices that can move mountains if we go all in. This is where I announce my next big choice. I'm retiring from baseball today to focus on more important issues in life. I'm happy to announce that Kim and I are going to be proud parents for the first time. It just goes to show you, it wasn't all baseball the last few months," said Blake, as he paused to laugh at his own comment.

"I'm going to work every day to be a better husband and now, a father. I'm going to work every day to be a more productive member of society. Baseball is great, it's the greatest game on earth and it provided me with huge financial rewards, but it's now time for me to find bigger meaning in life. I'm going to start training to work as an alcohol counselor, and one day, I hope Major League

Baseball will allow me to work with all teams to help athletes balance life with baseball. This season was a once-in-a-lifetime occurrence and it provided me with enough lessons to learn until the day I die. What a season it was. The last two months were absolutely crazy. We didn't win it all, but hey, we're the Cubs. We're apparently not supposed to win it all. It was great getting to the playoffs, but we had nothing left in the tank when we got there. That's on me, but we showed the nation and a lot of people what can be done against all odds. We didn't move mountains, although it sure felt like it a few times, but I hope I showed the nation how one person, the one person on the Chicago Cubs team that didn't die on that awful day, can still live to help others move their own personal mountains of change for the better. Thank you all. Now go out there and help someone else move their own mountain and I'll feel like my extended speech was worth it."

Blake walked back to his seat next to Kim and kissed her before sitting down. His path was finished as a major league baseball player and manager too, but his journey was just beginning as he looked forward to new directions. The challenges weren't finished; they were just moved as if he had been traded to another team.

About the Author

Timothy F. Bouvine began sports-blogging in 2010 and loved his new pursuit of writing so much that he decided to broaden his goals to include a novel. This, his first book, is a continuation of a lifelong love of baseball paired with the knowledge obtained from his own recovery from alcohol abuse.

tfbouvine@hotmail.com

TO ORDER ADDITIONAL COPIES OF

CATCHING LIGHTNING
Without the Bottle

Contact Savage Press by
visiting our webpage at

www.savpress.com

or see our
Savage Press
Facebook page.

Or Call

218-391-3070

to place secure credit card orders.

mail@savpress.com